Family Law

Family Law

by Harry D. Krause

Max L. Rowe Professor of Law, University of Illinois College of Law

David D. Meyer

Professor of Law, University of Illinois College of Law

FOURTH EDITION

WEST®

A Thomson Reuters business

Mat #40748999

Black Letter Series and Black Letter Series design appearing on the front cover are trademarks registered in the U.S. Patent and Trademark Office.

Copyright © 1988, 1996 WEST PUBLISHING CO.
© West, a Thomson business, 2004
© 2009 Thomson Reuters
    610 Opperman Drive
    St. Paul, MN 55123
    1–800–313–9378

ISBN: 978–0–314–19448–0

 PRINTED ON 10% POST CONSUMER RECYCLED PAPER

Preface

ABOUT "STUDY AIDS"

Having authored this Black Letter, it must seem near the height of hypocrisy to repeat the customary pious caution against over-reliance on "study aids." Well, we'll do it anyway. You know as well as we do that the one way of becoming an effective lawyer is to *think* along with the development of the subject matter by studying the cases themselves—or in any event their edited remains—in the *assigned* "study aid," your casebook. But you also find yourself under time pressures that make anything that abstracts the "black letter law" seem inevitably attractive. WEST established this "Black Letter" series to assure a level of quality that some more hastily prepared "outlines" lack. If it is to be done, it should be done well. Consistently with the need for brevity, we have tried to be reasonably accurate in synthesizing this fast-evolving area of law, even if some of the finer points have had to be compromised.

Over the years, and through several editions, a number of students and staff members of the University of Illinois College of Law have contributed their efforts to the creation of this Black Letter. For expert administrative assistance, special thanks are due Angela Martin, Stacey Ballmes and Carrie May–Borich, who helped ensure that the various revisions made it into print.

ORGANIZATION

The detailed organization of this Black Letter is traced in the Table of Contents. To summarize: A "capsule summary" for last-minute, final review broadly mirrors the organization of the main part. (While major headings are the same, some of the subheadings have been combined or altered to achieve greater brevity and clarity.) The "Capsule" is followed by more detailed exposition where the text is supported with summaries of illustrative cases. Quotation of original language is emphasized in order to maintain accuracy and to give "live" flavor to the law. True/false questions follow each substantive chapter. These questions— and even more, the answers—are to be taken with a grain of caution. As you well know, few things are wholly true or wholly false, especially in law. Most of the challenges presented there are "more true than false" or "more false than true." The questions should be reviewed in those terms. At the end, a practice essay examination is provided. A cross reference chart correlates coverage of subject matter in this volume and in leading casebooks. A Glossary, appropriately based on Black's Law Dictionary, and a detailed Index conclude this Black Letter.

AND STILL ANOTHER WORD ABOUT EXAMINATIONS

By now you have had so much advice on how to write a law examination that you have discovered that there is no universal rule, but you probably have a pretty good idea what works best for you. If it works, stick with that. A model answer has not been provided for the practice essay because quite different responses to the same question may merit (or receive) the same grade. Each person has to tailor his or her approach to her or his own style and (if only more were known about that) to the grader's personality and preferences. If there are time limitations—and on the typical law school examination there are—we would discount the oft-repeated morsel that you should first prepare an elaborate outline of your answer on scrap paper. Anyone who can, after brief reflection, find the proper starting point from which to develop the answer logically while going along, should do just that. This will leave more time to answer the question where it counts—in the bluebook, pursuing additional issues or elaborating on a basically correct answer. Those who think they are helped if they draw up an outline before answering the question should re-examine their mental resources whether they cannot train themselves to avoid the time-consuming duplication of thought and writing. Of course, if there is no significant time limit, by all means prepare an outline and even write drafts. It probably will improve your product.

Another variant (intended by the examiner to make you feel more flustered or more comfortable?) is the open book examination. With time constraints, an "open book" examination will tempt you to waste precious time on looking up things you do (or should) know. Again, this typically will be time you would be better off using to *write* your answer.

There is one universal rule. That rule mandates the fair (not necessarily equal) allocation of time and effort to *each* question, to each part of a multi-part examination. The marginal grade-boosting value of a few extra sentences (or even "issues") on one question will rarely come close to the return on getting at least a basic answer worked out to the next question. Do not "borrow" time. If you can't organize, simply stop answering one question and begin answering the next when your watch says so.

Beyond that, clear organization (or at least giving the impression thereof) is as good an indicator of clear thinking as you can provide the grader—and law examination grading is supposed to reward clear thinking. Here is where the value of a structured outline of your answer may come in. A structured response (with numbered subheadings, if appropriate) should begin at a logical starting point, the "core issue", and evolve logically, issue by issue. It will look *and very likely be* more "organized" than a rambling discussion that wanders panic-stricken from issue to issue, back and forth, even if you ultimately "hit" them all.

We'll say nothing about handwriting other than that the sheer physical legibility of your answer is much more important than is generally admitted. Remember that you are in law school, not medical school. Lawyers communicate in language, not in illegible code. Typed or printed answers have the attribute of being more transparent. A good answer will look more obviously good (*i.e.*, perhaps a little better than it really is), and a bad answer will look more obviously bad (*i.e.*, worse than it may actually be). *But there is the uncomfortable fact that the fast typist can add a considerable amount of volume to his or her answer!* Volume is worthless if it is mere verbiage—but if slow handwriting speed prevents you from putting down all the relevant information and analysis you have ready to pour out of your head, typing will put you ahead of the game. Today, of course, word processing computers have caused the near extinction of conventional typewriters—along with the skill needed to type without opportunity for instant and traceless erasure.

Good Luck! Remember it was you who decided to study law. All inevitable aggravations aside, "law" should be perceived by you as fun, and examinations as competitive games. Otherwise, the competitive life that follows law school will not be fun. If all else fails, think of Mr. Bumble's lawyer who mused: "The law may be a ass, but it sure is giving me a good ride!"

*

Summary of Contents

CAPSULE SUMMARY 1

I. THE NATURE OF MARRIAGE AND MARITAL CONTRACTS 13
    A. Religious Influence 15
    B. Contract or Status 15
    C. Controlling Factors Affecting the Marriage Contract 15
    D. Marriage and the Constitution 17
    E. The Marital Relationship at Common Law 26
    F. Married Women's Property Acts 26
    G. The Antenuptial Agreement 26
    H. Agreements During Marriage 37
    I. Conflicts Aspects of Marital Agreements 40
    J. Breach of Promise to Marry 41
    K. Gifts in Contemplation of Marriage 41

II. MARRIAGE REQUISITES AND COMMON LAW MARRIAGE 45
    A. Formal Requirements 47
    B. Substantive Requirements for Valid Marriage 61
    C. Conflicts of Laws 68
    D. Annulment 70

III. COHABITATION WITHOUT MARRIAGE 81
    A. Unmarried Cohabitation 82
    B. Same–Sex Relationships 89

IV. SPOUSES 93
    A. Support Obligations During Marriage 95
    B. Property Rights 100
    C. Torts and the Family 111
    D. Marriage and Criminal Law 120
    E. Family Names 124

V. DIVORCE—STATUS ISSUES 129
    A. Access to and Jurisdiction of Courts 130
    B. Traditional Grounds and Defenses 132
    C. Divorce Reform 142
    D. Separation 145

VI. DIVORCE—FINANCIAL CONSEQUENCES 149
    A. Alimony on Divorce 151

	B.	Property Division on Divorce	163
	C.	Separation Agreements	178
VII.		**THE PARENTAL CHILD SUPPORT OBLIGATION**	**189**
	A.	Definition of the Parental Obligation	191
	B.	Support Duty of Stepparents and Grandparents	191
	C.	Duration of the Obligation	191
	D.	Traditional Criteria for Awarding Support	197
	E.	Child Support Guidelines	197
	F.	Modification	199
	G.	Child Support Enforcement Sanctions	200
	H.	Conflicts of Laws Aspects of Child Support: The Uniform Interstate Family Support Act	201
	I.	Federal Child Support Enforcement Legislation	202
	J.	Full Faith and Credit	202
	K.	Reciprocity: The Child's Duty to Support Parents	203
VIII.		**CHILD CUSTODY**	**205**
	A.	Child Custody During Marriage	207
	B.	Child Custody Upon Divorce	207
	C.	Joint Custody	217
	D.	Rights of the Noncustodial Parent	219
	E.	Standards for Modification	223
	F.	Visitation Rights of Third Parties	225
	G.	Interstate Recognition of Custody Decrees	226
IX.		**THE PARENTAL OBLIGATION OF CARE AND CONTROL, AND THE JUVENILE COURT SYSTEM**	**235**
	A.	Child Dependency	237
	B.	Child Neglect and Abuse	237
	C.	Constitutional Rights	238
	D.	Parental Control Over a Child's Medical Care	243
	E.	Child Abuse	248
	F.	Disposition by the Juvenile Court	251
	G.	Criminal Procedure	254
X.		**CHILDREN'S RIGHTS**	**259**
	A.	History of Parental Control	260
	B.	Constitutional Rights	260
	C.	Emancipation	262
	D.	Minor's Capacity to Contract	262
	E.	Children and Tort Law	262
	F.	Property Rights	268
	G.	Education: State and Parents	268

XI. LEGITIMACY, ILLEGITIMACY AND PATERNITY 275
  A. **Legitimacy** 276
  B. **Illegitimacy** 277
  C. **Establishing Paternity** 280
  D. **Conflicts of Laws** 283

XII. ADOPTION 285
  A. **History and Development** 287
  B. **Social Functions** 287
  C. **The Adoption Process** 287
  D. **Qualifications of Adoptive Parents** 292
  E. **Consent to Adoption** 298
  F. **Anonymity** 305
  G. **Revocation of Adoption** 306
  H. **Legal Effect of Adoption** 307

XIII. PROCREATION 313
  A. **Constitutional Underpinnings** 314
  B. **Assisted Reproduction** 317

APPENDICES

App.
A. Answers to Review Questions 329
B. Practice Essay Questions 349
C. Text Correlation Chart 359
D. Glossary 365
E. Table of Cases 377
F. Index 385

*

Table of Contents

CAPSULE SUMMARY **1**

I.   **THE NATURE OF MARRIAGE AND MARITAL CONTRACTS** **13**

    A.   **Religious Influence**   15

    B.   **Contract or Status**   15

    C.   **Controlling Factors Affecting the Marriage Contract**   15

        1.   State Power   15

            a.   Contract Clause Inapplicable   15

            b.   State Reserve Power   15

            c.   Due Process Clause Inapplicable   16

        2.   Change of Residence   16

        3.   Private Marriage Contract   17

    D.   **Marriage and the Constitution**   17

        1.   Religious Freedom   17

        2.   Monogamy   18

            a.   Justification for Regulation   18

                1)   Religion and Tradition   18

                2)   Constitutionality   18

                3)   Modern Rationale   19

            b.   Criminal Sanctions   20

                1)   Enforcement Practice   20

                2)   "Enoch Arden" Defense   20

            c.   Civil Effects of Bigamous Marriage   20

        3.   The Right to Marry   21

        4.   Same–Sex Marriage   23

        5.   Marital and Sexual Privacy   25

    E.   **The Marital Relationship at Common Law**   26

    F.   **Married Women's Property Acts**   26

    G.   **The Antenuptial Agreement**   26

        1.   Individualizing Marriage by Contract   26

        2.   Validity of Antenuptial Agreements   27

            a.   Contract Requirements   27

                1)   Statute of Frauds   27

                2)   Consideration   28

                3)   Risk of Overreaching   28

                    a)   Full Disclosure   30

            b) Fair and Reasonable Provision—*What* Is
                "Unconscionable?" *When* Is the Deal to Be
                Evaluated—At Time of Execution or Enforcement? . . . 31
            c) Voluntariness and Advice of Counsel 33
        b. Subject Matter 34
            1) Disposition at Death 34
            2) Providing for Divorce 34
                a) Second Marriages 35
                b) Property Rights vs. Support Obligations and Other
                   "Essentials" of Marriage 35
            3) Regulating the Ongoing Marriage 36
                a) Judicial Policy of Noninterference in Marriage 36
                b) UPAA 36
                c) Usefulness of Unenforceable Provisions 37
        c. UMDA 37
        d. UPAA and UMPA 37
        e. Gift Tax Treatment of Antenuptial Agreements 37
  H.   **Agreements During Marriage** 37
    1. Postnuptial Agreements 38
        a. Consideration 38
        b. Statutory Limitations (Married Women's Property Acts) 38
        c. Overreaching 39
        d. Public Policy 39
        e. Gift Tax Consequences 39
    2. Reconciliation Agreements 40
    3. Separation Agreements 40
  I.   **Conflicts Aspects of Marital Agreements** 40
  J.   **Breach of Promise to Marry** 41
  K.   **Gifts in Contemplation of Marriage** 41
    1. Gifts Before Engagement 41
    2. Gifts During an Engagement 41
    3. Gifts From Third Parties 42
II.   **MARRIAGE REQUISITES AND COMMON LAW MARRIAGE** 45
  A.   **Formal Requirements** 47
    1. Consent 47
        a. Capacity 47
            1) Practical Relevance of Capacity Issue 49
            2) Consent of Guardian 49
        b. Intent 50
    2. Solemnization 50
        a. Marriage License 50
            1) Waiting Period 50
            2) Solemnization Without License 50

		b.	Ceremony	51
		c.	Public Record	51
		d.	Purposes of Solemnization	51
		e.	Proxy Marriages	51
		f.	"Confidential" Marriages	52
	3.	Common Law Marriage		52
		a.	Traditional Form	52
		b.	American Law	52
			1) Holding Out	54
			2) Abolition of Common Law Marriage	54
			3) Statutes Regulating Common Law Marriage	55
			4) Modern Rationale	55
			5) Conflict of Laws	56
			6) Uniform Marriage and Divorce Act	58
	4.	Presumptions Regarding Validity of Marriage		58
	5.	Valid Common Law Marriage Resulting From Removal of Impediment		59
	6.	Putative Spouse Doctrine		60
B.	**Substantive Requirements for Valid Marriage**			61
	1.	Consanguinity		61
		a.	Scope of Prohibition	61
		b.	Effect of Attempt to Enter into Incestuous Marriage	61
		c.	Criminality	62
		d.	Justification of Prohibition	62
			1) Genetics	62
			2) Social Arguments	63
		e.	Criticism of the Prohibition	63
		f.	Relationships of the Half Blood, through Illegitimacy, or Severed by Adoption	63
	2.	Affinity, Step–Relationship, Adoption		63
		a.	"Affinity" and "Step–Relationships"	63
		b.	Adoptive Relationships	63
		c.	Justification	63
		d.	Constitutionality	64
	3.	Age Requirements		64
		a.	Regulation	64
		b.	Justification of Age Requirements	66
		c.	Constitutional Limitation on Gender Distinctions	66
		d.	Effect of Noncompliance	66
			1) Who Can Attack	66
			2) Ratification	67
	4.	Physical Requirements		67
		a.	Blood Tests	67

	b.	Physical Capacity	67
	c.	Epilepsy	68
C.	**Conflicts of Laws**		68
1.	Law of Celebration		68
2.	"Most Significant Relationship" Test		69
3.	Uniform Marriage Evasion Act		69
4.	The Public Policy Exception		69
5.	Full Faith and Credit		69
D.	**Annulment**		70
1.	History		70
2.	Impediments		70
3.	Defenses		70
4.	The Void/Voidable Distinction		71
	a.	Void Marriage	71
	b.	Voidable Marriage	71
	c.	Significance of the Distinction	71
	d.	UMDA	72
5.	Annulment for Fraud		72
6.	Annulment for Duress		73
7.	Annulment of Marriage Entered in Jest		73
8.	Annulment of Sham Marriage		73
9.	Legal Incidents of Annulment		75
	a.	Effects Regarding Children and Financial Obligations	75
	b.	Non–Retroactive Annulment Under UMDA § 208(e), With Divorce–Like Consequences	76
	c.	Revival of Former Spouse's Duty of Support	76
	d.	Revival of Other Rights Related to Marriage	78
III.	**COHABITATION WITHOUT MARRIAGE**		**81**
A.	**Unmarried Cohabitation**		82
1.	*Marvin v. Marvin*		82
	a.	Family Law Statutes Do Not Govern a Non–Marital Relationship	82
	b.	Contracts Between Partners Are Enforceable, Unless the Consideration Is Meretricious	82
	c.	If There Is No Express Agreement—Other Remedies May Protect the Parties' Expectations	82
	d.	Outcome of *Marvin*	83
2.	Application of the *"Marvin* Doctrine"		83
	a.	Application to Facts Resembling Common Law Marriage	83
	b.	Application to Facts Not Resembling Common Law Marriage	85
	c.	Recovery for Services	87
3.	*Marvin* Doctrine Rejected		88
4.	*Marvin* Doctrine "Codified"		88

      5.   Domestic Partnership Under the ALI Principles 88

  B. **Same–Sex Relationships** 89

      1.   Cohabitation 89

      2.   Domestic Partnerships and Civil Unions 90

      3.   Transsexuals 90

IV. **SPOUSES** 93

  A. **Support Obligations During Marriage** 95

      1.   Historical Basis 95

      2.   Changing Status 95

      3.   "Necessaries" 95

          a.   Necessaries Defined 95

          b.   Merchant's Recovery 96

          c.   Gender Neutrality 96

      4.   Actual Agency Between Spouses 97

      5.   Judicial Refusal to Interfere in Ongoing Marriage 97

      6.   "Necessaries" After Separation or Pending Divorce 98

      7.   Constitutional Limitations 99

  B. **Property Rights** 100

      1.   Common Law 100

          a.   Scope 100

          b.   Circumvention of Rules 100

      2.   Married Women's Property Acts 100

          a.   Scope of Statutes 100

          b.   Purpose and Effect of Statutes 101

      3.   Separate Property States 102

          a.   Separate Property 102

          b.   Pros and Cons of Separate Property 102

          c.   Joint Ownership in Separate Property States 102

              1)   Forms of Joint Ownership 102

              2)   Interspousal Transfers, Joint Ownership and Presumptions of Gift or Advancement 103

              3)   Effect of the "Marital Property" Concept on "Gifts" 104

          d.   Devolution of Separate Property Upon Death 104

              1)   Election Against the Will 104

              2)   Uniform Probate Code 105

              3)   Intestacy 105

      4.   Community Property States 106

          a.   Historical Note 106

          b.   The Concept of Community Property 107

              1)   Definition of Separate and Community Property 107

              2)   Management and Control 108

                  a)   Louisiana 108

                  b)   Texas 108

		c)	Equal Management and Control	108
		d)	Modified Joint Control	108
		e)	Relative Merits of These Models	108
	c.	Community Property on Death		109
		1)	No Election Against a Spouse's Will	109
		2)	Intestacy	109
	d.	Presumptions		109
5.	Marital Property and the Conflicts of Laws			110
	a.	The Problem		110
	b.	The Solution		110

C.   Torts and the Family 111
  1. Torts Between Spouses 111
      a. Justification for Interspousal Immunity 111
      b. Reintroducing "Fault" into Divorce Settlements? 111
      c. Arguments Against Immunity 113
      d. Is the Immunity Unconstitutional? 114
      e. Intentional and Negligent Torts Distinguished 114
  2. Recovery for Loss of Consortium 115
  3. Tortious Interference With Family Relationships ("Heartbalm Actions") 115
      a. Breach of Promise to Marry 115
          1) Proof 115
          2) Tort Action 116
          3) Damages 116
      b. Criminal Conversation 117
          1) Elements of Cause of Action 117
          2) Defenses 118
      c. Alienation of Affections 118
          1) Elements of Cause of Action 118
          2) Criminal Conversation and Alienation of Affections Distinguished 119
      d. Modern Treatment of Heartbalm Actions 119

D.   Marriage and Criminal Law 120
  1. Immunities 120
  2. Testimonial Privilege 120
  3. Rape 121
  4. Marital Violence 122
      a. Order of Protection and "No Contact" Orders 122
      b. Police Protection 122
  5. The "Battered Wife Syndrome" 122

E.   Family Names 124
  1. Husband and Wife 124
  2. Unmarried Couples 124

3. Child 125

V. **DIVORCE—STATUS ISSUES** **129**
  A. **Access to and Jurisdiction of Courts** 130
    1. Residency Requirements 130
      a. Constitutionality of Residency Requirement 130
    2. Personal Jurisdiction 130
      a. Full Faith and Credit 130
        1) *Ex parte* Divorce 130
        2) Rule in *Sherrer* 131
      b. Comity 131
      c. Federal Jurisdiction Over Divorce Actions 131
    3. "Long–Arm" Jurisdiction 131
      a. Divorce 131
      b. Child Support 132
  B. **Traditional Grounds and Defenses** 132
    1. Historical Development 132
      a. English Origins 132
        1) Early English Law 132
          a) Divorce *a vinculo matrimonii* 133
          b) Divorce *a mensa et thoro* 133
        2) English Reform 133
      b. Application in America 133
    2. Divorce for Marital Fault 133
      a. Decline of Fault–Based Divorce Laws 133
        1) Bars and Defenses 133
        2) Loose Standards 134
        3) No–Fault Laws 134
      b. Modern Relevance of the Fault System 134
    3. Traditional Fault Grounds 134
      a. Adultery 134
      b. Physical Cruelty 135
      c. Desertion 136
        1) Time Period 136
        2) Constructive Desertion 137
        3) Reconciliation Offers 137
      d. Mental Cruelty 137
        1) Requirements 137
        2) Subjective Standard 138
        3) Opportunity for Collusive Divorce 138
      e. Habitual Drunkenness and Drug Addiction 138
      f. Impotence and Bigamy 138
      g. Insanity 138
        1) Plaintiff's 138

			2)	Defendant's	138
	4.	Traditional Bars and Defenses			139
		a.	Collusion		139
		b.	Recrimination		139
		c.	Provocation		140
		d.	Provocation and Recrimination Distinguished		140
			1)	Causal Connection	140
			2)	Defense vs. Bar	140
			3)	Misconduct vs. Ground for Divorce	140
			4)	Rationale	140
		e.	Connivance		140
		f.	Condonation		141
			1)	Proof of Intent	141
			2)	Conditional Condonation	141
		g.	Insanity		142
C.	**Divorce Reform**				142
	1.	Social Trends			142
	2.	Available Alternatives			142
		a.	Fault–Based Systems		143
		b.	No–Fault Systems		143
	3.	No–Fault Grounds			143
		a.	Living Separate and Apart		143
		b.	Marriage Breakdown		144
	4.	Covenant Marriage			145
D.	**Separation**				145
	1.	Divorce From Bed and Board			145
	2.	Separate Maintenance			146
	3.	Conversion Into Full Divorce			146
VI.	**DIVORCE—FINANCIAL CONSEQUENCES**				**149**
A.	**Alimony on Divorce**				151
	1.	Traditional Standards for Awarding Alimony			151
		a.	Historical Development		151
		b.	Mutuality of Alimony Obligation		151
	2.	Alimony Today			151
	3.	Determining the Amount of Alimony			153
		a.	Standard of Living Maintained During Marriage, Need and Ability to Pay		154
		b.	Recipient's Earning Potential and Assets		154
	4.	Fault as a Factor in Alimony Awards			156
	5.	Modification of Alimony			158
		a.	Recipient Spouse's Changing Need		158
		b.	Change in Obligated Spouse's Ability to Pay		158
		c.	Obligated Spouse's Bankruptcy		159

6. Termination of Alimony 159
    a. Death of Either Ex–Spouse 159
    b. Recipient Spouse's Remarriage 160
    c. Recipient Spouse's Cohabitation 161
7. Enforcement of Alimony by Contempt 162
8. Federal Tax Treatment of Alimony 163
9. Alimony and Property Award Distinguished 163

B. **Property Division on Divorce** 163
1. Separate Property States 163
    a. Property Transfers on Divorce 163
    b. Equitable Distribution 164
    c. "Marital Property" 164
    d. The Uniform Marriage and Divorce Act 165
    e. Marital Fault and Economic Fault ("Dissipation") 166
    f. Post–Divorce Joint Ownership 168
    g. Pre–Divorce Transfers of Separate Property 168
2. Community Property States 168
3. Conflicts of Laws Aspects of Property Division 169
4. Property Awards and Bankruptcy 170
5. Tax Treatment of Property Awards 171
6. Treatment of Professional Licenses and Practices 171
    a. The Professional License as a Factor in Determining Alimony . 171
    b. "Goodwill" Distinguished 172
    c. The Professional License as "Marital Property" 173
    d. "Career Enhancement" 175
    e. "Restitution" of Educational Contribution 175
7. Allocation of Pensions 176
8. The "Employee Retirement Income Security Act" (ERISA) and the
    "Qualified Domestic Relations Order" (QDRO) 178

C. **Separation Agreements** 178
1. Validity of Separation Agreement 179
2. Traditional Requirements for Enforceability 179
    a. "Facilitating" or "Encouraging" Separation or Divorce 179
    b. Consideration 179
    c. Full Disclosure, Fraud, Fairness and Representation by
        Attorney 180
3. The Divorce Decree and the Separation Agreement 182
    a. Specific Incorporation 182
    b. Incorporation by Reference 182
    c. No Incorporation 183
    d. Court's Review of Separation Agreement 183
    e. Reconciliation 184
        1) What Is Reconciliation? 184

2) Effect of Reconciliation on Separation Agreement 184

VII. **THE PARENTAL CHILD SUPPORT OBLIGATION** **189**

A. **Definition of the Parental Obligation** 191

B. **Support Duty of Stepparents and Grandparents** 191

C. **Duration of the Obligation** 191

    1. Majority 192

    2. Emancipation 194

    3. Reversion to Unemancipated Status 195

    4. Death of Parent 196

        a. Parents Not Divorced 196

        b. Parents Divorced 196

D. **Traditional Criteria for Awarding Support** 197

E. **Child Support Guidelines** 197

F. **Modification** 199

G. **Child Support Enforcement Sanctions** 200

    1. Civil Contempt 200

    2. Criminal Contempt 200

    3. Civil and Criminal Contempt Distinguished 200

    4. Criminal Prosecution for Non–Support 201

    5. Federal Crime 201

H. **Conflicts of Laws Aspects of Child Support: The Uniform Interstate Family Support Act** 201

I. **Federal Child Support Enforcement Legislation** 202

J. **Full Faith and Credit** 202

K. **Reciprocity: The Child's Duty to Support Parents** 203

VIII. **CHILD CUSTODY** **205**

A. **Child Custody During Marriage** 207

    1. Custody After Death of Parent(s) 207

    2. The Child Reaches Majority 207

B. **Child Custody Upon Divorce** 207

    1. Legal Custody Defined 207

    2. "Best Interests" Standard 208

        a. Discretion 208

        b. Historical Criteria 208

        c. Modern Criteria 208

            1) Preference of Child 208

            2) Court's Best Interests Findings 209

            3) Reports of Professionals 209

            4) Counsel for Child 209

    3. The "Tender Years" Presumption and the Maternal Preference Rule 210

    4. Religion 210

5. Race 211

6. Parent's Sexual Morality 212

7. The ALI Principles' "Approximation Standard" 214

8. Parent vs. "Third Party" 214

C. **Joint Custody** 217

D. **Rights of the Noncustodial Parent** 219

1. Visitation Rights 219

2. Restriction on Interstate Travel by Custodial Parent 220

3. Enforcement of Visitation Rights 222

E. **Standards for Modification** 223

1. Stability of Environment 223

2. Change in Circumstances 224

F. **Visitation Rights of Third Parties** 225

G. **Interstate Recognition of Custody Decrees** 226

1. "Forum Shopping" Under the "Old" Law 226

2. Early Judicial Responses 226

3. The Uniform Child Custody Jurisdiction Act 227

a. Purposes of UCCJA 227

b. Statutory Provisions 227

4. The Federal Parental Kidnapping Prevention Act 227

5. The Uniform Child Custody Jurisdiction & Enforcement Act 229

6. International Custody Disputes—Hague Convention 230

IX. **THE PARENTAL OBLIGATION OF CARE AND CONTROL, AND THE
JUVENILE COURT SYSTEM** 235

A. **Child Dependency** 237

B. **Child Neglect and Abuse** 237

1. Civil Standard 237

2. Criminal Sanctions 238

C. **Constitutional Rights** 238

1. Vagueness of Statutory Standards 238

2. Right to Counsel 239

3. Standard of Proof 240

4. Freedom of Religion 241

5. Home Visits and the Fourth Amendment 242

6. State's Responsibility to Intervene—Liability for Failure to
Protect? 242

D. **Parental Control Over a Child's Medical Care** 243

1. Physical Health 243

2. The First Amendment Issue 244

3. Mental Health 245

4. Minor's Consent to Medical Treatment 246

a. Abortion 246

b. Birth Control 248

		c.	Life–Saving Medical Care	248
	E.	**Child Abuse**		248
		1.	Abuse Reporting Statutes and Registries	248
		2.	The Battered Child Syndrome	250
	F.	**Disposition by the Juvenile Court**		251
		1.	Guardianship	251
		2.	Foster Care	251
		3.	Institutionalization	253
		4.	Termination of Parental Rights	253
	G.	**Criminal Procedure**		254
		1.	History and Development	254
		2.	The Need for Reform	254
		3.	Status Offenses and Delinquency	254
X.	**CHILDREN'S RIGHTS**			259
	A.	**History of Parental Control**		260
	B.	**Constitutional Rights**		260
	C.	**Emancipation**		262
	D.	**Minor's Capacity to Contract**		262
	E.	**Children and Tort Law**		262
		1.	"Wrongful Life"	262
			a. Recovery Allowed	262
			b. Recovery Denied	264
			c. Contract Actions	264
			d. Birth Defects	264
		2.	Wrongful Death	265
		3.	Suits Between Parent and Child—Erosion of the Tort Immunity	265
		4.	"Heartbalm" Actions	266
		5.	Childrens' Torts Against Third Parties—Parents' Liability?	267
		6.	Parents' Criminal Liability?	267
	F.	**Property Rights**		268
	G.	**Education: State and Parents**		268
		1.	Private Schooling	268
		2.	Constitutional Objections to Obligatory Schooling	269
		3.	Parental Control Over Classroom Content	269
		4.	Discipline in Schools	271
XI.	**LEGITIMACY, ILLEGITIMACY AND PATERNITY**			275
	A.	**Legitimacy**		276
		1.	Definition	276
		2.	Presumption of Legitimacy	276
	B.	**Illegitimacy**		277
		1.	Traditional Attitudes	277
		2.	The Constitutional Mandate	277

        a. Standard of Review 277
        b. Relationship to Mother 277
        c. U.S. Supreme Court Cases on the Father and Child
            Relationship 278
            1) Intestate Succession 278
            2) Right of Support 278
            3) Wrongful Death 278
            4) Government Benefits Based on Father and Child
                Relationship 279
    C. **Establishing Paternity** 280
        1. The Uniform Parentage Act 280
        2. Constitutional Requirements 280
        3. Statutes 281
            a. Burden of Proof 281
            b. Statute of Limitations 281
        4. The Unmarried Father's Custodial Interests 281
    D. **Conflicts of Laws** 283

XII. **ADOPTION** 285
    A. **History and Development** 287
    B. **Social Functions** 287
    C. **The Adoption Process** 287
        1. Agency Placement 287
        2. Independent Adoption 287
        3. "Sale" of Children and "Black Market" Adoption 288
        4. Subsidized Adoption 289
        5. Adult Adoption 290
        6. Equitable Adoption 291
    D. **Qualifications of Adoptive Parents** 292
        1. Marital Status 292
        2. Sexual Orientation 293
        3. Age 294
        4. Physical and Emotional Disabilities 295
        5. Religion 295
        6. Race 296
    E. **Consent to Adoption** 298
        1. Consent of Parents 298
        2. Consent of Unmarried Father 298
            a. Judicial (U.S. Supreme Court) Intervention 298
            b. Uniform Parentage Act, Uniform Putative and Unknown
                Fathers Act, Uniform Adoption Act 301
        3. Unreasonable Refusal of Consent 301
        4. Adoption by Stepparent: Consent of the Noncustodial Parent 302
        5. Consent of Agency or Guardian 303

	6.	Consent of the Child	303
	7.	Formalities of Consent	303
	8.	Finality and Revocation of Consent	303
		a. Birth Parents	303
		b. Reversal of Placement by Agency	304
F.	Anonymity		305
G.	Revocation of Adoption		306
H.	Legal Effect of Adoption		307
	1.	Custody	308
	2.	Name and Birth Certificate	308
	3.	Incest Laws	308
	4.	Obligation of Support	309
	5.	Inheritance	309
		a. From Adoptive Parents	309
		b. From Kin of Adoptive Parents	309
		c. From Natural Parents	309
		d. From Adoptee	310

XIII. PROCREATION ... 313
- A. Constitutional Underpinnings ... 314
  - 1. Contraception ... 314
  - 2. Abortion ... 315
  - 3. Sterilization ... 316
    - a. Compulsory Sterilization ... 316
    - b. Voluntary Sterilization ... 317
- B. Assisted Reproduction ... 317
  - 1. Artificial Insemination ... 318
    - a. Married Couple ... 318
    - b. Unmarried Persons ... 319
  - 2. *In Vitro* Fertilization and Ovum Transplantation ... 319
    - a. Husband's Sperm—Wife's Ovum ... 320
    - b. Donor's Sperm—Wife's Ovum ... 320
    - c. Donor's Ovum—Husband's or Donor's Sperm ... 320
    - d. Surrogate Mother—Husband's Sperm and Wife's Ovum ... 320
  - 3. Surrogate Motherhood for Pay ... 321
    - a. Surrogate Mother and Child ... 321
    - b. Legal Relationship Between "Purchaser's" Spouse/Partner and Child ... 325
    - c. Intermediary's Liability ... 326

APPENDICES

App.

A.	Answers to Review Questions	329
B.	Practice Essay Questions	349
C.	Text Correlation Chart	359
D.	Glossary	365
E.	Table of Cases	377
F.	Index	385

*

Capsule Summary

■ I. THE NATURE OF MARRIAGE

A. CONTRACT OR STATUS

Marriage is a status which is entered into by contract. While the state defines the rights and obligations due each party, the parties are allowed some variation by means of antenuptial or postnuptial agreements.

B. THE MARITAL RELATIONSHIP AT COMMON LAW

Husband and wife were regarded as one person in law. The legal existence of the married woman was essentially incorporated into that of the husband. The "Married Women's Property Acts" gave married women legal capacity to make contracts, own property, and more, but social and economic inequality continued to leave many women vulnerable if marriage ended.

C. ANTENUPTIAL (PREMARITAL) AGREEMENTS

Today, antenuptial agreements dictating the financial consequences of divorce or death are generally enforced if the following conditions are met: (1) the agreement is *voluntary*; (2) the agreement is *informed*, having been negotiated with adequate disclosure of each party's financial assets; and (3) the terms of the agreement are *not unconscionable*.

D. AGREEMENTS DURING MARRIAGE

Reconciliation and separation agreements are commonly enforceable so long as the terms are not unconscionable. Increasingly, states are beginning to permit married couples to enter into postnuptial agreements even when divorce or separation is not immediately on the horizon.

■ II. MARRIAGE REQUISITES

A. FORMAL REQUIREMENTS

Consent and solemnization, broadly defined, create a legally effective marriage.

B. COMMON LAW MARRIAGE

A minority of jurisdictions permit parties to enter marriage informally. "Common law marriage" is a valid marriage entered into by the parties' agreement, but without formal solemnization, where: (1) the parties have the *capacity* to marry; (2) they *intend* to be married; (3) they *hold themselves out* to others as married; and (4) they *cohabit* as a married couple.

C. PROPERTY RIGHTS IN THE ABSENCE OF MARRIAGE

1. Putative Spouse Doctrine
A "putative spouse" is one who has unwittingly, and in good faith, participated in an invalid marriage. Although not legally married, she or he may nevertheless be able to seek marriage-like property division and alimony.

2. **Cohabitation Without Marriage**

In some states, "quasi-marital" property and possibly support obligations may arise from non-marital cohabitation, when there is an express or implied cohabitation contract between the parties.

3. **Domestic Partnerships and Civil Unions**

In a growing minority of states, couples may enter into formal domestic partnerships or civil unions, acquiring all or nearly all of the property rights associated with marriage.

D. SUBSTANTIVE REQUIREMENTS FOR VALID MARRIAGE

Traditionally, states have insisted that persons wishing to marry be single, of different genders, of sufficient age and adequate health, and not closely related. At one time, many states also insisted that marriage partners be of the same race. Race-based restrictions were held unconstitutional in 1967 and, increasingly, the remaining restrictions have come under attack as well. The highest courts of California, Connecticut, and Massachusetts have each ruled that their state constitutions entitle same-sex couples to marry; in 2008, voters in California amended that state's constitution to reinstate the ban on same-sex marriage.

E. CONFLICT OF LAWS—VALIDITY

The law of the place of celebration usually governs the validity of the marriage, unless recognition would violate a strong public policy of the state in which recognition is sought.

F. ANNULMENT

Annulment is a judicial declaration that, by reason of some defect existing at its inception, a purported marriage does not exist and never has existed.

■ IV. SPOUSES

A. SUPPORT OBLIGATIONS DURING MARRIAGE

Spouses are obligated to support one another during marriage although courts seldom enforce the principle in intact families. In many states, one spouse may compel the other to pay for essential items, or "necessaries," by purchasing them on credit.

B. PROPERTY RIGHTS

1. **Common Law**
   At common law the husband gained possession of any property owned or acquired by the wife, but this rule was abrogated by the Married Women's Property Acts.

2. **Modern Law—Separate–Property States**
   The majority of states (41 in 2008) have separate property regimes, under which each spouse independently owns and controls whatever property he or she acquires during the marriage.

3. **Modern Law—Community Property States**
   In community property states, each spouse owns a present, undivided one-half interest in property acquired by either spouse during the marriage. Some states except from the scope of community property, property acquired by means of gift, inheritance, or passive returns on non-community property.

C. TORTS AND THE FAMILY

1. **Immunities**
   At one time, tort suits among family members were barred by intra-family tort immunities. In recent years, however, these immunities have been widely abandoned or curtailed.

2. **"Heart Balm" and Other Torts**
   Tort law once provided a wide range of remedies for the destruction of intimate relationships, including actions for seduction, criminal conversation, alienation of affections, breach of promise to marry, and more. The strong trend in recent decades, however, has been to abolish or sharply limit these actions.

D. MARRIAGE AND CRIMINAL LAW

The modern trend is to reduce or abolish traditional immunities between spouses that barred certain criminal prosecutions, such as the once-common immunity for marital rape. Today, states have enacted special statutes that deal with domestic violence and provide aid to victims, especially by way of protective orders.

E. FAMILY NAMES

Recent years have seen tradition give way to creativity in the adoption of family names, and the courts have generally acquiesced in this trend.

■ V. DIVORCE—STATUS

A. JURISDICTION

To establish jurisdiction, states typically require a divorce petitioner to establish residency in the state. Although courts may grant an *ex parte* divorce even without personal jurisdiction over the respondent spouse, in order to decide matters relating to child custody, property, or alimony, the other spouse must have sufficient contacts with the forum to permit the assertion of personal jurisdiction.

B. TRADITIONAL GROUNDS AND DEFENSES

At one time, a party seeking divorce had to prove that the other spouse had committed a designated "fault" ground, such as adultery, physical or mental cruelty, desertion, or habitual drunkenness. The other spouse could then defeat the divorce action by raising an enumerated defense, such as condonation, recrimination, provocation, or connivance.

C. NO–FAULT DIVORCE

Today, all states permit divorce without fault where a marriage is irretrievably broken, usually on a showing that the parties have lived separate and apart for a specified period.

■ VI. DIVORCE—FINANCIAL CONSEQUENCES

A. ALIMONY ON DIVORCE

Typically, courts have broad discretion in deciding whether to award alimony. A trend toward very limited, "rehabilitative" alimony awards in the 1970s and 1980s has given ground recently to recognition that indefinite alimony may in fact be justified upon the dissolution of some longterm marriages. Alimony may be modified if there is a subsequent change of circumstances and typically ends upon the death of either party or upon the remarriage of the recipient.

B. PROPERTY DIVISION ON DIVORCE

1. Marital and Community Property

If there is a divorce, the property systems of the community and separate property states operate similarly. Many separate property states classify property acquired during the marriage (except by gift, inheritance, or passive return on pre-marital property) as "marital property" which may be divided on divorce, much as "community property" is treated elsewhere.

2. Equitable Distribution

Although some states mandate an equal division of "marital" or "community" property, most mandate "equitable distribution." Under the latter rule, courts have considerable latitude to order a "fair" splitting of assets, taking into account the respective contributions of the spouses, their prospects for future earnings, their health and financial obligations, and numerous other factors. The states disagree over whether *marital* fault (*e.g.*, adultery) may be considered, but all agree that *economic* fault, or the wrongful dissipation of marital assets, is a proper factor.

C. SEPARATION AGREEMENTS

Separation agreements specifying the consequences of divorce are widely enforced by the courts. Ordinarily, terms respecting property and alimony are binding on the court, while terms dealing with child support or custody are subject to further scrutiny.

■ VII. THE PARENTAL CHILD SUPPORT OBLIGATION

A. WHO MUST PAY?

Parents are legally obligated to support their children. Some states also impose support duties on stepparents, but only during the duration of their marriage. Occasionally, courts have found non-parents liable for child support under theories of "equitable adoption."

B. HOW MUCH AND FOR HOW LONG?

Today, federal legislation has caused all states to legislate specific, usually mathematical, "guidelines" that determine the support obligation, with the primary or sole reference point being the absent parent's income. Departures from the "guidelines" are permitted if there are exceptional circumstances. The support obligation typically continues until the child reaches majority or becomes emancipated.

■ VIII. CHILD CUSTODY

A. "BEST INTERESTS" STANDARD

In disputes between parents, custody should be decided according to the "best interests of the child." Courts typically consider a wide range of factors in assessing a child's "best interests," including each parent's emotional relationship with the child, the respective home environments, and the assessments of experts. Under the "Tender Years Doctrine," states formerly applied a heavy presumption in favor of mother custody of young children. Today, courts use nominally gender-neutral standards.

B. PARENT VS. NON–PARENT

There is a strong presumption, rooted partly in constitutional doctrine, that parents are entitled to custody of their children. Accordingly, courts typically will award custody to a parent over a non-parent unless the parent is "unfit" to care for a child or, in some jurisdictions, unless parental custody would impose a serious detriment on the child.

C. VISITATION RIGHTS

1. Non–Custodial Parents

The non-custodial parent is entitled to visitation unless contact would pose a serious risk to the child. In order to facilitate this visitation, many courts have imposed restrictions on the relocation of the custodial parent, although the trend is to allow greater mobility.

2. Non–Parents

Statutes allowing non-parents, such as grandparents, to seek court-ordered visitation have come under increasing constitutional attack. The U.S. Supreme Court ruled in 2000 that courts considering such a request must give "special weight" to the parents' reasons for objecting to contact.

D. MODIFICATION

Custody orders may be modified upon proof of changed circumstances and a showing that change is in the best interest of the child.

■ IX. PARENTAL OBLIGATION OF CARE AND CONTROL AND THE JUVENILE COURT SYSTEM

A. STATE INTERVENTION FOR ABUSE & NEGLECT

The state may intervene to protect children from dependency, abuse, and neglect. Intervention may range from investigation and counseling to, in the worst cases, termination of parental rights and placement of the child in a new adoptive family. The federal Adoption and Safe Families Act of 1997 has prodded states toward more aggressive intervention.

B. CONSTITUTIONAL LIMITATIONS

Due process respects parental rights and demands that, in an action to terminate parental rights, the state prove its allegations of unfitness by "clear and convincing evidence." In some cases, indigent parents may be entitled to court-appointed counsel and to a waiver of filing fees on appeal. Abuse and neglect laws have been attacked—mostly unsuccessfully—on the ground that they are unconstitutionally vague.

■ X. CHILDREN'S RIGHTS

A. HISTORY OF PARENTAL CONTROL AND CONSTITUTIONAL RIGHTS

Parental prerogative is limited by the neglect, dependency and abuse laws and, increasingly, by the recognition that children have constitutional rights of their own.

B. EMANCIPATION

Emancipation generally occurs when a minor acts independently of his or her parents in a manner associated with adulthood. Emancipation terminates parental support obligations and eliminates minority as a defense to contracts.

C. MINOR'S CAPACITY TO CONTRACT

A contractual obligation incurred by an unemancipated minor generally is voidable, unless ratified when the minor reaches majority.

D. CHILDREN AND TORT LAW

With respect to the parent-child relationship, tort liability is limited by remnants of intra-family tort immunities. Statutes now permit parents to recover for the wrongful death of a child.

■ XI. LEGITIMACY, ILLEGITIMACY AND PATERNITY

A. LEGITIMACY

Since the late 1960s, using an intermediate standard of constitutional review, the U.S. Supreme Court has invalidated nearly all forms of legal discrimination against illegitimate children.

B. ESTABLISHING PATERNITY

All states provide for the judicial ascertainment of paternity. Scientific advances have made this determination far more certain. In most cases, however, paternity is established without proof of genetic fatherhood on the basis of a voluntary acknowledgment of paternity or a legal presumption created by marriage to the mother.

■ XII.   ADOPTION

A.   WHO MAY ADOPT?

Prospective adoptive parents are evaluated as to marital status, age, religion, ethnic origin, physical disabilities, emotional problems, residency and economic status. A growing number of states now permit unmarried persons, including same-sex couples, to adopt.

B.   CONSENT TO ADOPTION

Formal consents to an adoption ordinarily must be obtained from both parents, unless the father is unmarried and has shown very little interest in the child. Children above a certain age may be required to consent.

C.   LEGAL EFFECT OF ADOPTION

Adoption creates a new legal parent-child relationship and extinguishes all legal ties with the surrendering parents. In most states, adoption records remain secret, unless all parties indicate their desire for openness.

■ XIII.   PROCREATION

A.   CONTRACEPTION AND PRIVACY

The U.S. Supreme Court has recognized a constitutional right of privacy which includes the right of married and unmarried couples to access contraception.

B. ABORTION

The constitutional right of privacy includes a woman's right to elect abortion. The current rule is that states may regulate abortion to promote maternal or fetal health so long as the regulations do not impose an "undue burden" on free choice, and may prohibit abortion after fetal viability.

C. ASSISTED REPRODUCTION

New techniques for noncoital reproduction encompass artificial insemination, ovum donation, *in vitro* fertilization, embryo transfer, and "surrogate mother-hood." Although a married couple will readily be recognized as a child's parents if they each contributed genetically to the child's conception, more complicated questions can arise when third-party donors or surrogates are involved or when the intending parents are unmarried.

I

The Nature of Marriage and Marital Contracts

■ ANALYSIS

A. Religious Influence
B. Contract or Status
C. Controlling Factors Affecting the Marriage Contract
   1. State Power
   2. Change of Residence
   3. Private Marriage Contract
D. Marriage and the Constitution
   1. Religious Freedom
   2. Monogamy
   3. The Right to Marry
   4. Same–Sex Marriage
   5. Marital and Sexual Privacy
E. The Marital Relationship at Common Law
F. Married Women's Property Acts
G. The Antenuptial Agreement

1.   Individualizing Marriage by Contract
2.   Validity of Antenuptial Agreements

H.   Agreements During Marriage
1.   Postnuptial Agreements
2.   Reconciliation Agreements
3.   Separation Agreements

I.   Conflicts Aspects of Marital Agreements

J.   Breach of Promise to Marry

K.   Gifts in Contemplation of Marriage
1.   Gifts Before Engagement
2.   Gifts During an Engagement
3.   Gifts From Third Parties

A. Religious Influence

In England, the ecclesiastical courts' exclusive jurisdiction in matters of marriage and divorce lasted until the 1850s. *Holy* matrimony served as the setting for the procreation and rearing of children, as a haven from and defense against sin and crime (*i.e.*, fornication) and afforded spouses mutual society, help and comfort. Much of the law created by English church doctrine and religious courts entered into the common law of the United States.

B. Contract or Status

"Marriage is a personal relationship between a man and a woman arising out of a civil contract to which the consent of the parties is essential." UMDA § 201. Entered into by contract, *marriage is a status.* Rights and obligations are delineated ultimately by the state, not by the parties alone. Thus, although states now afford significant freedom to couples to control the financial consequences of divorce through contracts, states continue to specify many non-negotiable aspects of the marriage relationship. *Maynard v. Hill,* 125 U.S. 190, 8 S.Ct. 723, 31 L.Ed. 654 (1888), pronounced: "Other contracts may be modified, restricted, or enlarged, or entirely released upon the consent of the parties. Not so with marriage. The relation once formed, the law steps in and holds the parties to various obligations and liabilities."

C. Controlling Factors Affecting the Marriage Contract

1. State Power
The states have "reserve power" to modify the law of marriage and divorce, even when such a legislative change may interfere with the reasonable expectations of married parties. This has been upheld on the following rationales:

a. Contract Clause Inapplicable
U.S. Const. art. I, § 10 provides: "No State shall * * * pass any * * * Law impairing the Obligation of Contracts * * *." Marriage, however, has been held not to be a contract within the meaning of that article of the Constitution, because "[marriage] is an institution in the maintenance of which in its purity, the public is deeply interested * * *." *Maynard v. Hill, supra.*

b. State Reserve Power
Because marriage involves the public interest, marriage regulation incorporates the reserve power of the state to amend existing laws or enact additional laws.

Example: H and W married when a fault-based divorce statute was in effect. Much later, the state enacted no-fault divorce, and H filed for divorce. W contended that the state's implementation of no-fault divorce constituted an unconstitutional impairment of her contract rights because H would not have been able to divorce her under the fault-based statute in effect at the time they were married. (Result: Divorce granted. The marriage contract includes the reserve power of the state to amend the law.) *In re Walton's Marriage*, 28 Cal.App.3d 108, 104 Cal.Rptr. 472 (1972).

c.   Due Process Clause Inapplicable

"Status" as a married person is *not property* within the purview of the Due Process Clause. Even if that "status" were "property," a retroactive change in divorce laws would not deprive a person of that status *without due process of law.*

Example: W had prevailed in a separation action under fault-based New York divorce law. After the enactment of no-fault (living apart) divorce legislation in 1966, H claimed that the separation under the earlier decree was the basis for a no-fault divorce. This would deprive W of certain economic benefits and rights relating to her relationship with H that she had retained under the separation decree. (Result: Divorce granted. W did not have a vested right that was adversely affected as her "prospective right of inheritance is inchoate and expectant." "In short, the State, having the power directly to limit or abolish rights of accession to the property of a living person, may undoubtedly do so indirectly by providing a new ground for divorce. Since, then, no vested rights of the defendants have been adversely affected, there has been no denial of due process.") *Gleason v. Gleason*, 26 N.Y.2d 28, 308 N.Y.S.2d 347, 256 N.E.2d 513 (1970). In response to *Gleason*, New York *legislated* limited relief for such cases. D. R. L. § 170a.

2.   Change of Residence

The parties' reasonable expectations as to the incidents of their marriage may be altered by their move from one jurisdiction to another. While the *validity* of marriage generally is determined in accordance with the law of the place of celebration, the law of the parties' domicile generally governs the legal incidents of the *marital relationship* as well as requirements for and consequences of *divorce*.

Example: H and W married in Massachusetts in 1976 and later acquired property in Maine for their eventual retirement. In 2003, W moved to their property in Maine and later filed for divorce there, while H remained at the original marital home in Massachusetts. The court properly applied Maine law to classify and divide the couple's marital property, including their Massachusetts home. *Zeolla v. Zeolla*, 908 A.2d 629 (Me. 2006).

3. Private Marriage Contract

An antenuptial agreement, or to a lesser extent a post-nuptial agreement, between the parties may affect and alter the terms of the marriage relationship. (See G, below).

D. Marriage and the Constitution

Although marital relationships traditionally are defined and controlled by state law, the U.S. Supreme Court has applied constitutional interpretation to a host of family law issues. In this manner, numerous aspects of family law have been federalized and, incidentally but very importantly, unified throughout the United States. Increasingly, state courts have interpreted state constitutions to expand certain rights, as in the case of same-sex marriage (*e.g., In re Marriage Cases*, 43 Cal.4th 757, 76 Cal.Rptr.3d 683, 183 P.3d 384 (2008); *Goodridge v. Department of Public Health*, 440 Mass. 309, 798 N.E.2d 941 (2003)).

1. Religious Freedom

The state's power to regulate civil marriage coexists with the freedom of religions and religious believers to define marriage in their own way for religious purposes. The state may not deliberately target religious practice, but neither is it constitutionally required to conform the civil institution of marriage to private religious scruples.

Examples: (1) Reynolds, a member of the Church of Jesus Christ of Latter–Day Saints, was convicted of bigamy. He challenged his conviction as a violation of the First Amendment. (Result: Conviction upheld. "[I]t is impossible to believe that the constitutional guarantee of religious freedom was intended to prohibit legislation in respect to this most important feature of social life. . . . [T]he only question which remains is, whether those who make polygamy a part of their religion are excepted from the operation of the statute. If they are, then those who do not make polygamy a part of their religious belief may be found guilty and punished, while those who do must be acquitted and go free. This would be introducing a new element into criminal law.") *Reynolds v. United States*, 98 U.S. (8 Otto) 145, 25 L.Ed. 244 (1878).

(2) H was granted a divorce from W. Both were citizens of India and Hindus of high caste. W contended that the divorce violated her First Amendment (free exercise of religion) rights as the Hindu religion does not recognize divorce. She alleged that if she ever returned to India divorced, her family and friends would treat her as if she were dead. (Result: For H. The order dissolved only the civil contract of marriage and did not dissolve it ecclesiastically. "The wife here may take such view of their relationship after the decree as her religion requires, but as a matter of law the civil contract has been dissolved.") *Sharma v. Sharma*, 8 Kan.App.2d 726, 667 P.2d 395 (1983).

2. Monogamy

Marriage to more than one spouse at the same time (bigamy, polygamy) is invalid and subject to criminal sanctions. Aside from intentional bigamy for whatever—often fraudulent, sometimes religious—purpose, much "unintended" bigamy occurred in the days of difficult divorce, when a person remarried whose prior marriage had been divorced by ineffective legal process (*e.g.,* an invalid migratory divorce) or not at all. The continued practice of polygamy in the United States has received renewed attention after highly publicized raids and prosecutions in Texas, Arizona, and Utah; it is estimated that between 10,000 and 50,000 Americans are currently living in polygamous unions, mostly in western states.

a. Justification for Regulation

1) Religion and Tradition
Restrictions on bigamy and polygamy are founded in religious beliefs, moral taboos, and Western cultural tradition.

2) Constitutionality
In 1878, the U.S. Supreme Court upheld a statute prohibiting bigamy against attack under the First Amendment. The court held

that the public interest in preventing polygamy outweighed the interest of Mormons in practicing that aspect of their religion, noting that "[p]olygamy has always been odious among the northern and western nations of Europe." *Reynolds v. United States,* 98 U.S. (8 Otto) 145, 25 L.Ed. 244 (1878). Even while concluding that their state constitutions entitled same-sex couples to marry, the highest courts of both California and Massachusetts emphasized that laws banning polygamy stand on firmer constitutional ground. *In re Marriage Cases,* 43 Cal.4th 757, 76 Cal.Rptr.3d 683, 183 P.3d 384 (2008); *Goodridge v. Department of Public Health,* 440 Mass. 309, 798 N.E.2d 941 (2003).

3) **Modern Rationale**

Today, restrictions on polygamy are commonly justified as promoting the stability of the family and avoiding sexual and economic exploitation of the spouses and children of the polygamist.

Examples: (1) H & W, along with a second woman H also wished to marry, brought suit after county clerk refused marriage license to H and second intended wife. The three argued that Utah's refusal to allow "plural marriage" violated their constitutional rights to association, privacy, and religious exercise. (Result: Ps lose. "Monogamy is inextricably woven into the fabric of our society. It is the bedrock upon which our culture is built. * * * In light of these fundamental values, the state is justified, by a compelling interest, in upholding and enforcing its ban on plural marriage to protect the monogamous marriage relationship." On the constitutional issue of privacy, the court went on to say, "[W]e find no authority for extending the constitutional right of privacy so far that it would protect polygamous marriages. We decline to do so.") *Bronson v. Swensen,* 394 F.Supp.2d 1329 (D. Utah 2005) (quoting *Potter v. Murray City,* 760 F.2d 1065 (10th Cir.1985), *cert. denied,* 474 U.S. 849, 106 S.Ct. 145, 88 L.Ed.2d 120 (1985)), *vacated on other grounds,* 500 F.3d 1099 (10th Cir. 2007).

(2) H was convicted of bigamy and unlawful sexual conduct with a minor after he entered into a private, "celestial" marriage with his wife's 16–year-old sister.

He argued that the Constitution forbids a state from criminalizing a private, consensual intimate relationship. (Result: Conviction upheld. "[T]he behavior at issue in this case is not confined to personal decisions made about sexual activity, but rather raises important questions about the State's ability to regulate marital relationships and prevent the formation and propagation of marital forms that the citizens of the State deem harmful. . . . Further, it is not unreasonable to conclude that this case involves behavior that warrants inquiry into the possible existence of injury and the validity of consent. 'The practice of polygamy . . . often coincides with crimes targeting women and children. Crimes not unusually attendant to the practice of polygamy include incest, sexual assault, statutory rape, and failure to pay child support.' ") *State v. Holm*, 137 P.3d 726 (Utah 2006).

b. Criminal Sanctions

1) Enforcement Practice

For decades, criminal bigamy statutes were rarely enforced. A series of high profile prosecutions in recent years, including a nationwide FBI manhunt for polygamist sect leader Warren Jeffs in 2006, appears to mark a new willingness to enforce bigamy laws.

2) "Enoch Arden" Defense

When an individual's spouse has been missing for a specified period of time (such as seven or five years) and if he or she believed that his or her marriage had ended in divorce or through the partner's death, typical statutes provide a defense to criminal bigamy prosecution of a remarried individual. Based on a Tennyson poem, these statutes are commonly referred to as *"Enoch Arden"* statutes. They do *not* have civil effects, such as validating the later marriage.

c. Civil Effects of Bigamous Marriage

A marriage is void if entered while a previous marriage is still in force. Nevertheless, in many states even a bigamous marriage may have certain legal effects: (1) Statutes may declare the offspring of such marriages "legitimate"; (2) Statutes may authorize alimony to be paid to

[handwritten margin notes: "Alabama ↓ Common law"; "If Wife 1 died or get divorce W2 can be legal in common law states."; "HW¹ HW²"]

the "victim" of a void marriage; (3) The putative spouse doctrine (p. 60) may protect the interests of the partner who, in good faith, believed his or her partner to be eligible to marry; (4) A subsequent end of the first *[handwritten: Test]* marriage through divorce or the other spouse's death may validate the previously void marriage in states recognizing common law marriage; (5) A "presumption" may in certain cases uphold a marriage of dubious validity (p. 58); (6) UMDA § 207(b) expressly validates a previously invalid marriage as of the time the impediment is removed; (7) A declaration of invalidity may be granted *non*-retroactively under UMDA § 208(e) Alternative B: "Unless the court finds * * * that the interests of justice would be served by making the decree not retroactive, it shall declare the marriage invalid as of the date of the marriage" (p. 76).

3. The Right to Marry

In 1967, Virginia was one of sixteen states that still prohibited interracial marriage. Two Virginia residents, a black woman and a white man, had married in the District of Columbia in 1958. After returning to Virginia, they were convicted of violating the statutory prohibition. The sentence was one year in jail which was suspended on condition that they leave Virginia and not return together for twenty-five years. In *Loving v. Virginia*, 388 U.S. 1, 87 S.Ct. 1817, 18 L.Ed.2d 1010 (1967), the United States Supreme Court invalidated the state law. Very importantly, the court classified the right to marry as "fundamental": "The freedom to marry has long been recognized as one of the vital personal rights essential to the orderly pursuit of happiness by free men. * * * Marriage is one of the 'basic civil rights of man,' fundamental to *[handwritten: Test]* our very existence and survival." Given its facts, *Loving might have been*, but was not, interpreted to be limited to the particularly odious *racial* classification there involved. Instead, the concept of marriage as a fundamental right under the Due Process and Equal Protection Clauses has been used to attack and invalidate a broad variety of marriage restrictions, such as a Wisconsin statute conditioning the issuance of a marriage license on compliance with prior support obligations. *Zablocki v. Redhail*, 434 U.S. 374, 98 S.Ct. 673, 54 L.Ed.2d 618 (1978).

Examples: (1) Missouri prison regulations permitted an inmate to marry only with the permission of the superintendent, and provided that such approval should be given only "when there are compelling reasons to do so." The term "compelling" was not defined, but officials testified that generally only a pregnancy or the birth of an illegitimate child would be considered a compelling reason. (Result: The U.S. Supreme Court held: "We disagree * * * that *Zablocki* [*v. Redhail, supra*], does not apply to inmates. It is settled that a prison inmate 'retains those (constitutional) rights that are not inconsistent with his status as a prisoner or with the legitimate penological objectives of the corrections system.' * * * [T]he almost complete ban on the decision to marry is not reasonably related to legitimate penological objectives. We conclude, therefore, that the * * * regulation is facially invalid.") *Turner v. Safley,* 482 U.S. 78, 107 S.Ct. 2254, 96 L.Ed.2d 64 (1987).

(2) State law required males to be 21 years of age to obtain a marriage license without parental consent (18 with consent; 16 with court order) and females to be 18 without parental consent (16 with consent; 15 with court order). (Result: Statute unconstitutionally denies equal protection on account of sex, and *mandamus* may be used to compel issuance of marriage license to 20–year-old plaintiff.) *Phelps v. Bing,* 58 Ill.2d 32, 316 N.E.2d 775 (1974). Note: More recently, gender-related age discrimination was ruled out by the U.S. Supreme Court's *Stanton* cases. See p. 68.

(3) A debtor who had married while under protection of the U.S. bankruptcy code sought to modify his repayment plan. The trustee in bankruptcy characterized the debtor's marriage as a voluntary change in circumstances that should weigh against the proposed modification. (Result: Modification allowed. Referring to *Loving v. Virginia*, the bankruptcy court held: "Clearly there is no provision of the Code which is intended to inhibit the right to marry while in bankruptcy. Any such interpretation would turn public policy on its ear by requiring payments to creditors under a confirmed plan at the expense of the debtor's support of his family. * * * The obligation of financial support as it flows from the decision, albeit perhaps untimely, to marry or procreate, is not intended to be superseded by the creditor's rights under the Code. * * * Accordingly, the monthly payments will be reduced from $215.00 to $140.00, and the Plan will be extended to sixty months. The dividend to unsecured creditors will be reduced from 100% to 34%.") *In re Walker,* 114 B.R. 847 (Bkrtcy.N.D.N.Y.1990).

4. Same–Sex Marriage

Traditionally, the laws of all states limited marriage to the union of one man and one woman. In recent years, that limitation has come under constitutional attack in a number of states. Initially, those attacks failed, as courts ruled that the fundamental right to marry recognized in *Loving* was confined to those wishing to enter *traditional* marital unions. *See, e.g., Dean v. District of Columbia*, 653 A.2d 307 (D.C. 1995). In 2003, the U.S. Supreme Court struck down a criminal ban on sexual relations between same-sex partners as a violation of substantive due process. *Lawrence v. Texas*, 539 U.S. 558, 123 S.Ct. 2472, 156 L.Ed.2d 508 (2003). The Court carefully reserved the question of whether the Constitution would further require states to give "formal recognition" to same-sex relationships, but the reasoning of its decision—*i.e.,* that a state has no legitimate interest in privileging heterosexual intimacy on moral grounds—at least undermined traditional justifications for prohibiting same-sex marriage. Both before and after *Lawrence*, litigants have succeeded in challenging bans on same-sex marriage by asserting various theories under *state* constitutional law. Other courts have distinguished *Lawrence* and upheld the constitutionality of laws banning same-sex marriage.

Examples: (1) Same-sex couples who were refused marriage licences filed suit claiming that Hawaii's ban on same-sex marriage constituted a denial of substantive due process and equal protection under the state constitution. (Result: Ban does not deny due process because the fundamental right to marry is limited to traditional marriage. Ban *does* constitute "suspect" discrimination under state equal protection principles because the withholding of the license was based on the gender of the intending partners. *Baehr v. Lewin*, 74 Haw. 530, 852 P.2d 44 (1993). On remand, the trial court concluded that the state had not carried its strict-scrutiny burden of demonstrating a compelling state purpose for the discrimination against same-sex couples. *Baehr v. Miike*, 1996 WL 694235 (Haw. Cir. Ct. Dec. 3, 1996). While an appeal was pending, Hawaii voters amended the state constitution to limit marriage to opposite-sex couples. Hawaii then enacted legislation permitting same-sex couples to register as domestic partners in lieu of marriage.) *Test*

(2) Same-sex couples challenged Vermont's ban on same-sex marriage as a violation of the state constitution's "Common Benefits Clause," a provision roughly equivalent to the federal Constitution's Equal Protection Clause. (Result: The denial of

benefits associated with marriage to same-sex couples denies them equal benefits in contravention of the state constitution.) *Baker v. State*, 170 Vt. 194, 744 A.2d 864 (1999). In response to the state supreme court's mandate to enact corrective legislation, the Vermont legislature enacted a law permitting same-sex couples to enter into "civil unions" carrying essentially all the benefits under state law associated with marriage, although not "marriage" itself.

(3) Same-sex couples challenged Massachusetts' ban on same-sex marriage as a violation of the liberty and equality guarantees of the state constitution. (Result: The court did not resolve whether same-sex couples have a fundamental right to marry, because the state's ban on same-sex marriage is unconstitutional even under the rational-basis test. The exclusion of committed same-sex couples from the civil institution of marriage furthers no legitimate interest of the state; to the contrary, it "confers an official stamp of approval on the destructive stereotype that same-sex relationships are inherently unstable and inferior to opposite-sex relationships and not worthy of respect.") *Goodridge v. Department of Public Health*, 440 Mass. 309, 798 N.E.2d 941 (2003).

(4) Same-sex couples challenged California's ban on same-sex marriage as a violation of the liberty and equality guarantees of the state constitution. California law permitted same-sex couples to register as domestic partners, thereby gaining virtually all benefits of marriage under state law, but limited marriage to opposite-sex couples. (Result: Denying marriage to same-sex couples violates the fundamental right to marry and impermissibly discriminates on the basis of sexual orientation under the state constitution. "In light of the fundamental nature of the substantive rights embodied in the right to marry—and their central importance to an individual's opportunity to live a happy, meaningful, and satisfying life as a full member of society—the California Constitution properly must be interpreted to guarantee this basic civil right to *all* individuals and couples, without regard to their sexual orientation.") *In re Marriage Cases*, 43 Cal.4th 757, 76 Cal.Rptr.3d 683, 183 P.3d 384 (2008). In November 2008, California voters amended the state constitution to overturn the court's decision and reinstate the ban on same-sex marriage.

(5) Same-sex couples challenged New York's ban on same-sex marriage as a violation of the liberty and equality guarantees of the state constitution. (Result: "The right to marry someone of the same sex . . . is not 'deeply rooted' " in the nation's history and tradition and is therefore not a fundamental constitutional right. Furthermore, the ban on same-sex marriage does not discriminate against any suspect or quasi-suspect class. Applying the rational basis test, limiting marriage to opposite-sex couples is rationally related to the state's interest in promoting a stable environment for childrearing. "First, the Legislature could rationally decide that, for the welfare of children, it is more important to promote stability, and to avoid instability, in opposite-sex than in same-sex relationships," given that only opposite-sex couples can become parents by accident. Second, "[t]he Legislature could rationally believe that it is better, other things being equal, for children to grow up with both a mother and a father.") *Hernandez v. Robles*, 7 N.Y.3d 338, 821 N.Y.S.2d 770, 855 N.E.2d 1 (2006).

5. Marital and Sexual Privacy

Griswold v. Connecticut, 381 U.S. 479, 85 S.Ct. 1678, 14 L.Ed.2d 510 (1965), discovered a right to marital privacy in "emanations from" and the "penumbras of" numerous constitutional amendments based on society's traditional respect for the marital relationship. The Court then struck down a Connecticut statute prohibiting—even by married couples—the use of birth control drugs or devices. *Griswold* was followed by *Eisenstadt v. Baird*, 405 U.S. 438, 92 S.Ct. 1029, 31 L.Ed.2d 349 (1972), which invalidated a similar law applied to unmarried persons. *Eisenstadt* cast doubt on whether the right of privacy referred to in *Griswold* is based on the *marital* relationship: "Yet the marital couple is not an independent entity with a mind and heart of its own, but an association of two individuals each with a separate intellectual and emotional makeup. If the right of privacy means anything, it is the right of the individual, married or single, to be free from unwarranted governmental intrusion into matters so fundamentally affecting a person as the decision whether to bear or beget a child."

Although the idea of an unwritten constitutional right of privacy remains controversial, the U.S. Supreme Court has continued to recognize heightened constitutional protection for a widening range of "private" decisions relating to marriage, procreation (discussed at p. 314), abortion (discussed at p. 315), child-rearing (discussed at p. 238), and other aspects of family life. In 2003, the Court extended this line of precedent to include same-sex intimacy, striking down a Texas law that criminalized sodomy. *Lawrence v. Texas*, 539 U.S. 558, 123 S.Ct. 2472, 156 L.Ed.2d 508 (2003). The Court did not, however, expressly state that it was recognizing a fundamental privacy right.

E. The Marital Relationship at Common Law

Traditionally, the marital relationship was dominated by the husband. Blackstone's classic phrase was: "By marriage, the husband and wife are one person in law; that is, the very being or legal existence of the woman is suspended during the marriage, or at least is incorporated and consolidated into that of the husband." During marriage, all of the married woman's real and personal property was controlled by the husband. While the *single* woman had legal capacity at common law, a *wife* could not contract, neither with her husband nor with others, nor could she sue or be sued.

F. Married Women's Property Acts

Trust devices were developed to keep married women's property out of their husbands' control. In the late 1800's, some of the legal disabilities imposed on women were eliminated directly by so-called "Married Women's Property Acts." *Test* These typically allowed married women to own and convey property, make contracts, sue or be sued and much more, but they did not end all disabilities imposed on the wife by marriage. Tort immunities continue into the present, although in greatly diminished form. See Ch. IV, p. 111.

G. The Antenuptial Agreement

Traditionally, antenuptial (or prenuptial or premarital) contracts have been used by people who are wealthy, are elderly and/or are parents of children from a previous marriage in order to protect their estates. Today, increasing use of such contracts by intending spouses is due to the entirely different economic relationship between H and W in a dual career (or two-job) marriage, the ease with which divorce may be obtained, and the desire of many modern couples to shape the content of their marital relationship. Traditional antenuptial agreements typically dealt only with property division upon death. So limited, they were enforceable. More recently, antenuptial agreements dealing with support and property settlements upon divorce as well as contracts dealing with aspects of the ongoing marriage have become permissible.

1. Individualizing Marriage by Contract

 An antenuptial agreement seeks to individualize aspects of the parties' marriage by altering marital rights and obligations, personal or financial, that otherwise would be imposed by law.

2. Validity of Antenuptial Agreements

Valid antenuptial agreements must meet all of the usual requirements of *Law/ Test* contract law. Beyond that, antenuptial agreements have been subject to special scrutiny based on public policies relating to marriage, the parties' confidential and intimate relationship and, so it sometimes seems, even the court's hindsight.

a. Contract Requirements

1) Statute of Frauds → *Says that Most Agreements have to be in writing*

Test Most states require antenuptial agreements to be in writing, as did the original Statute of Frauds. Appropriate exceptions may be made if there was sufficient part performance, or enforcement would cause a fraud to be perpetrated, or one party's representations coupled with the other's reliance have led to a detrimental change in position. Some statutes require compliance with further formalities, such as requiring the agreement to be witnessed formally.

Examples: (1) H insisted that he would marry only if W agreed that each would remain employed throughout their marriage and that "each party's income and property would be treated as separate property." W orally agreed and the couple was married in 1986. By the time of the couple's divorce in 2001, W had become a very successful lawyer with annual income of more than $1 million; H argued that the oral prenuptial agreement was unenforceable under the statute of frauds. (Result: The oral prenuptial agreement was enforceable under the "part performance" exception to the statute of frauds. "The record reflects painstaking and meticulous effort to maintain separate finances and property" throughout the marriage, consistent with the oral agreement.) *DewBerry v. George*, 115 Wash.App. 351, 62 P.3d 525 (2003).

(2) H and W orally agreed that if she would marry him, he would treat the child, with whom she was pregnant, "as if it were his own." At the time of the agreement, both H and W knew that he was not the biological father of the child. H had his name listed as father on the birth certificate. During the four years of the marriage, he never denied being the child's father.

Upon separation H contended that as the agreement was oral, it was not enforceable under the Statute of Frauds and he had no further duty to support the child. (Result: For W. W acted in reliance on H's promises when she agreed not to put up the child for adoption at birth. Therefore, H is estopped from raising the Statute of Frauds.) *T. v. T.*, 216 Va. 867, 224 S.E.2d 148 (1976).

2) <u>Consideration</u> *Test*

The mutual promises to marry traditionally have served as consideration. The Uniform Premarital Agreements Act—enacted by about one-half of the states—purports to do without consideration: "It [a premarital agreement] is enforceable without consideration." UPAA § 2. However, that bold step is implicitly limited by UPAA § 4 which provides that "[a] premarital agreement becomes effective upon marriage." Accordingly, not much, if anything, has changed with respect to premarital agreements. The UPAA clause is significant in respect of post-marriage modification of agreements, where consideration had typically been more difficult to find, because married parties already have broad legal duties to each other.

3) <u>Risk of Overreaching</u> *Test*

The intimate relationship between intending marriage partners has caused courts to scrutinize antenuptial agreements for signs of overreaching. Many courts speak in terms of a fiduciary duty between the parties. Historically, courts have been more sensitive to wives' complaints about antenuptial agreements than to complaints of husbands, because the traditional wife was (or would through marriage become) economically dependent and was often financially less knowledgeable. Moreover, usually it was the wife who relinquished rights in the antenuptial agreement. Improvements in the legal and economic status of women have made it less important that courts stretch to protect wives, and newer cases are interpreting premarital agreements in accordance with their terms, even if the terms are harsh and the circumstances of execution less than "squeaky clean."

Example: H and W's antenuptial agreement limited W to support payments of $200 per week in the event of separation or divorce, subject to a maximum of $25,000. H's attorney presented the agreement to W on the eve of the wedding, and she signed the agreement without benefit of independent counsel, nor did H's attorney advise her regarding any legal rights that she surrendered. When they married, H was a 39–year-old neurosurgeon with an income of approximately $90,000 per year and assets worth approximately $300,000. W was a 23–year-old unemployed nurse. The couple separated after 7 years of marriage and commenced divorce proceedings 2 years later. (Result: Antenuptial agreement enforced. The court reviewed earlier cases that had required *either* a reasonable provision for the spouse *or* full and fair disclosure of both the parties' finances as well as of the statutory rights being relinquished. "[E]arlier decisions * * * rested upon a belief that spouses are of unequal status and that women are not knowledgeable enough to understand the nature of contracts that they enter. Society has advanced, however, to the point where women are no longer regarded as the 'weaker' party in marriage, or in society generally. Indeed, the stereotype that women serve as homemakers while men work as breadwinners is no longer viable. Quite often today both spouses are income earners. Nor is there viability in the presumption that women are uninformed, uneducated, and readily subjected to unfair advantage in marital agreements. Indeed, women nowadays quite often have substantial education, financial awareness, income, and assets. * * * By invoking inquiries into reasonableness, * * * the functioning and reliability of prenuptial agreements is severely undermined. * * * Further, everyone who enters a long-term agreement knows that circumstances can change during its term, so that what initially appeared desirable might prove to be an unfavorable bargain. Such are the risks that contracting parties routinely assume. Certainly, the possibilities of illness, birth of children, reliance upon a spouse, career change, financial gain or loss, and numerous other events that can occur in the course of a marriage cannot be regarded as unforeseeable. If parties choose not to address such matters in their prenuptial agreements, they must be regarded as having contracted to bear the risk of events that alter the value of their bargains.") *Simeone v. Simeone*, 525 Pa. 392, 581 A.2d 162 (1990).

a) Full Disclosure *Test*

Each party—traditionally the focus was primarily on the future husband—must make full disclosure of all material facts relating to the quantity, character, and value of property. Alternatively, a conscious waiver of full disclosure, especially when combined with adequate general knowledge of the partner's financial situation may be upheld.

Examples: 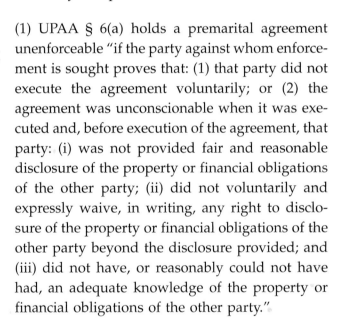 (1) UPAA § 6(a) holds a premarital agreement unenforceable "if the party against whom enforcement is sought proves that: (1) that party did not execute the agreement voluntarily; or (2) the agreement was unconscionable when it was executed and, before execution of the agreement, that party: (i) was not provided fair and reasonable disclosure of the property or financial obligations of the other party; (ii) did not voluntarily and expressly waive, in writing, any right to disclosure of the property or financial obligations of the other party beyond the disclosure provided; and (iii) did not have, or reasonably could not have had, an adequate knowledge of the property or financial obligations of the other party."

(2) H and W executed a home-made antenuptial agreement, neither party being represented by counsel. Under the agreement, W relinquished her rights to all property owned or later acquired by H. The agreement did not mention alimony or attorney's fees. At the time the agreement was entered into, W was keeping the books of H's businesses, and it was conceded that she knew as much about his financial circumstances as he did. (Result: Agreement valid. The fact that this agreement was "basically unfair and inequitable to the wife" was not sufficient to vacate or modify the

agreement. "[O]nce it is established that the agreement is unreasonable, 'a presumption arises that there was either concealment by the defending spouse or a presumed lack of knowledge by the challenging spouse of the defending spouse's finances at the time the agreement was reached.' Here * * * the wife had full and complete knowledge of the husband's finances. Thus this presumption was rebutted." The court added a *caveat*: "[W]hile the wife here may be awarded lump sum alimony in the discretion of the trial court, she may not be awarded lump sum alimony in order to accomplish equitable distribution of the husband's property because to do so would be violative of the terms and spirit of the antenuptial agreement.") *Cladis v. Cladis*, 512 So.2d 271 (Fla.App.1987).

b) **Fair and Reasonable Provision—*What* Is "Unconscionable?" *When* Is the Deal to Be Evaluated—At Time of Execution or Enforcement?**

Fair and reasonable economic provision for a dependent spouse may save the agreement even if disclosure was incomplete. Some courts will uphold antenuptial agreements if *either* full disclosure *or* appropriate economic provision is made; other courts expressly require *both*. In either event, as a practical rule, contracts involving *both* full disclosure *and* fair provision are much less likely to be upset. Jurisdictions disagree over whether "unconscionability" should be judged according to the circumstances known at the time the agreement was made or those existing at the time the agreement is enforced.

Examples: (1) UPAA § 6(c) provides: "An issue of unconscionability of a premarital agreement shall be decided by the court as a matter of law." What that may mean in practice is illustrated by UPAA § 6(b): "If a provision of a premarital agreement modifies or eliminates spousal support and that modification or elimination causes one party to the agreement to be eligible for support under a program of public assistance at the time of separation or marital dissolution, a court, notwithstanding the terms of the agreement, may require the other party to provide support to the extent necessary to avoid that eligibility." See UPAA § 6(a), p. 30.

(2) (Not decided under UPAA). H and W executed an antenuptial agreement under which W relinquished her interest in any property owned by H, whether acquired before or after the marriage. At the time of the marriage, H was an attorney and real estate investor with assets of approximately $1,400,000. W, with assets of approximately $100,000, directed nursing programs at two community colleges. Each party had children from their prior marriages and they had one child together. There was full and complete disclosure of earnings, property, and financial condition, and W was found to have waived her opportunity to seek advice from independent counsel. (Result: Remanded for a determination of the agreement's *fairness at both the time of execution and the time of enforcement.* "[T]he court should review the substantive fairness of the agreement in light of the circumstances existing at the inception. This will require appropriate inquiry into facts bearing upon the reasonable expectations of each signatory as to the scope and ultimate effect of the contract in the event the marriage should terminate by dissolution. The court should also review * * * whether in light of [the birth of the parties' child] enforcement would be oppressive and unconscionable. * * * Trial courts engaging in such a review must strike a balance between the law's policy favoring freedom of contract between informed consenting adults, and substantive fairness—admittedly a difficult task.") *McKee-Johnson v. Johnson*, 444 N.W.2d 259 (Minn.1989).

(3) (Not decided under UPAA). When H and W married, H was vice chairman of the board of an

advertising agency. W was his secretary. H's annual income was $285,000 and his net worth was approximately $1,800,000. W had no assets other than some jewelry. The day before the wedding, W signed an antenuptial agreement under which she waived her right to spousal support in excess of $1,000 per month. During their 15–year marriage, W did not work outside the home. On divorce, the parties agreed that she was to retain primary physical custody of their child. (Result: Remanded for a determination of whether the antenuptial agreement was *unconscionable at the time of divorce.* "To enforce a spousal support provision of a premarital agreement because it was reasonable at the time of execution of the agreement can result in unforeseen economic hardship to a spouse that may shock the conscience of the court due to relevant changes in the circumstances of the marriage by the time of the divorce. Public policy mandates against the enforcement of unconscionable support payments.") *Lewis v. Lewis,* 69 Haw. 497, 748 P.2d 1362 (1988).

c) Voluntariness and Advice of Counsel
To be enforceable, there must be no duress, coercion, or overreaching in the negotiation of the agreement. To eliminate all suspicion of overreaching, it is advisable that both parties be represented by independent counsel. However, typical state statutes, the Uniform Marital Property Act, and the Uniform Premarital Agreements Act do *not* specifically *require* counsel.

Example: On the eve of their wedding, H and W executed an antenuptial agreement under which W relinquished all rights to past, present, and future support, division of property, and any other property rights accruing because of the marriage. It was undisputed that there was adequate disclosure of H's assets. Although H's attorney had suggested that W consult with independent counsel, she had declined to do so. (Result: Agreement valid, because W was not denied a meaningful opportunity to consult counsel. The reviewing court added the *caveat*: "When an antenuptial agreement provides disproportionately less than the party challenging it would have received under an equitable distribution, the party financially disadvantaged must have a meaningful opportunity to consult with counsel. The presentation of an agreement a very short time before the wedding ceremony will create a presumption of overreaching or coercion if, in contrast to this case, the postponement of the wedding would cause significant hardship, embarrassment or emotional stress.") *Fletcher v. Fletcher*, 68 Ohio St.3d 464, 628 N.E.2d 1343 (Ohio 1994).

b. Subject Matter

1) Disposition at Death
Antenuptial agreements dealing with the disposition of property on either or both parties' *death* are valid, assuming that the contract requirements for validity are met.

2) Providing for Divorce
At one time, antenuptial agreements seeking to secure the financial consequences of *divorce* were held invalid. The courts saw such agreements as encouraging divorce in violation of public policy against divorce. Since the existence of an antenuptial agreement may actually deter divorce by making the parties aware of the cost of divorce in advance, the traditional rationale was always weak. Moreover, modern liberal divorce statutes negate any strong state policy against divorce. As a result, in recent years, states have moved widely to permit parties to make contracts contemplating the possibility of later divorce.

Example: An antenuptial agreement provided that, upon a legal separation or dissolution of the marriage, W would receive health insurance coverage and $75.00 per week as alimony but would have no further claim for support or H's property. (Result: Agreement not invalid *per se.* The court overturned its 75–year-old ruling that "the law will not permit parties contemplating marriage to enter into a contract providing for, and looking to, future separation after marriage," and rejected the "notion that divorce is promoted by an antenuptial agreement which contemplates such a possibility." The court upheld "the right of parties to enter into appropriate agreements." It recognized antenuptial agreements in contemplation of divorce, subject to (1) the requirement of full disclosure, and (2) the restriction that the agreement must not be *unconscionable at the time enforcement is sought.* The case was remanded for further proceedings on the issues of disclosure and unconscionability.) *Edwardson v. Edwardson,* 798 S.W.2d 941 (Ky.1990).

a) Second Marriages

If older parties or second marriages are involved, courts have more readily upheld antenuptial agreements making provision for divorce.

→ First

b) Property Rights vs. Support Obligations and Other "Essentials" of Marriage

Test

An antenuptial agreement settling the division of *property* upon divorce will be upheld more readily than one affecting *support* obligations. As a matter of public policy, the duty of support is seen as more "essential" to marriage than is the distribution of accumulated marital property. Other explanations are that: (1) parties should not predetermine a maintenance award at a time when the factors which should go into the determination of the award cannot be foreseen, and (2) the public has a direct stake in persons not becoming public charges due to loss of spousal support. UPAA § 3(a)(4) allows provisions negating support, but § 6(b) would enforce such a provision only to the extent a party is not thereby made eligible for public aid. It should be noted that the distinction between support and property is in many cases neither clear nor very useful, because modern divorce often involves parties with limited assets and incomes and their divorce settlements often involve trade-offs between property and support.

Example: H and W had entered into an antenuptial agreement which entitled W to a maximum of $200 alimony per month for 10 years if the couple should separate or divorce. W also was to receive one-half of the price received for the marital home, the personal property and possessions in their home, and one car. Attached to the antenuptial agreement was a statement of assets owned by each party. H's assets were valued at $550,000, W's at $5,000. The marriage lasted for 14 years. Upon divorce, H owned assets worth $8,000,000 and had an annual income of approximately $250,000. The trial court found the antenuptial agreement to be valid. The appellate court reversed, holding that such agreements were not enforceable by the party found to be at fault in a divorce proceeding. H appealed to Ohio's Supreme Court. (Result: (1) Marital misconduct does not abrogate an antenuptial agreement. (2) To determine the validity of the agreement, the court held that provisions covering the division of property are to be tested for unconscionability as of the time of execution, while public policy requires that provisions covering maintenance are to be tested as of the time of divorce.) *Gross v. Gross*, 11 Ohio St.3d 99, 464 N.E.2d 500 (1984). (Note: This case was *not* decided under UPAA).

3) Regulating the Ongoing Marriage

Today, some intending marriage partners enter into comprehensive agreements that seek to deal with any number of aspects of everyday marital life.

a) Judicial Policy of Noninterference in Marriage

Courts typically will *not* enforce agreements purporting to deal with support obligations *during* marriage, sexual behavior, family religion, promises not to defend a divorce action or not to seek a divorce, child rearing and other day-to-day aspects of married life.

b) UPAA

UPAA § 3(a) increases the range of permissible subject matter: "Parties to a premarital agreement may contract with respect to: * * * (8) any other matter, including their personal rights and obligations, not in violation of public policy or a statute imposing a criminal penalty."

c) **Usefulness of Unenforceable Provisions**

Even if an agreement concerning the ongoing marriage is not enforceable, it may serve a purpose if the "negotiation" causes a prospective couple to make plans for their future and thereby clarify their individual and marital expectations. *Caveat*: Given current trends, an antenuptial agreement that is unenforceable or of doubtful enforceability when made may ultimately turn out to be enforceable, by the time an issue arises.

c. UMDA

The UMDA makes no detailed provision for antenuptial agreements, but provides that agreements concerning *property* may be *considered* on divorce (UMDA § 307(a), Alternative A): "In making apportionment [of property and assets belonging to either or both spouses] the court shall *consider* the duration of the marriage, any prior marriage of either party, *any antenuptial agreement of the parties, * * *."*

d. UPAA and UMPA

The Uniform Premarital Agreement Act (enacted in one-half of the states) and the Uniform Marital Property Act (enacted in Wisconsin) broadly favor antenuptial agreements. They would allow almost all such agreements to stand unless "unconscionable" when "made" or "executed." (UPAA § 6(a), UMPA § 10(g)). Neither Act provides relief if the agreement has become "unconscionable" at the time it is sought to be enforced. (See above, p. 32.)

e. Gift Tax Treatment of Antenuptial Agreements   *Test*

Property transfers to a spouse prior to marriage are taxable as *gifts*. Even if the antenuptial agreement is otherwise valid, the exchange of mutual promises to marry has not been deemed adequate and full consideration in money or money's worth within the meaning of the Internal Revenue Code. Rev. Rul. 69–347, 1969–1 Cum. Bull. 227. Since property transfers between spouses are not subject to gift tax, property transfers should be deferred until after the parties are married.

Tax free. Get marriage first

H. Agreements During Marriage

Agreements made *during* marriage fall into three categories: (1) agreements made when separation is not immediately contemplated that seek to determine obligations within the ongoing marriage or the consequences of any future divorce ("postnuptial agreements"); (2) agreements effecting a reconciliation between estranged spouses ("reconciliation agreements"); and (3) agreements in anticipation of separation ("separation agreements").

1. Postnuptial Agreements → lacking Consideration

An agreement made by a couple while married that seeks to define or redefine personal and financial details of their relationship may present more serious legal problems than an antenuptial agreement, though enforcement is becoming more common.

a. Consideration

Lack of consideration may defeat a postnuptial agreement because—in contrast to an antenuptial agreement—the mutual promises to marry no longer serve as consideration. Mutual promises of support, housekeeping, or a promise to do or not do something implicit in the marriage relationship cannot serve as consideration because the promisor already is obligated by law to do or not do the same. A *reconciliation* agreement, however, is a common form of postnuptial contract and typically meets the consideration test, in that one or the other or both parties gives up a legal right, such as the right to seek a divorce or separation. (Note that UMPA and UPAA do not require consideration for marital agreements or for modification of premarital agreements.)

Example: H and W entered into postnuptial contract in which H, in consideration of their 25–year marriage, promised to share with W certain separate property he had inherited. When W later filed for divorce, H argued that the agreement was unenforceable. (Result: Postnuptial agreement is unenforceable for lack of valid consideration and mutuality. "[A]n existing marriage is past consideration and will not support a postnuptial agreement." Furthermore, "the element of mutual obligations does not exist in this agreement. . . . [T]here is no obligation or real liability upon [W] to do anything in consideration of [H's] promise to convey an interest in the Florida land to her.") *Simmons v. Simmons*, 98 Ark.App. 12, 249 S.W.3d 843 (2007).

b. Statutory Limitations (Married Women's Property Acts)

In the past, further difficulty sprang from traditional prohibitions against contracts between spouses for services or labor. Today, courts typically do not hesitate to enforce agreements between spouses relating to a business relationship that is not inherently dependent on the marriage.

Another exception involves marital contracts for services that are extraordinary and beyond the usual obligations implicit in marriage.

Example: H, a recipient of public funds, contracted with W for her services as an attendant and aiding him in activities he was unable to perform. (Result: Contract upheld. Although a husband is entitled to receive the domestic services of his wife, this right does not extend to "all services which she is capable of rendering that he may require," such as the personal care services rendered here. "To say that such is her duty is to say that the wife of a totally disabled man may not leave her home to seek employment without her husband's permission. It is law in Georgia that a husband is not entitled to the salary or wages of his wife, and shall not receive them without her consent. In the shadow of this statute, if nowhere else, stands the right of a married woman to the employment that will give her salary or wages. Her surrendering of this legal right to become a personal attendant to her husband is sufficient consideration for the express contract of employment, as she has suffered a legal detriment.") *Department of Human Resources v. Williams*, 130 Ga.App. 149, 202 S.E.2d 504 (1973).

c. Overreaching

Obviously, postnuptial agreements present even greater potential for overreaching and undue influence than antenuptial agreements. Courts therefore go to considerable lengths to scrutinize such agreements. Moreover, where consideration is still required, there is greater difficulty in finding consideration for a postnuptial agreement.

d. Public Policy

As in the case of antenuptial agreements, traditional public policy invalidated postnuptial agreements (other than separation agreements) that looked to divorce. With limited exceptions involving reconciliation agreements, postnuptial agreements attempting to deal with day-to-day aspects of marital life usually are not enforced. The policy reasons against involving the judiciary in day-to-day management of a marriage are the same as in the case of antenuptial agreements.

e. Gift Tax Consequences

Gift tax generally is not due in connection with property transfers under postnuptial agreements because an unlimited marital deduction applies to transfers between spouses.

2. Reconciliation Agreements

When parties *reconcile* by way of a formal agreement, consideration usually is found in their agreement to continue or to resume cohabitation or in their agreement not to sue or to abandon pending legal proceedings. The risk of overreaching is of less concern here because the marital conflict reduces the probability of undue influence. Another factor in favor of such agreements is that the courts traditionally favor resumption of marriage. Nevertheless, if such an agreement deals with rights upon a future divorce or separation, or seeks to alter an "essential" of marriage, public policy limitations may apply.

3. Separation Agreements

Even though they do precisely what courts used to hold antenuptial and ordinary postnuptial agreements may *not* do (*i.e.*, define the consequences of divorce), separation agreements entered *when separation or divorce is imminent*, have long been viewed as useful. If "fair," they have long been upheld. UMDA § 306(a) favors separation agreements concerning support, disposition of property and custody of children "to promote amicable settlement of disputes between parties to a marriage attendant upon their separation or the dissolution of their marriage." Such agreements, *except terms affecting children*, "are binding upon the court unless it finds * * * that the separation agreement is unconscionable." UMDA § 306(b). (See further discussion of separation agreements at p. 178).

I. Conflicts Aspects of Marital Agreements

Marital agreements may present conflicts of laws questions. Does the law of (1) the state where the agreement was entered, (2) the state where the couple was married, (3) the state where the couple had its usual marital domicile, or (4) the state where the couple is now domiciled, control the enforceability of a marital agreement? To answer this question, courts look to conflicts "policies," the relative weight of the interests of the jurisdictions with potentially applicable laws, and the intent of the parties, especially if expressed in the agreement.

Example: Hours before they married, H and W entered into an antenuptial agreement. H was a senior executive at General Motors Corporation and 25 years older than W, who had been a model but had little business experience. At the end of their 13–year marriage, assets approximated 20 million dollars and almost all were in the sole name of H. The couple had two children. H and W had executed the premarital agreement and married in California, but lived in New Jersey at the time they divorced. (Result: (1) California law applies.

"[W]hen an agreement is silent as to which law should be applied, the validity and construction of a contract shall be determined by the law of the place of contracting. But this agreement is not silent and expressly provides that it: 'shall be construed under the laws of the State of California and enforceable in the proper courts of jurisdiction of the State of California.' When the agreement was executed the parties had substantial contracts with California and reasonably expected to retain many of them which, indeed, has been the case. For these reasons the law of California must be applied in this case." (2) Antenuptial agreement is valid and enforceable. In New Jersey, a party to an antenuptial agreement is treated as a fiduciary on the theory that "parties who are not yet married are not presumed to share a confidential relationship." Not so in California. "So long as the spouse seeking to set aside such an agreement has a general idea of the character and extent of the financial assets and income of the other, that apparently is sufficient in California. * * * Accordingly, the court is satisfied that under California law there was a sufficient disclosure by the husband.") *DeLorean v. DeLorean*, 211 N.J.Super. 432, 511 A.2d 1257 (1986).

J. Breach of Promise to Marry

The cause of action for breaching a promise to marry is classified as a tort. It is one of the so-called "heartbalm" actions, discussed at p. 115.

K. Gifts in Contemplation of Marriage

Termination of an engagement may affect gifts made during the engagement by the prospective spouses to one another, as well as wedding gifts made to the couple by third parties during the engagement.

1. Gifts Before Engagement

Gifts exchanged by a couple *before* engagement generally are considered unconditional and usually need not be returned when the engagement is terminated. Today, when formal engagements are less common and extended periods of premarital cohabitation more common, this rule can no longer be regarded as very useful. The individual circumstances of each case (focusing on the donor's intent) should govern the outcome.

2. Gifts During an Engagement

Courts assume that most gifts made by one partner to the other during engagement are conditional on marriage. If the marriage does not occur, such gifts (the most obvious example being the engagement diamond) must be returned. In any particular case, whether a gift must be returned may depend upon how the engagement ended, who ended it, and the purpose for which the gift was made. If the gift was made on a birthday or holiday, it will more readily be held not to have been conditional on marriage and may thus not be returnable.

3. Gifts From Third Parties

Wedding gifts made to a couple by third parties usually are considered conditional upon the marriage taking place. They may thus be recovered when the engagement is terminated.

Review Questions

1. T or F   Most of the rights and obligations of marriage remain defined by common law rather than by statute.

2. T or F   Under the Contract Clause of the U.S. Constitution, statutes governing the parties' rights and obligations in marriage and upon divorce may be applied only prospectively.

3. T or F   The validity and legal incidents of a marriage are determined by the place of the marriage.

4. T or F   An antenuptial agreement between consenting adults will generally be upheld even if it materially changes the parties' economic position from one that would be imposed by the law of divorce.

5. T or F   Courts generally will not enforce antenuptial agreements that regulate the parties' finances and personal activities during the ongoing marriage.

6. T or F   The fairness of financial provisions in an antenuptial agreement is judged as it appears at the time of the divorce.

7. T or F   In the case of an *ante*nuptial agreement, contractual consideration is supplied by the change in legal position effected by marriage.

8. T or F   When the parties are already married and thus owe broad obligations to each other, their *post*nuptial agreements may be held invalid for lack of consideration.

9. T or F   Antenuptial gifts remain the property of the donee, even if the marriage never takes place or is followed quickly by divorce.

10. T or F   The so-called "Married Women's Property Acts" allow married women to own and convey property.

11. T or F   The UMDA validates H's bigamous second marriage to W_2 as of the time H's first marriage ends by divorce or by the death of W_1.

12. T or F   The UPAA requires invalidation of an antenuptial agreement if its consequences are unconscionable at the time of divorce.

13. T or F   The court is bound by a provision in H's and W's separation agreement that specifies that W will have custody of their children.

14. **T or F**   The court is bound by a provision in H's and W's separation agreement that specifies how much property and alimony is to be provided upon divorce.

II

Marriage Requisites and Common Law Marriage

■ ANALYSIS

A. **Formal Requirements**
   1. Consent
   2. Solemnization
   3. Common Law Marriage
   4. Presumptions Regarding Validity of Marriage
   5. Valid Common Law Marriage Resulting From Removal of Impediment
   6. Putative Spouse Doctrine
B. **Substantive Requirements for Valid Marriage**
   1. Consanguinity
   2. Affinity, Step–Relationship, Adoption
   3. Age Requirements
   4. Physical Requirements
C. **Conflicts of Laws**
   1. Law of Celebration

2. "Most Significant Relationship" Test
3. Uniform Marriage Evasion Act
4. The Public Policy Exception
5. Full Faith and Credit
D. Annulment
1. History
2. Impediments
3. Defenses
4. The Void/Voidable Distinction
5. Annulment for Fraud
6. Annulment for Duress
7. Annulment of Marriage Entered in Jest
8. Annulment of Sham Marriage
9. Legal Incidents of Annulment

To create a legally effective marriage, three requirements must be met: There must be (1) consent to the contract; (2) solemnization of the marriage (or in a minority of states, compliance with the rules of "common law marriage"); and (3) compliance with certain substantive prerequisites.

A. Formal Requirements

1. Consent

Valid marriage requires the free and voluntary consent of both parties who must (1) be competent and (2) intend to enter into marriage with each other at that time.

a. Capacity

Capacity to enter the marriage exists if, at the time of solemnization, the parties were capable of understanding the nature of the act. The wisdom of the parties' decision and their capacity to be adequate spouses or parents are *not* at issue.

Lack of capacity, rather than eugenic considerations, is the basis for statutory prohibitions against issuing marriage licenses to the mentally infirm, sometimes labeled as "insane," "feebleminded," "mentally incompetent," or those under the influence of liquor or drugs. A person who is mentally retarded may be capable of entering into a valid marriage so long as he or she satisfies the legal definition of capacity. UMDA § 208(a)(1) provides that a marriage shall be invalidated if "a party lacked capacity to consent to the marriage at the time the marriage was solemnized, either because of mental incapacity or infirmity or because of the influence of alcohol, drugs, or other incapacitating substances, or a party was induced to enter into a marriage by force or duress, or by fraud involving the essentials of marriage."

Examples: (1) Both H and W were mentally retarded. After being released from the Beatrice State Home, H lived and worked in Omaha under the auspices of Eastern Nebraska Community of Retardation. H and W were married five years later. After they had been married for two years, H's guardian petitioned to have the marriage declared void. At issue was whether H had sufficient mental capacity to marry. (Result: Marriage valid. H had mental capacity to enter into a marriage contract as he was able to understand the nature of the marriage contract and the duties and responsibilities incident to it at the time of marriage.) *Edmunds v. Edwards*, 205 Neb. 255, 287 N.W.2d 420 (1980).

(2) H, a elderly man, married W, his former nurse who was 43 years his junior. After H's death, the executor of his estate petitioned to annul the marriage on the ground that H lacked mental capacity to give consent. (Result: Marriage annulled. H "was extremely hard of hearing, suffered from severe short-term memory loss, had been hospitalized several times from 2001 to 2003, and suffered from severe arthritis. . . . The facts that he had not been diagnosed as suffering from any particular psychiatric or mental disease, and that he appeared at times to be lucid and alert, do not alter this conclusion, since the evidence showed that at best he was only somewhat functional and coherent.") *In re Joseph S.*, 25 A.D.3d 804, 808 N.Y.S.2d 426 (2006).

(3) H had been diagnosed as a chronic paranoid schizophrenic and had been in various mental institutions for much of his adult life. In 1975 he was released from a mental hospital pursuant to a judicial finding that he was not imminently dangerous to himself or others. As a condition of his release, H moved to a structured home environment where he was cared for by attendants who did his cooking, cleaning and driving. His guardian, a bank that managed the approximately $900,000 estate H had inherited from his father, paid for the home and services. H's only surviving relatives were an elderly aunt and several cousins, one of whom was chairman of the board of the guardian bank. In 1980 H met W at an outpatient mental health facility. W did not suffer from a mental disability but was confined to a wheelchair. They married and moved into H's home. Several months later, the guardian bank initiated an annulment action. A jury found that H had sufficient mental capacity and understanding on the day of his marriage to enter into a marriage contract. H's guardian appealed. (Result: No annulment. "A marriage of a person incapable of contracting for want of understanding is not void, but voidable. We find that prior adjudication of incompetency is not conclusive on the issue

of later capacity to marry and does not bar a party from entering a contract to marry. The mental capacity of a party at the precise time when the marriage is celebrated controls its validity or invalidity. * * * 'The general rule is that the test is the capacity of the person to understand the special nature of the contract of marriage, and the duties and responsibilities which it entails, which is to be determined from the facts and circumstances of each case' ".) *Geitner v. Townsend*, 67 N.C.App. 159, 312 S.E.2d 236 (1984).

1) Practical Relevance of Capacity Issue

Although capacity is a prerequisite for the issuance of a marriage license, the issue of capacity is litigated most often when one of the parties brings an annulment action. At that time the objecting party must prove that he or she or the other party had lacked the requisite mental capacity to consent to marriage *at the time of the marriage.*

2) Consent of Guardian

An incompetent may be allowed to marry or, in some jurisdictions, divorce with the consent of a guardian.

Examples: (1) (Marriage). H was struck by an automobile in 1972 and suffered severe brain damage. One year later H was divorced from the woman to whom he had been married at the time of the accident. Five years after the accident, H became romantically involved with his psychologist, W. That year W and her first husband were divorced, and H's father was appointed as H's guardian. H and W then married without H's guardian's approval. (Result: Guardian's petition to annul marriage is granted. State legislation required the guardian's approval before a ward may marry.) *Knight v. Radomski*, 414 A.2d 1211 (Me.1980).

(2) (Divorce). H sustained a permanently disabling head injury as a result of an automobile accident. W cared for H for six months after the accident but then abandoned her husband to his parents' care. H's mother was granted plenary guardianship over H and his person, and she filed for dissolution of H's marriage to W. W moved to dismiss on the ground that a

guardian does not have standing to bring an action for dissolution of a ward's marriage. (Result: No dissolution. "Research reveals a strong majority rule that, absent statutory authorization, a guardian cannot maintain an action, on behalf of a ward, for the dissolution of a ward's marriage. * * * Illinois follows the majority rule.") *In re Marriage of Drews*, 115 Ill.2d 201, 104 Ill.Dec. 782, 503 N.E.2d 339 (1986).

b. Intent

Both parties must intend to marry each other. The intent to marry may be vitiated by fraud, duress, jest, sham or ulterior purposes. (See discussion of annulment, pp. 72–74).

2. Solemnization

a. Marriage License

Prospective marriage partners must obtain a marriage license in advance of solemnization. Such a license is issued routinely if the parties' application indicates that there exist no impediments to their marriage, based on the state's prerequisites for marriage.

1) Waiting Period

To prevent hasty and impulsive marriages, many states impose a brief waiting period between the time of issuance of the license and the time of the marriage ceremony. Under UMDA § 204, a marriage license becomes effective three days after issuance and expires after 180 days.

2) Solemnization Without License

The policy in favor of upholding parties' expectations and protecting existing relationships—even in states not recognizing common law marriage—may in some states lead to a holding that a marriage solemnized without a license is valid. Similarly, a valid marriage may result even if the parties failed to solemnize a marriage after they had obtained a license, or if solemnization was performed by one not legally authorized to perform marriages.

Example: Twenty-five years before, H and W were married in the Roman Catholic church without obtaining a license. (Result: Valid marriage. "Most such cases arise long after the parties have acted upon the assumption that they are married, and no useful purpose is served by avoiding the long-standing relationship.") *Carabetta v. Carabetta,* 182 Conn. 344, 438 A.2d 109 (1980).

b. Ceremony

Except where common law marriage is recognized, marriage must be solemnized by a person authorized by the state, such as a designated civil official or a religious minister. A marriage solemnized by a person not authorized to do so often is upheld if at least one party was unaware of the disqualification. Consummation is not a condition to the validity of a properly solemnized marriage but may help shore up one with defects. UMDA § 206(a) provides, "[a] marriage may be solemnized by a judge of a court of record, by a public official whose powers include solemnization of marriages, or in accordance with any mode of solemnization recognized by any religious denomination, Indian Nation or Tribe, or Native Group."

c. Public Record

The marriage license must be completed by the person solemnizing the marriage and returned to the appropriate state office to be recorded.

d. Purposes of Solemnization

Solemnization gives public notice of the marriage; it provides a permanent record of the marriage; it impresses upon the parties the seriousness of their act; it satisfies religious tradition; and it aids in the collection of vital statistics.

e. Proxy Marriages

If one party is unable to attend the marriage ceremony, a number of states permit marriage to be performed by proxy. Proxy marriage has been of special utility during times of war, enabling soldiers stationed overseas to marry homebound partners. UMDA § 206(b) gives the person solemnizing a marriage the power to marry a couple when the party unable to be present has authorized in writing a third person to act as his or her proxy.

Federal law limits recognition of proxy marriages for immigration purposes: "The term 'spouse', 'wife', or 'husband' does not include a spouse, wife, or husband by reason of any marriage ceremony where the contracting parties thereto are not physically present in the presence of each other, unless the marriage shall have been consummated." 8 U.S.C.A. § 1101(a)(35).

f. "Confidential" Marriages

California Fam. Code § 500 allows persons "living together as husband and wife" to enter into a confidential marriage.

3. Common Law Marriage

Common law marriage is also referred to as informal marriage. It is a valid marriage entered into by the parties' agreement, but without formal solemnization. All substantive prerequisites for marriage must be met (no prior marriage, not within forbidden degrees of relationship, etc.). Today, approximately one fourth of the states continue to recognize common law marriages. Since the law of conflicts favors upholding the validity of marriage, a common law marriage that was valid where and when celebrated will generally be recognized as valid elsewhere as well. Accordingly, if the parties have or have had an adequate connection with a state recognizing common law marriage, a common law marriage may be found to be valid even in states that have abolished it.

a. Traditional Form

Older law knew two ways of entering into common law marriage: (1) by exchange of vows by the parties with words expressing their intent to be married in the present tense; and (2) by words in the future tense (engagement), followed by consummation. The chief difference between common law and ceremonial marriage is the absence of a public ceremony and record, and it is the difficulty of proof that has persuaded the courts or legislatures of most states to abolish common law marriage.

b. American Law

Brought to the United States, common law marriage underwent various modifications. Specific requirements vary somewhat among the jurisdictions. In addition to, and as proof of, their express, present agreement to marry, most states now require that the parties actually cohabit as husband and wife and "hold themselves out" to the public as married. Common law marriage does *not* require that the parties cohabit for any specific period of time. The marriage takes effect at the time of the contract.

Examples: (1) H and W moved in together in June 1983. They each deposited their paychecks in a common account, W began using H's surname, and the couple filed joint income tax returns beginning in 1984. In 1990, the couple had a ceremonial marriage, reportedly to enable W to claim benefits under H's health insurance. When the couple divorced in 2006, W sought a division of the property the couple had acquired since 1983, while H insisted that the marriage began only in 1990. (Result: The couple formed a valid common law marriage in June 1983, when they cohabited and held themselves out as married, manifesting a shared intention to be married. Accordingly, W was entitled to a division of marital property acquired since 1983.) *Gearhart v. Gearhart*, 2008 WL 62286 (Ohio Ct. App. 2008).

(2) H and W were divorced in July, and H died in December. Despite their divorce, they continued to live together. Though W was observed with H in his home on numerous occasions, it was general knowledge in the community that they had been divorced. W had told a close friend that they would remarry on Christmas. W had bought a new car, but had it registered in her maiden name and at her home address rather than at H's address. During that same period she had signed a bail bond for H, again using her maiden name and home address. (Result: No common law marriage. " * * * [W] and [H] * * * did not have a present intention to again become man and wife since they had already previously agreed to ceremoniously remarry in the future. Furthermore, cohabitation standing alone is not sufficient to supply the requisite mutual assent required for the common-law marriage; there must be words of present assent.") *Humphrey v. Humphrey*, 293 Ala. 118, 300 So.2d 376 (1974).

(3) H and W were married in 1960 and divorced in 1965. Shortly thereafter, they reconciled and lived together until H's death in 1976. During this time they filed separate income tax returns as single persons, and kept separate bank accounts. They purchased insurance as married persons. People in town considered them married. They planned to undergo a second marriage ceremony later in 1976. (Result: Common law marriage. The court found that their agreement to remarry did not negate "present agreement" which was inferred from their cohabitation and from public recognition.) *Skipworth v. Skipworth*, 360 So.2d 975 (Ala.1978).

1) Holding Out

"Holding out" as married usually is shown by representations made to friends, neighbors, business associates, and creditors, and by use of a common surname, as well as by jointly filed tax returns, and, depending on apparent intent, jointly held bank accounts or realty.

Examples: (1) W worked as H's live-in housekeeper. After three years, she accepted his marriage proposal. Due to opposition from H's children, they agreed to live together as H and W, but without marrying. Although they attended social events together, W retained her surname, they filed separate tax returns as single persons, and W registered herself as a single person when she was hospitalized following a miscarriage. (Result: No common law marriage. " 'Holding out' or open declaration to the public has been said to be the acid test. * * * In other words, there can be no secret common-law marriage.") *In re Dallman's Estate,* 228 N.W.2d 187 (Iowa 1975).

(2) H and W lived together from 1987 until H's death in 1996. During that time, they displayed a sign in front of their home announcing "Hunsakers, Home of the Classics," and together purchased a grandfather clock on which their first initials were engraved together along with a common "H" for "Hunsaker," H's surname. (Result: Common law marriage, entitling W to claim a spousal share of H's estate. "The sign in front of their home and the pendulum of the grandfather clock are evidence that [H] and [W] held themselves out as husband and wife to those who visited their home. The answering machine message [in which W's voice stated, 'this is the Hunsaker residence'] is evidence that [H] and [W] held themselves out as married to those who called their home.") *In re Estate of Hunsaker,* 291 Mont. 412, 968 P.2d 281 (1998).

2) Abolition of Common Law Marriage

Abolition of common law marriage began in 1753 in England with Lord Hardwicke's Act, which required a ceremony and public record. The purpose was to put marriages on a more certain footing, in the interests of the partners, their children, and third parties dealing with them. The inevitable consequence of the abolition of common law marriage is that some relationships of long standing will be dealt with inequitably. Today, states may allow some relief by recognition of unmarried cohabitation (see *Marvin v. Marvin*, p. 82) or through the putative spouse doctrine, p. 60.

3) Statutes Regulating Common Law Marriage

A few states have enacted statutes dealing with the definition and proof of common law marriages.

Examples: (1) Texas provides that a common law marriage may be established either (a) by registering a formal declaration of informal marriage on a prescribed form or (b) by informally agreeing to be married and thereafter living together in Texas and holding out as married. In the absence of formal registration, the statute creates a rebuttable presumption that there was no agreement to marry if no action is brought is brought within two years of the couple's separation. (Tex. Fam. Code Ann. §§ 2401, 2402).

Utah provides: "A marriage which is not solemnized * * * shall be legal and valid if a court or administrative order establishes that it arises out of a contract between a man and a woman who: (a) are of legal age and capable of giving consent; (b) are legally capable of entering a solemnized marriage * * *; (c) have cohabited; (d) mutually assume marital rights, duties, and obligations; and (e) who hold themselves out as and have acquired a uniform and general reputation as husband and wife." Recognition of a common law marriage, moreover, must be sought within one year of the end of the relationship. (Utah Code Ann. tit. 30, § 1–4.5).

4) Modern Rationale

Many courts seem to regard common law marriage less as a conscious alternative to formal marriage, and more as a means of vindicating the reasonable expectations of the parties, or at least one of them. A common law marriage may be found if a formal marriage proves invalid or when partners have lived together in the honest belief that they were married, when such a finding would alleviate inequities concerning property and support matters that would otherwise arise, especially on the death of one of the parties.

Example: H and W were married before a Roman Catholic priest. They divorced and later resumed cohabitation. Their priest told them that they need not remarry as they were "already married in the eyes of God." The couple accepted the priest's explanation, went home to resume cohabitation and assumed that they were married. No civil ceremony was ever performed. H died and W applied for dependency benefits under workmen's compensation legislation. (Result: Common law marriage. The court found that it would fulfill the purposes of the legislation to hold W to be a "dependent" under the Act.) *Parkinson v. J. & S. Tool Company,* 64 N.J. 159, 313 A.2d 609 (1974).

5) **Conflict of Laws**

A common law marriage validly entered under the laws of one state is generally recognized everywhere, even in states that have abolished common law marriage. Moreover, in states that have abolished common law marriage, courts sometimes strain to protect the reasonable expectations of the parties by "stretching" conflict of laws doctrine—focusing on the parties' sojourn to another state that recognizes common law marriage and holding that a valid marriage was entered there.

Examples: (1) Following divorces from other individuals, H and W began living together on July 5, 1958. H gave W a wedding band, W took H's surname, and they told friends and relatives that they had married. Subsequently, they celebrated July 5 as their anniversary, filed joint tax returns, and H listed W as his wife and beneficiary on his life insurance policy. For 20 years the couple had lived in New York which does not recognize common law marriage, and on approximately eight occasions, the partners had stayed at a Pennsylvania motel. Pennsylvania recognized common law marriage. Following H's death, W sought social security benefits as H's surviving spouse. (Result: Valid common law marriage. "The law to be applied in determining the validity of such a marriage is the law of the state in which the marriage occurred. Since plaintiff claims that she contracted a common-law marriage with her husband in Pennsylvania during their travels through the state, the appropriate law to apply is the law of Pennsylvania. * * * Generally, a common-law marriage may be created by uttering words in the present tense with the intent to establish a marital relationship, but where no such utterance is proved, Pennsylvania law also permits a finding of marriage based on reputation and cohabitation when established by satisfactory proof.") *Renshaw v. Heckler*, 787 F.2d 50 (2d Cir.1986). (In 2003, Pennsylvania joined the majority of states in abolishing common-law marriage.)

(2) H and W_2 lived together from 1961 until H died in 1983. H did not divorce W_1 until 1981. H and W_2 held themselves out as husband and wife, W_2 took H's surname, and W_2's four daughters considered H to be their father. At the time of H's death, the couple was domiciled in Nevada. Nevada does not recognize common law marriage. From 1961 until 1963, however, the couple had lived in Texas which recognizes common law marriage and, between 1981 and H's death, the couple made two or three trips to Texas. W filed for social security death benefits as H's surviving spouse. (Result: Valid common law marriage. "Nevada does not recognize common law marriages contracted within its borders, but does recognize common law marriages that arise in another state so long as that state's legal requirements are met." The court found that under Texas law H and W_2 "entered into a marriage which would have been valid if Mr. Orr had not been previously married." When H and W_1 divorced, H's and W_2's marriage became valid under a Texas statute which then provided: "A marriage is void if either party was previously married and the prior marriage is not dissolved. However, the marriage becomes valid when the prior marriage is dis-

solved if since that time the parties have lived together as husband and wife and represented themselves to others as being married.") *Orr v. Bowen*, 648 F.Supp. 1510 (D.Nev.1986). (The current version of the statute is Tex. Fam. Code Ann. § 6.202.)

6) Uniform Marriage and Divorce Act

The UMDA does not take a stand for or against common law marriage, but suggests that the issue be re-examined by the states, including those that have abolished common law marriage. It provides two alternate versions, one recognizing common law marriage, one not, to "permit each state to make its decision in accordance with its own view as to policy, and to change its law at any time desired without destroying the effect of its adoption of the Uniform Act." (UMDA § 211, Comment.)

4. Presumptions Regarding Validity of Marriage

The following presumptions are potentially in conflict: (1) Absent proof of divorce, there is a presumption in favor of the continuation of marriage. (2) When a person enters more than one marriage without dissolving a former marriage, a presumption arises in favor of the validity of the marriage last in time.

Example: Two women (W_1, W_2) married decedent (H) a few months prior to his death and both claimed to be H's widows. There was evidence that H's marriage to W_1 had been for the purpose of facilitating W_1's immigration from Canada, but that marriage had not been terminated when H married W_2. The trial court upheld the first marriage, but ruled that W_1 had waived her rights in an antenuptial agreement. Accordingly, neither W_1's nor W_2's claim was allowed. (Result: Affirmed. While the prior marriage may have been for a limited purpose, it was at most voidable and therefore could not be attacked collaterally. Two presumptions, (1) that the later of successive marriages is valid and (2) that continuation of a prior marriage is favored, may be considered in deciding which of successive marriages is valid. "In evaluating these conflicting presumptions, the court must look to the underlying policies intended to be served by the presumption and the extent to which those policies will actually be served under the facts of a particular case. We acknowledge that some commentators have indicated that the presumption favoring the validity of the later marriage should always prevail over the conflicting presumption that the earlier marriage continues, because the social policies underlying the former are more significant than the policies of probability and convenience which underlie the latter. But we think the better approach is to reserve discretion to weigh the various social policies in light of the facts of a particular case." In this case, policy reasons favoring the later marriage over the previous marriage were so weak that trial court properly found W_1's marriage to be valid.) *Appeal of O'Rourke,* 310 Minn. 373, 246 N.W.2d 461 (1976).

5. Valid Common Law Marriage Resulting From Removal of Impediment

UMDA § 207(b) provides that where there has been a marriage *ceremony,* even though one of the spouses was legally incapable of marrying at that time, the resulting cohabitation will automatically turn into a valid marriage upon removal of the impediment. Where the UMDA does not apply, courts may resolve such circumstances in terms of common law marriage.

Examples: (1) While H was still married to W_1, he went through a marriage ceremony with W_2. The latter "marriage," of course, was void. After being divorced from W_1, H continued to cohabit with W_2 but no new marriage ceremony was performed. After leaving W_2, H ceremonially married W_3 and their relationship continued until H's death. Both W_2 and W_3 filed for workmen's compensation benefits. (Result: No common law marriage to W_2; only W_3 is entitled to benefits. " * * * (T)he removal of an impediment to a marriage contract (the divorce in this case) does not convert an illegal bigamous marriage into a common law legal marriage. After the barrier to marriage has been removed, there must be a new mutual agreement, either by way of civil ceremony or by way of a recognition of the illicit relation and a new agreement to enter into a common law marriage arrangement.") *Byers v. Mount Vernon Mills, Inc.,* 268 S.C. 68, 231 S.E.2d 699 (1977).

(2) W and H_1 were married in 1944 and were never divorced. W and H_2 began living together in 1946. H_1 died in 1983. W and H_2 continued to live together until H_2's death in 1984. During this period W and H_2 held themselves out as married. W filed for her statutory share as a surviving spouse, and the executor of H_2's estate objected. (Result: Valid common law marriage.

"[W]hile no ceremony or particular words are necessary, there are common elements which must be present, either explicitly expressed or implicitly inferred from the circumstances, in order for a common-law marriage to exist. Those elements are: 1) capacity; 2) present, mutual agreement to permanently enter the marriage relationship to the exclusion of all other relationships; and 3) public recognition of the relationship as a marriage and public assumption of marital duties and cohabitation." The court held these requirements satisfied by the fact that W and H_2 had continued to live together and held themselves out as married in the year following H_1's death.) *Boswell v. Boswell*, 497 So.2d 479 (Ala.1986).

6. Putative Spouse Doctrine

The putative spouse doctrine has two elements: "(1) a proper marriage ceremony was performed, and (2) one or both parties had a good-faith belief that there was no impediment to the marriage and the marriage was valid and proper." *Williams v. Williams*, 120 Nev. 559, 97 P.3d 1124 (2004). UMDA § 209 elaborates:

"Any person who has cohabited with another to whom he is not legally married in the good faith belief that he was married to that person is a putative spouse until knowledge of the fact that he is not legally married terminates his status and prevents acquisition of further rights. A putative spouse acquires the rights conferred upon a legal spouse, including the right to maintenance following termination of his status, whether or not the marriage is prohibited or declared invalid. If there is a legal spouse or other putative spouses, rights acquired by a putative spouse do not supersede the rights of the legal spouse or those acquired by other putative spouses, but the court shall apportion property, maintenance, and support rights among the claimants as appropriate in the circumstances and in the interests of justice."

Example: After they separated, H assured W that he had obtained their divorce. W later purported to marry X in a formal ceremony and they lived together for 27 years, during which time they raised a daughter together. When W and X separated, W learned that H had never, in fact, obtained a divorce and that she therefore lacked capacity to marry X. (Result: W qualifies as a "putative spouse" and is therefore entitled to receive an equitable distribution of the couple's "quasi-community property." "[S]ubstantial evidence supports the district court's finding that [W] did not act unreasonably in relying on [H's] representations.") *Williams, supra.*

B. Substantive Requirements for Valid Marriage

Universally, societies have imposed substantive requirements upon parties to marriage. These have varied with time, religion and culture. There is general agreement on a few basics, such as the incest prohibition. Today, the validity of state regulation of marriage may be tested under the federal and state constitutions and may depend on a balancing of the individual's interest in marrying whom he wishes and the intensity of the state's interests in the particular regulation. *Loving v. Virginia*, 388 U.S. 1, 87 S.Ct. 1817, 18 L.Ed.2d 1010 (1967); *Zablocki v. Redhail*, 434 U.S. 374, 98 S.Ct. 673, 54 L.Ed.2d 618 (1978); *Turner v. Safley*, 482 U.S. 78, 107 S.Ct. 2254, 96 L.Ed.2d 64 (1987). Traditional prohibitions against same-sex marriages, for example, recently have been successfully challenged on state constitutional grounds (see p. 23).

1. Consanguinity

Marriage is prohibited between persons related by blood within certain degrees of kinship.

a. Scope of Prohibition

The scope of the prohibition varies from state to state. Marriages within the immediate family, between parent and child or brother and sister, are prohibited universally. Most states also prohibit marriage between an uncle and his niece or between an aunt and her nephew. Approximately one-half of the states prohibit marriage between first cousins.

b. Effect of Attempt to Enter into Incestuous Marriage

Traditionally, an attempted incestuous marriage is void. Depending on the intensity of the state's interest, this may hold true even when the marriage was valid when and where made. Note, however, that under more recent statutes and cases, even a void marriage may have considerable legal consequences.

Examples: (1) Decedent (D) validly married his niece in Italy. They resided in Connecticut for two years before his death. She applied for a widow's allowance from D's estate. (Result: Denied. The "marriage" was contrary to Connecticut's public policy and was invalid.) *Catalano v. Catalano*, 148 Conn. 288, 170 A.2d 726 (1961).

(2) H and W, first cousins, were lawfully married in Virginia before moving to Arizona in 1989. At the time of their move, Arizona law recognized their Virginia marriage as valid, even though Arizona law does not permit first cousins to marry in Arizona. In 1996, however, Arizona enacted legislation denying recognition of incestuous marriages, even if legally formed under the laws of another state. (Result: Statute would be applied to deny recognition of incestuous marriages of new migrants to Arizona but would not retroactively invalidate marriages already recognized at the time of the statute's enactment.) *Cook v. Cook*, 209 Ariz. 487, 104 P.3d 857 (Ct. App. 2005).

c. Criminality

Universally, statutes provide for criminal prosecution of incest involving close blood relationships. The definition of relationship for purposes of criminal "incest" varies in many states from that in marriage prohibitions (typically the criminal prohibition is narrower). In other states the definitions are coterminous.

d. Justification of Prohibition

Cultural and religious conceptions of the family are the origin of incest prohibitions. Today, incest statutes are defended as preventing genetically defective offspring, promoting family harmony, and discouraging sexual imposition on minors.

1) Genetics

The genetic argument has been criticized as insufficient to support the prohibition of marriage between extended relatives, because the probability of a "bad" gene affecting an offspring decreases markedly as the degree of kinship of the parents is extended. If the unfavorable gene is common in the population, consanguineous mating would not significantly increase the probability that the defective gene would be passed on to children. Moreover, the genetic argument only justifies prohibiting related individuals from having children, not from marrying or engaging in sexual relations. The latter point has been recognized in several state statutes allowing first cousins to marry if they are beyond child-bearing age, defined as 55 years old or older. In 2002, a study published in the *Journal of Genetic Counseling* concluded that the risk of birth defects among children born to parents who are first cousins is actually quite small.

2) Social Arguments

One social argument focuses on preventing sexual rivalries and jealousies between family members and preventing abuse of family authority. Incest prohibitions have also been defended in terms of the social good resulting from increased cultural diffusion and the broadening of family alliances.

e. Criticism of the Prohibition

The most significant argument against common incest prohibitions is that their reach is too broad. Some may be "over-inclusive" in defining prohibited relationships.

f. Relationships of the Half Blood, through Illegitimacy, or Severed by Adoption

Generally, incest statutes do not distinguish between relationships of the full and half blood, nor on the basis of illegitimacy or adoption.

Example: H and W were half-brother and half-sister by blood. W had been adopted and raised by another family. They were indicted for entering into a prohibited marriage. The couple argued that the prohibition of brother-sister marriage was inapplicable due to W's adoption. (Result: Adoption irrelevant. Half-sibling relationships are included under the prohibition despite not being enumerated. Adoption statutes that legally eliminate the tie between an adopted child and its natural relative do not impliedly change the consanguinity statute. The policy of maintaining secrecy of adoption records does not bar any and all inquiry into the facts of an adoption.) *State v. Sharon H.,* 429 A.2d 1321 (Del.1981).

2. Affinity, Step–Relationship, Adoption

a. "Affinity" and "Step–Relationships"

Marriages between persons related in various ways by "affinity" (through marriage) used to be widely prohibited. This prohibition has survived with respect to step-relationships (*e.g.,* stepfather-stepdaughter).

b. Adoptive Relationships

Most states continue to prohibit marriage between persons related by adoption.

c. Justification

No genetic arguments exist for marriage prohibitions based on affinity, step-relationships, or adoption, but justification has been drawn from the social, "family harmony" argument. "To authorize and encourage marriages of brothers and sisters by adoption would undermine the fabric of family life and would be the antithesis of the social aims and purposes which the adoption process is intended to serve." *Marriage of Mew and MLB,* 4 Pa.D. & C.3d 51 (1977).

d. Constitutionality

The prohibition on marriage of persons related by adoption has been attacked constitutionally.

Example: X and Y were brother and sister by adoption. They were not related by blood. Their parents had married when X was 18 and Y 13 years of age. Three years later, X and Y were denied a marriage license because of their relationship through adoption. Based on equal protection grounds, X and Y argued that the statute prohibiting their marriage was unconstitutional. (Result: Statute is unconstitutional as applied to brothers and sisters related through adoption as it does not have a rational relationship to a legitimate state interest.) *Israel v. Allen,* 195 Colo. 263, 577 P.2d 762 (1978). *Caveat:* It is probable that the court was influenced by the fact that the adoptive sibling relationship had been of short duration.

3. Age Requirements

a. Regulation

Typical state regulation consists of setting a minimum age for marriage and a higher age below which marriage requires parental consent.

UMDA § 203: "[T]he [marriage license] clerk shall issue a license to marry and a marriage certificate form upon being furnished: (1) satisfactory proof that each party to the marriage will have attained the age of 18 years at the time the marriage license is effective, or will have attained the age of 16 years and has either the consent to the marriage of both parents or his guardian, or judicial approval; [or, if under the age of 16 years, has both the consent of both parents or his guardian and judicial approval]."

Traditionally, many states allow marriage below the minimum age or without parental consent, if a court order is obtained.

UMDA § 205: "(a) The court, after a reasonable effort has been made to notify the parents or guardian of each underaged party, may order the [marriage license] clerk to issue a marriage license and a marriage certificate form: [(1)] to a party aged 16 or 17 years who has no parent capable of consenting to his marriage, or whose parent or guardian has not consented to his marriage; [or (2) to a party under the age of 16 years who has the consent of both parents to his marriage, if capable of giving consent, or his guardian.]" (Note: Bracketed language in Uniform Acts identifies suggested alternatives.)

The UMDA further provides that the court may approve the marriage of an underaged person "only if the court finds that the underaged party is capable of assuming the responsibilities of marriage and the marriage will serve his or her best interests." Pregnancy is expressly singled out as *not* alone establishing that the party's best interests will be served. This proviso discounts the past when courts typically reserved judicial approval of otherwise invalid under-age marriages for cases involving a pregnant bride-to-be. Marriage then was thought preferable to the social stigma attaching to unwed mothers and illegitimate children.

Examples: (1) A 14–year-old girl, alleging her love, her desire to marry and her physical fitness for marriage, petitioned the court for permission to marry the 22–year-old son of her father's second wife. Her father had consented to the marriage. (Result: Denied. The court held that something more than "the usual, ordinary or the mere urgent desire of the parties" is required before it can give its consent to the marriage.) *In re Barbara Haven,* 86 Pa.D. & C. 141 (Orphans' Ct. 1954).

(2) Plaintiff M was 15 years old. She was cohabiting with the 18–year-old father of her child and they wished to marry. New York law required that female applicants for marriage licenses between the ages of 14 and 18 must obtain written consent from both parents. Females between the ages of 14 and 16 must also obtain judicial approval. When M's mother refused to consent, M sought to have the law declared unconstitutional. (Result: Law upheld. "[The statute's] requirement of parental consent is rationally related to the State's legitimate interests in mature decision-making with respect to marriage by minors and preventing

unstable marriages. It is also rationally related to the State's legitimate interest in supporting the fundamental privacy right of a parent to act in what the parent perceives to be the best interest of the child free from state court scrutiny. [The statute], therefore, does not offend the constitutional rights of minors but represents a constitutionally valid exercise of state power.") *Moe v. Dinkins*, 533 F.Supp. 623 (S.D.N.Y.1981), *aff'd*, 669 F.2d 67 (2d Cir. 1982).

b. Justification of Age Requirements

Age requirements are justified by the state's interest (1) in protecting immature minors from entering into marriage, (2) promoting marital stability and (3) providing children resulting from marriage with the care of mature and responsible parents. Studies indicate a considerably higher divorce rate for teenage marriages than for marriages of older parties.

c. Constitutional Limitation on Gender Distinctions

Traditionally, there was a discrepancy in age limitations for males and females. In 1973, a judge in New York still upheld the constitutionality of this discrimination on the basis of the male's duty to provide for his family and his consequent greater need for time to establish his earning capacity. *Friedrich v. Katz*, 73 Misc.2d 663, 341 N.Y.S.2d 932 (1973). She was overruled on appeal (34 N.Y.2d 987, 360 N.Y.S.2d 415, 318 N.E.2d 606). U.S. Supreme Court cases involving similar age discrimination have held that such discrimination violates equal protection guarantees. *Stanton v. Stanton*, 421 U.S. 7, 95 S.Ct. 1373, 43 L.Ed.2d 688 (1975); *Stanton v. Stanton*, 429 U.S. 501, 97 S.Ct. 717, 50 L.Ed.2d 723 (1977). "[W]e do not find any compelling State interest which justifies treating males and females of the same age differently for the purpose of determining their rights to a marriage license." *Phelps v. Bing*, 58 Ill.2d 32, 316 N.E.2d 775 (1974).

d. Effect of Noncompliance

A marriage in which one party fails to meet state minimum age requirements is void or voidable, depending on the provisions of the particular statute or on the common law of the state.

1) Who Can Attack

The underaged party has standing to have the marriage annulled or to attack the marriage collaterally. A party who is of marriage age may not attack the validity of his or her marriage to an underaged person. In many states, the parents of an underaged person may have their child's marriage annulled. UMDA § 208(b): "A declaration of invalidity * * * may be sought * * * (3) for * * * [underage], by the underaged party, his parent or guardian * * *."

2) Ratification

If intent to ratify the marriage is manifested when a previously underaged marriage partner reaches the required age, the invalid marriage is validated. Generally, marital cohabitation past the required age validates such a marriage. UMDA § 208(b)(3) allows an underage marriage to be declared invalid only *"prior* to the time the underaged party reaches the age at which he could have married without satisfying the omitted requirement." (Emphasis added).

4. Physical Requirements

a. Blood Tests

Not long ago, state law commonly required a health examination for the issuance of a marriage license. Usually this consists of a blood test to determine presence of venereal disease, traditionally syphilis. Less frequently, tests are required for tuberculosis, measles, drug addiction or the Rh factor.

Reflecting the modern trend against such health screening, however, UMDA § 203(3) has made the requirement for a medical examination optional: "[T]he traditional forms of premarital medical examination, now required by the marriage laws of most of the states, need not be preserved. The premarital medical examination requirement serves either to inform the prospective spouses of health hazards that may have an impact on their marriage, or to warn public health officials of the presence of venereal disease. For the latter purpose, the statutes have been proved to be both avoidable and highly inefficient. Moreover, the cursory blood test which satisfied the requirements of most states provides very little service to the prospective spouses themselves." (Official Comment to UMDA § 203). Recently, many states have made health screening advisory only or have abandoned it altogether.

b. Physical Capacity

UMDA § 208 (a)(2) mirrors the traditional rule by providing that a marriage may be annulled if "a party lacks the physical capacity to consummate the marriage by sexual intercourse, and at the time the marriage was solemnized the other party did not know of the incapacity."

Example: 81–year-old H married W, a former tenant in his home, shortly before his death from cancer. After H's death, his sister sought to annul H's marriage (so as to prevent W from inheriting as a spouse) on the ground that he was impotent. (Result: Challenge to marriage rejected on this ground. "[O]nly a party to the marriage can be an applicant for annulment on the ground of impotency. . . . The unique proofs required for this ground lend credence to the notion that this is a private right of the parties to the marriage."). *In re Estate of Santolino*, 384 N.J. Super. 567, 895 A.2d 506 (Super. Ct. 2005).

c. Epilepsy

At one time, numerous states prohibited an epileptic from marrying. Medical advances led to the repeal of such statutes.

C. Conflicts of Laws

1. Law of Celebration

The law of the place of celebration generally governs the validity of a marriage.

Example: H and W_1 were divorced in Nebraska. The divorce decree ordered that neither party remarry within six months of the date of the decree. Before the six months expired, H married W_2 in Iowa. W_2 sought to divorce H in Missouri. H alleged that they were not married, as his first divorce was not final when the ceremony was celebrated. (Result: Marriage to W_2 held valid: "[I]n this case, the application of orthodox principles of conflict of laws leads us to the same conclusion we have reached by applying the presumption that the marriage was valid. The validity of the marriage in the first instance must be determined by looking to the law of the state where it was contracted. If we assume that Iowa would not recognize the marriage because the Nebraska decree had not terminated defendant's marital status, ordinary principles of choice of law would require us to look to Iowa's rules of conflict of laws. * * * When we do so, we find that Iowa clearly holds it is the law of the forum which determines whether a party is estopped to attack the validity of a foreign divorce decree. * * * The parties are domiciled here, and this court would hold the defendant estopped to deny the efficiency of the Nebraska decree even if it were shown that [W$_1$] was alive and well when the parties were married in Iowa.") *In re Marriage of Sumners*, 645 S.W.2d 205 (Mo.App.1983).

2. "Most Significant Relationship" Test

Restatement (Second) of Conflicts: "The validity of a marriage will be determined by the local law of the state which, with respect to the particular issue, has the most significant relationship to the spouses and the marriage * * *." A marriage satisfying requirements of the state where contracted is valid everywhere, "unless it violates the strong public policy of another state which had the most significant relationship to the spouses and the marriage at the time of the marriage." § 283. A state usually gives the same incidents to a valid foreign marriage that it gives to a marriage contracted within its territory. § 284.

3. Uniform Marriage Evasion Act

The Uniform Marriage Evasion Act provides that marriage may not be validly contracted in State B by a resident of State A, if such a marriage would be void in State A. Similarly, a marriage meeting all requirements in State A and contracted there by a nonresident party is void if prohibited in that party's state of residence. Only five states have adopted the UMEA, and one of those (Massachusetts) repealed its evasion law in 2008. The Commissioners on Uniform State Laws withdrew (*i.e.,* no longer recommend enactment of) the Act in 1943.

4. The Public Policy Exception

The general conflicts rule stated above permits states to refuse recognition to a marriage validly contracted in another jurisdiction if recognition would offend a "strong public policy" of the couple's home state. Accordingly, in recent years a majority of states have enacted "defense of marriage" statutes expressing their strong policy objections to the recognition of same-sex marriages.

5. Full Faith and Credit

Article IV, § 1, of the U.S. Constitution requires each state to give "full faith and credit" to the "public acts, records, and judicial proceedings of every other state." If a marriage license is a public "record" for these purposes, the

Full Faith and Credit Clause might suggest that other states must recognize out-of-state marriages notwithstanding local policy objections. In 1996, Congress sought to make this question moot by enacting the federal Defense of Marriage Act (28 U.S.C. § 1738C), part of which specifies that "[n]o State . . . shall be required to give effect to any public act, record, or judicial proceeding of any other State" conferring marriage on a same-sex couple. Congress enacted this legislation pursuant to its express authority under the Full Faith and Credit Clause to enact "general laws prescrib[ing] the manner in which such acts, records, and judicial proceedings shall be proved, and the effect thereof." As it stands now, therefore, federal law claims to exempt states from any constitutional full faith and credit obligation with respect to same-sex marriage, although there is some question whether the Full Faith and Credit Clause authorizes such nullifying legislation.

D. Annulment

Annulment (today often referred to as "Declaration of Invalidity," *e.g.*, UMDA § 208) is a judicial declaration that by reason of a defect or impediment that existed at its inception, a purported marriage does not exist. Depending upon the impediment on which the annulment is based, a defective marriage is classified as void or voidable. Traditionally, the declaration is retroactive in both circumstances: The marriage is treated as never having existed.

1. History

Annulment developed contemporaneously with limited divorce (legal separation) when full divorce with the right to remarry did not exist. Annulment of a prior marriage permitted remarriage, because, void or voidable, an annulled marriage was deemed never to have existed.

2. Impediments

Impediments (defects) sufficient to warrant annulment traditionally included failure of one or both parties to meet age requirements, fraud or duress, impotency, bigamy, religious orders, consanguinity, and affinity. To be the basis of a successful annulment action, the impediment must have existed at the time of the marriage.

3. Defenses

Generally, a party to an action seeking annulment of a voidable marriage may raise equitable defenses such as estoppel, ratification, and unclean hands. A void marriage, on the other hand, is not ratifiable and is without legal effect even without an annulment or declaration of invalidity. Nevertheless, a party to a void marriage who has "unclean hands" is often held estopped from asserting the voidness of the "marriage" and thereby gaining an unfair advantage.

4. The Void/Voidable Distinction

a. Void Marriage

A *void* marriage typically offends a strong public policy (such as the prohibition of incest or bigamy). It requires no judicial declaration or action to establish its invalidity. Nevertheless, such an action may be entertained by a court to provide certainty and to produce a public record that no valid marriage existed.

b. Voidable Marriage

A *voidable* marriage typically reflects encroachment upon some matter of lesser concern to the state, but of considerable concern to a party to the marriage (such as "fraud" or "duress"). A voidable marriage typically must be attacked during the life of the parties, attack may be allowed only to the parties, and some voidable marriages may be ratified by the parties' voluntary conduct, such as continued cohabitation after gaining knowledge of a fraud or after reaching marriage age.

c. Significance of the Distinction

The void/voidable classification may have potentially significant impact upon other legal interests. To illustrate, if a marriage is *void* and one partner dies, the surviving partner does not inherit as a spouse. (If the putative spouse doctrine or similar remedy applies, this rule may not hold.) If the marriage was *voidable* and has not been annulled, the surviving partner is considered a widow(er).

Example: Potential heirs of deceased W brought an action to annul W's marriage to H on grounds of mental incompetence and fraud. They alleged that W was of unsound mind at the time of the marriage and that H induced W to marry him in order to inherit from her, knowing that she was about to die. (Result: Annulment denied. Allegations would support only a finding of a voidable marriage. Since the action was not brought during W's lifetime, the marriage can no longer be annulled.) *Patey v. Peaslee*, 99 N.H. 335, 111 A.2d 194 (1955). *Contra, In re Santolino*, 384 N.J.Super. 567, 895 A.2d 506 (Super. Ct. 2005) (disallowing annulment action initiated by third party based on decedent's impotence, but permitting posthumous annulment based on decedent's mental incompetence).

d. UMDA

The UMDA reduces traditional distinctions between (1) void and voidable marriages and (2) between annulment and divorce. (See p. 77). UMDA § 208 defines and restricts the persons who may attack a defective marriage and when such an attack may or must be made.

5. Annulment for Fraud

As grounds for annulment of a marriage, a fraudulent misrepresentation (1) must have occurred before the parties' marriage, (2) must be material and must have been relied upon by the other party, and (3) must go to the "essence" of the marriage contract. What constitutes the "essence of marriage" is not defined uniformly. Courts have found fraud going to the essence of marriage when there were false representations regarding fertility, or serious misrepresentations concerning religious beliefs. Misrepresentations concerning wealth, character or past life, however, typically have not sufficed to invalidate a marriage, no matter how important the matter was to the other party.

Examples: (1) During their two-year marriage, H consistently refused to engage in sexual relations with W. Indeed, on their camping honeymoon in the Smoky Mountains, they slept in separate tents. (Result: Annulment granted. "[T]raditionally a sexual relationship is implicit in marriage vows and . . . an unstated intent, held at the time of the marriage ceremony, to utterly refuse to engage in a sexual relationship with the other party is a fraud that alters the very essence of the marriage.") *Janda v. Janda*, 984 So.2d 434 (Ala.Civ.App. 2007).

(2) Before their marriage, H falsely led W to believe that he was "a well-educated millionaire with expertise in real estate and finance." (Result: Annulment denied. "[F]raud or misrepresentation of a purely financial nature" is not sufficient to support annulment.) *In re Marriage of Meagher*, 131 Cal.App.4th 1, 31 Cal.Rptr.3d 663 (Ct. App. 2005).

(3) W represented to H_2 that H_1 was dead. In fact, she was divorced and H_1 was still living. As a practicing Roman

Catholic, H_2 credibly alleged that he would not have married W if he had known that H_1 was still alive. (Result: Annulment.) *Wolfe v. Wolfe*, 62 Ill.App.3d 498, 19 Ill.Dec. 306, 378 N.E.2d 1181 (1978), aff'd 76 Ill.2d 92, 27 Ill.Dec. 735, 389 N.E.2d 1143 (1979).

(4) Before marriage, H falsely represented himself to W as a practicing Orthodox Jew. (Result: Annulment. The court found that for this W, religion was an "essential of her marriage.") *Bilowit v. Dolitsky*, 124 N.J.Super. 101, 304 A.2d 774 (1973).

6. Annulment for Duress

To allow annulment of a marriage, duress (1) must have been perceived by the complaining party at the time of marriage and (2) must have been sufficient to prevent him or her from acting freely. Many cases seem to apply this test subjectively and may ask whether *this particular individual* was entering the marriage under duress, regardless of whether the belief was reasonable. Duress may be exercised by threats or application of physical force, or by threat of arrest or prosecution, and invalidates consent to marriage. Traditionally, a threat of criminal prosecution for seduction, fornication, or a similar offense was held *not* to invalidate a marriage thus induced, because marriage was a defense to such "crimes."

7. Annulment of Marriage Entered in Jest

"When two people participate in a mock marriage ceremony as the result of jest, exuberance, hilarity, or dare and harbor no intention to be bound thereby, most cases have allowed the marriage to be annulled, reasoning that the public interest would not be served by compelling these persons to accept the legal consequences of their imprudent conduct." *Mpiliris v. Hellenic Lines, Ltd.*, 323 F.Supp. 865 (S.D.Tex.1969). In 2004, the singer Britney Spears and a friend from high school tested this rule by spontaneously marrying at a Las Vegas wedding chapel in what she later described as "a joke carried too far." Fortunately, a Nevada court agreed to annul the marriage three days later. Spears later reassured MTV, "I believe in the sanctity of marriage—I totally do!"

8. Annulment of Sham Marriage

Occasionally, parties will enter into a marriage for a particular, limited purpose. They may marry to legitimate a child, to gain tax benefits, or to circumvent immigration quotas. Courts have not been consistent in their treatment of such marriages. If, at the time of the marriage, the parties intended to establish a life together or if the parties intended to partake of at least one of the inherent incidents of marriage (such as legitimation of a child), the marriage generally is upheld. Traditionally, courts were less likely to annul a marriage that had been consummated. The outcome may depend on who challenges the marriage. The "clean hands doctrine" may estop the parties, but not the federal government which, under specific provisions of the immigration laws, may challenge a sham marriage (or divorce) intended to take advantage of immigration preferences. U.S. law now imposes a 2–year duration test on marriages that lead to immigration preference, and requires a 2–year "exile" on the part of a would-be immigrant, if he or she enters a marriage with a U.S. citizen while deportation or exclusion proceedings are pending. (*E.g.,* Choin v. Mukasey, 537 F.3d 1116 (9th Cir. 2008); Acheampong v. Keisler, 250 Fed.Appx. 158 (6th Cir. 2007)). A marriage may be valid between the parties to the marriage or vis-à-vis most third parties, but this will not necessarily bind the immigration authorities. Conversely, if the parties later obtain an annulment or divorce, this does not allow the government to revoke an immigration visa granted on the basis of the marriage, unless the immigration laws specifically cover the situation. Similar situations may arise under federal tax laws.

Example: W, a native of Ghana, entered the United States unlawfully and applied for asylum. While her petition was pending, she married H, a U.S. citizen, and applied for lawful permanent resident status on that basis. After her two-year conditional residency period passed, W applied to remove the condition, as contemplated by federal immigration laws but immigration authorities determined that the marriage was a sham. (Result: Substantial evidence established that the marriage was a sham and that W was therefore deportable. "A marriage formed to help one spouse circumvent immigration law and not as the couple's good faith attempt to start a life together is called a 'fraudulent or sham marriage, and has not been recognized as enabling an alien spouse to obtain immigration benefits.' " Here, among other evidence, the couple gave conflicting accounts of their time spent together, repeatedly failed to acknowledge their marriage on tax, insurance, and other documents, and W was unable to "give the court information about [H's] job, religion, or even the medication he takes.") *Acheampong, supra.*

9. Legal Incidents of Annulment

a. Effects Regarding Children and Financial Obligations

Even if annulment declares a marriage never to have existed, many courts today recognize the relationship in some particulars, especially regarding the legitimacy of children and financial obligations.

Examples: (1) In an earlier decision, the state supreme court had held that H's common-law marriage to W was void *ab initio* because H had a wife living at the same time that W claimed to be H's wife. W did not know of the first wife until she filed for divorce. W filed this suit to determine her interest in personal and real property accumulated during the alleged marriage. (Result: Damages granted W. The court applied *Buckley v. Buckley*, 50 Wash. 213, 96 P. 1079 (1908): "Where a woman in good faith enters into a marriage contract with a man, and they assume and enter into the marriage state pursuant to any ceremony or agreement recognized by the law of the place, which marriage would be legal except for the incompetency of the man which he conceals from the woman, a status is created which will justify a court in rendering a decree of annulment of the attempted and assumed marriage contract upon complaint of the innocent party; and where in such a case the facts are as they have been found here, where the woman helped to acquire and very materially to save the property, the court has jurisdiction, as between the parties, to dispose of their property as it would * * * in a case of granting a divorce, awarding to the innocent, injured woman such proportion of the property as, under all the circumstances, would be just and equitable.") *Walker v. Walker*, 330 Mich. 332, 47 N.W.2d 633 (1951).

(2) H and W were married at a time when, unknown to W, H was married to another woman. W filed for divorce on the ground that the marriage was null and void *ab initio*. The trial court granted the divorce and awarded W alimony. H challenged the award of alimony. (Result: Alimony award upheld. "The key to the instant case, as we see it, is the legislative declaration that alimony is allowable whenever there is a decree for divorce. We read 'alimony'

not in the technical sense of the word, but as commensurate with 'support'. The inclusion of prevenient invalidity as a ground for divorce must be ascribed some meaning, and we think it shows a legislative intent to permit an award of alimony in a proper case. * * * In the absence of statute, alimony is generally not allowed in any case where the marriage is declared to be null and void *ab initio.* * * * But by statute in many states, support for the putative wife is allowed in all cases of divorce or annulment. In other states, the same result is reached, by construction of the divorce statutes to permit an award of alimony, even where the ground of divorce is that the marriage is a nullity. * * * We take the same view.") *Clayton v. Clayton,* 231 Md. 74, 188 A.2d 550 (1963).

b. Non–Retroactive Annulment Under UMDA § 208(e), With Divorce–Like Consequences

UMDA § 208(e) provides that "unless the court finds, after a consideration of all relevant circumstances, including the effect of a retroactive decree on third parties, that the interests of justice would be served by making the decree not retroactive, it shall declare the marriage invalid as of the date of the marriage. The provisions of this Act relating to property rights of the spouses, maintenance, support, and custody of children on dissolution of marriage are applicable to non-retroactive decrees of invalidity."

c. Revival of Former Spouse's Duty of Support

In many jurisdictions, an annulment does not revive a former spouse's duty of support that terminated upon the attempted remarriage. In some jurisdictions, however, whether an earlier support obligation is revived depends on whether the annulled "remarriage" was void or voidable: if void, the support duty is revived on the theory that there never was a remarriage; if voidable, the obligation will not be revived on the theory that the remarriage was valid until annulled. A third and smaller group of states simply decides the question case-by-case according to the particular equities.

Examples: (1) When they divorced in 2004, H's alimony obligation was made terminable on W's remarriage. In 2005, W remarried in Las Vegas, but promptly sought to annul the marriage after H sought to end his alimony payments.

(Result: W's remarriage terminated H's alimony duty, regardless of whether the Las Vegas marriage was void or voidable and later annulled. "By entering into another marriage, the alimony recipient has made an election to look to another for support. That election in no way hinged on how the later marriage worked out. That the subsequent marriage may later be determined not to be valid does not detract from such a result any more than would the untimely death of the recipient's new spouse or a sudden breakdown in their relationship soon after the marriage has taken place.") *Fredo v. Fredo*, 49 Conn.Super. 489, 49 Conn.Supp. 489, 894 A.2d 399 (2005).

(2) H's alimony obligation to W was terminable on her remarriage. Immediately following the divorce, W attempted to marry X, but the "marriage" was void because state law prohibited remarriage within six months of a divorce. Three months after the attempted remarriage, X deserted W and she sought to revive H's alimony obligation. (Result: Alimony revived. Although a voidable remarriage terminates a prior alimony duty, a void marriage is "a legal nullity" and therefore does not terminate H's duty.) *Watts v. Watts*, 250 Neb. 38, 547 N.W.2d 466 (1996).

(3) H's alimony obligation to W was terminable on her remarriage. Shortly after H and W divorced, W "remarried" X. But two months later W learned that X had never divorced his first wife, rendering his attempted marriage to W void. W obtained an annulment and sought to compel H to resume paying alimony. (Result: Case remanded for trial court to weigh the equities in deciding whether to revive alimony. "Under this method, the family court need not adhere to a bright-line rule and can consider relevant factors such as: length of the subsequent marriage, whether the payee spouse receives support and maintenance from the annulled marriage, whether the payor spouse is prejudiced by the revival of alimony payments, whether the subsequent marriage was properly annulled, and any change in the spouses' personal and financial circumstances after the subsequent marriage is annulled.") *Joye v. Yon*, 355 S.C. 452, 586 S.E.2d 131 (2003).

d. Revival of Other Rights Related to Marriage

If the "reconstitution" of the relationship preceding the annulment does not burden the former spouse but falls upon an employer, or on a state or federal program designed to support the spouse of a deceased employee, some courts are willing to disregard a subsequent invalid remarriage and allow revival of a right relating to a prior valid marriage.

Examples: (1) W received monthly death benefits as a widow of H_1, who was killed in the course of his employment. When she remarried, the death benefits terminated and she was awarded a 2–year lump-sum payment. Three years later and following the birth of their child, W learned that H_2 had a prior existing marriage that had never been terminated. The marriage between W and H_2 was annulled, and W filed for reinstatement of the monthly death benefits relating to H_1. Following a hearing, the benefits were reinstated as of the date of the void marriage, and the insurance carrier was credited with the 2–year lump-sum payment. The insurance carrier appealed. (Result: Award upheld. "Since the marriage [to H_2] was annulled, [W] is entitled to all of the benefits she would have received had there been no attempted marriage, subject only to the return of the amount paid in a lump sum. Here, the latter requirement was satisfied by crediting the amount of the lump sum payment to the benefits due.") *United States Fidelity and Guaranty Co. v. The Industrial Commission of Arizona*, 25 Ariz.App. 244, 542 P.2d 825 (1975).

(2) After W's marriage to H_2 was annulled, she filed an application for Social Security survivor's benefits based on H_1's earnings, with whom she had lived until his death. (Result: Benefits denied. " * * * [R]eference to state law is necessary * * * for the narrow purpose of determining whether the widow has entered into a relationship that will entitle her under state law to support from her second husband." The court found that she would be so entitled). *Nott v. Flemming*, 272 F.2d 380 (2d Cir.1959).

Review Questions

1. **T or F** Since a mentally incompetent person lacks capacity to marry, a guardian must consent to his/her marriage.

2. **T or F** A marriage will be annulled on the ground of fraud if the injured party can show his/her detrimental reliance on a misrepresentation.

3. **T or F** A marriage may be found even though the couple failed to have it solemnized.

4. **T or F** Proxy marriages generally are considered sham marriages and therefore are invalid.

5. M and W have lived together for five years. They have no children. They have told everyone that they are married, but no ceremony was ever performed. W now wants a divorce. In the typical state that recognizes common law marriage, which is the correct answer?

    A. Since M and W have no children, a valid common law marriage did not come into existence. Therefore, there can be no divorce.

    B. W may file for divorce in the same manner as if she had been married ceremonially.

    C. Since M and W have not cohabited for seven years, they do not have a common law marriage.

6. **T or F** The putative spouse doctrine protects a husband and wife who are not actually married, but who hold themselves out as married.

7–10. Questions 7 through 10 should be answered based on the following facts: H and W are married, and S is their 21–year–old son. G is a 16–year–old unrelated female. B is an 18–year–old unrelated male. A is W's 25–year–old sister.

7. **T or F** All states prohibit W from marrying S, but most allow S and A to marry.

8. **T or F** To marry B, G needs parental consent.

9. **T or F** If H and W had adopted G, some states would allow G to marry S.

10. **T or F** If the parties' religion requires a man to have several wives, a state law forbidding H to marry both W and G (if G's parents consent),

would be in violation of the constitutional guaranty of religious freedom.

11. **T or F**   Sam and Diane enter into a common law marriage in a state that recognizes common law marriage, meeting all the required prerequisites. Their marriage is not recognized in their home state which has abolished common law marriage.

12. **T or F**   Richard, age 25, and Liz, age 15, marry. One year later Richard has second thoughts and wants an annulment because Liz was underage at the time of their marriage. He may annul the marriage.

III

Cohabitation Without Marriage

■ ANALYSIS

A. **Unmarried Cohabitation**
 1. *Marvin v. Marvin*
 2. Application of the *"Marvin* Doctrine"
 3. *Marvin* Doctrine Rejected
 4. *Marvin* Doctrine "Codified"
 5. Domestic Partnership Under the ALI Principles

B. **Same–Sex Relationships**
 1. Cohabitation
 2. Domestic Partnerships and Civil Unions
 3. Transsexuals

A. Unmarried Cohabitation

1. *Marvin v. Marvin*

In the landmark *Marvin* case, Michelle Triola Marvin sued actor Lee Marvin to enforce an oral agreement purportedly giving her rights to support and one half of the property accumulated during the seven years the two cohabitated. The Supreme Court of California held:

a. Family Law Statutes Do Not Govern a Non–Marital Relationship

"No language in the Family Law Act addresses the property rights of nonmarital partners, and nothing in the legislative history of the act suggests that the Legislature considered that subject. The delineation of the rights of non-marital partners before 1970 had been fixed entirely by judicial decision; we see no reason to believe that the Legislature, by enacting the Family Law Act, intended to change that state of affairs."

b. Contracts Between Partners Are Enforceable, Unless the Consideration Is Meretricious

"The decisions in [earlier California] cases thus demonstrate that a contract between nonmarital partners, even if expressly made in con-templation of a common living arrangement, is invalid only if sexual acts form an inseparable part of the consideration for the agreement. In sum, a court will not enforce a contract for the pooling of property and earnings if it is explicitly and inseparably based upon services as a paramour. [One case] indicates that even if sexual services are part of the contractual consideration, any severable portion of the contract sup-ported by independent consideration will still be enforced."

c. If There Is No Express Agreement—Other Remedies May Protect [~ without words] the Parties' Expectations

"The courts may inquire into the conduct of the parties to determine whether that conduct demonstrates an implied contract or implied agreement of partnership or joint venture or some other tacit under-standing between the parties. The courts may, when appropriate, employ principles of constructive trust or resulting trust. Finally, a nonmarital partner may recover in quantum meruit for the reasonable value of household services rendered less the reasonable value of support received if he can show that he rendered services with the expectation of monetary reward." *Marvin v. Marvin*, 18 Cal.3d 660, 134 Cal.Rptr. 815, 557 P.2d 106 (1976).

d. Outcome of *Marvin*

Sent back down

The California Supreme Court remanded the *Marvin* case to the trial court which rejected Michelle's contract claim, but awarded her $104,000 for "rehabilitation." On further appeal, the California Appellate Court denied this recovery on the ground that "no basis whatsoever, either in equity or in law, exists for the challenged rehabilitative award." *Marvin v. Marvin*, 122 Cal.App.3d 871, 176 Cal.Rptr. 555 (1981). The California Supreme Court denied further review.

2. Application of the "*Marvin* Doctrine"

Despite the negative outcome of the case and the fact that *Marvin* was not the first such decision, *Marvin* now stands for the proposition that support and property obligations *may* arise from cohabitation without marriage. With the increase in unmarried cohabitation in today's society, the *Marvin* holding has been widely discussed and cited. Courts have allowed recoveries on the basis of express and implied agreements, as well as on the theory of unjust enrichment or quasi-contract and resulting and constructive trusts.

a. Application to Facts Resembling Common Law Marriage

Examples: (1) P and D lived together for 14 years, participated in a religious wedding ceremony, and had two children together, though they never legally married. During their relationship, the couple amassed more than $1 million in property, all of which was titled in D's name. In 2003, P and D were both killed in a car accident while on a family vacation. (Result: P and D "lived in a committed intimate relationship that would have been sufficient to justify equitable distribution of their jointly acquired property had their relationship terminated by dissolution rather than death. . . . By analogy to community property law, [P] had an undivided interest in the couple's jointly acquired property, even though it was titled in [D's] name. . . . We hold that when a committed intimate relationship is terminated by the death of both parties, the couple's jointly acquired property can be equitably divided between the partners' estates.") *Olver v. Fowler*, 161 Wash.2d 655, 168 P.3d 348 (2007).

(2) P and D lived together for 28 years. They never participated in a formal marriage ceremony or obtained a marriage license, but they held themselves out as married

and were regarded by others in the community as husband and wife. On three separate occasions they purchased real property jointly, as though a married couple. When they separated, P sued to establish a marriage between herself and D in order to become eligible for spousal social security benefits, and to equitably divide the couple's property. (Result: No common law marriage. Equitable division ordered. "[T]he citizens of this state, by way of the legislative process, have expressed a preference for the solemnization of marriage. Due to the presence of this statutory provision, we will not impose an alternative view. * * * We base our opinion on the principle that adults who voluntarily live together and engage in sexual relations are nonetheless as competent as any other persons to contract respecting their earnings and property rights. Of course, they cannot lawfully contract to pay for the performance of sexual services * * *. So long as the agreement does not rest upon illicit meretricious consideration, the parties may order their economic affairs as they choose, and no policy precludes the courts from enforcing such agreements. * * * [W]e hold that a court may order a division of property acquired by a man and woman who are unmarried cohabitants, but who have considered themselves and held themselves out to be husband and wife. Such order may be based upon principles of contract, either express or implied, or upon a constructive trust. Factors to be considered in ordering such a division of property may include: the purpose, duration, and stability of the relationship and the expectations of the parties. Provided, however, that if either the man or woman is validly married to another person during the period of cohabitation, the property rights of the spouse and support rights of the children of such man or woman shall not in any way be adversely affected by such division of property. The expectations of the parties under these circumstances would be equitable treatment by the other party in exchange for engaging in such a cohabiting relationship.") *Goode v. Goode*, 183 W.Va. 468, 396 S.E.2d 430 (W.Va.1990).

(3) P and D lived together for 12 years and had two children. They held themselves out to the public as hus-

band and wife, filed joint income tax returns and maintained joint bank accounts. D insured P as his wife on his medical insurance policy, and P and D purchased real and personal property as though husband and wife. P obligated herself on promissory notes to lending institutions as though D's wife, and she worked as a receptionist in D's business for 3 years. P also took care of the children and the house and contributed personal property. After a bitter separation, P sought an accounting and a share of accumulated property under family law statutes, marriage by estoppel, express or implied in fact contract, constructive trust based upon unjust enrichment, and partition. (Result: (1) Unmarried cohabitants are not a family within the meaning of the statute that authorizes the division of property in an action affecting the family. (2) The doctrine of marriage by estoppel is inapplicable. (3) P has valid claims for breach of contract, express or implied in fact, unjust enrichment, and partition. "We disagree with the circuit court's implicit conclusion that courts cannot or should not, without express authorization from the legislature, divide property between persons who have engaged in nonmarital cohabitation. Courts traditionally have settled contract and property disputes between unmarried persons, some of whom have cohabited. Nonmarital cohabitation does not render every agreement between the cohabiting parties illegal and does not automatically preclude one of the parties from seeking judicial relief, such as statutory or common law partition, damages for breach of express or implied contract, constructive trust and quantum meruit where the party alleges, and later proves, facts supporting the legal theory.") *Watts v. Watts*, 137 Wis.2d 506, 405 N.W.2d 303 (Wis.1987).

b. Application to Facts Not Resembling Common Law Marriage

Examples: (1) P began working as a receptionist in D's medical office when she was 23 years old. The two commenced an affair that eventually spanned 20 years, during which D repeatedly promised P that he would leave his wife, marry P, and have a child with P. When their relationship finally ended, P sought to enforce D's alleged promise to support her for life. The lower courts denied relief on the ground that cohabitation is essential to establishing the sort of "marital-type relationship" that will support a "palimony" claim under New Jersey law. (Result: Cohabitation is relevant but not strictly required to show a "marital-type relationship" capable of supporting a palimony claim. Nevertheless, the trial court properly found on the facts of the case that "the parties' relationship was best characterized as a dating relationship." "In concluding that the parties did not enjoy a marital-type relationship, the judge found that the parties did not live together; they did not spend significant periods of time together; they did not commingle their property or share living expenses; and they did not hold themselves out to the public as husband and wife. The trial judge correctly considered the lack of cohabitation as a factor in reaching its determination and appropriately analyzed all of the factors of the highly personalized relationship between the parties, including the fact that defendant continued to live with his wife.") *Devaney v. L'Esperance*, 195 N.J. 247, 949 A.2d 743 (2008).

(2) P had an intimate relationship with D, a celebrity defense lawyer, spanning 17 years and the birth of one child. During much of that time, D was married to two other women in succession, with whom he lived. When P sued to enforce a promise of lifetime support under *Marvin*, D argued that there could be no enforceable support duty because the parties had not "cohabited." (Result: *Marvin* claim reinstated and remanded. "To require nothing short of full-time cohabitation before enforcing an agreement would defeat the reasonable expectations of persons who may clearly enjoy a significant and stable relationship arising from cohabitation, albeit less than a full-time living arrangement. . . . Here, the parties had shared a long-term, stable and significant relationship. In this context, evidence that they lived together two to four days a week both before and at the time they entered their *Marvin* agreement is sufficient to raise a triable issue of fact that they cohabited under *Marvin*.") *Cochran v. Cochran*, 89 Cal.App.4th 283, 106 Cal.Rptr.2d 899 (2001).

c. Recovery for Services

Examples: (1) P and D had a 13– or 14–year relationship and lived together for seven of those years. In 1978 they purchased a home in Reading, Massachusetts. On the way to the closing, D told P that he would have to take title in his name alone in order to obtain Veterans' Administration financing, and the deed was so recorded. During the three years they lived together in Reading, D (a career army officer) attended law school at night and P (who had given up her career as a flight attendant to maintain a home for D) worked as a waitress. D paid the mortgage, taxes, utilities, and insurance on the house. P paid for food, household supplies, and much of the furniture. P did all of the housework. When D was transferred to Washington, D.C., P moved with him. Their relationship deteriorated and P, who wished to move back to Reading, sued to obtain title to the house as tenant in common with D. (Result: No tenancy in common, but D held one-half of the property in constructive trust in favor of P. "The judge's unchallenged findings of fact demonstrate that there was a fiduciary relationship between the parties and that the defendant violated his fiduciary duty to the plaintiff. Equitable principles impose a constructive trust on property to avoid the unjust enrichment of a party who violates his fiduciary duty and acquires that property at the expense of the person to whom he owed that duty.") *Sullivan v. Rooney,* 404 Mass. 160, 533 N.E.2d 1372 (Mass.1989).

(2) P brought an action for the reasonable value of services rendered and material furnished in the improvement and renovation of D's home. P and D had been cohabiting at the time the services were performed. (Result: P was entitled to recover funds he expended, the reasonable value of work he performed, and services he rendered in renovating and improving D's home, reduced by the reasonable value of benefits received by him. "[W]e cannot agree that the fact of unmarried cohabitation between the parties bars either party from asserting against the other a claim which would otherwise be enforceable under principles of law of general applicability. * * * [W]e regard the

position that the courts will not participate in resolving the disputes in accordance with general principles of law and, thus, will leave the parties to their own devices, to be unrealistic and unresponsive to social need.") *Mason v. Rostad,* 476 A.2d 662 (D.C. 1984).

3. *Marvin* Doctrine Rejected

In *Hewitt v. Hewitt,* 77 Ill.2d 49, 31 Ill.Dec. 827, 394 N.E.2d 1204 (1979), a man and woman had lived together as husband and wife for fifteen years. They had three children. No marriage ceremony had been performed, but H allegedly had told W that they were married, that no ceremony was necessary and that he would "share his life, his future, his earnings and his property" with her. Because Illinois does not recognize common law marriage and fearing that to allow her recovery would adopt the *Marvin* doctrine in derogation of what should be the legislature's prerogative, the Illinois Supreme Court held that H had no obligation to share any property earned by him throughout their years together or to pay her any support in the future. *Accord, Nichols v. Funderburk,* 881 So.2d 266 (Miss.Ct.App. 2003) (denying any division of property to woman who had cohabited with partner for 12 years, since she was 15 years old, during which time they had two children together).

[handwritten annotation: just live together]

4. *Marvin* Doctrine "Codified"

Minnesota Stat. Ann. § 513.075: "If sexual relations between the parties are contemplated, a contract between a man and a woman who are living together in this state out of wedlock, or who are about to commence living together in this state out of wedlock, is enforceable as to terms concerning the property and financial relations of the parties only if: (1) the contract is written and signed by the parties, and (2) enforcement is sought after termination of the relationship." § 513.076: "Unless the individuals have executed a contract complying with [the above] provisions, the courts of this state are without jurisdiction to hear and shall dismiss as contrary to public policy any claim by an individual to the earnings or property of another individual if the claim is based on the fact that the individuals lived together in contemplation of sexual relations and out of wedlock within or without this state."

5. Domestic Partnership Under the ALI Principles

In 2001, the *Principles of the Law of Family Dissolution* drafted by the American Law Institute proposed that states recognize as "domestic partners" long-term cohabitants who have established "a life together as a couple." *See* ALI

Principles of the Law of Family Dissolution § 6.01. The ALI would leave it to individual states to determine how long couples must cohabit to acquire this status, and directs courts to a range of common-sense considerations in deciding whether the couple has established "a life together," including whether the couple have children, pooled their financial resources, divided household roles, and so on. If the couple qualify as "domestic partners" under the ALI proposal, they would then be treated much like married partners if they later separated, empowering courts to divide property and award alimony (or, in the ALI's terminology, "compensatory payments"). Most controversially, the ALI's proposal would permit the recognition of domestic partnerships involving persons who were still married to others. No state has adopted the ALI's proposal.

B. Same–Sex Relationships

1. Cohabitation

The *Marvin* Doctrine has been applied to same-sex cohabitants.

Example: When P and D, both men, began living together, they orally agreed that P would quit school and devote himself full-time to being D's chauffeur, bodyguard, social and business secretary, partner in real estate investments, and spokesman. In turn, D agreed to give P one-half equity in all real estate thereafter acquired by D or jointly by D and P, to support P for life, and to permit P to withdraw from D's bank accounts and use D's credit cards. D also agreed to engage in a homosexual relationship with P. The parties further agreed that if any portion of the agreement was found to be unenforceable, that portion would be severable and the remaining provisions would remain in full force and effect. Seven years later D barred P from his premises. P sued for property rights based on the oral agreement. D argued that the agreement was unenforceable (1) under the statute of frauds and (2) because it was based upon illicit consideration, *i.e.*, sexual services. (Result: (1) D is estopped from raising a statute of frauds defense in light of P's detrimental reliance. (2) The agreement is enforceable even though the parties' sexual relationship was an express part of the consideration. "The issue here is whether the sexual component of the consideration is severable from the remaining portions of the contract. * * * The services which plaintiff alleges he agreed to and did provide included being a chauffeur, bodyguard, secretary, and partner and counselor in real estate investments. If provided, these services are of monetary value, and the type for which one would expect to be compensated unless there is evidence of a contrary intent. Thus, they are properly characterized as consideration independent of the sexual aspect of the relationship.") *Whorton v. Dillingham*, 202 Cal.App.3d 447, 248 Cal.Rptr. 405 (1988).

2. Domestic Partnerships and Civil Unions

A growing number of states and municipalities have acted to permit unmarried couples to register formally as "domestic partners" and thereby to qualify for a range of public benefits and programs ordinarily reserved for married couples. Jurisdictions differ on whether such partnerships are available to any unmarried couple or are limited to same-sex couples, who generally lack the option of marriage; jurisdictions also vary in terms of the generosity of benefits made available to registered partners. Hawaii created a domestic partnership registry in 1996 as a compromise measure after voters amended the state constitution to maintain the state's ban on same-sex marriage. Vermont similarly enacted legislation offering same-sex "civil unions" in 2000 in response to a ruling by the state supreme court that same-sex couples are entitled under the state constitution to the same benefits offered to married couples. Several other states (including Connecticut, New Hampshire, and New Jersey) have since followed Vermont's lead by enacting legislation permitting same-sex couples to enter into marriage-like "civil unions."

3. Transsexuals

In jurisdictions where same-sex marriage is not allowed, courts are divided on whether a couple born to the same gender may marry if one underwent a successful sex change operation *prior* to marriage.

Examples: (1) H completed female-to-male sex reassignment surgery prior to marrying W, a female. After nine years of marriage, H filed for divorce and W answered that their marriage was void. (Result: Marriage was void ab initio. "We agree with the Kansas, Ohio, and Texas courts in their understanding of the common meaning of male and female, as those terms are used statutorily, to refer to immutable traits determined at birth. Therefore, we also conclude that the trial court erred by declaring that [H] is male for the purpose of the marriage statutes.") *Kantaras v. Kantaras*, 884 So.2d 155 (Fla.App.Ct. 2004).

(2) H was born a female but identified as a male and began taking testosterone at age 21. When H married W, a female, H considered himself a man and was by all outward appearances a man, but had not completed sexual assignment surgery. When H later filed for divorce, W contested on the ground that their marriage was never valid. (Result: H remained a woman for legal purposes and therefore H's marriage to W was void. As a result, H was not the presumptive father of the child born to W through artificial insemination during their relationship and had no standing to seek custody.) *In re Marriage of Simmons*, 355 Ill.App.3d 942, 292 Ill.Dec. 47, 825 N.E.2d 303 (2005).

(3) W filed a complaint for maintenance. H defended that W was a male and, therefore, their marriage was void. W testified that she was born a male but had gone through surgery to make her a female before her marriage. (Result: For W. "Successful sex reassignment surgery harmonized W's gender and genitalia so that W became physically and psychologically unified and fully capable of sexual activity as a woman. Absent fraud, husband has a legal obligation to support her as his wife. If such sex reassignment surgery is successful and the postoperative transsexual is, by virtue of medical treatment, thereby possessed of the full capacity to function sexually as a male or female, as the case may be, we perceive no legal barrier, cognizable social taboo, or reason grounded in public policy to prevent that person's identification at least for purposes of marriage to the sex finally indicated.") *M.T. v. J.T.*, 140 N.J.Super. 77, 355 A.2d 204 (1976).

Review Questions

1–2. Questions 1 and 2 should be answered based on the following facts: Charles and Camilla lived together for many years but had no children and never married. When they separate, Camilla wants to sue for alimony.

1. **T or F**   She may recover alimony under the state's divorce statute.

2. **T or F**   In several states, she may recover support under the *Marvin* doctrine.

3. **T or F**   Francis has a sex change operation and changed his name to Francine. Thereafter, Francine marries George. Their marriage is valid.

4. **T or F**   Paul and Joanne lived together for two years but never married. Joanne worked in Paul's business without compensation, but relied on Paul's oral promise to pay her once the business began turning a profit. While Paul paid for Joanne's living expenses, he paid her no wages even after the business started turning a profit. When they separate, Joanne has no claim against Paul.

IV

Spouses

■ ANALYSIS

A. **Support Obligations During Marriage**
    1. Historical Basis
    2. Changing Status
    3. "Necessaries"
    4. Actual Agency Between Spouses
    5. Judicial Refusal to Interfere in Ongoing Marriage
    6. "Necessaries" After Separation or Pending Divorce
    7. Constitutional Limitations
B. **Property Rights**
    1. Common Law
    2. Married Women's Property Acts
    3. Separate Property States
    4. Community Property States
    5. Marital Property and the Conflicts of Laws
C. **Torts and the Family**
    1. Torts Between Spouses
    2. Recovery for Loss of Consortium
    3. Tortious Interference With Family Relationships ("Heartbalm Actions")
D. **Marriage and Criminal Law**
    1. Immunities

2.   Testimonial Privilege

3.   Rape

4.   Marital Violence

5.   The "Battered Wife Syndrome"

E.   Family Names

1.   Husband and Wife

2.   Unmarried Couples

3.   Child

A. Support Obligations During Marriage

Traditional law required the husband to support his wife during the marriage, irrespective of the wife's financial resources. Today, while the facts lag behind, the legal support obligation is mutual. Mutuality is required by constitutional guarantees of equal protection. (In *Orr v. Orr*, 440 U.S. 268, 99 S.Ct. 1102, 59 L.Ed.2d 306 (1979), the U.S. Supreme Court invalidated a sexually discriminatory *alimony* statute.) ⟶ women and both men have the same right.

1. Historical Basis

At English common law, the wife's legal identity was merged with her husband's. The husband had sole control over his *and her* legal estates in land and other property and any income therefrom. As the typical wife had no opportunity to earn money to support herself, the husband was obligated to support her. This one-sided support obligation survived even after married women were given the right to own and control property. It was carried into modern society as a concomitant of role-divided marriage which, until recently, was the norm.

2. Changing Status

A number of states had long imposed a conditional support duty on the wife, if her husband was "in need." Today, the mutual legal duty of support is equally applicable to husband and wife and, as women have entered the work force, courts are prone to minimize alimony, the husband's traditional obligation upon divorce.

3. "Necessaries"

The husband's legal obligation of support during the ongoing marriage extended only to "necessaries." The "necessaries doctrine" sometimes has been explained as an agency implied in law, resting on the spouse's legal support obligation. Beyond the narrow "necessaries doctrine," however, principles having their roots in the law of express or implied (in fact) agency, apply to hold one spouse liable for the other spouse's expenditures on a considerably broader scale.

a. Necessaries Defined

"Necessaries" purchased for the family by one spouse, for which the other would be held liable, include all things essential to the family's well being, such as food, apparel, medicine and medical care, transportation, housing, and even furniture. What in any given case constitutes "necessaries" varies with the obligated spouse's financial status.

Example: Arguing that she was indigent, W requested appellate review at public expense after her conviction for possession of a controlled substance and possession of marijuana. After her first trial which had been declared a mistrial, but prior to her second trial, W had married H. H had ample resources to pay for the appeal. (Result: Legal expenses are "necessary" when a criminal action is involved and the spouse's liberty is at stake. While related to an antenuptial act, this expense is not an antenuptial debt, for which H would not be responsible. Therefore, H's resources are considered in determining whether W is indigent for this purpose.) *State v. Clark,* 88 Wash.2d 533, 563 P.2d 1253 (1977).

b.   Merchant's Recovery

Under the "necessaries doctrine" the creditor had to show that (1) he supplied to the wife (in its original form, the doctrine was gender-specific) an item that was "necessary," and (2) the husband had failed to provide. Some courts have relieved the merchant of showing the latter, requiring the merchant to show only that the item sold was in the "necessaries" category. Continued use of an item in the home may give rise to the conclusion that (1) a disputed item actually is "necessary," or (2) an actual (express or implied) agency relationship existed, or (3) the husband ratified the purchase.

Example: W purchased a sofa from P. There was no evidence that W was acting on H's behalf. The family enjoyed a position of social and economic prominence in the area where they resided. P contended that the necessaries doctrine applied to hold H liable for the purchase. (Result: For P. "[H and W's] socio-economic standing justifies a finding that the sofa at issue here was a suitable and proper item for their household.") *Sharpe Furniture, Inc. v. Buckstaff,* 99 Wis.2d 114, 299 N.W.2d 219 (1980).

[handwritten margin note: If they get Divorce H will still have to pay the sofa]

c.   Gender Neutrality

The necessaries doctrine has come under attack, especially in its traditional form where it imposes the liability on the basis of gender. Some jurisdictions have responded by extending the necessaries doctrine for the benefit of husbands as well as wives; others have responded by abolishing the doctrine altogether.

Example: Medical provider (MP) sued H and W for medical services rendered to H. The trial court dismissed MP's claim against W on the ground that W had not executed an agreement to pay for the services. The appellate court reversed. (Result: MP does not collect from W. "Because constitutional considerations demand equality between the sexes, it follows that a husband can no longer be held liable for his wife's necessaries. We therefore abrogate the common law doctrine of necessaries, thereby leaving it to the legislature to determine the policy of the state in this area. We do not make a judgment as to which is the better policy for the state to adopt. We merely leave it to the appropriate branch to decide this question." Dissent: "I agree that the common law doctrine of necessaries in its present form violates the equal protection clause * * *. However, unlike the majority, I conclude that this Court, as a matter of policy, should extend the doctrine to apply to both spouses rather than abrogate it entirely. In doing so, I would make the spouse who incurred the debt primarily liable. * * * Under these circumstances, the extension of the doctrine fits like a glove by requiring the more able spouse to care for the needs of the household. I submit that the application of the doctrine is just as necessary in today's society as it was one hundred years ago. It is my strong belief that we should not repeal this doctrine; we should simply refine it to meet equal protection requirements, and, by doing so, strengthen the martial obligation.") *Connor v. Southwest Florida Regional Medical Center*, 668 So.2d 175 (Fla.1995).

4. Actual Agency Between Spouses

There is no flat presumption that one spouse is an agent for the other. If authority is express, few problems peculiar to the marriage relationship arise. Importantly, however, authority of one marriage partner to act on behalf of both or the other will be readily implied, so that a spouse may become liable on a contract made by his or her partner. Similarly, estoppel may bar the non-purchasing spouse's protest if his or her actions have reasonably indicated to the merchant that the purchasing spouse is acting as his or her agent. Finally, if the non-purchasing spouse fails to disclaim a transaction by the other spouse, liability may be predicated on agency by ratification.

5. Judicial Refusal to Interfere in Ongoing Marriage

The necessaries doctrine and agency principles primarily protect creditors and help the family only indirectly. Reluctant to interfere in an ongoing marriage, courts are unwilling to enforce the spousal support obligation "inside" the home. As long as the home is maintained and the parties are cohabiting, courts assume that any support obligation is being satisfied. Only when the home breaks up, courts have statutory authority to enter a support order pursuant to legal separation or while divorce is pending.

★ if before divorce you were providing insurance you have to maintain it,

★ car to son to go to school

Example: In a 1953 case, H and W had been married for approximately 33 years. During the four years preceding the action, H had not given W money to purchase furniture or other household necessities. The house had electricity but did not have running water. W's children gave W clothes to wear. H owned land valued at $83,960, had bank deposits in the sum of $104,500, and had an annual income of $8,000–9,000. W had a bank account of $5,960. W brought an action to recover suitable maintenance and support money. (Result: For H. The court considered public policy and common law and held "[i]n the light of the cited cases it is clear, especially so in this jurisdiction, that to maintain an action such as the one at bar, the parties must be separated or living apart from each other. The living standards of a family are a matter of concern to the household, and not for the courts to determine, even though the husband's attitude toward his wife, according to his wealth and circumstances, leaves little to be said in his behalf. As long as the home is maintained and the parties are living as husband and wife it may be said that the husband is legally supporting his wife and the purpose of the marriage relation is being carried out. Public policy requires such a holding.") *McGuire v. McGuire,* 157 Neb. 226, 59 N.W.2d 336 (1953).

6. "Necessaries" After Separation or Pending Divorce

Generally, the support obligation continues so long as the marriage continues. Recently, however, some courts have been willing to loosen the "necessaries" obligation when the parties no longer lived in an active marriage, particularly when high medical expenses were involved.

Example: H and W had separated more than 4 years prior to H's hospitalization. During this time they did not live together or support each other. They did not have a separation agreement, and neither had filed for divorce or legal separation. After H died, the hospital assigned H's $16,000 debt to P. P sought recovery from W. (Result: W not liable for necessaries supplied to H more than 4 years after separation. "We cannot regard the marriage as viable at the time of Jose's hospitalizations. Certainly the couple was not a financial unit at that time. Thus plaintiff's assignor, when it admitted Jose to its facility, could not have reasonably assumed that Isabel's assets would be available for payment of its bill. In the circumstances liability should not be imposed on her.") *National Account Systems, Inc. v. Mercado*, 196 N.J.Super. 133, 481 A.2d 835 (1984).

7. Constitutional Limitations

On equal protection grounds, the U.S. Supreme Court struck down an Alabama alimony statute which provided that only husbands, not wives, may be required to pay alimony. *Orr v. Orr*, 440 U.S. 268, 99 S.Ct. 1102, 59 L.Ed.2d 306 (1979): "Legislative classifications which distribute benefits and burdens on the basis of gender carry the inherent risk of reinforcing the stereotypes about the 'proper place' of women and their need for special protection." The Court rejected the argument that the classification was justified by a legislative purpose of providing help for the needier spouse, typically the wife. The Court also rejected the claim that the classification was justifiable as an attempt to compensate women for past discrimination: "[E]ven statutes purportedly designed to compensate for and ameliorate the effects of past discrimination must be carefully tailored. Where, as here, the State's compensatory and ameliorative purposes are as well served by a gender-neutral classification as one that gender-classifies and therefore carries with it the baggage of sexual stereotypes, the State cannot be permitted to classify on the basis of sex." Although *Orr* was concerned specifically with alimony, the Court's language suggests reevaluation of all laws which place greater or different obligations on the husband than on the wife, and *vice versa*.

Example: Hospital sued H and W for hospital bill representing necessary services rendered to W. Under the common law doctrine of necessaries, the lower court held H responsible (along with W). H appealed. (Result: H and W are each responsible for necessaries provided to the other, if the other is unable to pay. "We agree with the husband that equal protection requires that husbands and wives not be treated differently with respect to the responsibility of one spouse for necessaries provided to the other spouse. But we disagree that a husband may not be responsible for necessaries provided to his wife. * * * [W]e conclude that a wife may be responsible for necessaries provided to her husband. * * * [W]e also conclude that one spouse may not be responsible for necessaries provided to the other spouse unless the other spouse is unable to pay therefor.") *Webb v. Hillsborough County Hospital Authority*, 521 So.2d 199 (Fla.App.1988).

B. Property Rights

1. Common Law

Complex common law rules essentially precluded a wife from owning property in her own name, so long as her husband was alive. The wife's personal property became the husband's upon marriage. Her husband also gained possession of any real property she owned at the time of marriage or obtained subsequently. Conversely, the wife had a "dower" interest in all real property her husband owned during the marriage, which prevented him from alienating it without her concurrence.

a. Scope

If the wife survived her husband, she received back her realty and whatever personal property the husband had not "reduced into possession." If she predeceased her husband and the marriage had produced a child, her real property would stay with him for life.

b. Circumvention of Rules

Equity provided devices to overcome the rigid common law rules of marital property. Properly arranged through a trust, a married woman could have the use (though not legal ownership) of her property, convey it during her lifetime or upon death, make contracts enforceable against her estate, and sue or be sued in matters concerning her property.

2. Married Women's Property Acts

Since the late 19th century, the so-called "Married Women's Property Acts" have granted married women the right to own and manage their property on their own. Out of this, the separate property concept developed.

a. Scope of Statutes

The "Married Women's Property Acts" provided the married woman with a separate legal existence for most purposes. One long-term holdover from the common law was a disability that prevented the spouses from contracting with each other regarding compensation for labor and services. Today, that disability has been eliminated if the contract is not necessarily related to the marital relationship. Based on the common law concept of legal "oneness" of husband and wife, spousal tort immunity also was continued by these statutes, but has recently been largely abandoned. One result is that tort liability may now be litigated either alongside or separately from divorce and sometimes unexpectedly affect the financial outcome of divorce. Contracts between spouses and intending spouses directly affecting the marriage, however, continue to be treated differently.

Example: An Alabama law denied W the power of alienating or mortgaging her lands without the assent and concurrence of her husband, whereas H could convey his land without W's signature. W contended that this was unconstitutional under the equal protection clause of the *state* constitution. (Result: For W. "There is no provision of the Constitution which would permit the legislature to deny to married women rights possessed by all other adults.") *Peddy v. Montgomery,* 345 So.2d 631 (Ala.1977).

b. Purpose and Effect of Statutes

The "Married Women's Property Acts" were enacted to remedy inequities of the common law marital property regime. On their face, they did much to improve the married woman's legal status. In practice, however, the statutes fell short. Under the separate property scheme imposed by these acts, the property of each spouse, whether earned or acquired before *or after* marriage, is that spouse's and only that spouse's property during the marriage. Except by gift or inheritance, the non-earning spouse acquires no property interest in the earner's savings. Traditionally, the court's power to order upon divorce a transfer of one spouse's property to the other was severely restricted or non-existent. Because the husband typically was the sole earner and thus became the sole owner of all property acquired out of his earnings during the marriage, the "equality" provided by these acts remained largely theoretical.

Example: H turned over a weekly household allowance to W, more or less regularly. With savings resulting from W's dismissal of a maid, W purchased securities in her own account. Upon divorce, H claimed the funds. (Result: No valid gift. To constitute a gift, delivery, intent and transfer of absolute power of disposition must be shown. Absent such a showing, the saved funds remained H's.) *Hardy v. Hardy,* 235 F.Supp. 208 (D.D.C.1964).

3. Separate Property States

~~The separate property regime applies in 41 states. The 9 community property states are Arizona, California, Idaho, Louisiana, New Mexico, Nevada, Texas, Washington and Wisconsin.~~

a. Separate Property → GA.

Under the separate property scheme each spouse is entitled, *during marriage*, to sole ownership and control of his or her property, whether earned or however acquired, before or after the marriage. *On divorce*, courts have become increasingly willing to delve into a spouse's separate property in order to adequately provide for a financially dependent wife. Reforms in the law of divorce now recognize the partnership aspect of marriage in financial terms and have developed the concept of (distributable) "marital property." "Equitable distribution" may extend to all property, marital and separate, of either party. This is discussed in connection with divorce.

b. Pros and Cons of Separate Property

The traditional separate property regime ignored the fact that a married woman, especially if she had children, typically did not have the same opportunity as her husband to acquire property or earn income. Today, as most married women have become wage earners, social conditions give more meaning to the separate property concept. The "marital property" concept now generally applied on divorce—essentially an "override" of separate property—has proved a useful safety valve. An advantage of a separate property regime *during* marriage is ease of management and disposition.

c. Joint Ownership in Separate Property States

1) Forms of Joint Ownership

Spouses may avail themselves of various forms of joint ownership: (1) Tenancy in common, (2) joint tenancy, and (3) tenancy by the entirety. Joint tenancy and tenancy by the entirety give both spouses undivided interests in the property with the right of survivorship. Tenancy by the entirety closely resembles joint tenancy, but is a form of joint ownership available only to spouses. In contrast to joint tenancy, a tenancy by the entirety may be terminated only by dissolution of the marriage. Property held "by the entirety" traditionally was subject to the husband's sole control and possession. This historical relic has survived occasional constitutional attack because the parties are free to choose how to hold their jointly owned property.

2) **Interspousal Transfers, Joint Ownership and Presumptions of Gift
    or Advancement**

    If a spouse places separate property in joint tenancy or in tenancy by
    the entirety, a strong but rebuttable presumption arises that the
    spouse intends to make a gift of the one-half interest to the other
    spouse. Traditionally, this presumption covered only gifts from the
    husband to his wife. By contrast, if the wife acquired separate
    property and transferred an interest to her husband as a joint tenant,
    an opposite presumption (of "advancement") held that she did *not*
    intend a gift, and the husband was seen as holding his interest in the
    property for the wife's benefit. Today, however, courts generally
    apply a presumption of gift to both spouses.

    Examples: (1) Shortly after their marriage, H retitled his home in
    the names of H and W, as tenants by the entirety. That
    Valentine's Day, H also presented W with a new
    Porsche Boxster, purchased with his premarital funds.
    When they later divorced, H insisted that he added
    W's name to the deed of his home "only for estate
    planning purposes and that his intent was to transfer
    an interest to Gina only upon his death." (Result: Trial
    court properly found that H intended both the car and
    shared ownership of his home as gifts to W. "When,
    during the course of a marriage, title to property for
    which one spouse has paid the purchase price is
    acquired in the names of both spouses, the transaction
    is presumed to be a gift or advancement for the benefit
    of the other spouse.") *Shramek v. Shramek*, 901 A.2d 593
    (R.I. 2006).

    (2) While married, H and W took title to a parcel of
    land as tenants by the entireties and built a house on
    the land. W filed for divorce and requested the court to
    determine the property rights in the realty. The Master
    found that at least $16,000 of the total cost of $22,000
    had come from W. The Master held that "as a result of
    the actions of [H] in taking 'undue advantage' of his
    wife by having her transfer her assets into their names
    without consideration, a 'constructive trust' in the
    amount of $16,000.00 was created in favor of [W]." H
    appealed. (Result: Reversed. "[I]n a marital relation-

ship a gift to entireties property is presumed for contributions made by either husband or wife. A constructive trust will be imposed only when it appears that the parties are in fact in a confidential relationship with one party enjoying an advantage over the other because of superior knowledge or influence and that this domination caused a gift to entireties property to arise. Finally, it must appear that it would be manifestly unjust to allow one party to thereby profit at the expense of the other." The "presumption of advancement" was struck down and the "presumption of gift" extended to both parties under the state's ERA.) *Butler v. Butler,* 464 Pa. 522, 347 A.2d 477 (1975).

3) **Effect of the "Marital Property" Concept on "Gifts"**

To the extent traditional presumptions of "gift" or "advancement" remain in effect, they have been adjusted where a "marital property" regime applies on divorce. To illustrate, a "gift" of non-marital property by one spouse to the other is typically classified on divorce as marital property, not as the recipient's non-marital property.

d. **Devolution of Separate Property Upon Death**

At the time of a spouse's death, his or her separate property passes by will, or if there is no will, by the law of intestacy.

1) **Election Against the Will**

If a spouse is not provided for in a will, or is dissatisfied with the provision made, statutes in separate property states commonly allow the omitted spouse to elect against the will and take a "statutory share," typically one-third (or one-half if the deceased left no descendants) in *all* of the deceased spouse's property, whenever or however acquired. State laws, however, are lax in protecting this "indefeasible" right of inheritance against manipulation. In many states, the decedent may defeat this provision by transferring separate property during his or her life and leaving little or nothing of value in the estate for the surviving spouse to collect.

Examples: (1) W executed an *inter vivos* trust in which she placed substantially all of her assets. The trust provided that H was to receive as much of the income and principal as necessary to meet any emergency situation for his "reasonable support, medical, and burial expenses." This provision was limited by another provision which advised the trustee to consider other sources available to H and the needs of certain of W's family before making any payments to H. After W's death, H asked that the trust be set aside as it deprived him of his marital rights in the property held in trust. (Result: Trust upheld. "We conclude that an *inter vivos* transfer of property is valid as against the marital rights of the surviving spouse unless the transaction is tantamount to a fraud as manifested by the absence of donative intent to make a conveyance of a present interest in the property conveyed.") *Johnson v. La Grange State Bank,* 73 Ill.2d 342, 22 Ill.Dec. 709, 383 N.E.2d 185 (1978).

(2) H made gratuitous transfers of property acquired by the joint efforts of H and W with the intent to deprive W of the property. W did not have knowledge of these transfers. Suit was brought by W for one half of the gifts. (Result: For W. "While we do not agree that a wife has a vested interest in jointly acquired property * * *, a married man cannot make gifts of jointly acquired property during his lifetime without the consent of or knowledge of his wife where the transfer is in fraud of the wife's marital rights.") *Sanditen v. Sanditen,* 496 P.2d 365 (Okl.1972).

2) Uniform Probate Code

To protect the surviving spouse, the Uniform Probate Code provides a detailed statutory scheme of "augmenting" the decedent's estate by disregarding certain *inter vivos* transfers for the purpose of calculating the survivor's statutory share. In an important break with tradition, 1993 UPC revisions abandon the traditional, rigid (typically one-third) share in the deceased spouse's estate and provide instead a share that slowly accrues until, after fifteen years, it reaches one-half of the decedent's estate.

3) Intestacy

If a spouse dies without a will, state intestacy laws govern the distribution of his or her separate property. Intestacy statutes typically provide for the surviving spouse to take all if there are no children or parents of the decedent, or a one-half or one-third share if there are children or parents. The remainder goes to the children, or if there are no children, to the parents.

The Uniform Probate Code § 2–102 suggests the following model for separate property states:

"The intestate share of the surviving spouse is: (1) if there is no surviving issue or parent of the decedent, the entire intestate estate; (2) if there is no surviving issue but the decedent is survived by a parent or parents, the first [$50,000], plus one-half of the balance of the intestate estate; (3) if there are surviving issue all of whom are issue of the surviving spouse also, the first [$50,000], plus one-half of the balance of the intestate estate; (4) if there are surviving issue one or more of whom are not issue of the surviving spouse, one-half of the intestate estate."

4. Community Property States

Nine states employ a community property system: Arizona, California, Idaho, Louisiana, New Mexico, Nevada, Texas, Washington, and, in a 1984 adaptation, Wisconsin. Traditionally a separate property state, Wisconsin adopted a revised version of the Uniform Marital Property Act in 1984 and 1985 and thereby became the first (and so far only) common law property state to enact a modern version of community property.

a. Historical Note

The traditional community property states—the first eight listed above—derived their marital property regimes from civil law sources. The rest of the United States followed the common law, and separate property reigned until the late 1940's. A number of separate property states then adopted community property schemes to obtain a federal income tax rate advantage arising from the fact that one-half of the husband's earning would be treated as his wife's income. To avert this trend, the 1948 Revenue Act allowed married couples to "split" incomes by filing joint returns. (In effect, each partner would henceforth pay income tax as though he or she had received one-half of the joint income. When tax rates were highly progressive and one partner was a high earner, this translated into potentially huge tax savings). The separate property jurisdictions that had adopted a form of community property subsequently reverted to separate property regimes. At the time of divorce reform in the 1960's and 1970's, the unfairness of the traditional separate property system was reconsidered, and separate property states adopted various regimes of "equitable distribution" on divorce. In 1984, late in the reform discussion, the Commissioners on Uniform State Laws proposed the Uniform Marital Property Act (UMPA) which would impose a modern form of community property. Twenty years later, UMPA had been adopted only in Wisconsin.

b. The Concept of Community Property

American community property regimes differ in detail. Generally, each spouse owns a *present* one-half interest in what is defined as community property. Principal distinctions among states concern (1) the definition of what is separate and what is community property, (2) the rights of each spouse to manage and control the community property, and (3) the distribution on divorce of separate and community property.

1) Definition of Separate and Community Property

In any marriage there may be four types of property: (1) the wife's separate property; (2) the husband's separate property; (3) joint property; and (4) "community" or "marital" property. Typically, separate property includes property owned before the marriage and property acquired during the marriage by inheritance or gift to one spouse or, with exceptions, by a recovery for personal injury by one spouse. Recovery for lost earnings typically is community or marital property, as the earnings would have been. Joint property is titled jointly, as discussed above. Community or marital property (the latter being the term separate property states use for property deemed divisible on divorce), generally is defined as including all property not designated by law as separate or joint property. One significant difference between states—community and separate property—concerns the classification of post-marriage income from a spouse's separate property. The majority of community property states consider such earnings separate property, in contrast to Texas and Louisiana which consider them community property. In defining marital property on divorce, the common law property states also have split on this issue. A further distinction is made in a few states (and by UMPA § 4(d) and (g)(3)) between (1) income on and (2) appreciation of separate property. "Income" becomes community or marital property and "appreciation" stays separate. *Caveat*: In classifying an item as income or appreciation, the courts will *not* necessarily look to federal income tax definitions of "interest," "dividends" or "capital gains."

2) **Management and Control**

A spouse's right to manage and control community property varies among the community property regimes. Several models have emerged:

a) **Louisiana**

A Louisiana statute gave the husband exclusive control over the disposition of property jointly owned with his wife. This statute was struck down in *Kirchberg v. Feenstra*, 450 U.S. 455, 101 S.Ct. 1195, 67 L.Ed.2d 428 (1981). In *Kirchberg*, H had executed a mortgage on a house he owned jointly with W as security for a promissory note. Under the statute, W was not required to be informed and, in fact, she was not informed. W learned about the mortgage when the mortgagee threatened to foreclose if W did not pay off the outstanding balance on H's promissory note. W did not pay and the attorney foreclosed on the mortgage. The U.S. Supreme Court held that the statute imposed gender-based discrimination and was in violation of the Equal Protection Clause.

b) **Texas**

Under the Texas model, each spouse has sole management and control of the community property that he or she would have owned if single. Any community property that is commingled, however, becomes subject to the joint management and control of the spouses, unless the spouses provide otherwise.

c) **Equal Management and Control**

With certain important restrictions, California and Arizona allow each spouse, equally and independently, to manage and even dispose of community property.

d) **Modified Joint Control**

In several community property states, both spouses must consent to community property transactions in excess of a statutory limit. Remedies such as restitution and temporary restraining orders are available if one spouse transfers or attempts to transfer community property without the other's consent.

e) **Relative Merits of These Models**

Under the Texas model, the non-earning spouse's situation *during* marriage does not differ materially from that of the non-earning spouse in separate property states. The equal management model better protects the non-earning spouse, but has the disadvantage that one spouse might spitefully or unwisely dissipate community assets. A modified joint control model sets limits for one-party autonomy.

c. Community Property on Death

At the death of a spouse, one-half of the community property passes by his or her will or, if no will exists, by the law of intestacy.

1) No Election Against a Spouse's Will

In community property states, the surviving spouse already owns his or her half of the community property upon the other's death. In view of that provision, community property states do not allow a dissatisfied spouse to elect a further share against a decedent spouse's disposition by will of his or her one-half interest in community property or all of his or her separate property.

2) Intestacy

Except for the absence of a right to elect against a spouse's will (which is compensated by the surviving spouse's ownership of one-half of the community property upon the partner's death), the intestate succession laws in community property states are similar to those in separate property jurisdictions.

The intestate regime recommended by UPC § 2–102A for adoption in community property states tracks the provision for separate property quoted above (p. 114) and adds: "as to community property (i) the one-half of community property which belongs to the decedent passes to the [surviving spouse]."

d. Presumptions

In community property states, presumptions may help classify property acquired by spouses as joint tenants or in separate names.

Example: H appealed from a judgment that determined H's and W's ownership interests in their residence and in a motor home. Both items had been purchased with a combination of community and separate funds. The home was held in joint tenancy and the motor home title was in W's name. (Result: Residence is community property and motor home is W's separate property. Where the only findings were that neither party intended a gift to the other, the joint tenancy title makes the residence community property. Where H was aware of W's sole title and did not object, there was evidence that H intended a gift of his community interest in the motor home to W.) *Lucas v. Lucas,* 166 Cal.Rptr. 853, 27 Cal.3d 808, 614 P.2d 285 (1980).

5. Marital Property and the Conflicts of Laws

a. The Problem

H and W live in state X, a separate property state. H owns land in X, and W is protected by her right to elect against H's will and/or inchoate dower rights. H sells the land, W releases her rights of dower and they move to state Y, a community property state, where H reinvests the proceeds in securities in his name. H dies, leaving nothing to W in his will. W has now lost the protection of the law of state X (dower and the right to elect against H's will), and receives no protection from state Y, because the proceeds used to buy the securities were H's separate funds. A similar scenario may be imagined upon divorce where there would be no community property to divide. See R. Weintraub, Conflict of Laws 441 et seq. (3d ed. 1986) and P. Hay, Conflict of Laws 118–21 (West's Blackletter 2d ed. 1994). The reverse scenario obtains when spouses move from a community property state to a separate property state: On one spouse's death, is the other entitled to a forced share in the decedent's half of the community property they brought along?

b. The Solution

The Uniform Disposition of Community Property at Death Act, enacted in about a dozen (of 41) separate property states, does *not* allow the surviving spouse elective share rights in the decedent's half of community property.

Several community property states have enacted remedial statutes that, in essence, eliminate unfair results by treating property (regardless of its technical classification) in accordance with the attributes it had where it was acquired. Such reclassified property is referred to as "quasi-community property." Statutes differ in detail, some apply only on death, some on divorce and others on both occasions. (See p. 169).

C. Torts and the Family

1. Torts Between Spouses

Traditionally, one spouse could not maintain a tort action against the other. At first the Married Women's Property Act carried this immunity forward; today the immunity has been almost wholly eliminated by legislation or in the courts, usually with no distinction made between intentional and negligent torts.

a. Justification for Interspousal Immunity

The fact that the common law gave the husband control over his wife's property and disabled the wife from suing in her own name supported interspousal tort immunity: Any recovery against H on W's behalf would be paid out of H's right pocket into his left, quite aside from H having to sue himself! Later, the argument was that the tort immunity helps preserve the peace and harmony of the home and, still later, that it prevents possible collusion to collect on liability insurance. Abrogating the doctrine, *Beaudette v. Frana*, 285 Minn. 366, 173 N.W.2d 416 (1969), nevertheless cautioned: "Interspousal immunity * * * has been * * * firmly rooted in the common law, both historically and ideologically, based upon the unique unity of a husband and wife within the marriage relationship. * * * Collusion in making spurious claims is an undeniable temptation where a member of the family is insured."

Unwilling to abolish the immunity completely, some courts had for some time refused to apply the defense when the family harmony and collusion arguments did not apply. To illustrate, courts refused to allow immunity when the spouse was dead at the hands (or car) of the other, and the action was for wrongful death, or after the marriage had otherwise terminated.

b. Reintroducing "Fault" into Divorce Settlements?

The abolition of interspousal tort immunity has been criticized for its potential for bringing fault issues back into divorce settlements.

Examples: (1) During their marriage, H berated W in public and in private. H had screamed at her because she could not drive a boat, slammed a door so hard it gouged a hole in the wall, threw a cup of coffee at the wall, and pulled food from the refrigerator onto the floor. He never physically abused her, although H once sprayed beer on W. H tightly limited the money he permitted W to spend. When he (accurately) suspected that W has having an affair, he angrily confronted W and her lover. When he thought she was drinking too much, he went through her garbage looking for evidence. In the divorce action, W sought damages for H's intentional infliction of emotional distress and the jury awarded W $362,000 in distress damages. H appealed. (Result: Award upheld. "[I]n a divorce proceeding a spouse may recover for intentional (but not negligent) infliction of emotional distress.") *Massey v. Massey*, 867 S.W.2d 766 (Tex.1993).

(2) After 10 years of marriage, H and W separated and H filed to dissolve the marriage. W countered alleging intentional infliction of emotional distress. The trial court found that during the marriage, H had assaulted and battered W, had insulted and screamed at her at home and in the presence of others, had once locked W out of the residence overnight in winter when she wore nothing but a robe, had made repeated demeaning remarks about W's sexuality, and had refused to allow W to pursue schooling and hobbies. The trial court also found that W had been legally incompetent during the last 4 years of the marriage, and medical experts agreed that W was temporarily emotionally disabled at the time of the hearing. The trial court awarded damages to W. H appealed. (Result: Reversed. W's claim can be disposed of summarily, because H's "insults and outbursts" fail to meet the legal standard of outrageousness. The court reasoned: "Conduct intentionally or recklessly causing emotional distress to one's spouse is prevalent in our society. This is unfortunate but perhaps not surprising, given the length and intensity of the marital relationship. * * * Not only should intramarital activity ordinarily not be the basis for tort liability, it should also be protected against disclosure in tort litigation. Although the spouse who raises a claim has no right to complain of the exposure of matters relevant to the claim, the courts must be sensitive to the privacy interests of the defending spouse. Any litigation of a claim is certain to require exposure of the intimacies of married life. This feature of the tort distinguishes it from intramarital torts already

recognized in New Mexico. For example, a suit by one spouse against the other arising out of an automobile accident poses no such risk. Nor does one ordinarily think of exposure of an incident of battery as implicating legitimate privacy interests. * * * A cautious approach to the tort of intramarital outrage also finds support in the public policy of New Mexico to avoid inquiry into what went wrong in a marriage. * * * [I]n determining when the tort of outrage should be recognized in the marital setting, the threshold of outrageousness should be set high enough—or the circumstances in which the tort is recognized should be described precisely enough, *e.g.,* child snatching, that the social good from recognizing the tort will not be outweighed by unseemly and invasive litigation of meritless claims.") *Hakkila v. Hakkila*, 112 N.M. 172, 812 P.2d 1320 (N.M.App.1991).

c. Arguments Against Immunity

Rejecting the family harmony argument, courts reason that (1) a personal injury action is not likely to disrupt family peace more than a property or contract action that now is universally allowed; (2) one spouse being willing to sue the other signals such a lack of "harmony" that to disallow the action would hardly mend the rift; (3) if insurance is present, a judgment against a spouse will have no impact on intra-family peace, since outside (insurance) money will compensate for the injury; (4) although the presence of insurance offers opportunity for fraud and collusion, courts and juries provide adequate protection.

Example: H allegedly assaulted and battered W. W sued H to recover for her injuries. The trial court dismissed W's complaint. W appealed. (Result: Doctrine of interspousal tort immunity is abrogated. "A survey of all states and the District of Columbia reveals that at present 31 states have fully abrogated the doctrine of interspousal immunity. Eight states have abrogated the rule for vehicular torts, four states have abrogated the rule for intentional torts; one state for all personal injury actions; and one state where death of either spouse intervenes between tortuous [sic] act and commencement of suit. One state has immunity imposed by statute while five states plus the District of Columbia continue to acknowledge and sustain the doctrine. One state has a cause of action but no remedy to enforce it. * * * The idea that maintenance of interspousal immunity will promote the public interest in domestic tranquillity is wholly illusory. If one spouse commits against the other an act which, but for the immunity, would constitute a tort, the desired state of matrimonial tranquillity is necessarily destroyed. But common sense suggests the peace is destroyed by the act of the offending spouse, not the lawsuit filed by the other. Beyond that, maintenance of the immunity surely cannot prevent injured spouses from harboring ill will and anger. Seen in this light, our traditional rule of interspousal immunity appears incapable of achieving the end claimed for it. Instead it leaves injured spouses without adequate or complete remedies. It is also noted that remedies incident to divorce and criminal prosecution are not adequate of the protection sought in this type of intentional tort.") *Burns v. Burns*, 518 So.2d 1205 (Miss.1988).

d. Is the Immunity Unconstitutional?

Moran v. Beyer, 734 F.2d 1245 (7th Cir.1984), held that the interspousal tort immunity denies the spouses equal protection.

e. Intentional and Negligent Torts Distinguished

In terms of the interspousal immunity, somewhat different policy arguments apply to intentional and negligent interspousal torts. In some states, courts allowed tort claims for intentional torts between spouses, while clinging to immunity for negligence, reasoning that any concern for family harmony was diminished where one spouse had intentionally harmed the other. In other jurisdictions, courts proceeded in the opposite direction, removing immunity for negligence claims first on the theory that any negligence judgment would likely be paid by insurance. With the rapid retreat of interspousal immunity generally, however, such distinctions are fading fast.

Example: On their honeymoon, H lost control of their car, causing an accident in which H was killed and W was seriously injured. W later sued H's estate for negligence. (Result: Utah first abrogated interspousal with respect to intentional torts, but now rejects immunity for negligence claims as well. "[T]he two primary rationales used to justify interspousal

[handwritten margin note: H or W could not sue each other Unless it was intentional tort.]

immunity—marital discord and collusion—are ultimately without merit.") *Ellis v. Estate of Ellis*, 169 P.3d 441 (Utah 2007).

2. Recovery for Loss of Consortium

Derived Claim

At common law, a husband could recover for loss of his wife's consortium (companionship and services) caused by injury to her. Today, the cause of action is available to both spouses. Very recently, a very small number of jurisdictions have extended recovery for consortium beyond marriage to domestic partners. E.g., *Lozoya v. Sanchez*, 133 N.M. 579, 66 P.3d 948 (2003).

Example: H was seriously injured at work when a 600–pound pipe fell and struck his head, causing "severe spinal cord damage which left him totally paralyzed in both legs, totally paralyzed in his body below the midpoint of the chest, and partially paralyzed in one of his arms." H was unable to care for himself, and W quit her job to devote her full energies to him. H and W filed suit against H's employer for H's physical injuries as well as for the consequences to W. The lower court denied W's cause of action and W appealed. (Result: Reversed. "We * * * declare that * * * each spouse has a cause of action for loss of consortium * * * caused by a negligent or intentional injury to the other spouse by a third party.") *Rodriguez v. Bethlehem Steel Corp.*, 12 Cal.3d 382, 115 Cal.Rptr. 765, 525 P.2d 669 (1974). *Caveat*: A few courts have used the sex discrimination argument to *deny* recovery to both the husband and the wife.

3. Tortious Interference With Family Relationships ("Heartbalm Actions")

Although declining in number, some states still recognize tort actions for wrongful interference with family relations, collectively known as heartbalm *Test* actions.

a. Breach of Promise to Marry

1) Proof

Short of a formal engagement, difficulty in proving the existence of an express promise to marry has led courts to imply an agreement to marry from circumstances indicating such promises. Evidence may include the gift of an (engagement?) ring, activities undertaken together, expressions of affection, preparations for a wedding, and any other relevant circumstances.

2) Tort Action

Test Breach of promise to marry is in tort, not contract. This is particularly relevant in determining damages, especially punitive damages.

punishment (Normally on purpose)

3) Damages

In a breach of promise action, the plaintiff may seek actual financial damages, such as the cost of a wedding dress, relinquishment of a job and the like, as well as recovery for injury to feelings, health and reputation. In 2008, for example, a Georgia jury awarded $150,000 in damages to a woman whose fiancé jilted her after inducing her to leave a high-paying job in Florida and move to Georgia. An Illinois statute limits recovery to *actual* damages. Other states exclude recovery for loss of expected benefits, such as social and financial position. Since these injuries "to the heart" are incapable of precise measurement, awards of damages are unpredictable and sometimes may seem excessive. Beyond that, if the defendant is shown to have acted maliciously, punitive damages may be awarded. Of late, heartbalm awards have been more readily reversed or reduced on appeal than have other tort awards.

Examples: (1) During their courtship, D told P that he was worth over $2 million, that he planned to retire in two years after which they would travel, that P would never have to work again, and that D would support P's children. After their engagement, P placed her house for sale, sold most of the furniture, reserved a church, engaged a minister, ordered a wedding dress and a dress for the matron of honor, and arranged the reception. Two months after the engagement, D broke it off. This caused P medical problems, expense in ordering new furniture, and considerable embarrassment. P sought damages to compensate for these losses and to compensate for her loss of expected security. (Result: For P on direct damages, against P on loss of expectancies. "[W]e have decided that the breach-of-promise-to-marry action should be retained as a quasi-contract, quasi-tort action for the recovery of the foreseeable special and general damages which are caused by a defendant's breach of promise to marry. However, the action is modified to the extent that a plaintiff cannot recover for loss of expected financial and social position, because marriage is no longer considered to be a property transaction.") *Stanard v. Bolin,* 88 Wash.2d 614, 565 P.2d 94 (1977).

(2) P, a Chicago attorney, and D, an Oregon cattle rancher, met in January of 1992 and became engaged in March of 1992. D began having second thoughts, and broke off the engagement in April of 1992. P sued D under the Illinois Breach of Promise Act. A jury awarded P $178,000 ($25,000 for past and future medical costs, $93,000 for pain and suffering, and $60,000 for lost business profits). The court remitted the award to $118,000, concluding that the lost business profits were not attributable to the broken engagement. D appealed. (Result: Award reversed on the technical point that P had failed to provide the date of the engagement in the notice of intent to sue.) *Wildey v. Springs,* 47 F.3d 1475 (7th Cir.1995).

b. Criminal Conversation

The common law tort of "criminal conversation" allows a spouse to recover damages against a third party for adulterous conduct with the plaintiff's spouse.

1) Elements of Cause of Action

To prosecute an action for criminal conversation successfully, the plaintiff must only prove sexual intercourse between the defendant and his or her spouse. The plaintiff does not have to prove that defendant was aware of the spouse's marital status. Actionable sexual intercourse includes rape. Damages are presumed.

Examples: (1) H sued X for criminal conversation, alleging that X had an affair with W, H's then-wife. (Result: Evidence was sufficient to support judgment for H. Jury could infer adultery in forum state by circumstantial evidence showing motive and opportunity, including X and W's admissions that they regularly met for sexual encounters in other states and that they met twice at hotels in the forum state.) *Smith v. Lee,* 2008 WL 906323 (W.D.N.C. 2008).

(2) H brought a criminal conversation action against D. D admitted that he had had sexual relations with W while H and W were married. Based on D's admission, the lower court granted judgment for H. D appealed. (Result: The Supreme Court of Pennsylvania abolished the tort of criminal conversation, holding that in today's society it is unreasonable to impose such harsh results upon a defendant without looking to the role of the plaintiff's spouse and the quality of the plaintiff's marriage. "[T]he Court in 1959 * * * laudably rejected the fictitious notion that a wife, like a servant, was the personal property (chattel as it were) of the husband and that an action in criminal conversation was a right sacrosanct to none but the master. Still, the Court's extension to married women of the right to bring such a cause of action only delayed what today demands; that is, the total abolition of a pious yet unrighteous cause of action.") *Fadgen v. Lenkner,* 469 Pa. 272, 365 A.2d 147 (1976).

2) Defenses

Traditionally, the only defense available to the defendant is proof of the *plaintiff's* consent. It is not a defense that the plaintiff's spouse consented or was the aggressor or seducer.

c. Alienation of Affections

1) Elements of Cause of Action

The tort of "alienation of affections" allows a spouse to recover for a third party's conduct that has caused the plaintiff's spouse to transfer his or her affections to another, not necessarily to the defendant. Most states have abolished the cause of action, and many have restricted it.

Example: H developed a sexual relationship with D. H moved out of the marital home and W filed for divorce. One day before the divorce was granted, W filed a civil complaint against D, alleging alienation of affections. A jury awarded W $10,000, and the appellate court affirmed. D moved for review whether the cause of action for alienation of affections should be abolished. (Result: Reversed. "We conclude that the tort of intentional interference with the marital relation should be abolished because foundation of this action is based on the misperception that spousal affection is capable of theft by a third party.") *Hoye v. Hoye*, 824 S.W.2d 422 (Ky.1992).

2) Criminal Conversation and Alienation of Affections Distinguished

The tort action of "criminal conversation" allows recovery for the defendant's wrongful interference with the plaintiff's right to an exclusive sexual relationship with his or her spouse. Traditionally, proof of actual loss of affection or marital breakup was *not* required. By contrast, "alienation of affections" allows recovery for the defendant's wrongful interference with the spouse's emotions. Sexual intercourse is not a prerequisite, although it may be an element of proof and may aggravate damages.

d. **Modern Treatment of Heartbalm Actions**

In most states, heartbalm actions have been abolished or limited. The preamble to an Illinois statute that limits recovery to actual damages sums up the case against heartbalm actions:

"[T]he remedy heretofore provided by law for the enforcement of the action for criminal conversation has been subjected to grave abuses and has been used as an instrument for blackmail by unscrupulous persons for their unjust enrichment, due to the indefiniteness of the damages recoverable in such actions and the consequent fear of persons threatened with such actions that exorbitant damages might be assessed against them. * * * [T]he award of monetary damages in such actions is ineffective as a recompense for genuine mental or emotional distress." 740 ILCS 50/1.

The ingenuity of lawyers has sought to revive heartbalm actions in many disguises. Some "cohabitation cases" fit into this context. Modern "retreads" also may include cases seeking damages for the infection of a sexual partner with venereal disease, or for intentional infliction of emotional distress, or for certain types of "professional malpractice."

Examples: (1) P sued D, Orthodox Jewish rabbi, for breach of fiduciary duty after the end of their three-year sexual relationship. P alleged that D used his religious authority to counsel P and induce her to submit to his sexual advances. (Result: Claim dismissed. In light of New York's statutory abolition of heart balm recovery, "no cause of action can be maintained for an extended voluntary sexual affair between consenting adults, even if [P] could prove that her acquiescence was obtained through lies, manipulation or other morally opprobrious conduct.") *Marmelstein v. Kehillat New Hempstead*, 11 N.Y.3d 15, 862 N.Y.S.2d 311, 892 N.E.2d 375 (2008).

(2) H and W began marriage counseling with D, a licensed psychologist. Most sessions were joint, but on some occasions D met only with W. A sexual relationship developed between D and W. In counseling sessions, D advised H to be distant from W and not to engage in sexual contact with her. On D's advice, H ultimately separated from W. H's suit against D for intentional infliction of emotional distress and professional negligence was dismissed. H appealed. (Held: The gravamen of P's claims was not merely the sexual act or the alienation of his wife's affections. Instead, it was the entire course of conduct engaged in by his *therapist*, D. Therefore H's claims were not barred by the abolition of actions for criminal conversation and alienation of affections.) *Figueiredo-Torres v. Nickel*, 321 Md. 642, 584 A.2d 69 (Md.1991).

D. Marriage and Criminal Law

1. Immunities

Immunities traditionally granted to spouses (or more usually wives) served to bar criminal prosecutions in certain circumstances, particularly when the charge involved conspiracy or alleged that the wife was an accessory in her husband's crime. Modern reality has supplanted the common law, and the trend is to abolish criminal immunities: "[E]ven when a husband and wife conspire only between themselves, they cannot claim immunity from prosecution for conspiracy on the basis of their marital status." *People v. Pierce*, 61 Cal.2d 879, 40 Cal.Rptr. 845, 395 P.2d 893 (1964).

2. Testimonial Privilege

The common law disqualified a person from testifying against his or her spouse. This rule has undergone substantial modification. In the context of a federal prosecution, the U.S. Supreme Court held: "[T]he witness-spouse alone has a privilege to refuse to testify adversely; the witness may be neither compelled to testify nor foreclosed from testifying." Information "privately disclosed between husband and wife in the confidence of the marital relationship" remains protected. *Trammel v. United States,* 445 U.S. 40, 100 S.Ct. 906, 63 L.Ed.2d 186 (1980). The testimonial privilege has no application in cases of spousal or child abuse. *Test*

3. Rape

At common law and under once-typical criminal statutes, a husband could not be guilty of rape of his wife. Instead, if force was used, the act was punishable as a criminal assault. A 17th century English treatise (1 Hale, History of the Pleas of the Crown 629) stated the rule and rationale: "But the husband cannot be guilty of a rape committed by himself upon his lawful wife, for by their mutual matrimonial consent and contract the wife hath given up herself in this kind unto her husband, which she cannot retract." States now allow criminal prosecution of a husband for the rape of his wife, with varying emphasis on the question whether the spouses were living together or were separated at the time of the incident. Some states provide for lesser penalties for rape in cases involving spouses.

Examples:

Husband can be convicted for Rape while in marriage Yes

(1) H was convicted of three counts of aggravated rape of his wife. (Result: Conviction overturned. H was indicted for aggravated rape, for which spouses cannot be prosecuted, instead of spousal rape, which is governed by a separate statute with differing elements. At the time, a husband could be prosecuted for raping his wife only if he was armed, caused serious bodily injury, or the couple was living apart after filing for divorce or legal separation.) *State v. Dominy,* 6 S.W.3d 472 (Tenn. 1999). *Caveat:* In 2005, the Tennessee legislature abolished all separate treatment for spousal rape, treating it identically with other instances of rape.

(2) H and W were living apart pursuant to a family court order of protection. In the presence of their 2–year-old son, H forcibly raped and sodomized W. (Result: H's conviction upheld. The Court of Appeals of New York held the "marital exemption" from the criminal rape statute unconstitutional. "We find that there is no rational basis for distinguishing between marital rape and nonmarital rape. The various rationales which have been asserted in defense of the exemption are either based upon archaic notions about the consent and property rights incident to marriage or are simply unable to withstand even the slightest scrutiny. We therefore declare the marital exemption for rape in

the New York statute to be unconstitutional.") *People v. Liberta*,
64 N.Y.2d 152, 485 N.Y.S.2d 207, 474 N.E.2d 567 (1984).

4. Marital Violence

Traditionally, the law has been reluctant to intervene in domestic matters.
Recently, many states have addressed the significant incidence of domestic
violence by specific legislation and by instituting programs to aid victims.

a. Order of Protection and "No Contact" Orders

Orders of "protection" or "no contact" orders now are widely available.
The key element of this new remedy is that may cover a potentially very
wide list of conduct that in itself would not (necessarily) amount to a
crime or even a tort. A *criminal* contempt citation follows a violation.
Caveat: A conviction for criminal contempt (with possibly lesser sanction)
may bar a later criminal protection for the same act. *United States v.
Foster/Dixon*, 509 U.S. 688, 113 S.Ct. 2849, 125 L.Ed.2d 556 (1993).

b. Police Protection

In the absence of very special circumstances, the police are not liable for
failure to protect one spouse from the other.

> *Example:*   H, in violation of a restraining order, abducted his three
> daughters from W's front lawn. W repeatedly called police
> and urged H's arrest, even providing information about his
> location, but police took no action. Meanwhile, H murdered
> the three children. W sued the municipality, alleging that
> police failure to enforce the restraining order violated her
> rights to Du Process. (Result: No Due Process violation.
> State law did not entitle W to police enforcement. Therefore,
> she had no "property interest" in police enforcement pro-
> tected by the Due Process Clause. "Even if the statute could
> be said to have made enforcement of restraining orders
> 'mandatory' because of the domestic-violence context of the
> underlying statute, that would not necessarily mean that
> state law gave *respondent* an entitlement to *enforcement* of the
> mandate.") *Town of Castle Rock v. Gonzales*, 545 U.S. 748, 125
> S.Ct. 2796, 162 L.Ed.2d 658 (2005).

5. The "Battered Wife Syndrome"

The existence of a battered wife syndrome has been asserted to defend a wife
who has retaliated against an abusive husband. This defense differs from the

usual definition of self-defense in that the threat is not immediate. The theory underlying the syndrome is "that it is not unusual for a battered woman who has been abused over a long period of time to remain in such a situation, that a battered woman's self-respect is usually very low and she believes she is a worthless person, that a battered woman typically believes that the man is not going to repeat the abuse when he promises not to do it again, that the battered woman becomes increasingly afraid for her own well-being, and that the primary emotion of a battered woman is fear." *Smith v. State,* 247 Ga. 612, 277 S.E.2d 678 (1981). Not all courts admit psychiatric or other expert testimony on this syndrome, but some states have passed statutes defining and favoring the defense. *GA allows it*

Examples: (1) During the seven years that H and W were married, H had periodically attacked W. When W fatally stabbed H with a pair of scissors, W claimed that H had attacked her on the same afternoon. At her trial, W claimed that she had acted in self-defense. The trial court ruled that expert testimony about the battered women's syndrome was inadmissible. W appealed from her conviction. (Result: Reversed and remanded for new trial. "[T]he battered woman's syndrome has a sufficient scientific basis to produce uniform and reasonably reliable results.") *State v. Kelly,* 97 N.J. 178, 478 A.2d 364 (1984).

(2) During a 15–year marriage, W was repeated abused by H. H had kicked W until she required hospitalization, held a shotgun to her head and threatened to kill her, and beat her with a baseball bat. Allegedly H also sexually abused W's 12–year-old daughter from a previous marriage. When H ordered W to kill and bury her daughter W filed for divorce and voluntarily left H for the first time. Shortly thereafter, W was hospitalized following an overdose of psychiatric medication and agreed to move back in with H. On the evening of her return, H insinuated that he planned to take W's life. When H had fallen asleep, W shot and killed H. The judge instructed the jury on self-defense, and W was found not guilty. (Result: The self-defense instruction was erroneous. A battered woman cannot reasonably fear imminent life-threatening danger from her sleeping spouse. "Where self-defense is asserted, evidence of the deceased's long-term cruelty and violence towards the defendant is admissible. In cases involving battered spouses, expert evidence of the battered woman syndrome is relevant to

Battered Wife Syndrome allowed that Defense be heard

the determination of the reasonableness of the defendant's perception of danger. Other courts which have allowed such evidence to be introduced include those in Florida, Georgia, Illinois, Maine, New Jersey, New York, Pennsylvania, Washington, and Wisconsin. However, no jurisdictions have held that the existence of the battered woman syndrome in and of itself operates as a defense to murder. In order to instruct a jury on self-defense, there must be some showing of an imminent threat or a confrontational circumstance involving an overt act by an aggressor. There is no exception to this requirement where the defendant has suffered long-term domestic abuse and the victim is the abuser. In such cases, the issue is not whether the defendant believes homicide is the solution to past or future problems with the batterer, but rather whether circumstances surrounding the killing were sufficient to create a reasonable belief in the defendant that the use of deadly force was necessary.") *State v. Stewart*, 243 Kan. 639, 763 P.2d 572 (Kan.1988).

E. Family Names

1. Husband and Wife

Tradition, custom and common understanding to the contrary, the Wisconsin Supreme Court found that the common law has never *required* a married woman to adopt the surname of her husband. Instead, she acquires the husband's name by express choice or usage. On divorce, a wife who has assumed her husband's surname may request the court to legally restore her original surname.

> *Example:* W had never used H's surname as her own. Her employer insisted that, for group insurance purposes, she either use H's surname or "legally" change her surname back to her maiden name. When W petitioned the court for a name change, the trial court refused her request on the basis of "well settled * * * common-law principles and immemorial custom that a woman upon marriage abandons her maiden name and assumes the husband's surname." W appealed. (Result: Reversed. "[W] was never compelled to change her name, nor did she ever in fact adopt the surname [of H] by usage.") *Kruzel v. Podell*, 67 Wis.2d 138, 226 N.W.2d 458 (1975).

2. Unmarried Couples

Ordinarily, the law permits anyone to call himself or herself by any name, so long as no fraud is intended and the name itself is not somehow offensive to

Test

public policy. Recently, courts have upheld the right of unmarried couples—including same-sex couples—to adopt a common surname, overcoming objections by trial courts that this would undermine state policies favoring marriage and the traditional family. *E.g., In re Miller*, 824 A.2d 1207 (Pa. Super. 2003); *In re Bicknell*, 96 Ohio St.3d 76, 771 N.E.2d 846 (2002); *In re Application of Bacharach*, 344 N.J.Super. 126, 780 A.2d 579 (2001).

3. Child

Traditionally, the child of a marriage has taken the husband's surname. This is no longer assumed. Many courts have held that parents have the right to give their child any surname they wish, whether that is the name of either or both parents or a hybrid or combination name. On divorce or remarriage, litigation over a child's name often results when a mother having custody of a child who bears the father's name wishes to change the child's name to her own name or to her new married name. Few courts still think in terms of the father's common law right to have his child bear his surname. Instead, they look to the child's best interests when deciding such cases.

Examples: (1) H and W sued after the state refused to let them give their son the surname of "Jebef," which was a contracted combination of their surnames. The state would have allowed them to use either H's last name or a hyphenated combination of both of their last names. (Result: For Jebef. "Plaintiffs have a constitutionally protected right to give their own child any surname they choose.") *Jech v. Burch,* 466 F.Supp. 714 (D. Haw. 1979).

(2) H and W separated when W was four months pregnant. When their child (C) was born, W registered C's name on the birth certificate under her maiden name. The divorce decree awarded custody of C to W, but ruled that W must change C's surname to that of H. W appealed. (Result: Reversed. "[W] had the right to a determination of surname, based on the legal standard of the child's best interest.") *In re Marriage of Schiffman,* 28 Cal.3d 640, 169 Cal.Rptr. 918, 620 P.2d 579 (1980).

(3) M and F, an unmarried couple, had a child, C. They agreed that C would have M's surname. When M later married, she sought to change C's name to that of her new husband, but F objected. The trial court ruled that M had not carried the burden of showing that a change of name was in C's best interests. (Result: Refusal to change name affirmed. The evi-

dence did not support M's concern that C would feel left out of her new family if he had a different last name. "As for [C's] identification with a family unit, there was no evidence presented that [C] would be more or less likely to identify himself with a family unit with or without a change in his surname. Another factor which we have identified as relevant to a court's determination regarding a change in name is the child's preference. The only evidence presented at trial regarding [C's] preference was [M's] unsubstantiated testimony that [C] has been using the [new] name Watts in preschool and telling his teachers that his surname is Watts. [M's] testimony does not, in and of itself, indicate [C's] preference.") *In re Change of Name of Slingsby*, 276 Neb. 114, 752 N.W.2d 564 (2008).

Review Questions

1. **T or F** Statutes that hold only the husband liable for alimony have withstood constitutional challenge. The reasoning is that the reasonable and legitimate purpose of such statutes is to compensate women for past discrimination and to adjust for the economic reality that wives, as a class, are more often economically dependent on their husbands than husbands are dependent on their wives.

2. **T or F** On a "no-returns" sale, W bought a dining room set. H has returned the set to the store and refuses to pay for it. W has no funds. The creditor's best course of action is to seek payment from H under the "necessaries" doctrine.

Questions 3 through 6 should be answered on the assumption that H and W are married and live in a separate property state.

3. **T or F** Property owned by each spouse *prior* to marriage is their separate property, while property acquired *during* marriage belongs to both.

4. **T or F** If H and W divorce, the separate property of each spouse is not considered in making an equitable distribution of property.

5. **T or F** H and W can take title to property as tenants by the entirety, but not by tenancy in common or as joint tenants.

6. **T or F** By making lifetime transfers of her property, W can assure that H inherits none of her separate property, including savings from her earnings during the marriage.

7–9. Questions 7 through 9 should be answered on the assumption that H and W are married and live in a community property state.

7. **T or F** Separate property is limited to what each spouse acquired *prior* to marriage; community property is everything acquired by either spouse *after* marriage from any source, including earnings.

8. **T or F** The amount of control H has over the portion of community property earned by him varies, depending on the specific community property state in which the parties reside.

9. **T or F** If W dies, her will only can distribute her separate property, because the community property automatically passes to the survivor.

10. **T or F**   So-called "heartbalm" actions have been abolished universally, because of the difficulty of proof, the uncertainty of damages, the possibility of blackmail, and/or the notion that—in our liberated society—these "torts" are outdated.

11. **T or F**   In a criminal prosecution, one spouse may testify against the other only if the defendant spouse consents.

12. **T or F**   Neither a wife nor her children are required to take the husband's surname.

13. **T or F**   Courts will intervene in an ongoing marriage to ensure that a financially dependent spouse receives suitable maintenance and support.

14. **T or F**   All of the community property states derive their property regime from civil law sources.

15. **T or F**   Most states now permit recovery for loss of consortium by cohabitants.

16. **T or F**   Most states have abolished the traditional exemption for marital (spousal) rape.

17. **T or F**   H and W are married and live in a separate property state. W gives H a house during their marriage. If they should divorce, the gift is H's separate property.

18. **T or F**   H and W are married and live in a separate property state. If the recent Uniform Probate Code revisions are in effect when H dies with a will disinheriting W, the amount of W's statutory forced share will depend on how long W and H were married.

V

Divorce—Status Issues

■ ANALYSIS

A. **Access to and Jurisdiction of Courts**
    1. Residency Requirements
    2. Personal Jurisdiction
    3. "Long–Arm" Jurisdiction
B. **Traditional Grounds and Defenses**
    1. Historical Development
    2. Divorce for Marital Fault
    3. Traditional Fault Grounds
    4. Traditional Bars and Defenses
C. **Divorce Reform**
    1. Social Trends
    2. Available Alternatives
    3. No–Fault Grounds
    4. Covenant Marriage
D. **Separation**
    1. Divorce From Bed and Board
    2. Separate Maintenance
    3. Conversion Into Full Divorce

A. Access to and Jurisdiction of Courts

1. Residency Requirements *Test*

State statutes conferring jurisdiction over divorce actions typically require the plaintiff to have been a resident of the state for a specified period of time prior to commencement of the divorce action, such as 90 days or a year.

> *Example:* UMDA § 302 provides that a court has jurisdiction over the action if *either party* was domiciled in the state for 90 days prior to commencement of the divorce action.

a. Constitutionality of Residency Requirement

The Supreme Court has upheld Iowa's one year residence requirement against a challenge that the statute violated the divorce seeker's constitutional right to interstate travel and due process. A state has sufficient interest in the incidents of marriage to require persons seeking divorce to show "attachment to the state." Iowa's reasonable (one year) residency requirement is justified by the state interest in avoiding interference with the interest of other states in their residents' marital status and in having its own decrees respected elsewhere, *i.e.,* avoiding the increased risk that divorce decrees not based on adequate jurisdictional facts may be subject to collateral attack in other states. *Sosna v. Iowa,* 419 U.S. 393, 95 S.Ct. 553, 42 L.Ed.2d 532 (1975). (*Cf. Shapiro v. Thompson,* 394 U.S. 618, 89 S.Ct. 1322, 22 L.Ed.2d 600 (1969), the interstate-travel/welfare-eligibility case, and *Boddie v. Connecticut,* 401 U.S. 371, 91 S.Ct. 780, 28 L.Ed.2d 113 (1971), the no-fee-for-indigent's-divorce decision).

2. Personal Jurisdiction

a. Full Faith and Credit → *without the other party.*

1) *Ex parte* Divorce

If plaintiff is a domiciliary of the state, a state court may grant him or her a divorce decree whether or not there is personal jurisdiction over the defendant. A divorce decree thus obtained is valid in the state issued and is entitled to Full Faith and Credit in other states. *Williams v. North Carolina,* 317 U.S. 287, 63 S.Ct. 207, 87 L.Ed. 279 (1942)("Williams I"); *Williams v. North Carolina,* 325 U.S. 226, 65 S.Ct. 1092, 89 L.Ed. 1577 (1945)("Williams II"). The full faith and credit effect of an *ex parte* decree, however, does not extend to the incidents of divorce, especially financial dispositions. *Estin v. Estin,* 334 U.S.

541, 68 S.Ct. 1213, 92 L.Ed. 1561 (1948); *Vanderbilt v. Vanderbilt*, 354 U.S. 416, 77 S.Ct. 1360, 1 L.Ed.2d 1456 (1957).

2) Rule in *Sherrer*

If plaintiff and defendant made personal appearances and thus were subject to the court's jurisdiction and had an opportunity to contest the issue of the plaintiff's domicile, neither party may later collaterally attack the decree on the ground that the court lacked jurisdiction. The effect of a "migratory" decree thus obtained extends to all matters properly adjudicated, *including incidents of divorce. Sherrer v. Sherrer*, 334 U.S. 343, 68 S.Ct. 1087, 92 L.Ed. 1429 (1948). The effect of such a decree may extend to third parties, such as children (*Johnson v. Muelberger*, 340 U.S. 581, 71 S.Ct. 474, 95 L.Ed. 552 (1951)) or a second spouse (*Cook v. Cook*, 342 U.S. 126, 72 S.Ct. 157, 96 L.Ed. 146 (1951)).

b. **Comity**

Recognition of a divorce decree obtained in a foreign, non-U.S. jurisdiction is not constitutionally compelled. However, unless an important state policy is violated (for instance, the divorcing parties are domiciliaries of the state and could not have obtained their divorce locally) such decrees will ordinarily be recognized and enforced on the basis of comity.

c. **Federal Jurisdiction Over Divorce Actions**

Under specific legislation, federal courts exercise jurisdiction over certain matters ancillary to domestic relations disputes, such as interstate child custody and child support enforcement. Despite the theoretical applicability of diversity jurisdiction to domestic relations actions in which the spouses are citizens of different states and the amount in controversy meets the federal standard, federal courts—following century-old dicta—decline to take jurisdiction over domestic relations matters. For a time, some federal courts tended to discount the traditional rule, though most continued to refuse to involve themselves in any family law matters. In 1992, the U.S. Supreme Court reaffirmed the continued existence of the abstention rule. *Ankenbrandt v. Richards*, 504 U.S. 689, 112 S.Ct. 2206, 119 L.Ed.2d 468 (1992).

Federal Court: NO DIVORCE

→ *regarding getting involved in a divorce case*

3. **"Long–Arm" Jurisdiction**

a. **Divorce**

Many state "long-arm statutes" contain provisions subjecting both parties to personal jurisdiction in the state of "marital domicile."

Additional, specific jurisdictional bases vary considerably and, of course, must meet the test of procedural due process. *Lieb v. Lieb*, 53 A.D.2d 67, 385 N.Y.S.2d 569 (1976). In 1990, the U.S. Supreme Court reaffirmed the traditional rule that "jurisdiction based on physical presence alone constitutes due process." The context was a divorce action a wife had brought in California where personal service was had on the out-of-state father when he visited the children in California. Aside from physical presence, no additional "minimum contacts" were needed. *Burnham v. Superior Court of California*, 495 U.S. 604, 110 S.Ct. 2105, 109 L.Ed.2d 631 (1990).

b. Child Support

In *Kulko v. Superior Court*, 436 U.S. 84, 98 S.Ct. 1690, 56 L.Ed.2d 132 (1978), the father resided in New York. The mother (who resided in California) sued him in California for child support. The father's only contacts with California included (1) two brief transit visits to the state while in the military years ago and (2) recently allowing his daughter of whom he had custody to reside with her mother in California. The U.S. Supreme Court held that these contacts with California were insufficient to give the California court personal jurisdiction over the father. The court noted that California's interest in securing support for its residents is protected by the Uniform Reciprocal Enforcement of Support Act.

B. Traditional Grounds and Defenses

★ Divorce started in England

1. Historical Development

Traditional American divorce laws allowed divorce only upon proof of marital fault, as defined by statute.

a. English Origins

The American fault-based divorce system derived from English divorce laws, which, in turn, derived from ecclesiastical (canon) law.

1) Early English Law

Until the mid-nineteenth century, ecclesiastical courts had jurisdiction over marital cases in England. Marriage was viewed as an indissoluble union. Even after other countries began to recognize divorce and the right to remarry, England continued to allow only two exceptions:

a) Divorce *a vinculo matrimonii* _Fraud_

Where impediments to marriage existed at the time of marriage or the marriage was not validly entered, any attempted marriage was a nullity. Divorce *a vinculo* (annulment) allowed the parties to "re"marry.

b) Divorce *a mensa et thoro* → _Natural fault._

Based on marital fault, the courts would grant a divorce *a mensa et thoro* (from bed and board). This remedy gave the parties permission to live apart (indeed it required them to do so) and provided for alimony, but did not allow them to remarry. This remedy has evolved into modern law governing legal separation or separate maintenance.

2) English Reform

Test In the mid–1850s, the English common law courts obtained jurisdiction over marital actions. The body of law concerning "divorce *a mensa et thoro*" was extended to a type of divorce that included the right to remarry. As it had for divorce *a mensa et thoro,* the law required proof of marital fault.

b. Application in America

The English divorce-for-fault system was applied in the American colonies and was taken over into the law of the states.

Not fault = most popular.

2. Divorce for Marital Fault

a. Decline of Fault–Based Divorce Laws

Today, no state retains fault as the sole basis for divorce, though many retain fault-based divorce as an alternative to no-fault divorce. The fault system eroded in stages. Arcane complexity and evasionary tactics contributed to its decline.

1) Bars and Defenses

To illustrate, "collusion" between the parties—perhaps as little as acquiescence—was a bar to divorce. "Recrimination" barred a divorce if both parties were "guilty" of a marital offense. Defenses included provocation, connivance, condonation and insanity. As matters developed, courts silently acquiesced in the parties' collusion or overlooked recrimination and, by granting divorces in uncontested actions without serious insistence on proof of allegations of marital fault, became participants in evading the strict divorce-for-fault laws. See detailed treatment of bars and defenses at p. 139.

2) Loose Standards

The requisite degree of marital fault was diminished when "looser" grounds, such as "mental cruelty," were added to the list of fault grounds. Judicial definition of mental cruelty often seemed to include more or less "normal" marital conflicts.

3) No–Fault Laws

Today, all states offer no-fault divorce. More or less token proof of the "breakdown" of the marital relationship, typically by showing a period of separation, is the current standard. The no-fault laws go beyond the collusive (consent) divorces that had long been procured under the fault system in that most states allow "unilateral divorce"— divorce at the will of one party.

b. Modern Relevance of the Fault System

The fault-based system remains relevant because a majority of states have retained fault as an alternative ground for divorce actions, along with more recently enacted no-fault standards. Whether a divorce is obtained on a fault or a no-fault ground may, in some jurisdictions, affect property division, alimony, and child custody, as well as how quickly a party can procure a divorce. (No-fault divorce typically requires a period of living apart, whereas a fault-based divorce carries no such requirement.)

[handwritten marginal note: Fault states= Jury trial / todo el dirty close delante / de la Corte / GA= If you have childrens / 3 months, r No / childrens 30 days. / No fault states easier]

[handwritten: Test]

3. Traditional Fault Grounds

The most important fault grounds for divorce are adultery, physical cruelty, mental cruelty, desertion or abandonment, impotency, habitual drunkenness and, less commonly, "indignities," and "insanity." (Note that "insanity" may in a fault-based system also function as a defense as it negates "fault.")

a. Adultery

For purposes of divorce law, adultery is defined as voluntary sexual intercourse between a married person and someone other than that person's spouse. Disputes rarely go to the definition and more often concern proof. Circumstantial evidence, including evidence of mutual affection, an adulterous inclination, and an opportunity to commit adultery, typically is sufficient, though many jurisdictions demand that the evidence be "clear and convincing."

Examples: (1) W's adulterous conduct was established by evidence given by a private investigator that W's alleged paramour was in W's home almost daily from early evening until one or two hours after midnight, that when seen together in public W had her arm around the alleged paramour, and that certain entries by W in her diary constituted confessions of adultery. *Leonard v. Leonard,* 259 So.2d 529 (Fla.App.1972).

(2) W was granted divorce based in part on H's adultery with X, a neighbor. (Result: Reversed. Evidence that H and X cared deeply for one another, spent time together in a local park, and that X was observed emerging from H's apartment one morning in a bathrobe did not constitute "clear and convincing" evidence of adultery. "[T]he evidence must be . . . inconsistent with a reasonable theory of innocence.") *Spence v. Spence,* 930 So.2d 415 (Miss.Ct.App. 2005).

(3) W filed for divorce. H counterclaimed, alleging that W's lesbian relationship constituted adultery. W argued that a non-heterosexual relationship cannot constitute adultery. The trial court ruled for H, and W appealed. (Result: For H. "[A]dultery exists when one spouse rejects the other by entering into a personal intimate sexual relationship with any other person, irrespective of the specific sexual acts performed, the marital status, or the gender of the third party. It is the rejection of the spouse coupled with out-of-marriage intimacy that constitutes adultery.") *S.B. v. S.J.B.,* 258 N.J.Super. 151, 609 A.2d 124 (1992).

b. Physical Cruelty

Divorce based on physical cruelty traditionally required a showing of "extreme and repeated" cruelty. A single act may suffice if it endangers life, limb or health. Recently, courts have grown less tolerant of acts of physical violence in marriage, even if isolated.

Examples: (1) W was denied a divorce when she relied on a *single* instance of physical abuse by H to support her claim of cruelty. H's claim for a divorce on grounds of W's desertion was also denied, because he had provoked her desertion when he struck her. *Capps v. Capps,* 216 Va. 382, 219 S.E.2d 898 (1975).

(2) After 26 years of marriage, H sought a divorce alleging cruel and inhuman treatment. H alleged that W struck him with objects, including a lamp and a vase, threatened him with a knife, attempted to choke him, and frequently berated him. The trial court granted H a divorce on the grounds of cruel and inhuman treatment. The appellate court reversed. H appealed. (Result: No divorce. Given the length of the marriage, H made an insufficient showing of cruelty. "[W]hether a plaintiff has established a cause of action for a cruelty divorce will depend, in part, on the duration of the marriage in issue. The existence of a long-term marriage does not, of course, serve as an absolute bar to the granting of a divorce for cruel and inhuman treatment, and even in such a marriage 'substantial misconduct' might consist of one violent episode such as a severe beating.") *Brady v. Brady*, 64 N.Y.2d 339, 486 N.Y.S.2d 891, 476 N.E.2d 290 (N.Y.1985).

(3) W was granted divorce partly on ground of physical cruelty, and H appealed, insisting that his conduct never "endangered [W's] life, person, or health." (Result: Divorce affirmed. "Verbal and physical abuse may have been tolerated in another era, and our predecessors at bar may have placed the continuity of the marital bond above the well-being of individual participants, but our values are different today." Here, general testimony that H engaged in "hitting, pinching, pulling hair, etc.," and a broader pattern of "controlling behavior," resulting in issuance of a protective order, was sufficient to show requisite cruelty.) *Das v. Das*, 133 Md.App. 1, 754 A.2d 441 (Ct.Spec.App. 2000).

c. Desertion ⟶ Dejar la pareja

Required elements of desertion include the absent party's intent not to resume cohabitation, separation for the statutory period, no consent to the separation by the opposing party and absence of provocation. Test (The latter two "ingredients" may also be seen in terms of defenses.)

1) Time Period

The statutory time period for desertion commences when the parties separate or when the intent to desert is formed, if the latter is later.

The time period must run without interruption. If a temporary reconciliation is followed by a second desertion, the time periods may not be added together.

2) Constructive Desertion *Test*

Courts may find "constructive desertion" in misconduct of the "deserting" spouse. In an appropriate setting it may be held that the spouse who physically departed was actually the one deserted—if the absence was provoked.

> *Examples:* (1) The refusal to fulfill a basic obligation of marriage (such as permanent and inexcusable denial of sexual intercourse) constitutes abandonment. *Diemer v. Diemer,* 8 N.Y.2d 206, 203 N.Y.S.2d 829, 168 N.E.2d 654 (1960).
>
> (2) A wife's refusal to have uncontracepted intercourse with her husband was held not to constitute desertion where the husband consented, albeit reluctantly. *Zagarow v. Zagarow,* 105 Misc.2d 1054, 430 N.Y.S.2d 247 (1980).
>
> (3) Deliberate attempts to force a spouse from the marital home, such as removal of the husband's clothes from the marital dwelling and a change of locks, constitute constructive desertion. *Fort v. Fort,* 270 S.C. 255, 241 S.E.2d 891 (1978).

3) Reconciliation Offers

An offer to reconcile, made by the absent spouse in good faith and rejected by the non-deserting spouse without justification, may stop the running of the period of desertion. The (formerly innocent) spouse who refuses such an offer may then become the "deserter."

d. Mental Cruelty

1) Requirements

Statutes providing for divorce based on mental cruelty often require "extreme and repeated" mental cruelty, but provide no definite guideline. Courts have construed these statutes to include anything from inexcusable denial of sexual intercourse over an extended period to humiliating and degrading treatment of a spouse. Some courts have refused to find mental cruelty based on false accusations of infidelity, unwillingness to have children, or occasional strife and disharmony.

2) Subjective Standard

Test

What constitutes mental cruelty may depend upon the particular parties involved rather than on objective criteria. Relevant considerations may include family tradition, ethnic and religious backgrounds, local customs and standards, and other cultural differences. Moreover, the definition of "mental cruelty" seems to differ in contested cases and in uncontested cases. In uncontested cases, standards often are considerably less stringent, and standards may be at their strongest when a marriage of long duration is at issue.

3) Opportunity for Collusive Divorce

Because mental cruelty is such a vague standard, it was (ab)used in obtaining what amounted to consent divorces, before the spread of the no-fault option made this approach less attractive.

e. Habitual Drunkenness and Drug Addiction

In some states, habitual drunkenness and drug addiction specifically are fault grounds for divorce. Under one such statute, alcohol or drug abuse must be "gross" or "continuous" or "habitual" or continued "for the space of 2 years" to justify divorce. Elsewhere, these habits may provide evidence of (mental) cruelty.

f. Impotence and Bigamy

Though traditionally grounds for annulment when present at the time of marriage, some states allow impotence and bigamy as grounds for divorce.

g. Insanity – Crazy.

1) Plaintiff's

Courts disagree as to how an incompetent spouse may obtain a divorce. A court-appointed guardian generally may act on behalf of the ward; however, some courts hold that an action for divorce may not be maintained by the incompetent spouse's guardian without express statutory authorization or that due process requires a case-by-case determination of the issue.

2) Defendant's

A spouse's insanity constitutes a ground for divorce in some states, but in other states may be a defense to fault-based divorce. Divorce statutes seldom provide a definition of insanity, leaving the matter to judicial interpretation. Some statutes require that the insanity have existed for some specified time period, or that it be permanent or incurable, or that there have been confinement to a mental institution for a stated period or a formal adjudication of insanity.

Example: H's unusually bizarre sexual fixations were held to be "indignities" sufficient as W's *ground* for divorce, but *not* sufficient as H's (insanity) *defense* to divorce. *Steinke v. Steinke,* 238 Pa.Super. 74, 357 A.2d 674 (1975).

→ Court will not allowed you have the divorce

4. Traditional Bars and Defenses

Collusion and recrimination are traditional *bars* to a divorce action based on fault grounds. Traditional *defenses* include provocation, connivance, condonation, and insanity. In traditional fault-based practice, the bars and defenses provided an often effective (if sometimes unsavory) negotiating tool to "facilitate" settlement of property and alimony claims.

a. Collusion   will bars a divorce   [this was before ~~someone~~ fault had to be prove]

Collusion is an agreement between the spouses to procure a divorce. The traditional rule was that evidence of an agreement between the spouses to get a divorce may bar a divorce even if the marital offense did in fact occur. More recently, the view was that collusion bars the divorce only if the alleged marital offense did not actually occur or when, pursuant to agreement between the spouses, one spouse committed a marital offense to provide the other a ground for divorce.

Quite at odds with the law on the books, the vast majority of divorce actions in fault-based jurisdictions had long been uncontested. These divorces typically were based on thoroughly collusive agreements negotiated between the parties, with careful attention to financial and child custody consequences. Generally, the courts did not question such agreements, unless the parties were too flagrant about their consent and collusion.

b. Recrimination   will bar a divorce

Traditionally, recrimination barred a divorce when *both* spouses had committed a marital offense. The theory was that "the law is for the relief of an oppressed party, and the courts will not interfere in quarrels where both parties commit reciprocal excesses and outrages." *Mogged v. Mogged,* 55 Ill.2d 221, 302 N.E.2d 293 (1973). Some states limited the operation of the bar to offenses of a similar nature or to adultery on both sides. Even before the demise of for-fault-only divorce, many courts and legislatures had either abolished recrimination outright or had eroded the operation of recrimination by making application of the bar discretionary with the court, or transforming the bar into an affirmative defense, *i.e.,* by requiring it to be specifically raised by defendant in the pleadings.

c. Provocation

The defendant in the divorce action proves provocation by showing that the plaintiff provoked the defendant's marital offense. Defendant must show that the marital offense was not excessive in relation to the provocation. If defendant succeeds, the plaintiff is denied a divorce.

d. Provocation and Recrimination Distinguished

1) Causal Connection

"Provocation" requires a causal connection between the marital offense and the other spouse's provoking conduct. "Recrimination" does not require a causal connection between both parties' grounds for divorce.

2) Defense vs. Bar

Provocation is a *defense* which is waived if it is not raised by the party whereas recrimination traditionally was a *bar* to a divorce and would be raised by the court if relevant evidence came to light. It could not be waived by the parties.

3) Misconduct vs. Ground for Divorce

To constitute the valid defense of "provocation," the plaintiff's misconduct need not itself constitute a ground for divorce. "Recrimination," however, applies only when both parties have been guilty of marital offenses that constitute grounds for divorce.

4) Rationale

Both provocation and recrimination rest on the "clean hands" theory that, under the fault system, only an innocent and injured spouse is entitled to a divorce.

e. Connivance – plan – agree

The defense of connivance derives from the maxim that one who has consented to misconduct is not injured by it. Connivance, however, is more than the plaintiff's consent to the defendant's misconduct. Plaintiff must have actively created an opportunity for the other to commit the marital offense of which he now complains. If the plaintiff has merely acquiesced in the opportunity rather than helped to create it, the defense of connivance is not available. (In such a situation, the defense of "condonation" may apply.)

Example: H hired a private detective to employ a number of persons to entice W to engage in immoral conduct, for the purpose of giving H grounds for a divorce. Although W ultimately succumbed, H was denied a divorce because of his connivance. *Greene v. Greene*, 15 N.C.App. 314, 190 S.E.2d 258 (1972).

f. Condonation
Condonation is the intentional and voluntary forgiveness of a marital offense. Because the defense turns on the mental state of the offended party (who is resisting the defense), problems of proof may be serious.

1) **Proof of Intent**
Intent to condone may be inferred from the spouse's conduct. Courts have divided on the question whether condonation occurs when the offended spouse, with knowledge of the marital offense, engages in sexual intercourse with the guilty spouse. Generally, continued cohabitation after obtaining knowledge of the offense is sufficient to prove condonation, unless the cohabitation is the result of necessity.

Example: W sought divorce on ground of H's adultery, but trial court refused. (Result: Affirmed. H admitted to adultery during marital counseling with W. "The parties continued to live together for several years following [H's] admission, and there was no evidence that this living arrangement was continued out of necessity. Moreover, [H] testified that he and [W] shared the same room, shared domestic duties, and continued sexual relations until petitioner filed for divorce in May 2001. Based on this evidence, we conclude that the trial court's finding on the issue of condonation is not against the manifest weight of the evidence.") *In re Marriage of Hightower*, 358 Ill.App.3d 165, 294 Ill.Dec. 450, 830 N.E.2d 862 (2005).

2) **Conditional Condonation**
Jurisdictions were divided on whether condonation was conditional on the offending spouse's future good behavior. If conditional, a

later act of misconduct would revive the original (condoned) marital offense and reconstitute it as a ground for divorce. Conditional condonation was criticized as a blackmail tool in the hands of the offended spouse. Proponents argued that conditional condonation facilitated reconciliation because it afforded an opportunity to attempt reconciliation without jeopardizing a ground for divorce. Some statutes provided that under certain circumstances reconciliation attempts do not constitute condonation. Since all states now offer no-fault divorce, the "preservation" of a ground for divorce has become unnecessary, and the issue is largely irrelevant. (Note that if a jurisdiction still correlates financial consequences with divorce-for-fault, the revival of a fault ground may be worth pursuing.)

g. Insanity

In traditional usage, insanity constituted a defense to a fault ground for divorce in the sense that insanity negates fault. (*Anonymous v. Anonymous*, 37 Misc.2d 773, 236 N.Y.S.2d 288 (1962)).

C. Divorce Reform

1. Social Trends

Dissatisfaction with the fault-based divorce system provided impetus for reform of the divorce laws. In theory too restrictive, the fault system also had become too "wide open," as demonstrated by the overwhelming majority of collusive consent divorces. Disgust with the airing of the couples' private life in a judicial proceeding combined with the view that even if "fault" manifests itself in a statutorily recognized marital offense, the offense may be more a symptom than the cause of marital disharmony. For many reformers, it was persuasive that the legal system had effectively lost control over divorce. Concern with the integrity of a legal system that fostered collusion and perjury ran deep.

2. Available Alternatives

Alternatives available to the reformers included 1) modernization of the fault-based system, 2) consent divorce, 3) a solely no-fault system, and 4) adding a "no-fault option" to the traditional fault system. Today, while all states offer no-fault divorce, only a minority of states have opted for a pure no-fault approach. The majority of states have retained traditional fault grounds and added some form of "no-fault" as an alternative basis for divorce. A few states have updated their catalogue of marital fault. In New

York, no-fault divorce requires the consent of both parties in a "written agreement of separation." N.Y. Dom. Rel. L. § 170(6). Of course, collusive consent divorce remains available under the fault option, and as a practical matter, the uncontested "irretrievable breakdown" ground in no-fault divorce also typically involves a consent divorce.

a. Fault–Based Systems

The arguments in favor of abandoning fault-based divorce have been summarized. Traditional defenders of the fault-based system contended that it promotes stability of marriages and that society has too great an interest in the institution of marriage to let it be terminated at the will of the parties or one of them. One pragmatic argument for *retaining* some sort of fault-based system was that the power to block a divorce provides the "innocent" spouse with a bargaining tool to facilitate settlement of issues collateral to divorce (*e.g.,* spousal and child support, property, and child custody).

b. No–Fault Systems ~~Right Now~~

The advantages of no-fault divorce are obvious. The major argument *against* no-fault divorce focuses on the notion that the decision to terminate a marriage should not be allowed to rest with the party who is in the "wrong," and should not be allowed to be made against the will of an "innocent" party. Critics of no-fault divorce argue that it allows a divorce to be obtained too easily, while proponents counter that this is in accord with modern social reality.

3. No–Fault Grounds

Common no-fault grounds for divorce include "living separate and apart," "irretrievable breakdown" of the marital relationship, and "incompatibility." *Most common Ground to divorce* For most practical purposes, no-fault divorce is "irresistible."

a. Living Separate and Apart

A common no-fault ground requires separation for a specified period of time. Statutes vary and range from six months to two years. A statute may require separation pursuant to a separation agreement or a court order; others are satisfied if the parties have voluntarily lived apart for the statutory period, regardless of the reason for or method of separation. (The element of consent distinguishes such separation from the fault ground of desertion.) Delaware regards separation "under the same roof" as effective "provided * * * the parties occupy separate bedrooms and do not have sexual relations with each other." Illinois counts six months' separation as sufficient if the partners agree, but requires two years of separation if one party objects.

Example: (1) H was sleeping at his mother's home and had not had sexual relations with W for the statutory period of separation. Except for this change, the couple had continued their relationship substantially the same as it had been prior to H's moving from the marital domicile. When H was not working or attending classes, he spent basically all of his waking hours with W at the former marital home. (Result: The parties had not lived separate and apart. The mere finding that their relationship was bereft of positive qualities is insufficient to support a divorce on ground of separation.) *Ellam v. Ellam,* 132 N.J.Super. 358, 333 A.2d 577 (1975).

b. Marriage Breakdown

Breakdown is proved by a showing that the marriage is "broken" or "dead," or that the parties' differences are irreconcilable and that a meaningful marriage no longer exists. Typically, the statutes require some objective proof (usually separation for a specific period of time) beyond the mere assertion by one party or both parties that the marriage is dead, but courts do not require an elaborate (or even any) investigation.

Examples: (1) H and W married in 1947 and had 5 children whose ages ranged from 17 to 28 years at the time of the 1978 dissolution proceedings. H was an alcoholic and the 3 youngest children had serious drug and behavioral problems, all of which contributed to the couple's marital discord. After H moved out of the marital home in 1976, he made several unsuccessful attempts at reconciliation. By the time of these proceedings H believed that no hope of reconciliation remained. W claimed the marriage could be saved if H were treated for alcoholism and sought a court order dismissing H's dissolution petition unless H completed a treatment program. The trial court dissolved the marriage. W appealed. (Result: Upheld. (1) Record supports the trial court's findings of serious marital discord and irretrievable breakdown. (2) Evidence of H's untreated alcoholism does not defeat findings of serious marital discord and irretrievable breakdown warranting dissolution.) *Hagerty v. Hagerty*, 281 N.W.2d 386 (Minn.1979).

(2) Twenty-one years after H and W married, H left W and moved in with X, another woman. (Also living with X were her teenage daughter as well as the father of her daughter, to whom X was not married.) Efforts at reconciliation were futile, H sought dissolution, and the trial court dissolved the marriage. W appealed, arguing that the marriage could be saved if H were removed from X's influence. (Result: Affirmed. "Respondent's appeal borders on the frivolous. Her contentions merit little discussion. It is sufficient to say the record discloses a reasonable effort to effect reconciliation has been made and it is obvious the petitioner has no desire to continue the marriage relationship. The evidence clearly supports the trial court's finding, the marriage was irretrievably broken.") *Roberts v. Roberts*, 200 Neb. 256, 263 N.W.2d 449 (Neb.1978).

4. Covenant Marriage

In recent years, no-fault divorce has come under attack from a variety of critics who argue that it has weakened marital bonds or left economically dependent spouses excessively vulnerable. One response, first adopted by Louisiana in 1997 and later by Arizona and Arkansas, is "covenant marriage." Under this system, marrying couples are permitted to choose between a standard marriage (dissoluble by no-fault divorce) and a "covenant marriage" (dissoluble only on narrow fault grounds or satisfaction of an unusually long separation period).

D. Separation

1. Divorce From Bed and Board

Traditional statutes that provide limited divorces (divorce *a mensa et thoro*— from bed and board) allow for adjudication of the parties' rights similar to that which would occur in an ordinary divorce proceeding. The major points of distinction are that remarriage is not available to parties to a limited divorce, and that limited divorce may preserve certain entitlements (*e.g.*, inheritance rights, pension rights or tax or social benefits) that may be lost by divorced spouses. Many states have abandoned "limited divorce" and provide only for full divorce and (temporary) legal separation, in the sense of separate maintenance. Some states allow the latter as an option to limited or full divorce.

2. Separate Maintenance

Most states allow a spouse to obtain spousal support by bringing an action for separate maintenance. Typical statutes allow a "needy" spouse, sometimes only if "innocent," to obtain court ordered support from the other spouse while the parties are separated. Separate maintenance does not involve the division of property that is available in limited divorce.

3. Conversion Into Full Divorce

Some statutes provide for conversion of a separation or limited divorce into full divorce at the request of either party. This is no longer a serious issue because the same result may be achieved if a "living-apart" no-fault ground is later used to obtain a full divorce. Questions may arise regarding the relitigation of financial consequences that were previously fixed on the occasion of a limited divorce. (Following *Gleason v. Gleason*, 26 N.Y.2d 28, 308 N.Y.S.2d 347, 256 N.E.2d 513 (1970), New York enacted a statute allowing compensation for financial loss upon conversion of an earlier limited divorce into a later full divorce. N.Y. Dom. Rel. Law. Art. 10 § 170.)

Review Questions

1. **T or F** — H left W in their marital home in Iowa, moved to Wisconsin, established domicile and obtained a divorce which denied W any alimony. Although notified by registered mail, W refused to appear. Because Wisconsin did not have personal jurisdiction over W, Iowa need not recognize the Wisconsin decree.

2. **T or F** — Same facts as in Question #1, but W brings the divorce action against H in Iowa, H refuses to appear, and W obtains the divorce along with a substantial alimony award. The alimony award is unenforceable in Wisconsin.

3–4. For questions 3 and 4, choose the correct terms to fill in the blanks: A=Divorce *a vinculo matrimonii*; B=Divorce *a mensa et thoro*.

3. **A** was the rough equivalent of today's annulment. Traditionally it was the only form of "divorce" that allowed the parties to remarry. It was granted where an impediment to marriage existed at the time of the marriage or where the marriage was not validly entered.

4. **B** was the rough equivalent of today's legal separation or limited divorce. It did not allow the parties to remarry. Traditionally, this remedy was based on marital fault and gave the parties permission to live apart.

5. **T or F** — H wants a divorce from W. Neither party is guilty of any "fault." Today, H may obtain the divorce against W's opposition.

6. **T or F** — Even before no-fault divorce, divorce was widely available by consent of the parties.

7. **T or F** — No-fault divorce typically is granted on the sole basis of at least one of the parties' assertion that the marriage has broken down.

8. **T or F** — With the universal acceptance of no-fault divorce, fault grounds and defenses to fault grounds have become irrelevant.

9. **T or F** — Provocation and recrimination are really the same defense.

10. **T or F** — "Desertion" under a fault-based divorce system is really the same as "living apart" under a no-fault system.

11. **T or F** — Despite the abstention rule, federal courts have increasingly heard cases involving family law.

12. T or **F** W leaves H and moves to Maine, a state neither H nor W had visited before, taking along H's beloved cat. W initiates divorce proceedings against H in Maine. H travels to Maine solely to retrieve his cat. While H is there, he is served with process. The Maine court does not obtain jurisdiction over H because H lacks the requisite minimum contacts with Maine.

13. T or **F** Under a divorce-for-fault regime, H provokes W to leave him. W has deserted H.

14. T or **F** Under a divorce-for-fault regime, H helped create the opportunity for W's adultery. W can claim the defense of collusion.

VI

Divorce—Financial Consequences

■ ANALYSIS

A. **Alimony on Divorce**
1. Traditional Standards for Awarding Alimony
2. Alimony Today
3. Determining the Amount of Alimony
4. Fault as a Factor in Alimony Awards
5. Modification of Alimony
6. Termination of Alimony
7. Enforcement of Alimony by Contempt
8. Federal Tax Treatment of Alimony
9. Alimony and Property Award Distinguished

B. **Property Division on Divorce**
1. Separate Property States
2. Community Property States
3. Conflicts of Laws Aspects of Property Division
4. Property Awards and Bankruptcy
5. Tax Treatment of Property Awards
6. Treatment of Professional Licenses and Practices
7. Allocation of Pensions

8. The "Employee Retirement Income Security Act" (ERISA) and the "Qualified Domestic Relations Order" (QDRO)

C. Separation Agreements
1. Validity of Separation Agreement
2. Traditional Requirements for Enforceability
3. The Divorce Decree and the Separation Agreement

A. Alimony on Divorce

1. Traditional Standards for Awarding Alimony

a. Historical Development

When full divorce with the right to remarry was not available and limited divorce (*a mensa et thoro*) did not dissolve marriage but only terminated cohabitation, alimony represented the continuation of the husband's marital support obligation. When full divorce became available, the obligation to pay alimony was carried forward. Critics argue that, when divorce terminates the marriage, the continuation of the marital support obligation does not make sense.

b. Mutuality of Alimony Obligation

Based on the husband's one-sided legal obligation to support his wife, the traditional right to alimony extended only to the wife. The U.S. Supreme Court has held that such discrimination violates equal protection. *Orr v. Orr*, 440 U.S. 268, 99 S.Ct. 1102, 59 L.Ed.2d 306 (1979). Accordingly, in today's divorces, either spouse may be entitled to alimony, although, as a practical matter, relatively few husbands are awarded alimony.

Example: At W's request, H quit his job as a toy salesman after one and a half years of marriage. For the remaining seven and a half years of marriage, W supported H with contributions from her father and from her own separate estate. H was now 37 years old. The trial court awarded H $30,000 in lump-sum alimony, $5,000 a month rehabilitative alimony for 18 months, and $30,000 for H's attorneys. (Result: Affirmed.) *Pfohl v. Pfohl*, 345 So.2d 371 (Fla.App.1977).

2. Alimony Today

Due to the radical divorce reforms of the 1970s as well as greatly improved employment opportunities for women, courts now award alimony less often, for shorter periods and typically less generously than in the past. Another reason is that property transfers incident to divorce are now common, in contrast to the not-so-distant past when the traditional separate property systems did not allow the non-earning spouse (typically the wife) to share. Reinforcing this trend, the UMDA is phrased so as to make an award of alimony seem to be an exceptional case. (See especially 3.b., below).

Where a pre-divorce separation agreement or an antenuptial agreement does not provide otherwise, the trend is away from awarding large amounts of alimony for extended periods of time, even to a dependent spouse who does not receive or have much property. Courts emphasize the concept of "rehabilitative alimony" which is intended to allow a dependent spouse to become self-supporting.

Examples: (1) H, aged 65 years, and W, aged 63 years, were divorced after 37 years of marriage. The trial court awarded W approximately 70 percent of the couple's community property, including W's pension (valued at $84,000) and equity in real property valued at somewhat more than $100,000. W appealed, challenging trial court's refusal to award alimony. (Result: Denial of alimony affirmed. "In addition to the requirement that the marriage have lasted at least ten years, [the relevant Texas alimony statute] requires that the spouse . . . seeking maintenance payments show that she lacks sufficient property, including property distributed incident to the divorce, to provide for her minimum reasonable needs and that she 'clearly' lacks earning ability in the labor market adequate to provide support for such reasonable needs. . . . There is no evidence in the record to indicate that Carmen attempted to return to work during the period of separation, and the record does not contain an explanation of why her ailments prevent her from returning to work as a bookkeeper. . . . [Moreover,] the trial court awarded [W] significant assets in the property division.") *Chafino v. Chafino*, 228 S.W.3d 467 (Tex.App.2007).

(2) At the time of the parties' marriage in 1954, W was a skilled executive secretary. After the birth of a child, W never returned to the job market. H became executive vice president of a major corporation and ultimately earned in excess of $120,000 per year. At the time of the divorce, W was 45 years old. The trial court found that with some additional training, W could earn from $12,000 to $18,000 per year and awarded W rehabilitative alimony for a period of four years, in addition to property valued at $225,000. (Result: Affirmed, based on a statute patterned after the UMDA.) *Otis v. Otis*, 299 N.W.2d 114 (Minn.1980).

Because of their limited duration and potentially harsh effect, awards of rehabilitative alimony often receive close scrutiny by appellate courts.

Although most courts feel that marriage should not be a "ticket to a perpetual pension," the earner-spouse's support responsibility remains long-term— and may extend for life—when the dependent spouse has no realistic employment opportunities and the marriage was of considerable duration. *Test*

Examples: (1) H and W were married for 26 years. During the last six years, W was employed for only three months. Beyond a high school education, W had no formal training. The trial court awarded W rehabilitative alimony for nine months. (Result: Reversed. " * * * (I)t is not likely that she (W) will be able to obtain a job paying more than one-quarter of what her husband now earns. In view of this, the husband should be required to assist her in her support on a permanent basis subject always to the right of obtaining relief under changed circumstances.") *Lash v. Lash,* 307 So.2d 241 (Fla.App.1975).

  (2) When H and W divorced after 27 years of marriage, H was a commercial airline pilot earning $75,000 per year and W was a reading specialist earning $43,000 per year. H and W did not have children. During the marriage W had worked continu- ously and had supported H while he obtained a private pilot's license and flight instructor's license, studied architecture for 2 years, and earned two degrees. The couple moved at least six times during the marriage because of H's educational, military, and employment commitments, and W lost seniority and retirement benefits with each move. Upon divorce, H was ordered to pay W temporary monthly alimony of $1,300 for the first year and $1,000 for a second year. Both parties appealed. (Result: Alimony awarded to W held inadequate and unfair. Court extended alimony of $1,000 per month for an additional 10 years. "The magnitude of Ruth's contribution to the com- munity over many years is not fairly recognized by the two- year alimony award she received when the marriage was terminated.") *Gardner v. Gardner,* 110 Nev. 1053, 881 P.2d 645 (1994).

3.   Determining the Amount of Alimony

Statutes typically leave the amount of the alimony award to the court's discretion, limited by stated factors. UMDA § 308(b) sums up a modern approach:

"The maintenance order shall be in amounts and for periods of time the court deems just, without regard to marital misconduct, and after considering all relevant factors including: (1) the financial resources of the party seeking maintenance, including marital property apportioned to him, his ability to meet his needs independently, and the extent to which a provision for support of a child living with the party includes a sum for that party as custodian; (2) the time necessary to acquire sufficient education or training to enable the party seeking maintenance to find appropriate employment; (3) the standard of living established during the marriage; (4) the duration of the marriage; (5) the age and the physical and emotional condition of the spouse seeking maintenance; and (6) the ability of the spouse from whom maintenance is sought to meet his needs while meeting those of the spouse seeking maintenance."

a. Standard of Living Maintained During Marriage, Need and Ability to Pay

Traditionally, the amount of the alimony award was based on the receiving spouse's needs and the paying spouse's ability to pay, as reflected by the pre-divorce standard of living. (See factors (1), (3), (6) in the UMDA excerpt above.)

b. Recipient's Earning Potential and Assets

Employment opportunities for women have improved dramatically and the ability of a spouse to be self-supporting now is a major consideration in awarding alimony. Today's question is not so much whether the typical ex-spouse *can* go to work, but whether she or he *must* and if so, in what position. Factors against forcing an ex-spouse into paid employment are (1) the presence of young children of whom the spouse has custody, and (2) long-term dependency with attendant loss of job skills. Earning *capacity* and assets, especially marital assets distributed on divorce, have become another major factor. UMDA § 308(a) explicitly *conditions* spousal maintenance on these elements, before looking at any other factors related to ability to pay or need: "[T]he court may grant a maintenance order for either spouse, only if it finds that the spouse seeking maintenance: (1) lacks sufficient property to provide for his reasonable needs; and (2) is unable to support himself through appropriate employment or is the custodian of a child whose condition or circumstances make it appropriate that the custodian not be required to seek employment outside the home."

Examples: (1) W and H agreed that W would work to put H through law school instead of completing her biology degree.

During that part of the marriage W became proficient as a secretary. H later became an attorney in a prominent law firm. After their separation, W returned to college in a pre-medical course. The trial court awarded her $200 weekly as alimony and child support, to allow her to obtain her medical education. (Result: Reversed. The wife can be self-supporting as a secretary and her "goal in medicine * * * was never in the contemplation of the parties during marriage.") *Morgan v. Morgan*, 52 A.D.2d 804, 383 N.Y.S.2d 343 (1976).

(2) H and W's marriage lasted 22 years before they separated in May of 1987. W had a college degree in business, did not work outside the home during the marriage and had difficulty obtaining employment following the separation. H was a self-employed businessman who had founded a software company that was acquired by a large company. H regularly engaged in stock transactions, and his average gross monthly income in 1987 was more than $40,000. By March of 1988 it was "only" about $16,000. The couple owned more than $3,000,000 in assets, and these were equitably divided by the trial court upon divorce, with each party receiving in excess of $1,000,000. The trial court also awarded W permanent monthly alimony of $4,000 per month. Neither party appealed the property division, but H appealed the alimony award, the district court of appeal reversed, and W appealed. (Result: Alimony reinstated. The trial court had authority to award permanent alimony even though the recipient had also received a substantial distribution of marital assets.) *Hamlet v. Hamlet*, 583 So.2d 654 (Fla.1991).

(3) H and W had been married for 15 years. H was a pathologist. For the first seven and a half years of marriage, W had worked as a qualified medical technician. The youngest of their four minor children was five years old. The trial court awarded child support, made a property division and awarded $1,000 per month alimony for a period not to exceed 144 months. (Result: Affirmed. "The contention [that W is employable] ignores the interests of

the children, and the desire of the wife to continue to care for them properly.") *Morris v. Morris,* 201 Neb. 479, 268 N.W.2d 431 (1978).

4. Fault as a Factor in Alimony Awards

Traditionally, if the wife was at fault in the divorce (especially if she was guilty of adultery), she could not obtain alimony. Worse, in a separate property state, there was no right to share in property earned by H. Conversely, H's fault was a prerequisite to an alimony award (as it was, of course, a prerequisite for the divorce itself), and some courts gave increased awards of alimony to an innocent wife, if the husband was guilty of a serious matrimonial offense. Along with acceptance of no-fault grounds for divorce, today's statutes often expressly prohibit the courts from considering the parties' marital misconduct when awarding alimony, dividing property or deciding on child custody. UMDA § 308(b) provides that "the maintenance order shall be in amounts and for periods of time the court deems just, without regard to marital misconduct * * *." In jurisdictions where fault grounds continue in effect as an *alternative* to no-fault divorce, fault usually remains relevant if the divorce is granted on a fault ground. However, some such states will now disregard marital fault even where the divorce itself is granted for fault. Conversely, in a few no-fault states, fault (not necessarily defined by traditional grounds for divorce) may be considered even when the divorce is awarded on a no-fault ground.

Examples: (1) W ran a beauty salon and H worked for the postal service. They divorced after 18 years of marriage. During the trial W established that H was having an affair, and the trial court took H's fault into account when it awarded W alimony of $500 per month for 100 months. H appealed. (Result: Reversed and remanded for a determination of alimony without regard to marital fault. "We conclude that in domestic relations actions it was the legislative intent that, in all but extremely gross and rare situations, financial penalties are not to be imposed by a trial court on a party on the basis of fault.") *Marriage of Sommers,* 246 Kan. 652, 792 P.2d 1005 (1990).

(2) H was president of an insurance firm, and W did not work outside the home during their 9–year marriage. W admitted to post-separation adultery, and H was granted a divorce on that ground. The trial court found that to deny W alimony would create manifest injustice and awarded her $1,200 per month. H

appealed. (Result: Alimony award upheld. "Even though one party may have been the major force in creating the 'fault during the marriage' which led to its dissolution and the other spouse may have been relatively blameless, those conditions constitute but one of the factors the court must weigh. The court must also weigh and consider the parties' relative economic positions in deciding whether it would be manifestly unjust to deny a spousal support award. * * * The judge expressly noted and considered that the wife had committed adultery. The adultery, however, occurred after the parties were separated and, according to the finding of the trial judge, after the marriage had been irretrievably lost * * * due to gradual dissolution caused by mutual inattention and fault from both parties. * * * The evidence supports the trial judge's conclusion that, based on the parties' respective degrees of fault during the marriage and their relative economic circumstances, a denial of spousal support to the wife would be manifestly unjust.") *Barnes v. Barnes*, 16 Va.App. 98, 428 S.E.2d 294 (1993).

(3) W and H were granted a divorce after 18 years of marriage. The trial court reserved the issues of alimony, property division, and child support. Several weeks later, W sought to have H murdered, but the man with whom she contracted was an undercover agent for the Wisconsin Dept. of Justice. After W's arrest, W and H agreed on property division and child custody (to H), and H agreed to pay her $230 per month in temporary alimony. W pleaded guilty to solicitation in connection with first degree murder and was incarcerated for 10 months. Upon her release, she moved for increased alimony. The relevant statute listed 10 factors to be considered in determining eligibility for monthly alimony. Under factors 1–9, W was eligible, but the court denied alimony altogether based on factor 10, "[S]uch other factors as the court may in each individual case determine to be relevant." W appealed. (Result: Denial of alimony affirmed. Unlike adultery, which is *marital* misconduct, solicitation to kill one's spouse is not in that sense conduct against the marital relationship. "Requiring [H] to pay maintenance to the person who tried to have him killed is fundamentally unfair. Additionally, the trial court did not punish [W] by refusing her maintenance, it merely refused to reward her for

her failure; if [W] had been successful in having [H] killed, she would receive no maintenance.") *Brabec v. Brabec*, 181 Wis.2d 270, 510 N.W.2d 762 (1993).

5. Modification of Alimony

When (1) alimony (even a nominal amount) is awarded in the original divorce decree, or (2) jurisdiction is reserved to consider the issue of alimony at a later date, or (3) a statute so provides, an alimony award may be modified upon a showing of changed circumstances. Any such change must occur after the alimony decree.

a. Recipient Spouse's Changing Need

A significant change of circumstances in the dependent spouse's needs may allow modification of alimony.

Example: Ex–H brought proceedings against ex-W to have his alimony obligation of $350 per month terminated because she had become employed as a school teacher. (Result: Alimony reduced to $100 per month, rather than terminated. "[I]t should be the policy of the law to encourage one receiving alimony to seek employment. This purpose would not be served if a wife who manifests sufficient initiative and industry to get a job is penalized by having her alimony cut off entirely.") *Carter v. Carter*, 584 P.2d 904 (Utah 1978).

b. Change in Obligated Spouse's Ability to Pay

When ascertaining the obligor's ability to pay, courts may consider not only the actual earnings of the obligor, but also his or her *potential* earning capabilities. Thus, courts will not necessarily decrease alimony payments when earnings are lowered through a change in employment or retirement, and will deny modification if circumstances show that the change was voluntary and for the purpose of reducing alimony payable. Many courts refuse to consider changes in employment made for *bona fide*, but non-essential reasons. It is disputed whether an ex-spouse's remarriage, resulting in decreased ability to pay or decreased need, warrants a change in alimony payments.

Examples: (1) When they divorced, H was earning more than $150,000 yearly as a corporate vice president and agreed to pay W $4,300 per month in alimony. Thereafter, H was terminated in a corporate reorganization and took a job at a state university paying $62,000 yearly. The trial court reduced H's alimony obligation to $3,600 per month, but H protested that this amount still nearly equaled his new net monthly earnings of $3,792. (Result: Modification upheld. If need be, H could draw on his assets of $449,000 to meet his alimony obligations. "[T]he alimony awarded in the present case would not deplete the plaintiff's estate for almost 12 years based on his current financial situation, and could last substantially longer if plaintiff's income increases in accordance with the earning potential he has demonstrated.") *Swain v. Swain,* 179 N.C.App. 795, 635 S.E.2d 504 (2006).

(2) Following 42 years of marriage, H and W divorced and W was awarded $2,000 monthly alimony. When H won $20 million in the Wisconsin "Megabucks" lottery, W moved to modify alimony. The trial court granted the motion, increasing W's monthly maintenance to $5,333. H appealed, claiming the increase was unjustified. W appealed, claiming the amount was too low. (Result: Lottery winnings could be considered a change in H's financial circumstances justifying an increase in alimony. W, however, was entitled only to an amount that would afford her the same standard of living she enjoyed during the marriage. Case remanded to determine the increase that would achieve this goal.) *Gerrits v. Gerrits,* 167 Wis.2d 429, 482 N.W.2d 134 (1992).

c. Obligated Spouse's Bankruptcy

The obligor's bankruptcy does not discharge alimony or child support obligations. (Obligations based on property settlements, on the other hand, are dischargeable in some bankruptcy proceedings. See p. 170).

6. Termination of Alimony

a. Death of Either Ex–Spouse

Generally, the alimony obligation terminates at the death of either the payee or the payor. When the premarital or separation agreement expressly so specifies, the alimony obligation may continue after the payor's death as a charge against his estate. If the obligation is to continue beyond death, the agreement should provide for a method to determine a present value, or specify a lump sum payment at the obligor's death, to facilitate administration of the estate. In practice, protection for the recipient spouse often is achieved by the maintenance in her favor of a life insurance policy on the obligor's life. When this is accomplished in a separation agreement, no issue arises. When, at the time of divorce, a court orders an obligor to maintain a life insurance policy in favor of his or her spouse, the order may be attacked as inappropriately continuing the alimony obligation beyond death. Some courts have rationalized such orders as being in the nature of current alimony, as premiums are paid during the obligor's lifetime.

Example: Ex–W sought continued payment of alimony against the estate of her deceased ex-H. A separation agreement incorporated into their divorce decree provided that alimony would terminate upon ex-W's remarriage. Ex–W contended that this should be interpreted to mean that remarriage was the exclusive factor to terminate the obligation. (Result: Ex–W loses. "The failure to expressly provide for continuation of alimony payments after death should be viewed as evidence of a contrary intent.") *Estate of Kuhns v. Kuhns*, 550 P.2d 816 (Alaska 1976).

b.   Recipient Spouse's Remarriage

If the premarital or separation agreement does not provide otherwise, the receiving spouse's remarriage usually terminates an alimony obligation relating to a prior marriage. This may occur either (1) automatically (by operation of a statute or under the terms of the divorce decree), or (2) pursuant to a new court order based on changed circumstances. Depending on the purpose and circumstance of the award (*e.g.*, is it in lieu of property?), alimony specifically ordered for a defined period may not terminate. Similarly, "rehabilitative" alimony may be held not to terminate upon the recipient's remarriage because rehabilitative alimony is paid for a specific purpose that is not necessarily superseded by remarriage.

Example: Prior to entry of a decree of divorce, H and W entered into a property settlement agreement. In the agreement H agreed to pay "W for her maintenance and support during her lifetime * * *." A payment schedule was set out for the first twenty years. This agreement was incorporated into their divorce decree. Two months after the divorce decree, W remarried. H made payments for over five years before bringing suit for modification or termination of the payments. (Result: Modification denied. The court found that H had a duty to continue making the payments "because the payments were for 'contractual support' and not alimony.") *In re Marriage of Mass,* 102 Ill.App.3d 984, 58 Ill.Dec. 941, 431 N.E.2d 1 (1981).

c. Recipient Spouse's Cohabitation

The alimony recipient's unmarried cohabitation with another person may be sufficient to justify reconsideration of an alimony award. Many courts have held that unmarried cohabitation does not necessarily require termination of alimony. Interpreting separation agreements, some courts have construed the word "remarriage" to include cohabitation, but most have not. By statute, several states provide for automatic termination of an alimony obligation if the party receiving the alimony cohabits with another person on a resident or longer-term basis. New York speaks in terms of termination of alimony if the recipient is "habitually living with another man and holding herself out as his wife." California employs a presumption of "decreased need" if "the supported party is cohabiting with a person of the opposite sex." Illinois looks to termination "if the party receiving maintenance cohabits with another person on a resident, continuing conjugal basis." It is disputed whether an alimony obligation that was once terminated by cohabitation revives when cohabitation ends.

Examples: (1) Ex–H petitioned to terminate alimony obligation on basis of ex–W's alleged cohabitation with another man. (Result: Termination denied. "In the present case, the former wife and Archer have spent the night together, have had sexual relations, have gone out on dates, have shared meals, and have taken trips together and shared a hotel room. Archer, however, did not keep any clothing or personal items at the former wife's home, and he did not materially or habitually contribute to the former wife's expenses. Further, the former wife testified that she has dated men other than Archer and that she and Archer have never shared a residence. Based on the foregoing, we conclude that the trial court acted within its discretion in declining to terminate the former husband's periodic-alimony obligation.") *Decker v. Decker,* ___ So.2d ___, 2008 WL 2854820 (Ala.Civ.App. 2008).

(2) Ex–W filed a contempt complaint against ex-H for his failure to make support payments. The decree of divorce incorporated a separation agreement which provided for alimony to end upon, *inter alia,* "the wife's living together with a member of the opposite sex, so as to give the outward appearance of marriage * * *." Ex–W cohabited on a regular basis with a man in his apartment, sharing the bedroom. She did not use her lover's surname, nor did she represent that she and her lover were married. (Result: Contempt denied, alimony terminated. Evidence was sufficient to support conclusion that divorced wife lived "together with a member of the opposite sex, so as to give the outward appearance of marriage" within meaning of the contingency in the parties' incorporated separation agreement. Alimony terminated despite lack of evidence that her lover financially supported ex-W.) *Bell v. Bell,* 393 Mass. 20, 468 N.E.2d 859 (1984).

(3) When H and W divorced after 30 years of marriage, H was ordered to pay W monthly alimony of $750. Several years later, H moved to terminate the alimony payments under the applicable statute, alleging that W was cohabitating with a man (A) "on a resident, continuing conjugal basis." W and A went out together socially, traveled together, and exchanged birthday and Christmas gifts. They did not sleep in the same bedroom, and A alleged that he was impotent. The circuit court and the appellate court held that a *sexual* relationship was an essential element of a conjugal relationship under the statute. H appealed. (Result: Reversed; W's alimony terminated. "We believe that a relationship can have a conjugal basis even though there is an absence of any sexual relationship.") *Marriage of Sappington,* 106 Ill.2d 456, 88 Ill.Dec. 61, 478 N.E.2d 376 (1985).

7. Enforcement of Alimony by Contempt

Along with the usual remedies for the enforcement of money obligations, alimony has the additional advantage—to the recipient—that it is enforceable by contempt. This means that the sanctions may include jail.

[handwritten note: Person receiving has to pay taxes on it]

8. Federal Tax Treatment of Alimony

Generally, alimony is deductible by the payor and included in the recipient's federal taxable income. The definition of alimony was substantially changed in the 1980s. Rules for alimony under pre–1985 decrees and separation instruments continue in effect for pre–1985 obligations. For current divorces, the definition of "alimony" guards against disguising as alimony a non-deductible payment, such as child support or an installment property settlement. The following rules apply: (1) The payment must be in cash or its equivalent. (2) The parties must not designate that the payment is not alimony. (3) If the parties are separated under a decree of divorce or separate maintenance, the parties must not be members of the same household when the payment is made. (4) There must be no liability to make payments after the death of the recipient spouse. (5) The payment must not be described or treated as child support. (6) If amounts exceeding $10,000 per calendar year are to be paid, they must be payable in each of the first three post-separation years. Generally, if annual payments decrease by more than $15,000 during the three-year period, there will be a "recapture" of excess alimony deductions.

9. Alimony and Property Award Distinguished

The terms of the settlement agreement or of the divorce decree may help assure the classification and thereby the legal consequences of post-marital payments. The parties' or court's designation, however, is not necessarily controlling for all purposes. Specific payments may be classified differently under different laws and for different purposes (*e.g.*, bankruptcy, or taxation, or enforcement).

B. Property Division on Divorce

1. Separate Property States

With some variations, separate property states hold that each marital partner owns and controls property he or she owned before marriage, plus property acquired by him or her during the marriage through personal earnings, gift, inheritance, interest and dividends on investments or their appreciation, or separately acquired in any other manner.

a. Property Transfers on Divorce

In traditional separate property states, courts would order a transfer of property between divorcing spouses only for the purpose of sorting out the spouses' commingled separate property. Jointly titled property was subject to the presumptions of gift or advancement, discussed at p. 103.

Any other transfer of separate property would be labeled "in lieu of alimony" or "lump sum alimony" or "alimony in gross."

b. Equitable Distribution

Adherence to the pure separate property scheme left the non-earning spouse (typically the wife) without assets, despite vital services she or he may have contributed to the marriage. Largely in the 1970s, courts and legislatures adopted various schemes to rectify this state of affairs. Today, statutes in separate property states commonly provide, or are interpreted by the courts to provide, for an "equitable distribution" of property acquired during marriage. The current theory is that marriage is a shared enterprise, and equitable distribution is the division of the assets of the shared enterprise, based on the partners' presumably equal contributions and other equities.

c. "Marital Property"

Several separate property states have adopted detailed definitions of "marital property." In its technical concern for distinguishing between separate property and marital property, this approach closely resembles a community property scheme. However, in contrast to community property which vests in both parties when it is acquired by one party to a marriage, this scheme comes into effect only upon divorce. It then deals with distribution of property as if a community property regime had been in effect all along. This approach has been unsuccessfully attacked as a "retroactive impairment of contract" (*Kujawinski*, below), or a deprivation of "vested rights" (*Fournier*, below).

Example: (1) An Illinois statute presumed all property acquired by either spouse during the marriage to be marital property upon divorce. Exceptions included property acquired by gift or devise. H sought a judgment that retroactive application of that statute was unconstitutional, arguing that transfer of an interest in his property to W impaired his contractual relations with third parties. (Result: Application of the statute is *not* unconstitutional. "Had the legislature chosen to apply the concept of equitable distribution of property only to property acquired after the Act became effective, the full impact and purposes of the new Act would not have been felt for at least a generation. Such prospective application would continue the very inequity which the legislature sought to remedy and would place the present generation of married couples at a decided disadvantage in comparison with subsequent generations of married couples. Moreover, in each dissolution proceeding involving property, courts would be presented with the impracticable dilemma of applying, depending upon the acquisition date of any disputed property, differing sets of laws and policies. * * * [W]e conclude that the State interest to be promoted by applying the section retrospectively greatly outweighs the asserted property interest, which is only slightly more impaired by such application.") *Kujawinski v. Kujawinski*, 71 Ill.2d 563, 17 Ill.Dec. 801, 376 N.E.2d 1382 (1978).

(2) A Maine statute classified as marital property all property acquired by either spouse during the marriage. Statutory exceptions included property acquired by gift, devise, or descent. During the marriage, W acquired by intestate succession a 33% interest in beach property and shortly thereafter obtained full title by purchasing the similarly acquired interests of her father and sister. Upon divorce, the trial court ruled that the beach property was marital property, with the exception of W's 33% interest acquired by descent. W appealed, arguing that the statute deprived her of vested property rights. (Result: Statute is constitutional. "In enacting [the statute], the legislative purpose was to provide a more equitable method of distributing property upon the termination of a marriage and not to affect property titles retrospectively. * * * [T]he Act becomes operative when a divorce or separation proceeding is involved [and] limits the definition of 'marital property' to the 'purposes of this section only.' The Act does not prevent married persons from owning property separately during marriage and disposing of it in any fashion either of them may choose, assuming neither a separation nor a divorce intervenes. Viewed in this light, the defendant's claim that [the Act] deprived her of vested property rights without due process of law is without merit.") *Fournier v. Fournier*, 376 A.2d 100 (Me.1977).

d. The Uniform Marriage and Divorce Act

The UMDA's provisions on the distribution of property on divorce have been influential, even if not followed precisely. § 307 provides:

Alternative A (recommended generally for adoption)

"In a proceeding for dissolution of a marriage, [or] legal separation * * * the court, without regard to marital misconduct, shall, and in a proceeding for legal separation may, finally equitably apportion between the parties the property and assets belonging to either or both however and whenever acquired, and whether the title thereto is in the name of the husband or wife or both. In making apportionment the court shall consider the duration of the marriage, any prior marriage of either party, any antenuptial agreement of the parties, the age, health, station, occupation, amount and sources of income, vocational skills, employability, estate, liabilities, and needs of each of the parties, custodial provisions, whether the apportionment is in lieu of or in addition to maintenance, and the opportunity of each for future acquisition of capital assets and income. The court shall also consider the contribution or dissipation of each party in the acquisition, preservation, depreciation, or appreciation in value of the respective estates, and the contribution of a spouse as a homemaker or to the family unit."

Alternative B (included for consideration by community property states)

"In a proceeding for dissolution of the marriage [or] legal separation * * * the court shall assign each spouse's separate property to the spouse. It also shall divide community property, without regard to marital misconduct, in just proportions after considering all relevant factors including: (1) contribution of each spouse to acquisition of the marital property, including contribution of a spouse as homemaker; (2) value of the property set apart to each spouse; (3) duration of the marriage; and (4) economic circumstances of each spouse when the division of property is to become effective, including the desirability of awarding the family home or the right to live therein for a reasonable period to the spouse having custody of any children."

e. Marital Fault and Economic Fault ("Dissipation")

Under most no-fault divorce statutes and some fault statutes, the division of property on divorce is not subject to consideration of marital fault. "Economic fault," by contrast, is increasingly considered in the apportionment of property. Typically, courts define as "dissipation" or "economic fault" payments or gifts made by one spouse (a) after a breakdown in the marriage, (b) for a "non-marital purpose." The amount of these losses may then be charged against what otherwise would have been the "guilty" spouse's share of the marital property. Sometimes it is not altogether clear whether marital or economic fault is being punished.

Examples: (1) H and W were married for 30 years and both parties worked continuously throughout the marriage. H had been a department store vice president earning $85,000 per year, but had lost this job as a result of a corporate takeover. During the last year of the marriage H earned $12,000. W was a nurse earning $41,000 per year. The marital property was valued at $500,000, of which $300,000 represented H's pension and IRA. Upon divorce, the trial court awarded 60 percent of the marital property to W upon a finding that H's same-sex relationships may have placed W at risk of acquiring AIDS and therefore affected her future economic circumstances. H appealed. (Result: Reversed and remanded for an equal division of the marital property. "[I]f the husband is also at risk for AIDS to the same (or even greater) extent as the wife, we can conclude as a matter of law that this risk has an identical impact upon the husband's future economic circumstances. Therefore, absent the injection of fault into the analysis, the trial court's division of the marital estate in favor of the wife—based upon the risk that the wife might develop a communicable disease for which the husband shares the same risk—is clearly against the logic and effect of the facts and the reasonable inferences to be drawn therefrom and constitutes an abuse of discretion. We conclude that the trial court's 'health and economic circumstances' justification for an unequal division of marital assets in favor of the wife is based upon insufficient evidence and is implicitly based upon [marital] fault.") *R.E.G. v. L.M.G.*, 571 N.E.2d 298 (Ind.App.1991).

(2) When they married in 1979, W was a college sophomore and H had just been drafted by the New York Jets to play professional football. W had not finished college and did not work during the marriage. H played with the Jets for nine years and his final annual contract salary was $775,000 plus $50,000 in bonuses. The parties had bought a $550,000 resort home and spent much of H's salary on other luxury items, including a power boat, a Rolls Royce

and four other cars. In 1988, H met an actress (A), with whom he had an intimate relationship. When A developed cancer, H broke his football contract to accompany A to chemotherapy treatments. H played only six of the 16 games of the 1988 season, forfeiting $484,437 in salary, or $324,573 in net pay after taxes. After H broke his contract, he was unable to sign with a U.S. football team and earned only $20,000 in the Canadian Football League in 1989 before he was cut. Thereafter, he earned no money, and at the time of the divorce the only marital asset of value remaining was $264,000 in equity in the couple's New York home. (Result: Marital assets held to *include* the NFL salary H forfeited, *i.e.*, $324,573. Together with the home equity, the assets thus totaled $591,573, of which W was awarded 33%, or $194,229. Because H owed W $71,707 in past due support, W was awarded the full equity in the New York home plus a judgment for the balance, *i.e.*, $1,936.) *Gastineau v. Gastineau*, 151 Misc.2d 813, 573 N.Y.S.2d 819 (1991). (Note: This was *not* the usual "dissipation of marital assets" case, where the marital community is reimbursed for what one spouse actually has spent for his or her nonmarital purposes.)

f. Post–Divorce Joint Ownership

"Continued joint ownership following divorce is the exceptional case 'reserved for the unusual situation where the economics involved call for such a solution.' " *Hopkins v. Hopkins*, 597 S.W.2d 702, 706 (Mo.App.1980). Upon divorce, a tenancy by the entireties automatically converts into a tenancy in common and is subject to partition, unless the court provides for joint tenancy.

g. Pre–Divorce Transfers of Separate Property

Generally, a spouse has the right to dispose of his or her separate property during marriage without the consent of the other spouse. As discussed above, the notion of "dissipation" of marital property may be applied at the time of divorce to compensate one spouse for losses through the other spouse's wrongful misapplication of marital property.

2. Community Property States

Under community property regimes, all property acquired during marriage generally is community property, and is owned by *both* spouses as of the time it is acquired. Pre-marital properties and properties acquired during marriage by gift or inheritance or, depending on the state, as earnings on or appreciation of separate property, remain separate property unless commingled. On divorce, the court assigns the separate property to the owners and divides the community property equally or, in several states, "equitably."

Examples: (1) Upon their divorce, W was awarded approximately 70 percent of the community property acquired during the 37–year marriage. She appealed, contending that H's adultery warranted granting her an even greater share of the community property. (Result: Trial court's equitable distribution affirmed. "While [H's] conduct, both in and out of the courtroom, may well have provided the trial court with a reasonable basis for awarding an unequal property division in equity, [W] is not entitled to additional assets to punish her former spouse for his behavior.") *Chafino v. Chafino,* 228 S.W.3d 467 (Tex.App.2007).

(2) In dividing community property, the trial court "rewarded" H for his "successful efforts" in preserving and protecting the community property estate, and "punished" W for destroying any meaningful father-daughter relationship between H and his children. W was awarded land valued at $27,400. H was awarded land estimated to be worth as much as $170,000. W appealed the unequal distribution. At issue was whether the required "equitable" distribution must be "equal." (Result: For W. The court felt that the distribution of community property was "whimsical and arbitrary" and that, in the absence of sound reason, division "must be substantially equal." The lower "court's unequal property distribution was arbitrary, unreasonable and an unconstitutional deprivation of the appellant's vested property interest in the community.") *Hatch v. Hatch,* 113 Ariz. 130, 547 P.2d 1044 (1976).

3. Conflicts of Laws Aspects of Property Division

The law of the matrimonial domicile at the time of acquisition generally determines ownership of property acquired by the husband and wife, as well as its characterization as separate or community property.

Example: H and W lived their marriage in New Jersey, a separate property state. They acquired property in the form of securities and bank accounts. H left W and moved to Idaho, a community property state, taking the property with him. H then obtained a divorce in Idaho. No distribution to W was made of the property. W appealed. (Result: For W. The Idaho court looked to the fact that Idaho's concept of "separate property" differed significantly from New Jersey's and held that the law of the state (New Jersey) where the separate property was acquired should apply to give W the equitable share to which she would have been entitled in New Jersey.) *Berle v. Berle*, 97 Idaho 452, 546 P.2d 407 (1976).

Several other community property states provide for this problem by statutes that create so-called "quasi-community property."

Example: Tex. Fam. Code § 7.002 provides: "[I]n a decree of divorce or annulment the court shall also order a division of the following real and personal property, wherever situated, in a manner that the court deems just and right, having due regard for the rights of each party and any children of the marriage: (1) property that was acquired by either spouse while domiciled elsewhere and that would have been community property if the spouse who acquired the property had been domiciled in this state at the time of the acquisition; or (2) property that was acquired by either spouse in exchange for real or personal property, and that would have been community property if the spouse who acquired the property so exchanged had been domiciled in this state at the time of its acquisition."

4. Property Awards and Bankruptcy

Before 2005, bankruptcy law treated alimony and child support obligations as non-dischargeable (meaning that they survived a bankruptcy), but generally allowed for the discharge of debts arising from a division of property in divorce. As a result, ex-spouses were sometimes tempted to file for bankruptcy as a way of avoiding property debts, spawning recurring litigation over whether a divorce obligation was properly in the nature of alimony (non-dischargeable) or property division (dischargeable). Amendments to the bankruptcy code in 2005 eliminated this distinction in Chapter 7 bankruptcies, so that future obligations to transfer property to a former spouse are treated like alimony, child support, and other "domestic support obligations" not subject to discharge. The 2005 amendments did not, however, eliminate the distinction in Chapter 13 bankruptcies; in that context, debts arising from divorce property divisions continue to be dischargeable under a test that balances hardships to the debtor and the debtor's ex-spouse. Moreover, the 2005 revisions specify that debts pursuant to a "domestic support order" can include those owed to the government as well as to a former spouse. 11 U.S.C.A. § 101(14A).

Example: D received excess payments under a child care assistance program (she had failed to report all of her income, which would have reduced her eligibility). As a result, she was obligated to repay the state $1,850. (Result: D's debt to the state was not dischargeable in her bankruptcy. "The term 'domestic support obligation' is broad and includes a wide variety of obligations. Prior to the 2005 amendments, the Code provided that the debt in question must be one owed to a spouse, former spouse or child of the debtor. . . . The new definition encompasses *all* debts to a governmental unit related to support, such as the child care subsidy at issue here."). *In re Schauer,* 391 B.R. 430 (Bankr., E.D. Wis. 2008).

5. Tax Treatment of Property Awards

The recipient of property in a divorce settlement takes the transferor's adjusted basis for that property. Before 1984, the transfer by one spouse to the other of property was a taxable event, if the fair market value of the property differed from its basis. To illustrate, if the property had appreciated in value, the transferor was liable for capital gains tax to the extent of the appreciation. If the property had lost value, there was a loss for tax purposes. *United States v. Davis,* 370 U.S. 65, 82 S.Ct. 1190, 8 L.Ed.2d 335 (1962).

person that transfers, liable [handwritten annotation]

6. Treatment of Professional Licenses and Practices

When a divorce occurs shortly after (or before) one spouse completes advanced education and qualifies for a professional license, an award of generous alimony provides a ready remedy, if (or indeed, whether or not) the other spouse has made a significant contribution either in cash or services to the earning of the license. Because of their antipathy to alimony, a few courts have classified a professional license as an "asset" and "divided" it upon divorce, by awarding a specific percentage of the "present value" of the license to the other spouse as property. Other courts have taken the license into account under a variety of theories.

a. The Professional License as a Factor in Determining Alimony

Example: When W and H married in 1976, W had finished 3 years of college and H was entering medical school. During H's first

3 years of medical school, W left college and worked as a department store clerk until the couple's first child was born. After 7 years of marriage, when H had one year left to complete his medical residency, H left W and moved in with another woman. In H and W's divorce, W was awarded child support, rehabilitative maintenance of $500 per month, and restitution of the salary she had earned while H attended medical school. W appealed, seeking a maintenance award reflecting H's increased earning potential resulting from his degree. (Result: Rehabilitative maintenance and restitution awards vacated; remanded to determine appropriate alimony and property division. "[W]hen one spouse obtains a professional degree during the marriage, but the marriage ends before the benefits of the degree can be realized, the future value of the professional degree is a relevant factor to be considered in reaching a just and equitable maintenance award.") *Downs v. Downs*, 154 Vt. 161, 574 A.2d 156 (1990).

b. "Goodwill" Distinguished

A professional degree or license should be distinguished from the actual value of an existing practice, *i.e.*, goodwill.

Example: W supported H while he attended college and law school. H became the sole shareholder in a professional corporation specializing in personal injury and medical malpractice cases. W raised their children and never worked outside the home. When the couple divorced after 23 years of marriage, H appealed the distribution of marital assets, arguing that the court improperly included his professional goodwill. (Result: It is not improper to divide professional goodwill as a marital asset, if the goodwill has monetary value over and above the tangible assets and cases in progress and is separate and distinct from the attorney's professional reputation. "[T]he courts of at least twenty states have held that professional goodwill is a marital asset that, if it exists in a particular case, should be distributed upon dissolution. * * * Goodwill is property of an intangible nature commonly defined as the expectation of continued public patronage. * * * It should be emphasized that such goodwill, to be a marital asset, must exist separate and apart from the

reputation or continued presence of the marital litigant. * * * Generally, clients come to an individual professional to receive services from that specific person. Even so, if a party can produce evidence demonstrating goodwill as an asset separate and distinct from the other party's reputation, it should be considered in distributing marital property.") *Thompson v. Thompson*, 576 So.2d 267 (Fla.1991).

c. **The Professional License as "Marital Property"**

The majority of courts continue to consider one spouse's contribution to the other spouse's education as an important factor influencing the alimony award or the division of property. Only a few states, prominently New York, characterize the degree or license as marital property and attempt to "divide" it.

Examples: (1) H and W were married for nine years. At the time of their marriage, W had a bachelor's degree. She held a temporary teaching certificate and needed about 18 months of postgraduate training to receive permanent certification. During the marriage, she pursued her education. H had nearly completed college when they married. During the marriage, he completed his bachelor's degree and medical school. H initiated divorce proceedings two months after receiving his medical license. The trial court found that W had contributed 76% of the household's income, exclusive of a $10,000 student loan obtained by H. Finding H's medical degree and license to be marital property with a present value of $188,800, the court awarded W 40%, to be paid in eleven annual installments. The appellate court reversed. W appealed (Result: (1) A license to practice medicine, acquired during marriage, is marital property subject to equitable distribution; (2) a working spouse is entitled to equitable portion of the license, not a return of funds advanced; (3) there was no suggestion that W was guilty of fault sufficient to shock the conscience of court, to be a proper consideration in equitable distribution of marital property. "Limiting a working spouse to a maintenance award, either general or rehabilitative, not only is contrary to the economic partnership concept underlying the statute but also retains the uncertain and inequitable economic ties of dependence that the Legislature sought to extinguish by equitable distribution.") *O'Brien v. O'Brien,* 66 N.Y.2d 576, 498 N.Y.S.2d 743, 489 N.E.2d 712 (1985).

(2) W postponed her degree in nursing and worked full-time to put H through law school. W also did all of the household work. H blamed the fights he started with W on the stresses of law school. W claimed that by the end of their marriage, her whole life revolved around trying not to agitate H. The parties separated when H admitted that he had occasionally dated another woman while W was working. Upon divorce, the trial court determined that H's law degree was a marital asset, and H appealed. (Result: Remanded for valuation of W's equitable interest in H's law degree. Where an advanced degree is the end product of a concerted family effort, involving the mutual sacrifice, effort, and contribution of both spouses, there arises a marital asset subject to distribution, and the non-student spouse has an equitable claim against this asset. "[T]he goal is to attempt to financially return to the nonstudent spouse what that spouse contributed toward attainment of the degree. Because such an award is not premised upon the notion that a nonstudent spouse possesses an interest in the degree itself, we do not believe the actual value of the degree is a relevant consideration. * * * [T]he focus of an award involving an advanced degree is not to reimburse the nonstudent spouse for 'loss of expectations' over what the degree might potentially have produced, but to reimburse that spouse for unrewarded sacrifices, efforts, and contributions toward attainment of the degree on the ground that it would be equitable to do so in view of the fact that that spouse will not be sharing in the fruits of the degree.") *Postema v. Postema,* 189 Mich.App. 89, 471 N.W.2d 912 (1991). *Caveat:* Michigan courts retain equitable discretion in assessing contributions in this context. *Berger v. Berger,* 277 Mich.App. 700, 747 N.W.2d 336 (2008) (holding that trial court did not err in rejecting expert testimony about alleged present value of W's MFA degree where "[a]t best, [H] tolerated [W's] educational pursuits" but did not sacrifice to support them).

d. "Career Enhancement"

At least in New York, courts analogize the enhancement of a spouse's career during the marriage to the acquisition/creation of a marital asset and award the "silent" partner a share in the other's "career."

Example: When W and H married, W had just embarked on her career as an opera singer. Seventeen years later, when the marriage was ending, W (Frederica von Stade) had become a celebrated artist with the Metropolitan Opera Company as well as an international recording artist and television performer. During the marriage, H sacrificed his own career as a singer to advance W's career, traveled with W to her performances, cared for the couple's children, photographed W for album covers and magazine articles, and worked as her voice coach for 10 years. Upon divorce, H argued that his efforts would not be sufficiently compensated unless W's career as a performing artist and celebrity would be subject to equitable distribution. (Result: W's career and celebrity status is marital property. "We agree with the courts that have considered the issue, that the enhanced skills of an artist such as the plaintiff, albeit growing from an innate talent, which have enabled her to become an exceptional earner, may be valued as marital property subject to equitable distribution.") *Elkus v. Elkus*, 169 A.D.2d 134, 572 N.Y.S.2d 901 (1991).

e. "Restitution" of Educational Contribution

A number of jurisdictions award the spouse who has financed the other's education a form of restitution. In its most basic form this amounts to a return of funds advanced, plus interest.

Examples: (1) H and W were married for about seven years. Both had undergraduate degrees when they married. With the exception of a one and one-half year period when H earned his M.B.A. degree, they shared household expenses during their marriage. While H was attending school, W contributed $24,000 to the household, and H made no contribution. About $6,500 of H's educational expenses were covered by veterans' benefits and the Air Force. W began a part-time graduate program during the same period. Her educational expenses were paid by her employer, and she continued to work full-time. The Appellate Division held that W was not entitled to reimbursement. W appealed. (Result: Reversed. The court refused to hold H's degree to be property, but held that W had a right to be reimbursed. "Valuing a professional degree in the hands of any particular individual at the start of his or her career would involve a gamut of calculations that reduces to little more than guesswork." Concerning reimbursement the court said: "Where a partner to marriage takes the benefits of his spouse's support in obtaining a professional degree or license with the understanding that future benefits will accrue and inure to both of them, and the marriage is then terminated without the supported spouse giving anything in return, an unfairness has occurred that calls for a remedy.") *Mahoney v. Mahoney,* 91 N.J. 488, 453 A.2d 527 (1982).

(2) In California, a statute prescribes an elaborate version of the reimbursement of expenditures concept, "with interest at the legal rate." Cal. Fam. Code § 2641(b).

(3) In Illinois, a statute requires that "contributions * * * to the education, training, career or career potential, or license of the other spouse" must be considered in the determination of alimony. 750 ILCS 5/504.

7. Allocation of Pensions

In community property states, pensions derived out of community funds are community property and subject to division on divorce. In separate property states, the non-earning spouse had a right to the continuation of alimony after the earner's retirement and thus shared in pension rights. With the general move toward "equitable distribution" or the concept of "marital property," courts today commonly treat pension rights (whether vested or nonvested) as "marital property" subject to division at divorce to the extent they were earned during the marriage. The valuation of pension interests, however, presents great difficulty, especially when a final adjustment at the time of divorce is contemplated, or when the pension is not vested.

Examples: (1) When H and W divorced after 15 years of marriage, W was awarded alimony of $100 per month. The community property was divided evenly, with the exception of H's retirement plan, over which the court retained jurisdiction. Six months following the divorce, H first became eligible to retire. His monthly benefit would then have been $717.18, of which W's interest was $177.14. H did not retire, however, and represented that he intended to work for some years in the future. W moved to require H to pay her share of his pension immediately, retroactive to the date he became eligible to retire. (Result: W is entitled to immediate distribution of her share of H's retirement benefits. "Under the cases and statutory law, H cannot time his retirement to deprive W of an equal share of the community's interest in his pension. It is a settled principle that one spouse cannot, by invoking a condition wholly within his control, defeat the community interests of the other spouse. * * * H would deprive W of the immediate enjoyment of an asset earned by the community during the marriage. In so doing, he would subject W to the risk of losing the asset completely if H were to die while he was still employed. Although H has every right to choose to postpone the receipt of his pension and to run that risk, he should not be able to force W to do so as well. * * * H's claim that he is being forced to retire misses the point. He is free to continue working. However, if he does so, he must reimburse W for the share of the community property that she loses as a result of that decision.") *Gillmore v. Gillmore*, 29 Cal.3d 418, 174 Cal.Rptr. 493, 629 P.2d 1 (1981).

(2) H and W divorced after 20 years of marriage. In dividing the marital property, the trial court awarded H's nonvested pension with a then-present value of $27,000 to H and offsetting assets to W. H appealed, arguing that a nonvested pension is not a marital asset. In the alternative, H argued that the trial court should not have used the present value method to value the pension. (Result: A nonvested pension is a marital asset, but its valuation should not be determined using the present value method; instead, the court should retain jurisdiction and, upon request of the nonemployee spouse, value and divide the pension after it has vested. "The trend * * * is to consider pensions as marital property regardless of whether they have vested. * * * Supporting this trend is the reasoning that the contingent nature of a nonvested pension presents simply a valuation problem, not bearing on the non-employee spouse' entitlement to a just share of the marital assets. * * * Since

[under the present value method] the non-employee spouse receives his or her share in a lump sum at the time of the divorce, the method unfairly places all risk of possible forfeiture on the employee spouse.") *Laing v. Laing*, 741 P.2d 649 (Alaska 1987).

8. The "Employee Retirement Income Security Act" (ERISA) and the "Qualified Domestic Relations Order" (QDRO)

Divorce can not take it

ERISA applies to employee benefit plans that are maintained by an employer engaged directly or indirectly in commerce. The Act supersedes state laws on the subject. The Act provides: "Each pension plan shall provide that benefits provided under the plan may not be assigned or alienated." 29 U.S.C.A. § 1056(d)(1). A 1984 amendment expressly applies the restriction to a "domestic relations order," unless it is a "qualified domestic relations order." 29 U.S.C.A. § 1056(d)(3)(A).

"[T]he term 'qualified domestic relations order' means a domestic relations order—(I) which creates or recognizes the existence of an alternate payee's right to, or assigns to an alternate payee the right to, receive all or a portion of the benefits payable with respect to a participant under a plan, and (II) with respect to which the requirements of subparagraphs (C) and (D) are met, and (ii) the term 'domestic relations order' means any judgment, decree, or order (including approval of a property settlement agreement) which—(I) relates to the provision of child support, alimony payments, or marital property rights to a spouse, former spouse, child, or other dependent of a participant, and (II) is made pursuant to a State domestic relations law (including a community property law.)" 29 U.S.C.A. § 1056(d)(3)(B).

A QDRO must specify names and addresses, amounts or percentages to be paid, applicable periods and the plan to which the QDRO applies. A QDRO must *not* require the plan to provide any benefit not otherwise provided under the plan, require the plan to provide increased benefits, or require payment of benefits which have previously been divided in a qualified domestic relations order to another alternative payee. 29 U.S.C.A. § 1056(d)(3)(D). The ordering of payment of benefits to an alternative payee on or after the date the employee attains the earliest retirement age, as if he or she had actually retired on that date, meets these requirements. 29 U.S.C.A. § 1056(d)(3)(E).

C. Separation Agreements

A separation agreement is made during marriage in contemplation of divorce. The agreement specifies the parties' wishes as to the settlement of their economic affairs and may extend to questions relating to children.

1. Validity of Separation Agreement

Traditional law governing the validity of separation agreements involved conflicting policies. On the one hand, contracts facilitating divorce were considered void as contrary to the public policy against divorce. On the other hand, it has long been obvious that it is in the public interest for parties to settle their own affairs without unnecessary recourse to the courts. Resolving this conflict on the side of practicality, the courts have upheld separation agreements when the parties' separation or divorce had already occurred or was about to occur, the agreement was supported by consideration, and the agreement was fair.

2. Traditional Requirements for Enforceability

a. "Facilitating" or "Encouraging" Separation or Divorce

Traditionally, to render the agreement valid, the parties' separation must have been accomplished or about to occur.

Example: While separated, and in contemplation of divorce, H and W executed a separation agreement in which H agreed to pay for upkeep on the marital home where W lived, make one-half of the mortgage payments as long as W did not remarry or either of the couple's children remained at home, and to pay child and spousal support. H argued that the agreement was void on the grounds that it violated public policy by being premised on the consideration of divorce. (Result: Agreement valid. "In line with the policy favoring family settlements, even where made in contemplation of divorce, in order to render an agreement unenforceable some *overt* manifestation of mutual assent with respect to a bargained for divorce must appear.") *Wife, B.T.L. v. Husband, H.A.L.*, 287 A.2d 413 (Del.Ch.1972).

b. Consideration

A promise to perform duties imposed by the marital relationship generally is not effective consideration. However, separation agreements rarely founder on the consideration issue. Courts have upheld agreements supported by the wife's promise to take custody of the children, the husband's promise to support his wife, or the release by a spouse of property or support rights which he or she may have.

c. Full Disclosure, Fraud, Fairness and Representation by Attorney

Separation agreements may be invalidated if there was no full disclosure, or if the agreement is grossly unfair. If both partners are represented by separate counsel, a resulting agreement is far more secure than it is when only one or neither party is represented by counsel. Traditionally, it was postulated that the confidential relationship between husband and wife required the dominant partner (H) to bear the burden of proving the fairness of the agreement. The modern view is that whether or not such a relationship exists depends on the facts of the particular case, and courts will invalidate a separation agreement only upon a showing of *actual* fraud, misrepresentation, coercion, or undue influence. Under UMDA § 306 only an "unconscionable" separation agreement is not binding on the court. (Note: Provisions in separation agreements relating to child custody or child support are *not* binding on the court, whether or not they are "conscionable.")

Examples: (1) W's attorney prepared a separation agreement. H made two significant changes (reducing child support from $700 to $300 per month and adding the disposition of eleven houses owned by the couple). H's secretary retyped the agreement. H asked W to come to his office to sign the agreement. When W arrived, H suggested they discuss the agreement in private. He did not mention the changes, but informed W that he knew of her affair with a police lieutenant and that he would go to the newspapers if W did not sign the agreement. W requested that she be able to talk to her attorney and threatened to leave several times. H threatened to "start the ball rolling." W negotiated several changes in the agreement and then signed it. H received $163,000, and W received $45,000 under the agreement. W sued for cancellation of the separation agreement on the grounds that it was obtained by duress or undue influence. (Result: For H. The evidence sustained finding that there was a lack of trust and confidence between parties necessary to the establishment of a confidential relationship between them. "[T]here is no rule of law that precludes a woman from giving away a substantial portion of her property to save her reputation, if it is her voluntary act.") *Bell v. Bell,* 38 Md.App. 10, 379 A.2d 419 (1977).

Right to review all records

(2) H owned an interest in a closely held insurance business. When H and W divorced, H assured W that the business furnished him only a salary and that its stock had no market value. H produced financial records to support this representation. Several years after the divorce was final, W learned that the business had been sold just prior to the divorce and that H had received $340,000 for his share; H thus had concealed 99.5 percent of his net worth. W sought to reopen the divorce. The trial court denied her motion because she had failed to exercise due diligence. W appealed. (Result: Judgment reopened and new trial ordered on the property distribution issues. "Of paramount significance * * * is the court's express finding that in concealing his assets, the defendant had perpetrated a fraud on the court. * * * The defendant's conduct was a deliberate, fraudulent and egregious concealment of assets. The record clearly shows that, at the time he filed his affidavit, the defendant knew exactly how much he would be receiving from the sale of his business. If we allow such a deliberate and fraudulent statement of assets to go unchallenged, the role of the financial affidavit will be reduced to a meaningless formality, as will the court's role in reviewing it. We will not permit such a result.") *Greger v. Greger*, 22 Conn.App. 596, 578 A.2d 162 (1990).

(3) H and W negotiated the details of their separation agreement without legal representation. Their divorce was uncontested. The attorney for H's car dealership drew up the agreement, filed the divorce and told the parties that he could represent them only if there were no disagreements regarding the terms of the divorce. He did not advise W, and nothing in the record indicates that he advised H that their interests might be adverse, or that each should be represented by a separate attorney. Following the divorce, W consulted another attorney and sought to have the judgment set aside. (Result: Judgment affirmed. "[T]here is no evidence that H failed to disclose assets or misrepresented their value. Nor is there an allegation or evidence of active collusion between H and the attorney representing W to deprive W of her rightful share of marital property. W's own evidence demonstrates that she was aware of all

of the assets of the marriage and agreed on their division. A party is not entitled to relief from choices freely and deliberately made.") *Kolmosky v. Kolmosky*, 631 A.2d 419 (Me.1993).

3. The Divorce Decree and the Separation Agreement

Generally, courts incorporate separation agreements into divorce decrees. This may be accomplished by specific reference or by expressly setting forth the terms in the decree. Validity, modifiability and enforceability of the separation agreement are affected by the relationship between the agreement and the divorce decree.

a. Specific Incorporation

When the decree expressly sets forth (and orders compliance with) the terms of the separation agreement, the agreement obtains the status and enforceability of a judgment. Among other consequences, failure to comply will be contempt of court. Moreover, the incorporated agreement may be modified only in accordance with the rules for modifying judgments. (UMDA § 306(e) *additionally* allows enforcement as a contract.)

b. Incorporation by Reference

If the terms of the agreement are not expressly set forth in the decree, but the agreement is incorporated by reference, the issue of validity of the agreement is assured (*res judicata*). However, the agreement is not enforceable as a judgment.

Example: While separated, H and W entered into a separation agreement. The agreement provided that it was to be incorporated by reference in the divorce decree, but that it would not merge with it. The divorce decree ordered incorporation by reference. Eight years later, H petitioned to set aside the agreement on the basis that, during negotiations, he had suffered from a mental disease. (Result: The court held that the separation agreement was not merged, but that H was precluded from attacking the agreement. "[W]here, as in the instant case, the agreement provides that it shall be incorporated but not merged in the decree, it is patent that the parties did not intend merger and the agreement survives as a separate and independent contractual arrangement between the parties. * * * [W]here, as in the instant case, the property settlement agreement is presented to the court for approval and is approved by the court and incorporated in the divorce decree, the validity of the agreement is conclusively established and the doctrine of res judicata operates so as to preclude a collateral attack on the agreement.") *Johnston v. Johnston,* 297 Md. 48, 465 A.2d 436 (1983).

c. No Incorporation → No Contempt of Court

A separation agreement entered into by the parties, but not incorporated into the divorce decree, is enforceable as a contract, subject to the various inhibitions applying to marital agreements.

> *Example:* Prior to H and W's divorce in 1986, they entered into a separation agreement providing that, when H retired, W was to receive 50% of H's pension and social security benefits. Their agreement was *not* incorporated into the final divorce decree. After H retired, he paid W these benefits for 2 years. When H stopped paying, W filed suit to enforce the separation agreement. (Result: Summary judgment under a breach of contract theory for W in the amount of H's arrearages up to the date of the judgment. W, however, was *not* entitled to specific performance of the unincorporated agreement, nor could H be held in contempt for breach of the agreement.) *Eickhoff v. Eickhoff,* 263 Ga. 498, 435 S.E.2d 914 (1993).

d. Court's Review of Separation Agreement

Courts usually accept the separation agreement as offered by the parties. Nevertheless, judicial discretion to accept or reject is considerable. Traditionally, scrutiny ran almost exclusively in favor of the wife. UMDA § 306(b) reduces traditional judicial discretion by providing that a separation agreement, except to the extent it provides "for the support, custody, and visitation of children," is "binding upon the court unless it finds, after considering the economic circumstances of the parties and any other relevant evidence produced by the parties * * * that the separation agreement is unconscionable."

> *Example:* When they divorced after 27 years of marriage, H and W executed a separation agreement that provided for an equal division of the couple's $1.6 million marital property as well as maintenance for W. The agreement contemplated that H would pay W her share of the marital property (which

consisted primarily of H's ownership interest in a closely held oil business) in monthly installments spread out over 10 years. On further consideration, W disavowed the agreement as unfair. (Result: Agreement is invalid because "unconscionable." First, W testified that she did not fully understand the agreement, had poor math skills, and relied on her father to explain the terms. Second, allowing H to keep the marital property while paying out W's share over 10 years without interest meant that "husband, whose income is substantially greater than wife's, obtained the considerable benefit of retaining the use, enjoyment, and investment value of the unpaid balance." Finally, the court appeared influenced by the fact that "[t]he family lived for many years in various oil field camps in desolate parts of Wyoming," while W cared for the children and worked in low-wage jobs, before H came to wealth near the end of the marriage.) *In re Marriage of Thornhill,* ___ P.3d ___, 2008 WL 3877223 (Colo.App. 2008).

e. Reconciliation

The parties' reconciliation generally terminates their separation agreement, but does not override a court decree. Executed provisions of the agreement, such as completed property transfers, are not affected. Specific action by the court is needed to vacate a court decree.

1) What Is Reconciliation?

Holdings differ on what constitutes reconciliation. Some courts require renewed cohabitation; others may find that even isolated acts of sexual relations accomplish reconciliation.

2) Effect of Reconciliation on Separation Agreement

It has been argued that, after reconciliation, the separation agreement turns into an invalid post-nuptial agreement since it still contemplates divorce. More reasonably, reconciliation constitutes a change of circumstances that amounts to an implied revocation of prospective, but not of executed, provisions of the separation agreement.

Example: H was obligated to pay W $80,000 under a settlement agreement that was merged into their divorce decree. H paid $30,000 upon execution of the agreement, but never paid the remaining installments. Seven months later the parties remarried, but six years later their second marriage also ended in divorce. The court assigned to divide the marital estate for the second divorce declared the settlement agreement from the first divorce "null and void," and W appealed. (Result: Reversed. "This property settlement was not merged into the second marriage, and according to the record, H still owes for this judgment. Those assets from the judgment are W's separate assets.") *Marriage of Nordberg*, 265 Mont. 352, 877 P.2d 987 (1994).

Review Questions

1. **T or F**   Most courts now embrace the idea of short-term or intermediate-term "rehabilitative alimony" and no longer award lifetime alimony.

2. **T or F**   Even where a fault ground is used for divorce, "fault" no longer is a consideration with regard to alimony or property division.

3. **T or F**   Modern "no-fault" statutes dispense with proof of "marital fault" insofar as the divorce itself is concerned, but typically allow consideration of marital fault in determining the financial consequences of divorce.

4–7.   Questions 4 through 7 should be answered based on the following facts: H and W divorced after 10 years of marriage. Their separation agreement was incorporated verbatim in the divorce decree. H agreed to pay W "rehabilitative" alimony of $500 per month for 6 years. In addition, W was given a one third interest in stock which H had purchased out of his earnings during the marriage.

4. **T or F**   H quits his job, sells his furniture, moves in with his parents, and starts writing a book about divorce. He has no current income. Because of this significant change in circumstances, his alimony payments will be eliminated or modified to a much lower amount.

5. **T or F**   Three years after the divorce, H dies of a heart attack. W will not collect any further alimony payments from H's estate.

6. **T or F**   Two years after the divorce, W remarries. H petitions to terminate the alimony payments alleging her change in circumstances. H's petition will be granted.

7. **T or F**   H goes through bankruptcy with no assets available for his creditors. After discharge, H continues to be liable to pay W alimony, but W has no claim for the value of stock not yet transferred to her.

8. **T or F**   Upon a showing of the payor's or the recipient's changed circumstances, an alimony award may generally be modified up or down.

9. **T or F**   For federal income tax purposes, alimony is deductible by the payor and is included in the recipient's taxable income.

10. **T or F**   For federal income tax purposes, a property settlement upon divorce is treated as a nontaxable event.

11. **T or F** Today, a professional license or academic degree earned during the marriage is typically treated as marital property upon divorce.

12. **T or F** After the parties' reconciliation, their separation agreement remains in force to govern property rights upon a subsequent divorce.

*

VII

The Parental Child Support Obligation

■ ANALYSIS

A. Definition of the Parental Obligation
B. Support Duty of Stepparents and Grandparents
C. Duration of the Obligation
    1. Majority
    2. Emancipation
    3. Reversion to Unemancipated Status
    4. Death of Parent
D. Traditional Criteria for Awarding Support
E. Child Support Guidelines
F. Modification
G. Child Support Enforcement Sanctions
    1. Civil Contempt
    2. Criminal Contempt
    3. Civil and Criminal Contempt Distinguished
    4. Criminal Prosecution for Non–Support
    5. Federal Crime
H. Conflicts of Laws Aspects of Child Support: The Uniform Interstate Family Support Act

I. Federal Child Support Enforcement Legislation
J. Full Faith and Credit
K. Reciprocity: The Child's Duty to Support Parents

A. Definition of the Parental Obligation

Traditionally, the duty to support the family was imposed primarily on the father and only secondarily on the mother. Today the duty to support children rests equally upon both parents, although the custodial parent (still typically the mother) generally fulfills the obligation by providing care. A child's independent wealth or income normally does not relieve the parents of their support obligation. Because courts are reluctant to intervene in family relationships, litigation concerning child support issues typically is limited to situations where the obligated parent is separated, divorced or not married. The neglect and dependency laws assure a minimum level of child support in the ongoing family. When the parents cannot adequately support the child, government welfare programs have long provided relief. Federal welfare reform legislation enacted in 1996 both limited eligibility for benefits, however, and prodded states to step up their efforts to collect support payments from parents. The child support obligation continues after a child is removed from the home or moves out voluntarily, although, in such cases, enforcement of adequate support is often impossible. Termination of parental rights ends the obligation of support.

B. Support Duty of Stepparents and Grandparents

Persons who are not legal parents are ordinarily under no duty to support a child, even if they share a family relationship as stepparents or grandparents. Some jurisdictions have imposed support duties on stepparents during the marriage to the child's parent, but these duties end if there is a divorce. Del. Code Ann., tit. 13, § 501(b); *Kelley v. Iowa Department of Social Services,* 197 N.W.2d 192 (Iowa 1972). And some have occasionally imposed duties on former stepparents or other caregivers under theories of estoppel or "equitable adoption." *E.g., L.S.K. v. H.A.N.,* 813 A.2d 872 (Pa. Super. 2002); *accord Zellmer v. Zellmer,* 188 P.3d 497 (Wash. 2008) (stating that "a stepparent is not subject to the family support statute unless he or she has established a loco parentis relationship with a child, which requires more than merely taking a child into one's home or exercising temporary custody and control"). Both maternal and paternal grandparents may also be liable for the support of a child born to unemancipated minors. *E.g., Whitman v. Kiger,* 139 N.C.App. 44, 533 S.E.2d 807 (2000).

C. Duration of the Obligation

The obligation to support a child runs until the child reaches majority or becomes emancipated, or until either the parent or the child dies. Under certain circumstances, a divorced or separated parent may be liable for the cost of higher education. If the child is disabled and unable to provide for itself, the obligation may be wholly open-ended.

Example: Twenty-three-year-old C suffered from severe mental illness and was incapable of supporting and caring for herself. After reaching age 21, C had moved into her own apartment and held a job for a time, but later moved back in with M because of her disability. M and F were divorced, and M sought support for C from F. The trial court denied support, finding that the duty to support an adult child exists only when the disability precedes majority and that, when she attained the age of majority, C was not disabled. The appellate court reversed. (Result: Support obligation upheld. "[T]he appellant would draw a distinction in the parents' support obligation based upon the time that the child's disability arose. We do not agree. * * * Unlike physical injuries, mental disabilities often develop over time. The evidence in the instant case traced the roots of Janette's mental disability into her childhood. Yet, her mental difficulties, though present all along, did not become disabling, according to the master's finding, until after she passed the age of majority. * * * The arbitrary age chosen for the age of majority should not override the clear policy expressed in plain language by the legislature * * *. We cannot accept the inconsistency and inequity that would follow from applying an emancipation rationale as urged by appellant.") *Sininger v. Sininger*, 300 Md. 604, 479 A.2d 1354 (1984).

1. Majority

Widespread change in the statutory age of majority from 21 to 18 years of age generally has ended parental responsibility for support after age 18. Several states extend parental liability to cover higher education past majority, but typically only in situations where the parents are divorced or separated. No clear rule defines the extent to which the support-paying parent may control the adult child's lifestyle or choice of studies; however, in regard of choice of school (private or public) a reasonableness test (measuring the child's ability against the parent's educational background and financial resources) is emerging.

Examples: (1) F was held obligated to finance his 18–year-old son's continuing education because the latter suffered from dyslexia and would need further education in order to support himself and pay future medical bills. *Elkins v. Elkins*, 262 Ark. 63, 553 S.W.2d 34 (1977).

(2) C attacked an Illinois statute allowing courts to order divorced parents to provide for the education of children who have reached the age of majority even though undivorced, married parents do not have the same obligation. (Result: No Equal Protection violation. The statute does not require that divorced parents provide majority age children with education in all cases. The situation of the child of divorced parents differs from that of the intact family. "Unfortunately, it is not the isolated exception that noncustodial divorced parents * * * cannot be relied upon to voluntarily support the children of the earlier marriage to the extent they would have, had they not divorced. * * * If parents could have been expected to provide an education for their child absent divorce, it is not unreasonable for the legislature to furnish a means for providing that they do so after they have been divorced.") *Kujawinski v. Kujawinski*, 71 Ill.2d 563, 17 Ill.Dec. 801, 376 N.E.2d 1382 (1978). (*Contra: Curtis v. Kline*, 542 Pa. 249, 666 A.2d 265 (1995), where divorced F succeeded in ending his child support obligation on the child's majority. The following statute was held *unconstitutional*: "[A] court may order either or both parents who are separated, divorced, unmarried or otherwise subject to an existing support obligation to provide equitably for educational costs of their child whether an application for this support is made before or after the child has reached 18 years of age." The Pennsylvania Supreme Court held: "In the absence of an entitlement on the part of any individual to post-secondary education, or a generally applicable requirement that parents assist their adult children in obtaining such an education, we perceive no rational basis for the state government to provide only certain adult citizens with legal means to overcome the difficulties they encounter in pursuing that end.")

(3) When his parents separated, C was a senior in high school. C lived with M for 3 months following the separation. Relations between M and C became strained, and C moved in with F. Prior to his departure, C had shoved M and spat at her during a fight. After this C did not communicate with or visit M. F paid all of C's college expenses during C's freshman year, and C continued to live with F when not in school. When C was accepted as a transfer student to a more expensive private college, he commenced an action against M and F to secure

financial assistance for his college expenses. The trial court found that the estrangement between M and C was not a bar to support and directed M to pay $3,250 per year to C. M appealed. (Result: Reversed. "Perhaps the single most compelling piece of evidence in this case is [M's] testimony that her son 'spat in my face and shoved me so that I fell over. He never spat but once. He did push me more than once. He struck me at least twice.' That any father would condone, let alone encourage, a son who has so abused his mother in taking legal action against her shocks the sensibilities of this writer. The dissent would add insult to injury by finding that [C] is entitled to exact funds for college from his mother's already strained resources. Such compounding of the tragedy of this family cannot be countenanced. * * * If as an adult, a child repudiates a parent, that parent must be allowed to dictate what effect this will have on his or her contribution to college expenses for that child.") *Milne v. Milne*, 383 Pa.Super. 177, 556 A.2d 854 (1989).

2. Emancipation

Through emancipation, a minor becomes legally independent of his or her parents, ending parental rights and duties, and becomes fully responsible for his or her own acts and contracts. The following acts or events point toward emancipation: marriage, enlistment in the military, providing for self support, or any other circumstance that shows the minor has assumed the position of an adult to the point where the legal rights and obligations of adulthood should go with it.

Examples: (1) F was excused from supporting his 18–year-old daughter (C) who had left home to have a child, when C was supported by public assistance. "[W]e cannot agree with the commissioner that whenever an older child chooses to leave home, for any reason, the parents must pay for the child's separate maintenance, or contribute support, if the child applies for public assistance. The courts must still consider the impact on the family relationship and the possibility of injustice in the particular case. Of course the fact that the child is eligible for public assistance may, as is evident here, permit her to avoid her father's authority and demands however reasonable they may be. But it does not follow that the parent must then finish what has been begun by underwriting the lifestyle which his daughter chose against his reasonable wishes and repeated counsel." *Parker v. Stage,* 43 N.Y.2d 128, 400 N.Y.S.2d 794, 371 N.E.2d 513 (1977).

(2) M and F were divorced. Under their divorce agreement, F was obligated to support C until she married, died, turned 21, or became "otherwise emancipated." After graduating from high school, C continued to live with M, but began working full-time for a hospital at an annual salary of approximately $15,000. F moved to end his support obligation. (Result: F not obligated to pay support. C became "otherwise emancipated" when she began working on a full time basis and earned a liveable salary). *Ware v. Ware,* 10 Va.App. 352, 391 S.E.2d 887 (1990).

(3) At the age of 16½, C refused to enter an in-patient facility for a psychiatric evaluation. F locked her out of the house and refused to continue to support her. C maintained herself with a part-time job and the help of friends and neighbors. C petitioned for support from F. (Result: F's support obligation continues. "The obligations of parents cannot be avoided merely because the child is at odds with her parents or has disobeyed their instructions. Even a child's delinquent behavior will not, of itself, relieve a parent of the obligation to support. * * * Additionally, petitioner's part-time employment since leaving her home is insufficient to sustain her, and therefore, does not result in her emancipation. Inasmuch as respondent has refused to allow petitioner to return to her home, 'there is no injustice in having him provide for her support elsewhere.' ") *Jennifer S. v. Marvin S.,* 150 Misc.2d 300, 568 N.Y.S.2d 515 (1991).

3. Reversion to Unemancipated Status

An emancipated minor may revert to unemancipated status if the state of facts that caused the emancipation ceases to exist. In that case, the minor may again be entitled to support from his or her parents until again becoming emancipated or reaching the age of majority.

Example: Divorced F was obligated to pay child support for his daughter, B. When B was 16 years old, she married with her mother's consent. B's emancipation ended F's child support obligation, but B annulled her marriage seven months later on grounds of fraudulent inducement. F refused to resume support for his then–17–year-old daughter. (Result: F's support duty reinstated. "[U]pon annulment of [B's] marriage before she would have otherwise become emancipated, she was returned to unemancipated status and Father's child support obligation likewise revived.") *State ex rel. Dept. of Econ. Security v. Demetz*, 212 Ariz. 287, 130 P.3d 986 (App. 2006).

4. Death of Parent

a. Parents Not Divorced

The death of parent or child terminates the support obligation. In nearly all jurisdictions a parent may disinherit a minor child. In some states disinheritance must stop short of putting a minor child on welfare. A parent may freely disinherit an adult child. Pretermitted heir laws guard against unintentional disinheritance. Intestacy laws provide children with a portion of the estate when the parent leaves no will. In (civil law) Louisiana, disinheritance of minor and even adult children is restricted.

b. Parents Divorced

UMDA § 316(c) breaks with the traditional rule in the event of divorce: "Unless otherwise agreed [ordered] * * *, provisions for the support of a child are terminated by emancipation of the child *but not by the death of a parent obligated to support a child.* When a parent obligated to pay support dies, the amount of support may be modified, revoked or commuted to a lump sum payment, to the extent just or appropriate in the circumstances." (Emphasis added).

Example: The Supreme Court of Illinois upheld a similar provision against equal protection challenge: "Two reasonable justifications are given by defendant for singling out divorced parents. First, though a nondivorced parent may disinherit a dependent child, he may not disinherit his family. The surviving parent may renounce the will of the deceased parent and demand a statutory forced share of the deceased parent's estate. The forced share then becomes available for the support of the dependent child because the surviving parent remains obligated to support the child. In effect, a child of a nondivorced parent has some indirect security against the possible loss of support due to disinheritance. The dependent child of a divorced parent has no similar protection because a surviving divorced spouse is not entitled to a forced share of a former spouse's estate. * * * In balance, section 510(c) mitigates rather than aggravates inequality. Second, while it is comparatively rare for a nondivorced parent to leave a spouse and their children out of a will, it is not so uncommon for a divorced parent to do so. A divorced parent may establish a new family which may command primary allegiance in a subsequent will." *Kujawinski v. Kujawinski*, 71 Ill.2d 563, 17 Ill.Dec. 801, 376 N.E.2d 1382 (1978).

D. Traditional Criteria for Awarding Support

In awarding support, courts consider all relevant facts, including the needs of the child, the standard of living and circumstances of the parents, the relative financial means of the parents, the earning ability of the parents, the need and capacity of the child for education, including higher education, the age of the child, the financial resources and the earning ability of the child, the responsibility of the parents for the support of others, and the value of services contributed by the custodial parent. In cases of divorce, the UMDA § 309 lists similar factors and would also consider the standard of living the child would have enjoyed had the marriage not been dissolved.

E. Child Support Guidelines

Prodded by federal legislation, all states now have much more specific, often formulaic, child support guidelines that primarily orient themselves on the obligated (typical the non-custodial) spouse's income, or on the joint income of both parents. All states are mandated to have such guidelines, but they have freedom to experiment. State approaches range from assessing specific percentages (increasing with the number of children) of the non-custodial, absent parent's net or gross income, to extremely complex formulae.

Examples: (1) The divorce decree awarded custody of C to M. F was ordered to pay $275 a month in child support. Five years later, M filed to increase F's child support payments, alleging C's increased needs and F's increased income. At that time, M's net monthly income was $2,046 and F's net monthly income was $1,986. The trial court found that M had sustained her burden of proving C's increased needs and F's increased income. The court increased F's support obligation to $400 per month finding that it was obligated to follow the legislated child support guidelines that state the obligation in terms of specified percentages of the absent parent's income (20% for one child, progressing up to 50% for six children), with little room for discretion. F appealed. (Result: Affirmed. Child support guideline statute (1) did not violate the separation of powers clause requirement of the state Constitution, (2) did not deprive the noncustodial parent of procedural or substantive due process, and (3) did not infringe on the noncustodial parent's right to equal protection under the law.) *Boris v. Blaisdell*, 142 Ill.App.3d 1034, 97 Ill.Dec. 186, 492 N.E.2d 622 (1986).

(2) When C was born, M and F were married to other persons. M's marriage was dissolved. F remained married and had two children from his marriage. M filed for child support. The state child support guideline provided four separate charts based on the number of children. F argued that his obligation to support his two children from his existing marriage, in addition to C, justified use of the chart for three children. The trial court determined F's obligation to C using the chart for one child. (Result: Affirmed. Unable to present evidence of any special circumstances that would make a support obligation based on the one-child chart unjust or inappropriate, F failed to overcome the presumption that the trial court's application of the one-child chart was correct.) *Gilley v. McCarthy*, 469 N.W.2d 666 (Iowa 1991).

(3) M and F had two minor children but were never married. F, an actor, earned in excess of $300,000 per month and had agreed to pay $3,500 per month in child support as well as the children's medical expenses. F and his parents also voluntarily provided child care, a housekeeper, vacations, food, transportation, private schooling, and a 4–bedroom house with beach and tennis facilities. M sought to modify the support order to comply with statutory child support guidelines, and moved for full disclosure of F's assets. F stipulated that he had had a gross income of at least $1.4 million in each of the past three years, and stated that he could pay any reasonable amount the court determined to be necessary for the support of his children. The trial court ordered discovery regarding F's income, expenses and assets. (Result: Reversed, on the basis of *White v. Marciano*, 190 Cal.App.3d 1026, 235 Cal.Rptr. 779 (1987), where the court determined "evidence of detailed lifestyle and net worth to be relevant only in those situations where the ability of the noncustodial parent to make adequate support payments may be affected by the unwise expenditure of income to the detriment of the supported minor.

Where there is no question of the noncustodial parent's ability to pay any reasonable support order, we conclude that evidence of detailed lifestyle [is] irrelevant to the issue of the amount of support to be paid and thus protected from discovery and inadmissible in determining the support order.") *Estevez v. Superior Court*, 22 Cal.App.4th 423, 27 Cal.Rptr.2d 470 (1994).

(4) F had an extramarital affair with M. C was born, and F had no further contact with M or C. Initially, F was ordered to pay $200 per month in child support. When F's income increased dramatically, M petitioned to increase F's child support obligation. The trial court ordered F to pay $3,092 per month, with $1,780 reserved for a trust fund established for C's college education. The appellate court reversed, limiting the support payment to $1,312 per month (based on the first $6,250 of F's monthly income, the top income to which the statutory support guidelines explicitly applied, multiplied by 21 percent, the percentage applicable to one child). The appellate court disallowed the trust, finding that it improperly extended support beyond majority. (Result: Reversed. (1) The court may take into account income that exceeds the highest amount listed in the child support guidelines, and (2) an educational trust is not an award of post-majority support. "Obviously, to treat the monthly income figure of $6,250.00 as a cap and automatically to limit the award to 21 percent of that amount for a child whose non-custodial parent makes over $6,250.00 may be 'neither appropriate nor equitable.' * * * Rather than adopting either of these diametrically opposed approaches, we conclude that the trial court should retain the discretion to determine—as the guidelines provide, 'on a case-by-case basis'—the appropriate amount of child support to be paid when an obligor's net income exceeds $6,250.00 per month, balancing both the child's need and the parents' means.") *Nash v. Mulle*, 846 S.W.2d 803 (Tenn.1993).

F. Modification

Child support obligations are modifiable if circumstances change. Typical changes obligors assert are (1) unfavorable income and employment changes, (2) the needs of a subsequent family, or (3) disability. On behalf of the child, assertions for more support include (1) increase in the cost of living, (2) a special need, such as medical care, (3) increased need by reason of age, and (4) the obligated parent's increased income.

G. Child Support Enforcement Sanctions

Courts sometimes confuse or fail to distinguish sharply between superficially similar remedies, especially civil and criminal contempt. A century ago, the matter seemed quite clear: "If the contempt consists in the refusal of a party to do something which he is ordered to do for the benefit or advantage of the opposite party, the process is civil, and he stands committed till he complies with the order. The order in such a case is not in the nature of a punishment, but is coercive, to compel him to act in accordance with the order of the court. If, on the other hand, the contempt consists in the doing of a forbidden act, injurious to the opposite party, the process is criminal, and conviction is followed by fine or imprisonment, or both; and this is by way of punishment. In one case the private party is interested in the enforcement of the order, and, the moment he is satisfied, the imprisonment ceases, on the other hand, the state alone is interested in the enforcement of the penalty, it being a punishment which operates in terrorem, and by that means has a tendency to prevent a repetition of the offense in other similar cases." *State v. Knight,* 3 S.D. 509, 54 N.W. 412 (1893).

1. Civil Contempt

Civil contempt applies to a parent who has failed to pay, but who is able to meet the obligation. It may involve an open-ended jail sentence, allowing the defaulter to leave jail as soon as the specified payment is made.

2. Criminal Contempt

Criminal contempt applies to a willful default on a support judgment and carries a specific sentence.

3. Civil and Criminal Contempt Distinguished

The U.S. Supreme Court sees the difference between criminal and civil as follows: "[T]he critical features are the substance of the proceedings and the character of the relief that the proceeding will afford. 'If it is for civil contempt the punishment is remedial, and for the benefit of the complainant. But if it is for criminal contempt the sentence is punitive, to vindicate the authority of the court.' The character of the relief imposed is thus ascertainable by applying a few straightforward rules. If the relief provided is a sentence of imprisonment, it is remedial if 'the defendant stands committed unless and until he performs the affirmative act required by the court's order,' and is punitive if 'the sentence is limited to imprisonment for a definite period.' If the relief provided is a fine, it is remedial when it is paid to the complainant, and punitive when it is paid to the court, though a fine that would be payable to the court is also remedial when the defendant can avoid paying the fine simply by performing the affirmative act required by the court's order. These distinctions lead up to the fundamental proposition that criminal penalties may not be imposed on someone who has not been afforded the protections that the Constitution requires of such criminal proceedings, including the requirement that the offense be proved beyond a reasonable doubt." *Hicks on Behalf of Feiock v. Feiock*, 485 U.S. 624, 108 S.Ct. 1423, 99 L.Ed.2d 721 (1988).

4. Criminal Prosecution for Non–Support

A criminal prosecution for non-support may also be available, based on state statutes that focus on the existence of the duty to support or on a specific judgment. A sentence for criminal contempt or for criminal non-support may be suspended on condition that payment is made.

5. Federal Crime

The Child Support Recovery Act of 1992 makes willful failure to support a child in another state a federal crime. (18 U.S.C.A. § 228). Prosecution is available for arrearages exceeding $5,000 or remaining unpaid for longer than one year. Penalties range from imprisonment to fines. First offenses are misdemeanors. Repeat offenses are felonies. Federal courts may make the payment of spousal and child support a condition of probation. The federal act was amended in 1998, by the (officially titled) Deadbeat Parents Punishment Act, to add tougher felony penalties for the failure to pay arrearages outstanding for more than two years or in excess of $10,000. The constitutionality of the federal act has been repeatedly challenged as beyond Congress' legislative authority under the Commerce Clause, but has been widely upheld. *E.g., United States v. Kukafka*, 478 F.3d 531 (3d Cir. 2007); *United States v. Faasse*, 265 F.3d 475 (6th Cir. 2001) (en banc).

H. Conflicts of Laws Aspects of Child Support: The Uniform Interstate Family Support Act

Until relatively recently, jurisdiction in child support matters was governed by the Uniform Reciprocal Enforcement of Support Act (URESA), which had been adopted by all states. In 1992, encouraged by federal endorsement, the Uniform Interstate Family Support Act (UIFSA) began to replace URESA. UIFSA provides an updated approach to interstate support that runs in tandem with pervasive federal legislation in this field. Federal welfare reform legislation enacted in 1996 required states to enact UIFSA as a condition of receiving federal welfare funds, and all states have now done so. For the (now historical) record, URESA allowed a support action to be filed in the jurisdiction where the dependent resided. The action would then be heard where the obligor resided. This avoided the need for travel and overcame possible difficulties with personal jurisdiction. If the court at the obligor's residence found the obligor owing, the judgment would be enforced there. The award would then be forwarded to the initiating court to be paid to the dependent. UIFSA retains most of URESA's good features. It contains comprehensive long-arm provisions that enable a state to take jurisdiction over an absent party who has a significant connection with the state. When a state has taken jurisdiction and is the state of residence for any party, that state retains exclusive jurisdiction. If simultaneous proceedings are initiated in more than one state, the home state of the child takes priority in adjudicating the dispute.

I.   Federal Child Support Enforcement Legislation

Since 1975, federal legislation has strengthened nationwide enforcement of child support obligations. Washington imposes broad burdens on state welfare programs if they wish to participate in the federal scheme. The original purpose was to reduce the cost of welfare assistance then under the guise of the Aid to Families with Dependent Children (AFDC) program. In 1996, comprehensive federal welfare reform through the Personal Responsibility and Work Opportunity Reconciliation Act (PRWORA) replaced AFDC with the Temporary Assistance to Needy Families (TANF) program and further strengthened federal child support enforcement efforts. The new law requires mothers to cooperate in identifying fathers, facilitates establishment of paternity through voluntary acknowledgments without need for court action, and created a national "New Hire" database to help locate parents owing support. For a small fee, the child support enforcement is available to persons not receiving public aid. Wage withholding remains a key weapon and the states are required to apply guidelines to determine the level of child support awards. The federal pressure has resulted in a general strengthening of state child support laws across the United States.

J.   Full Faith and Credit

Under Article IV of the federal Constitution, "full faith and credit" is due to valid and final sister-state judgments. This rule means generally that accrued installments, reduced to a money judgment, are entitled to full faith and credit, whereas accrued installments *not* reduced to judgment are due full faith and credit only if the accrued installments are not modifiable where the judgment was rendered. Under the traditional rule, full faith and credit was not due to modifiable accrued installments nor to future support (which is always modifiable). Since 1994, the "Full Faith and Credit for Child Support Orders Act" (28 U.S.C.A. § 1738B) requires that if a sister-state child support order meets federal standards it may be (1) enforced in any state and (2) modified only in very limited circumstances. The

Act sets jurisdictional requirements substantially similar to those of the Parental Kidnaping Prevention Act. (Note: Full faith and credit does not extend to judgments rendered in a *foreign country*, although such judgments may be and often are accorded recognition under principles of "comity.")

K. Reciprocity: The Child's Duty to Support Parents

Traditionally, children were required to contribute to the support of their indigent parents. Many states continue to have such laws on the books, although they are rarely enforced. Courts have upheld such laws against constitutional challenge on the ground that they further the legitimate state purpose of alleviating some of the burden of caring for the indigent. In early 1996, welfare reform proposals sought to impose broad reimbursement liability on children of Medicaid recipients, especially children of elderly parents in nursing care.

Example: The California Supreme Court held constitutional a civil code provision that required adult children of parents receiving aid to the aged to contribute to their parents' support according to a fixed schedule. "Since these children received special benefits from the class of 'parents in need', it is entirely rational that the children bear a special burden with respect to that class." *Swoap v. Superior Court of Sacramento County*, 10 Cal.3d 490, 111 Cal.Rptr. 136, 516 P.2d 840 (1973).

Review Questions

1–3. Based on the following facts answer Questions 1 through 3: H and W are divorced and have one daughter, D. W has custody of D, and H is obligated to pay D's support. W is remarried to H_2, and they live in a state in which the age of majority is 18.

1. **T or F** At age 17, D inherits $500,000 from a paternal aunt. Since D now has sufficient means to support herself, H is no longer obligated to support her.

2. **T or F** H_2 has no obligation to support D.

3. **T or F** H moves to Kansas and defaults on his child support obligation. W must file an action in Kansas to enforce the support obligation.

4. **T or F** The common law imposed the duty to support the family's children on the father.

5. **T or F** The parents of a disabled child have no further duty of support when the child reaches the age of majority.

6. **T or F** A child of married parents in an intact family is entitled to enforce support for higher education, if a state statute makes such support available to children of divorced parents.

7. **T or F** Once emancipated, a minor child cannot revert to unemancipated status.

8. **T or F** Unlike alimony, child support obligations are not modifiable.

9. **T or F** It is unconstitutional for a state to require adult children to support their indigent parents.

10. **T or F** Generally, a parent's child support obligation ends upon the parent's or the child's death or the child's emancipation or reaching the age of majority.

11. **T or F** Freddie-the-Lout, a famous rock star, earns $50 million a year and must pay child support for one child. The state's statutory child support guideline percentage for one child is 20 percent. Freddie must pay $10 million per year.

VIII

Child Custody

■ ANALYSIS

A. **Child Custody During Marriage**
  1. Custody After Death of Parent(s)
  2. The Child Reaches Majority
B. **Child Custody Upon Divorce**
  1. Legal Custody Defined
  2. "Best Interests" Standard
  3. The "Tender Years" Presumption and the Maternal Preference Rule
  4. Religion
  5. Race
  6. Parent's Sexual Morality
  7. The ALI Principles' "Approximation Standard"
  8. Parent vs. "Third Party"
C. **Joint Custody**
D. **Rights of the Noncustodial Parent**
  1. Visitation Rights
  2. Restriction on Interstate Travel by Custodial Parent
  3. Enforcement of Visitation Rights
E. **Standards for Modification**
  1. Stability of Environment
  2. Change in Circumstances
F. **Visitation Rights of Third Parties**

G. Interstate Recognition of Custody Decrees
1.   "Forum Shopping" Under the "Old" Law
2.   Early Judicial Responses
3.   The Uniform Child Custody Jurisdiction Act
4.   The Federal Parental Kidnapping Prevention Act
5.   The Uniform Child Custody Jurisdiction & Enforcement Act
6.   International Custody Disputes—Hague Convention

A. Child Custody During Marriage

Parents are "natural guardians" of their child. During marriage, both parents jointly have custody. Short of violating the neglect, dependency, abuse, school attendance and other protective laws, the parents have full discretion to make all decisions related to the welfare of their child. While this prominently includes medical care, the U.S. Supreme Court has formulated exceptions for the case of abortion involving a "mature minor." Under state statutes, various (usually medical) decisions may be made by a mature minor without involving the parents.

1. Custody After Death of Parent(s)

When one parent dies, the survivor takes over custody and guardianship. If the parents are separated or divorced and the custodial parent dies, the noncustodial parent is first in line for custody. In special circumstances (especially if the surviving parent cannot offer a suitable home), custody and guardianship may be awarded to a third party such as a grandparent or stepparent. If the second parent dies, the court appoints a guardian for a minor child. The court may designate separately a guardian of the child's person and a guardian of the child's estate, although the same person usually serves both functions. If a guardian is designated in the deceased parents' or last-to-die parent's will, courts usually approve the appointment of that guardian, although they are not bound by such a designation.

2. The Child Reaches Majority

Parental control and obligations terminate when a child reaches majority or is emancipated. If the adult child cannot manage his or her own affairs, a parent may retain or regain guardianship under statutes providing for judicial appointment of conservators. In some cases, parents have success-fully used these statutes to "kidnap" their *adult* children away from religious cults in order to have them "deprogrammed." Unless the parents proceed as judicially appointed guardians, they may incur civil and criminal liability.

B. Child Custody Upon Divorce

1. Legal Custody Defined

On divorce of the child's parents, the court has power to award custody of the child to one parent, with or without visitation rights to the other, or jointly to both parents. During the pendency of divorce proceedings, the court may order temporary custody of children. Legal custody encompasses the right to make all decisions concerning the child's welfare, education, religion, growth and development. UMDA § 408(a) provides:

"[T]he custodian may determine the child's upbringing, including his education, health care, and religious training, unless the court after hearing, finds, upon motion by the noncustodial parent, that in the absence of a specific limitation of the custodian's authority, the child's physical health would be endangered or his emotional development significantly impaired."

2. "Best Interests" Standard

Most state statutes give the courts broad discretion in awarding custody upon divorce. The "best interests of the child" is the governing consideration, at least when the parties vying for custody are the child's parents.

a. Discretion

Because of the inexactness of statutory and common law child custody criteria, as a practical matter the custody decision (at least between two fit parents) is in the discretion of the trial judge, whose decision is seldom upset on appeal.

b. Historical Criteria

Prior to the widespread adoption of the "best interests" test, other factors, both statutory and common law, determined who received custody of the child on divorce. Under the old law, the father was entitled to custody. Later, the "tender years" presumption gave a strong preference to the mother of young children. Religion, race, and morality played important roles. Although these criteria have not been retained in full force or at all, they still influence many judges' custody decisions.

c. Modern Criteria

The UMDA § 402 provides that "[t]he court shall not consider conduct of a proposed custodian that does not affect his relationship to the child" and that "[t]he court shall determine custody in accordance with the best interest of the child. The court shall consider all relevant factors including: (1) the wishes of the child's parent or parents as to his custody; (2) the wishes of the child as to his custodian; (3) the interaction and interrelationship of the child with his parent or parents, his siblings, and any other person who may significantly affect the child's best interest; (4) the child's adjustment to his home, school and community; and (5) the mental and physical health of all individuals involved."

1) Preference of Child

The child's preference is considered when the child is of sufficient age to express an intelligent preference. In an exceptional case, this has included a seven year old child. *Flaherty v. Smith*, 87 Mich.App. 561, 274 N.W.2d 72 (1978). More typically, a child's preference will not be considered (or even elicited) unless the child is substantially older and more mature. Generally, the child is asked to express his or her preference in the privacy of the judge's chamber and not in open court. UMDA § 404(a) provides that "[T]he court may interview the child in chambers to ascertain the child's wishes as to his custodian and as to visitation. The court may permit counsel to be present at the interview. The court shall cause a record of the interview to be made and to be part of the record in the case."

2) **Court's Best Interests Findings**

A trial court is not required to use the words "best interests of the child" in its findings, but sufficient factual findings must be made to enable a reviewing court to determine whether the award is based on the child's best interests.

3) **Reports of Professionals**

Psychiatric testimony or the advice of social work professionals often is sought or offered in custody proceedings to aid the court in ascertaining the child's best interests. UMDA § 404(b) provides:

"The court may seek the advice of professional personnel, whether or not employed by the court on a regular basis. The advice given shall be in writing and made available by the court to counsel upon request. Counsel may examine as a witness any professional personnel consulted by the court."

Courts typically place considerable reliance on professional investigative reports. Such reports are often admitted by stipulation. Otherwise, the limits on hearsay evidence may prevent the use of such reports without the preparer and possibly other witnesses being present in court.

4) **Counsel for Child**

Since there may be a conflict if an attorney representing one of the parents also seeks to act for the child, the child's best interests may require that an attorney be appointed for him or her. UMDA § 310 provides:

"The court may appoint an attorney to represent the interests of a minor or dependent child with respect to his support, custody, and visitation. The court shall enter an order for costs, fees, and disbursements in favor of the child's attorney. The order shall be made against either or both parents, except that, if the responsible party is indigent, the costs, fees and disbursements shall be borne by the [appropriate agency]."

A guideline detailing the child's attorney's duties and responsibilities was provided by the bench and bar of a Wisconsin county and is quoted with approval in *Veazey v. Veazey,* 560 P.2d 382 (Alaska 1977).

3. The "Tender Years" Presumption and the Maternal Preference Rule

Under 13 →   Other things being equal, if the child was of "tender years" (generally pre-teenage), recent tradition all but automatically gave custody to the mother. Once hailed as one of the strongest presumptions in the law, today's trend in courts and legislatures is to eliminate the tender years doctrine, at least nominally. Several states have struck down the doctrine as violative of equal protection or of a state ERA. Others upheld the doctrine against constitutional challenge. Many courts, expressly or subconsciously, are still influenced by the doctrine, especially where it has been "repackaged" in overtly sex-neutral terms. Under the "primary caretaker" rule, for example, courts are permitted in assessing a child's "best interests" to consider whether one parent has taken primary responsibility in the past for the child's day-to-day care. One study found that for each child going to the father, seven go to the mother (Maccoby & Mnookin, 1992).

Example: The parents divorced after having been involved in an auto accident. M had been in a coma for 6 weeks. F alleged that M's mental condition resulting from the accident made her unfit. The appellate court reversed a custody award to F, stating "[w]hen the child will be equally well cared for by either parent, the mother, in preference to the father, is entitled to its custody. The latter is especially so where the child is of tender years." *Funkhouser v. Funkhouser,* 158 W.Va. 964, 216 S.E.2d 570 (1975).

4. Religion

Courts sometimes take the parents' religion (or lack thereof) into account in their determination of custody. This risks an award of custody based on the court's approval or disapproval of the parents' religious views, and may raise First Amendment issues. On solid ground, courts have considered whether a parent's religious beliefs or practices threaten the physical health or well-being of the child. If psychological effects are alleged, the difficulty is more serious.

Examples: (1) The district court awarded custody to F. The Maine Supreme Court remanded, concluding that the district court had given undue weight to the fact that, as a Jehovah's Witness, M would not consent to a blood transfusion for the son. "If and only if the court is satisfied that an immediate and substantial threat to the child's well-being is posed by the religious practices in question" need the court proceed to a balancing of interests. Any order should make the "least possible intrusion upon the constitutionally protected interests of the parent." *Osier v. Osier,* 410 A.2d 1027 (Me.1980).

(2) Trial court awarded custody to F, noting that M had been less willing to facilitate visitation than F and concern over testimony that "she practiced sado-masochism, was a bisexual and a pagan." (Result: Affirmed. "In urging reversal, [M] contends that this case is analogous to [*Pater v. Pater,* 63 Ohio St.3d 393, 588 N.E.2d 794 (1992)]. However, in *Pater,* the trial court's award of custody to the father was based solely on the fact that the mother was a Jehovah's Witness. . . . The Supreme Court of Ohio reversed the trial court's decision, finding that it was grounded in religious bias. Here, the facts are distinguishable. Unlike *Pater,* the trial court's decision was not based entirely on its biases or beliefs regarding appellant's personal choices. Rather, the decision was made after the court considered other relevant factors that supported its determination that it was in the best interest of the child that [F] be named the custodial parent.") *Dexter v. Dexter,* 2007 WL 1532084 (Ohio Ct. App. 2007).

5. Race

The U.S. Supreme Court has made it clear that courts may not consider race as the *sole* factor in determining the "best interests" of the child. A few courts have continued to suggest, however, that race or ethnic background may be considered as *one* factor among others in deciding custody.

Examples: (1) When M and F were divorced in Florida, M was awarded custody of their 3–year-old daughter. The following year, F filed to modify the custody order alleging changed conditions, specifically that M was then living with an African–American man whom she later married. Without addressing the parental qualifications of F, M, or M's new husband, the trial court reasoned that the daughter would be stigmatized by growing up in a racially mixed household and awarded custody to F. The appellate court affirmed, and M appealed. (Result: Reversed. The U.S. Supreme Court held that race may not be the sole determinant of a custody decision. "The Constitution cannot control such prejudices but neither can it tolerate them. Private biases may be outside the reach of the law, but the law cannot, directly or indirectly, give them effect. * * * The effects of racial prejudice, however real, cannot justify a racial classification removing an infant child from the custody of its natural mother found to be an appropriate person to have such custody.") *Palmore v. Sidoti*, 466 U.S. 429, 104 S.Ct. 1879, 80 L.Ed.2d 421 (1984).

(2) Trial court awarded custody of infant daughter to M, an African American woman, rather than F, a white male, partly on the rationale that "as an African–American woman, [M] could provide [child] with a 'breadth of cultural knowledge' as to her African–American heritage." F objected that trial court's reliance on race to assign custody was unconstitutional. (Result: Affirmed. In *Palmore*, "[t]he Supreme Court determined that the custody award was unconstitutional, not because the trial court considered race, but because the trial court considered *solely* race. . . . [I]t appears that so long as race is not the sole consideration for custody decisions, but only one of several factors, it is not an unconstitutional consideration.") *In re Marriage of Gambla*, 367 Ill.App.3d 441, 304 Ill.Dec. 770, 853 N.E.2d 847 (2006).

6. Parent's Sexual Morality

Traditionally, courts placed great emphasis on the custodial parent's sexual morality. An adulterous mother, or a parent who had engaged in a homosexual relationship stood a good chance of losing a disputed custody case. Today much less emphasis is placed on the parent's sexual morality. The prevailing view is that unless the (sexual) activities of the custodial parent have a direct and demonstrable effect on the child, they are irrelevant and UMDA § 402 provides specifically: "The court shall not consider conduct of a proposed custodian that does not affect his relationship to the child." As a practical matter, the issue of a parent's sexual morality is most frequently litigated in the context of attempts to obtain modification of a prior custody award.

Examples: (1) Upon their divorce, trial court awarded custody to M based partly on F's adultery. (Result: Although "an extramarital affair may not be a reliable indicator of the party's parenting ability," here "[t]he trial court instead used the defendant's affair with plaintiff's cousin, who was the children's nanny, as evidence of character flaws that do reflect directly on defendant's parenting ability. Specifically, defendant chose self-gratification over the children's interests and lacked insight and judgment regarding the potential effect of his actions on others, including the children.") *Berger v. Berger,* 277 Mich.App. 700, 747 N.W.2d 336 (2008).

(2) When M and F divorced after a six-year marriage, F was awarded custody of their child based partly on M's adulterous affair, alcohol use, and traffic violations. M argued that trial court erred by over-emphasizing her affair and disregarding F's own affair and viewing of internet pornography on home computers. (Result: Custody award to F affirmed. Given F's denials and the inability of M's computer expert to determine which user downloaded the pornographic images on the home computers, trial court was justified in finding that "moral fitness" factor favored F.) *DeVito v. DeVito,* 967 So.2d 74 (Miss. App. 2007).

(3) When M and F divorced, the trial court awarded custody of their three-year-old daughter to F on the ground that M had set a bad moral example by becoming involved in a sexual dating relationship with another man after her separation but before her divorce. Two years later, M sought to regain custody after learning that F had also been involved in sexual relationships during their separation. (Result: F's undisclosed affairs constituted a material change of circumstances justifying a transfer of custody to M. "[T]he evidence showed that the child had originally been placed with [F] due in large part to the trial court's conclusion that he would provide a better moral example than [M,] a conclusion that has now proven to be incorrect. [F] has engaged in sexual relationships outside of marriage on at least two occasions since being granted custody of O.H. Further, he placed O.H. in the primary care of his new wife, who herself had one illegitimate child from a previous relationship and who was pregnant by [F] at the time of their marriage.

Clearly, [F] never had a claim to the moral high road and has demonstrated that he is less able than [M] to provide a good moral example to O.H.") *Harrison v. Harrison*, 102 Ark.App. 131, 2008 WL 943915 (2008).

7. The ALI Principles' "Approximation Standard"

Reflecting widespread dissatisfaction with the indeterminacy of the prevailing "best interests" standard, in 2000 the American Law Institute's *Principles of the Law of Family Dissolution* proposed that the goal of trial judges should not be to decide which custodian is "best" for a child, but rather to "approximate" as closely as practical whatever custody arrangements existed before the family's breakup. Rather than select a "winner" who gains "sole custody" while the "losing" parent is relegated to the role of non-custodial "visitor," the ALI encourages parents to craft a "parenting plan" that reflects their own unique division of caregiving and decision-making roles. The premise of this approach is that it is better for the child to have continuity of past parenting roles and better for the parents, to the extent possible given the reality of the family's breakup, to preserve their own established patterns of interaction with the child. To date, West Virginia is the only state to have formally adopted the ALI's approximation standard. Previously, West Virginia had presumed that a parent who had been a child's "primary caretaker" should be awarded sole custody. Additional jurisdictions have accepted "the approximation principle [a]s a factor to be considered by the courts" in determining a child's "best interests." *E.g., In re Marriage of Hansen*, 733 N.W.2d 683 (Iowa 2007).

8. Parent vs. "Third Party"

A strong presumption holds that it is in the best interests of the child to be in the custody of a parent. Indeed, parents are *prima facie entitled* to have custody, and a statute authorizing courts to award custody to a third party without a finding that the parents are unfit or that some other extraordinary circumstances exist may violate due process. The N.Y. Court of Appeals noted: "Neither the lawyer nor judge in the judicial system nor the experts in psychology or social welfare may displace the primary responsibility of child raising that naturally and legally falls to those who conceive and bear children." *Bennett v. Jeffreys*, 40 N.Y.2d 543, 387 N.Y.S.2d 821, 356 N.E.2d 277 (1976). Accordingly, a court may not award custody to a third person merely because that person can do a "better job" than the parent of raising the child. Courts in different jurisdictions use somewhat different legal standards in deciding parent-versus-third-party custody cases. Some states entitle parents to custody unless they are "unfit" to parent. A larger number of states give courts somewhat more flexibility, allowing an award of custody to a non-parent where exceptional circumstances show that parent custody would be detrimental to a child. A few jurisdictions nominally use a "best interests" standard, but heavily weigh parent status in assessing a child's interests.

Examples: (1) M left her four-year-old son, C, in the care of her parents. Two months later, her parents obtained a court order for permanent custody of C, citing M's drug use. M later sought to regain custody, "stating that she had complied with the court's order that she rehabilitate herself, that she was married, and that she was leading a stable life." (Result: Remanded for reconsideration. "Historically, a parent's superior right to custody, as opposed to a non-parent, is paramount and generally requires that a third party prove that the parent is unfit by clear and convincing evidence.") *Baker v. Combs*, 248 S.W.3d 581 (Ky.App. 2008). *Caveat:* A Kentucky statute, Ky. Rev. Stat. § 403.270, makes a limited exception for "de facto custodians," defined as persons who have raised and supported a child as a "primary caregiver" for an extended period (six months if the child is younger than three years old, or one year if older); "de facto custodians" may seek to retain custody against a parent under the ordinary "best interests" standard.

(2) After M and F's divorce, their 13–year-old daughter, C, spent a summer living with her paternal aunt in Aspen, Colorado. In a subsequent custody battle between M and F, the paternal aunt intervened and the trial court granted her primary residential custody, finding that C was thriving in Colorado and wished to remain there. F challenged the custody decision as violating his constitutional rights as a parent. (Result: Remanded for reconsideration in light of properly refined standards. To avoid constitutional infirmity, standing to wrest custody from parents must be limited to third parties who have established "a parent-like relationship with the child." Such third parties, moreover, may gain custody only by showing "exceptional circumstances" and "that it would be clearly damaging, injurious or harmful for the child to remain in the parent's custody. . . . [T]he standard is qualitatively different from a best interests test because it does *not* allow the court to rely on its own subjective lifestyle preferences but

requires the court to focus on the level of harm that the child would suffer should the parent retain custody," though unfitness need not be shown.) *Fish v. Fish*, 285 Conn. 24, 939 A.2d 1040 (2008).

(3) When they divorced, H was awarded custody of four children born during their 15–year marriage, the youngest of whom was fathered by another man during a brief separation. M appealed, arguing that she was entitled to custody of the youngest child over F, a non-parent. (Result: Custody to H affirmed. Although Indiana law formerly entitled parents to custody unless unfit, recent case law has diminished the strength of parental preference. Now, "before placing a child in the custody of a person other than the natural parent, a trial court must be satisfied by clear and convincing evidence that the best interests of the child require such a placement. The trial court must be convinced that placement with a person other than a natural parent represents a substantial and significant advantage to the child. The presumption will not be overcome merely because 'a third party could provide the better things in life for the child.' " Here, H had assumed a full parental role with respect to all four children; granting custody to M would mean a move to Louisiana, uprooting five-year-old child from stable, extended family ties in Indiana.) *In re Marriage of Huss*, 888 N.E.2d 1238 (Ind. 2008).

(4) In a celebrated case, the deceased M's parents were awarded custody over F's objections. The Supreme Court of Iowa held that the best interests of the seven-year-old boy required that his 60–year-old maternal grandparents, who had been asked by F to take temporary charge of the child after M's death two years before and who had provided a "stable, dependable, conventional, middle-class, middlewest background," be awarded permanent custody as against F who had since remarried. The Court emphasized the likelihood of a seriously disrupting and disturbing effect upon the boy's development that could result from his return to the "unstable, unconventional, arty, Bohemian, and probably intellectually stimulating" household of F. *Painter v. Bannister,* 258 Iowa 1390, 140 N.W.2d 152 (1966). (Note: Don't be too concerned; the boy ultimately ended up in his father's custody.)

C. Joint Custody

Under "joint custody," both parents share legal and may share physical custody of the child. California provides: "In making an order for custody with respect to both parents, the court may grant joint legal custody without granting joint physical custody." West's Ann. Cal. Fam. Code § 3085. Joint legal custody entails shared authority in making major childrearing decisions (such as schooling, religious upbringing, and health care), while joint physical custody implies a more or less equal division of residential time with the child. A majority of the states have enacted legislation providing for joint custody as an alternative disposition. Several states make joint legal custody the preferred alternative and presume that joint custody is in the child's best interest. Most states are neutral on the question, and a few lean in the other direction and recognize a presumption that joint custody is ordinarily *not* in the child's best interests. Based on sometimes sad experience, there has been some retreat from the initial enthusiasm that had greeted the new "doctrine."

Examples: (1) After repeated instances of domestic violence by F, M took their infant daughter and fled from Idaho to Oregon, where she obtained a protective order. F filed for custody in Idaho and the court ordered M to return to Idaho to share custody with H. (Result: Reversed. "[A]lthough [W] argued that [F's] habitual domestic violence overcame the presumption that joint custody was in [child's] best interest, the magistrate made no findings and did not decide this issue. Under Idaho law, it is presumed that a continuing relationship with both parents is in the child's best interest. However, this presumption can be overcome if the court finds one parent is a habitual perpetrator of domestic violence.") *Schultz v. Schultz*, 145 Idaho 859, 187 P.3d 1234 (2008).

(2) Upon their separation, trial court granted primary physical custody of the couple's two children to M; the court also granted M and F joint legal custody under which M "shall have decision-making authority regarding all issues affecting the minor children except for sports and extracurricular activities, which shall be decided jointly between the parties." F appealed. (Result: Reversed in part. "There is no presumption in favor of joint custody; however, it must be considered by the trial court upon the request of either parent. Thus, the trial court may grant legal custody only to one party, joint custody to both, or, if proper findings are made, joint legal custody with a split in decision-making authority." Here, evidence

(including that F had "body slammed" M 20 to 50 times during the marriage) supported trial court's conclusion that primary physical custody with M was in children's "best interests." However, trial court failed to justify its decision limiting F's role in joint legal custody. "On remand, the trial court may allocate decision-making authority between the parties again; however, were the court to do so, it must set out *specific findings* as to why deviation from 'pure' joint legal custody is *necessary*. Those findings must detail why a deviation from 'pure' joint legal custody is in the *best interest of the children*. As an example, past disagreements between the parties regarding matters affecting the children, such as where they would attend school or church, would be sufficient, but mere findings that the parties have a tumultuous relationship would not."). *Hall v. Hall*, 655 S.E.2d 901 (N.C. App. 2008).

(3) Upon divorce, trial court awarded joint legal and physical custody of the parties' three children to M and F, with residential custody to alternate between parents every six months. M did not contest joint legal custody, but challenged award of joint physical custody as contrary to children's best interests. (Result: Reversed. Traditionally, Iowa courts disfavored joint physical custody on the grounds that "divided custody is destructive of discipline, induces a feeling of not belonging to either parent, and in some instances can permit one parent to sow seeds of discontent concerning the other." Statutory enactments in 1997 and 2004 now "require that courts consider joint physical care at the request of any party and that it make specific findings when joint physical care is rejected." While this legislation creates no presumption in favor of joint physical custody, "the notion that joint physical care is strongly disfavored except in exceptional circumstances is subject to reexamination in light of changing social conditions and ongoing legal and research developments. Increasingly in Iowa and across the nation, our family structures have become more diverse. While some families function along traditional lines with a primary breadwinner and primary caregiver, other families employ a more undifferentiated role for spouses or even reverse 'traditional' roles. A one-size-fits-all approach in which joint physical care is universally disfavored is thus subject to serious question given current social realities." Here, evidence that M had been the children's primary caregiver and that the parents had "significant difficulties in communications," "considerable mutual distrust and a high level of conflict" established

that the children's best interests would be served by sole physical custody with M.) *In re Marriage of Hansen*, 733 N.W.2d 683 (Iowa 2007).

D. Rights of the Noncustodial Parent

Traditionally, courts have awarded sole custody of a child to one parent. Typically, that parent obtains legal and physical custody, and the other parent is awarded visitation rights. Recently, the concept of joint and shared custody has made significant inroads on the traditional sole custody concept. "Joint custody" provides a "decision-participating" role for the parent who does not have physical custody and who, typically, pays support.

1. Visitation Rights

Courts have held that the right of a parent to the companionship of his or her child is a fundamental constitutional right that may not be restricted without evidence that the parent's activities may tend to impair the child's emotional or physical health. Courts have rejected the argument that this entitles each parent to a 50 percent split of legal and physical custody. *E.g., In re Marriage of Arnold*, 270 Wis.2d 705, 679 N.W.2d 296 (App. 2004). But courts have accepted that non-custodial parents may be constitutionally entitled to reasonable visitation. Jurisdictions differ on the strength of showing that must be made to deny or take away visitation rights. First amendment issues may arise when the custodial parent complains that the noncustodial parent uses visitation to instruct the child in the noncustodial parent's religion. Granting that the custodial parent has the right to make ultimate decisions concerning the child's religious upbringing, some courts have nevertheless held that a noncustodial parent cannot be enjoined from discussing religion with his child or involving his child in religious activities in absence of a showing that the child would be thereby harmed. *E.g., In re Marriage of Murga*, 103 Cal.App.3d 498, 163 Cal.Rptr. 79 (1980).

UMDA § 407 provides:

"(a) A parent not granted custody of the child is entitled to reasonable visitation rights unless the court finds, after a hearing, that visitation would endanger seriously the child's physical, mental, moral, or emotional health. (b) The court may modify an order * * * whenever modification would serve the best interest of the child; but the court shall not restrict a parent's visitation rights unless it finds that the visitation would endanger seriously the child's physical, mental, moral, or emotional health."

Example: Upon their divorce, M and F were granted joint legal custody, while child lived primarily with F. On F's request, trial court later modified order, granting sole custody to F and terminating all contact with M. (Result: Denial of visitation reversed. "There is little case law defining the contours of the 'extreme' grounds that permit a trial court to deny, rather than merely limit, the access and visitation rights of a parent. This perhaps indicates that the remedy is so strict that courts only apply it in rare circumstances. . . . In the present case, there is insufficient evidence to establish that [M's] behavior constituted 'extreme' grounds meriting a denial of access and visitation rights. The most damaging piece of evidence presented by [F] is the audio tape in which [M] is heard threatening to do harm to herself and the two children. This is hardly stable and appropriate behavior, but even indulging all assumptions in favor of affirming the trial court—assuming that the tape is properly authenticated and that [M] was not merely 'joking,' as she contends—this conduct cannot be considered 'extreme' under our jurisprudence.") *In re M.S.R.*, 2007 WL 3228072 (Tex.App. 2007).

2. Restriction on Interstate Travel by Custodial Parent

To protect the exercise of the noncustodial parent's visitation rights, it was once common for courts to order the custodial parent not to take the child out of the jurisdiction without the court's specific permission. A violation of the court's order could be prosecuted as contempt. Recently, such restrictions have been challenged as unconstitutionally limiting the custodial parent's right to interstate travel, though most courts have rejected the claim. *E.g., Meadows v. Meadows,* ___ So.2d ___, 2008 WL 3582691 (Ala.Civ.App. 2008); *In re Marriage of Robison*, 311 Mont. 246, 53 P.3d 1279 (2002).

The trend in recent years has been to liberalize the custodial parent's ability to relocate. If the custodial parent's reasons for wishing to move are *bona fide* (*e.g.,* a significantly better professional opportunity beckons), and it appears that defeating the other parent's visitation rights is not the real motivation, permission to move usually (though not always) will be granted. A compensating change in visitation arrangements may then be made. For instance, the noncustodial parent may be granted longer-term summer visitation, instead of frequent weekend visitation.

Examples: (1) Following the parties' divorce in 2000, M was awarded primary custody of their two children. In 2001, M sought to move from Arkansas to Tennessee, where her new husband was stationed in the military and the trial court ordered a change of custody to F. The trial court reasoned that "it was not in the best interest of the children to move to Tennessee, because of the disruption in the relationship between the children and [F] and the strong family ties the children had formed in Northwest Arkansas." (Result: Reversed. "[R]elocation of a primary custodian and his or her children alone is not a material change in circumstance [permitting modification of a custody award]. We announce a presumption in favor of relocation for custodial parents with primary custody. . . . The custodial parent who bears the burden and responsibility for the child is entitled to seek a better life for herself or himself and the children, as enjoyed by the noncustodial parent." The noncustodial parent must rebut the presumption in favor of relocation by offering persuasive evidence that a move would be contrary to the child's best interests.) *Hollandsworth v. Knyzewski*, 353 Ark. 470, 109 S.W.3d 653 (2003).

(2) Following the parties' divorce in 1999, primary physical custody of the two children was awarded to F, but both parents remained actively involved in caring for the children on substantially equal terms. In 2001, F sought to move from Georgia to Alabama "to enhance his economic opportunity and to leave behind the pre-divorce chapter of his life." M objected and successfully sought a change of custody. (Result: Change of custody upheld. "When exercising its discretion in relocation cases, as in all child custody cases, the trial court must consider the best interests of the child and cannot apply a bright-line test." In this case, the trial court reasonably found "that Dr. Bodne's decision to move out of state seriously affected an important aspect of the parties' divorce agreement, namely, that Ms. Bodne continue her equal involvement in the children's lives, and had a direct negative effect on the children as testified to by numerous witnesses, including the children's pediatrician, minister, and family friends.") *Bodne v. Bodne*, 277 Ga. 445, 588 S.E.2d 728 (2003).

(3) When conflicts developed in their marriage, M left marital home in Birmingham, Alabama, taking the couple's infant son, C, to live with her at her parents' home in Schaumburg, Illinois.

In subsequent divorce, Alabama trial court granted custody to M on condition that she return to Alabama and continue to live within 60 miles of county where F resided. (Result: Affirmed. "[T]he policy of our state . . . is to value close and frequent contact between a child and both of his or her parents. The child flourished in the Birmingham area in the care and company of both parents and his extended paternal family, and, from what appears in the record, the child was exposed to similar educational and cultural experiences in both Schaumburg and the Birmingham area. Based on the evidence in the present case, the trial court could certainly have determined, based on the conflicting testimony, that the distance between Schaumburg and Alabama and the cost of visitation would make the father's visitation more difficult and would negatively impact the amount of contact the father would have with the child, thus forming the basis for a conclusion that the territorial restriction is in the best interest of the child. Because the child's best interest is served by the restriction, it is not an unconstitutional infringement on the mother's right to travel.") *Meadows v. Meadows*, ___ So.2d ___, 2008 WL 3582691 (Ala.Civ.App. 2008).

3. Enforcement of Visitation Rights

If the custodial parent interferes with the non-custodial parent's visitation rights, the proper remedy is judicial enforcement of the custody order, not self-help. Suspending the payment of child support without a specific court order is not a legitimate response. UMDA § 315 provides: "If a party fails to comply with a provision of a decree or temporary order or injunction, the obligation of the other party to make payments for support or maintenance or to permit visitation is not suspended; but he may move the court to grant an appropriate order."

Custody orders are enforceable by the court's civil or criminal contempt power. In addition, a custodial parent's protracted denial or frustration of the other parent's visitation rights may be grounds for a change in custody. Finally, some jurisdictions also allow non-custodial parents to recover tort damages for interference with visitation rights.

Examples: (1) Upon their divorce, M was awarded primary custody with "standard" visitation rights to F. F later repeatedly asked the court to hold M in contempt for obstructing his exercise of visitation rights. Trial court ultimately transferred custody to F and deferred determination of M's possible contempt of visitation order. (Result: M's appeal dismissed, pending trial court's resolution of contempt proceedings.) *Greenwood v. Greenwood*, ___ So.2d ___, 2008 WL 3983852 (Ala.Civ.App. 2008).

(2) M was held in contempt for interfering with F's visitation rights. She unsuccessfully invoked her right to free speech when she had been specifically ordered "to do everything in her power to create in the [children's] minds a living, caring feeling toward the father * * * and to convince the children that it is the mother's desire that they see and love their father." The Florida Supreme Court found that "[t]he cause of the blind, brainwashed, bigoted belligerence of the children toward the father grew from the soil nurtured and tilled by the mother." *Schutz v. Schutz*, 581 So.2d 1290 (Fla.1991).

(3) Upon their divorce, M and F were each granted custody of one of their two children, with visitation rights to the other. Thereafter, M fled to her native Egypt with both children. F sued M and her mother in tort for interfering with his custody and visitation rights and recovered a judgment of more than $3 million in compensatory and punitive damages. (Result: Affirmed. Maryland law recognizes a cause of action in tort for wrongful interference with both custodial and visitation rights. The damage award here was reasonable, and a parent need not plead economic loss. "Evidence of the ongoing absence of the children also indicates to us that [F] will never be fully compensated for the loss of society and companionship that he has suffered at the hands of the Appellants.") *Khalifa v. Shannon*, 404 Md. 107, 945 A.2d 1244 (2008).

E. Standards for Modification

Once a final (non-temporary) custody order is made, the typical court will modify the award only upon proof of substantially changed circumstances that indicate that modification is in the best interests of the child.

1. Stability of Environment

Judicial reluctance to modify a custody award is based on the perception that "shuffling" a child between parents is disruptive and harmful to the child's emotional development. Secondly, if access to modification is too easy, the child may become the victim of a continuing legal battle between the parents.

2. Change in Circumstances

A change of circumstances sufficient to change custody typically involves activities of the custodial parent that are likely to affect the child adversely. A change in circumstances that improves the *non*custodial parent's ability to raise the child rarely suffices to obtain a change in custody, unless combined with a significant deterioration in the custodial parent's ability to function as a parent. To reduce vexatious custody litigation brought by unhappy noncustodial parents, the UMDA significantly raised the hurdles against changes in custody. § 409 allows a change during the first two years after a custody award only if there is "reason to believe the child's present environment may endanger seriously his physical, mental, moral, or emotional health." After two years, UMDA makes modification available only if (a) the custodial parent agrees; (b) the child "has been integrated into the family of the petitioner with consent of the custodian"; or (c) "the child's present environment endangers seriously his physical, mental or emotional health, and the harm likely to be caused by a change of environment is outweighed by its advantages to him."

Examples: (1) "[W]e cannot hold the statute is satisfied where the court finds only that the interests of the children would be 'best served' by a change in custody, and that such a change would be 'to the environmental benefit' of the children. For the court in this case to have jurisdiction to modify a custody decree under [the UMDA], there must be a finding of danger to the physical, mental, moral, or emotional health of the children in their present environment, and a finding that the harm likely to be caused by such a change is outweighed by its advantages to them." *In re Custody of Dallenger*, 173 Mont. 530, 568 P.2d 169 (1977).

(2) Upon their divorce, Alaska trial court approved custody agreement directing that six-year-old daughter, C, would live with M in Alaska during the school year and with F in Illinois during summer vacations. Toward the end of C's first summer in Illinois, M and F orally agreed to "reverse" the custody arrangement so that C would remain in Illinois for the school year. M shortly thereafter changed her mind, leading F to seek a modification of the custody order. Trial court granted modification, citing C's integration into F's household once the school year began. (Result: Reversed. To justify a modification of custody, the "movant must prove a substantial change in

circumstances as a threshold matter." Here, C "was scheduled to spend the summer with [F] in Illinois under the existing agreement. Her integration into [F's] household was a natural consequence of visitation, not a substantial change in circumstances, and her return to Alaska at the end of the summer was anticipated by the custody arrangement, and did not amount to a disruption in her stability.") *McLane v. Paul*, 189 P.3d 1039 (Alaska 2008).

F. Visitation Rights of Third Parties

By 2000, every state had enacted legislation permitting certain non-parents to seek court-ordered visitation with a child. The statutes varied considerably, some limiting visitation to grandparents while others listed additional persons with standing to seek contact; many statutes permitted court intervention only in families where the parents were already separated by death or divorce, but some allowed court action even against intact families.

In *Troxel v. Granville*, 530 U.S. 57, 120 S.Ct. 2054, 147 L.Ed.2d 49 (2000), the U.S. Supreme Court recognized substantial constitutional limitations on these measures. In that case, a mother had challenged a visitation order issued pursuant to a particularly broad Washington statute that permitted "any person" to obtain visitation if a judge determined that contact would be in the child's "best interests." The order had been entered at the request of grandparents following the death of their son, the children's father. The Supreme Court, in a deeply fractured decision, held that the visitation order violated the mother's fundamental constitutional right to make basic child-rearing decisions. At a minimum, Justice O'Connor's plurality opinion stated, a trial court must give "special weight" to a parent's objections to contact before ordering visitation. The visitation order in *Troxel* failed this requirement because the trial judge had presumed that contact with grandparents is beneficial for children without deferentially considering the mother's reasons for wishing to curtail contact. Importantly, however, the Court in *Troxel* did *not* strike down Washington's visitation law on its face or hold that parents are constitutionally entitled to block all visitation with non-parents.

State courts have responded inconsistently to *Troxel*'s splintered holding. Some have gone well beyond *Troxel* in holding facially unconstitutional grandparent visitation laws that were considerably narrower than the statute *Troxel* itself left standing. *E.g., In re Marriage of Howard*, 661 N.W.2d 183 (Iowa 2003); *Wickham v. Byrne*, 199 Ill.2d 309, 263 Ill.Dec. 799, 769 N.E.2d 1 (2002). Others have applied the decision much more narrowly, sustaining visitation statutes and orders that gave due deference to parental objections. *E.g., Glidden v. Conley*, 175 Vt. 111, 820 A.2d 197 (2003); *Blixt v. Blixt*, 437 Mass. 649, 774 N.E.2d 1052 (2002).

Example: After *Troxel*, Arkansas rewrote its grandparent visitation statute to recognize a presumption that a fit parent's decisions concerning visitation by non-parents are in the best interests of their children. The statute permits grandparents to overcome that presumption by showing that (1) they have "established a significant and viable relationship with the child" and (2) visitation would serve the "best interests" of the child. Applying this statute, a trial court awarded visitation to maternal grandparents following the death of their daughter, over the objection of the custodial F. (Result: Grandparents indisputably had established a "significant and viable relationship" with their grandson. Yet, "[b]ecause the [grandparents] did not prove a loss of the relationship between them and [child] that would likely harm [child], they failed to establish that court-ordered visitation was in [child's] best interest and therefore failed to rebut the statutory presumption.") *Oldham v. Morgan*, 372 Ark. 159, ___ S.W.3d ___ (2008).

G. Interstate Recognition of Custody Decrees

1. "Forum Shopping" Under the "Old" Law

Because a custody determination remains modifiable if circumstances change, it was not viewed as a final order and was not entitled to Full Faith and Credit in sister states. *May v. Anderson*, 345 U.S. 528, 73 S.Ct. 840, 97 L.Ed. 1221 (1953).

Modifiability of custody awards led to forum shopping. A typical scenario involved a dissatisfied parent who "kidnapped" the child and took it to another state where a sympathetic court would be asked for modification of the custody determination on the basis of "changed circumstances." Until relatively recently, if the child was present in the jurisdiction and the petitioning parent alleged conduct by the other parent that was detrimental to the child, many courts were willing to hear such cases and redetermine custody. Note that kidnapping one's own child in violation of a court order was not a crime under state or federal kidnapping laws, although it was punishable by contempt.

2. Early Judicial Responses

To reduce abuses, some courts adopted a "clean hands" doctrine under which they would refuse jurisdiction over a custody dispute brought to them by a parent who had obtained custody of the child in violation of an existing custody order. Today, the problem is covered by state (UCCJA) and federal (PKPA) statutes.

3. The Uniform Child Custody Jurisdiction Act

In 1968, the National Conference of Commissioners on Uniform State Laws promulgated the Uniform Child Custody Jurisdiction Act (UCCJA). The Act responded to the then rapidly growing problem of parental "kidnapping" by fostering cooperation among states involved in a custody dispute. The Act was soon adopted (with some modifications) in every jurisdiction.

a. Purposes of UCCJA

The UCCJA sought to (1) provide means to avoid jurisdictional competition and conflict between courts of different states in matters of child custody, and (2) assure that litigation concerning custody takes place in the state with which the child and his family have the closest connection.

b. Statutory Provisions

Under the UCCJA one court assumes full and continuing responsibility for the custody of a particular child. Usually this is the court with the best access to relevant information about the child and its family. That court's judgment is to be enforced in other states who "shall not modify" it (UCCJA § 14). All modifications are to be made by the original court, unless the parties and the child no longer have appreciable ties with that court, or that court declines to exercise its jurisdiction.

UCCJA § 8 provides that a court may decline to exercise jurisdiction if the petitioner: (1) "has wrongfully taken the child from another state or has engaged in similar reprehensible conduct", or (2) "without consent of the person entitled to custody, has improperly removed the child from the physical custody of the person entitled to custody or has improperly retained the child after a visit or other temporary relinquishment of physical custody." UCCJA §§ 12, 13, 14 provide that any custody decree rendered pursuant to the Act must be respected and enforced, subject to modification only if the court which rendered the original decree did not have jurisdiction *and* the modifying court has jurisdiction. The Act also provides a procedure for the filing and enforcement of custody orders in other states.

Right to make own decisions

4. The Federal Parental Kidnapping Prevention Act

Since 1980, federal legislation mandates that Full Faith and Credit be given to sister-state custody decrees. Exceptions are (1) where the original forum did not have jurisdiction, or (2) where it declines to exercise jurisdiction, or (3) when an emergency (*e.g.,* abuse, neglect, abandonment) requires intervention to protect the child. The parties must have had notice and an opportunity to be heard. The parent locator facilities developed under the child support enforcement program are made available.

Examples: (1) M and F's North Dakota divorce decree awarded custody to M. Following the divorce, M continued to live in North Dakota with the couple's two sons. F moved to Pennsylvania to live with his parents. Following an extended visit with his sons in Pennsylvania, F refused to return them to M and sought custody in a Pennsylvania court. F was granted custody and M appealed. (Result: Decision vacated. The PKPA required that Pennsylvania relinquish jurisdiction to North Dakota, which had proper subject matter jurisdiction to enter the original decree and had not lost that jurisdiction.) *Barndt v. Barndt,* 397 Pa.Super. 321, 580 A.2d 320 (1990).

(2) M and F divorced when their son (S) was three years old. M was granted custody by a Washington court. Three years later, M accepted a job in Germany and enrolled S in a German boarding school where S lived until he was 10, seeing M irregularly on holidays and weekends. M and S returned to the United States and began living in California, moving 4 times during the next 2 years. During this period, visitation with F in Washington state resumed. When S was twelve years old, M entered law school and S lived with M's former boyfriend, seeing M on weekends and F during school vacations. During his visits with F, S saw a counselor who ultimately recommended that custody be changed to F. F then petitioned a Washington court to modify custody, the court changed custody to F, and M appealed on jurisdictional grounds. The appeals court reversed, and F appealed. (Result: Washington had continuing jurisdiction to modify custody under UCCJA and PKA. "It appears that the majority of appellate courts which have addressed the issue presented here hold that the state in which the initial decree was entered has exclusive continuing jurisdiction to modify the initial decree if: (1) one of the parents continues to reside in the decree state; and (2) the child continues to have some connection with the decree state, such as visitation.") *Greenlaw v. Smith,* 123 Wash.2d 593, 869 P.2d 1024 (1994).

In the case of interstate or international child-snatching, the PKPA invokes FBI assistance under the Fugitive Felon Act, but only if the violation of a judicial custody order is a *felony* under state law. A majority of the states now have enacted such felony statutes. Note: Parental kidnapping of a child remains exempt from criminal prosecution under the federal kidnapping statute (18 U.S.C.A. 1201): "The federal kidnaping statute, enacted initially in 1932, * * * was limited to cases of kidnaping involving interstate commerce in which the victim was held 'for reward or ransom'. * * * The obvious purpose of such restricted scope for that crime ('for reward or ransom') was to eliminate from the statute's coverage the kidnaping, conspiracy to kidnap or aiding and abetting in the kidnaping by a parent of his or her child." *United States v. Boettcher,* 780 F.2d 435 (4th Cir.1985).

5. The Uniform Child Custody Jurisdiction & Enforcement Act

The UCCJA has been supplanted almost everywhere by a new uniform act, the Uniform Child Custody Jurisdiction and Enforcement Act (UCCJEA). The UCCJEA was offered in 1997 to clarify the jurisdictional rules provided by the complex interaction of the UCCJA and the PKPA. In general, UCCJEA continues the UCCJA model but directs that the child's "home state" shall have exclusive and continuing jurisdiction over custody disputes until the state determines that it has lost all significant connections with the parties. The Act also bars states from modifying the custody orders issued by other states and provides for various enforcement mechanisms. As of 2008, UCCJEA had been adopted in all but four states.

Example: In 2000, a Maine trial court entered a custody order awarding primary custody of a child, C, to M, a Maine resident, with visitation each July with F, a resident of Alabama. After the July 2005 visit, F refused to return C to Maine. When M sought to enforce the Maine custody order in Maine eleven months later, F informed the court that he had filed his own custody action in Alabama. The Maine trial court thereafter ceded jurisdiction to the Alabama court on the ground that the child's "home state" was now Alabama. (Result: Vacated and remanded. Under the PKPA, Maine has exclusive, continuing jurisdiction over custody matters in this case because it properly exercised jurisdiction in the initial custody order and Maine remains the resident of the child or one of the parents. "As a result, a court of another state may not modify Maine's custody or visitation determination in this case unless and until the Maine court has declined to exercise its jurisdiction to modify such determination." "Pursuant to the UCCJEA, a Maine court 'may decline to exercise its jurisdiction at any time if it determines that it is an inconvenient forum under the circumstances and that a court of another state is a more appropriate forum.' " Here, the Maine trial court failed to make sufficient findings that Alabama is a more convenient forum, instead finding that the child's holdover from the summer visit had made Alabama the child's new "home state." "[A]lthough a determination as to a child's 'home state' is required under the PKPA when determining which state court should assume *initial* jurisdiction for the purpose of making child custody determinations, this analysis does not apply to a court's decision to *retain* jurisdiction. Second, pursuant to the PKPA, the court in Alabama may assume jurisdiction only if the court in Maine first declines jurisdiction for inconvenient forum; the Maine District Court does not cede its exclusive jurisdiction in response to Alabama's purported assumption of jurisdiction.") *Cole v. Cushman*, 946 A.2d 430 (Me. 2008).

6.   International Custody Disputes—Hague Convention

In 1985, the U.S. Senate ratified the Hague Convention on the Civil Aspects of International Child Abduction. The Convention facilitates the return of abducted children and the exercise of visitation rights across international boundaries giving jurisdiction to the court at the place of the child's "habitual residence." By 2008, the treaty was in effect between the United States and more than 70 countries. The Hague Convention and U.S. implementing legislation (International Child Abduction Remedies Act, 42 U.S.C.A. § 11601 *et seq.*), are powerful weapons in the orderly resolution of international child custody disputes. U.S. courts have not hesitated to return even U.S.–born children abroad, where an American parent had brought his or her child to the United States in violation of a foreign custody order. In the U.S., the "International Parental Kidnapping Crime Act" (18 U.S.C.A. § 1204) has added criminal clout to the Convention's civil sanctions.

Example: F, a German citizen, and M, a U.S. citizen stationed with the U.S. Army in Germany, married and had one son (S) in Germany. After several trial separations, F ordered M to leave their apartment with S and put most of their belongings in the hallway. Four days later, after F had visited with S several times, M took S to the U.S. and filed for divorce in Ohio where she was awarded temporary custody of S. In Germany, F sought and was awarded custody of S by a German court. F also filed a petition in U.S. federal court, alleging that M had wrongfully removed S from Germany in violation of the Hague Convention. The district court denied F's claim, and he appealed. (Result: Reversed and remanded; F's claim reinstated. "Under the Convention, the removal of a child from one country to another is wrongful when: (a) it is in breach of rights of custody attributed to a person, an institution or any other body, either jointly or alone, under the law of the State in which the child was habitually resident immediately before the removal or retention; and (b) at the time of removal or retention those rights were actually exercised, either jointly or alone, or would have been so exercised but for the removal or retention. * * * The district court appears to agree that before the argument of July 27, 1991, Thomas was a habitual resident of Germany. The district court, however, found that Thomas's habitual residence was 'altered' from Germany to the United States when Mr. Friedrich forced Mrs. Friedrich and Thomas to leave the family apartment. Habitual residence cannot be so easily altered. Even if we accept the district court's finding that Mr. Friedrich forced Mrs. Friedrich to leave the family apartment, no evidence supports a finding that Mr. Friedrich forced Mrs. Friedrich to remove Thomas from Germany.") *Friedrich v. Friedrich*, 983 F.2d 1396 (6th Cir.1993).

Review Questions

1. T or **F** After parents are divorced, and one parent has obtained custody of their children, the custodial parent has discretion to specify in his/her will who will get custody of the children upon his/her death.

2. **T** or F In their will, parents may specify a guardian for their surviving child.

3. T or F Which of the following criteria may be important factors in awarding custody?

   A. Parent's wishes

   B. Child's wishes

   C. Moral/sexual conduct of each proposed custodian

   D. Child's adjustment to his/her home, school and community

   E. Parents' premarital agreement

   F. Parental role division prior to divorce

4. **T** or F If a court awards legal custody to only one parent, the noncustodial parent has a right to visitation.

5. T or **F** A joint custody arrangement divides physical custody between the parents, but only one parent has ultimate decision-making power, *i.e.*, legal custody.

6. **T** or F A noncustodial parent's petition for change of custody will not be granted on the sole ground that he or she has experienced a substantial improvement in circumstances.

7. T or **F** Under the UMDA, once a visitation order is entered it may not be modified for two years.

8. **T** or F Under the UMDA, a parent's visitation rights may be restricted if it can be shown that this would be in the child's best interest.

9. **T** or F A court must determine child custody "in the best interests of the child."

10. T or F   Natural parents have a constitutional right to the companionship of their child.

11. T or F   Joint custody gives both parents legal custody.

12. T or F   If in the child's best interests, a court will enforce a grandparent's visitation rights to his or her grandchild notwithstanding the objections of married parents in an intact family.

13. T or F   The "tender years presumption" favoring the mother as custodian of young children has all but disappeared from custody statutes and case law.

14. T or F   There is a strong presumption that it is in the "best interest" of a child to be in the custody of a parent, even if a foster parent or third party could seemingly do a better job.

15. T or F   The court may award custody *sua sponte*, even if the decision resolves the dispute against the wishes of both parents.

16. T or F   M blocks F from visiting their children. F is entitled to refuse to make child support payments.

17. T or F   When M and F divorce, F (who is unemployed) is awarded custody of the children. M is ordered to pay child support from her modest income as a lawyer. F wins the "Powerball" lottery. M may have the support order terminated based on F's enormously improved ability to provide for the children.

18. T or F   Although modifiable, judicial child custody determinations are entitled to Full Faith and Credit.

*

IX

The Parental Obligation of Care and Control, and the Juvenile Court System

■ ANALYSIS

A. **Child Dependency**
B. **Child Neglect and Abuse**
    1.   Civil Standard
    2.   Criminal Sanctions
C. **Constitutional Rights**
    1.   Vagueness of Statutory Standards
    2.   Right to Counsel
    3.   Standard of Proof
    4.   Freedom of Religion
    5.   Home Visits and the Fourth Amendment

6. State's Responsibility to Intervene—Liability for Failure to Protect?

D. Parental Control Over a Child's Medical Care

1. Physical Health
2. The First Amendment Issue
3. Mental Health
4. Minor's Consent to Medical Treatment

E. Child Abuse

1. Abuse Reporting Statutes and Registries
2. The Battered Child Syndrome

F. Disposition by the Juvenile Court

1. Guardianship
2. Foster Care
3. Institutionalization
4. Termination of Parental Rights

G. Criminal Procedure

1. History and Development
2. The Need for Reform
3. Status Offenses and Delinquency

Juvenile courts hear three types of proceedings: (1) Child neglect and dependency, including child abuse, that may result in the appointment of a guardian and/or the termination of parental rights; (2) Status offenses; and (3) Delinquency. Only the first category directly involves "family law" and will be dealt with here. The other two categories are referred to briefly.

Through the juvenile court, the state may intervene to protect young children from parental absence, neglect or abuse. Inadequate parents may lose (1) custody of or (2) all rights (and obligations) to their children. The parental obligation of care and control is most poignantly at issue in actions to terminate parental rights.

A. Child Dependency

According to one typical statute, a "dependent" child is one "without proper parental care or control necessary for his physical, mental, or emotional health, or morals." *In re C.P.*, 836 A.2d 984 (Pa. Super. 2003) (quoting 42 Pa. C.S.A. § 6302). In short, the child *depends* upon the state for its support and well-being. The actual conditions supporting a finding of "dependency" closely resemble those spelling "neglect," but in "dependency" there is less or no emphasis on parental fault. Similarly, the legal consequences are essentially the same. An adjudication of neglect involves: (1) a determination that the parent or household is unfit or that the child is abandoned, abused, or neglected; (2) a decision that, in the child's best interest, the parent should not have custody or full legal control over the child; and (3) the placement of the child with a court-appointed guardian, a state facility or agency, or, if no immediate harm threatens, placement back with the offending parent, under supervision.

B. Child Neglect and Abuse

1. Civil Standard

Definitions of child "neglect" vary from state to state. It is difficult to spell out precise conditions of neglect in a statute. In consequence, judges tend to have broad discretion in finding neglect. "Abuse" tends to involve clearer situations because it slides over into intentional misconduct and usually involves a quite obvious transgression of minimum tolerable standards.

Example: When Andrew, Sarah's fourth child, was born, the state immediately placed him in foster care and sought to have him designated a "child in need of assistance" based upon his mother's neglect of Andrew's older siblings. The Maryland Court of Special Appeals held that the mother could be found to have "neglected" her newborn son based upon her prior conduct with other children. The statutory definition of "neglect" means "the leaving of a child unattended or other failure to give proper care and attention to a child by any parent [or other custodian] . . . under circumstances that indicate: (1) That the child's health or welfare is harmed or placed at substantial risk of harm; or (2) That the child has suffered mental injury or been placed at substantial risk of mental injury." Under this definition, a parent's pattern of neglect of other children may be evidence of a "substantial risk of harm" to a newborn child. *In re Andrew A.*, 149 Md.App. 412, 815 A.2d 931 (2003).

2. Criminal Sanctions

In serious cases of child neglect or abuse, specific statutes apply criminal sanctions separately from the civil proceeding.

Example: C, then fifteen years of age, absented herself from school for part of the day. When she returned home that evening, M, having learned of her daughter's absence from school, struck C on the legs several times with a belt. According to C, F then took the belt and beat her with it, striking her 15 to 20 times on the back, neck, arm and legs. (Result: F was convicted under the state's criminal child abuse law. A parent is not permitted to resort to punishment which would exceed that properly required for disciplinary purposes or which extends beyond the bounds of moderation. Excessive or cruel conduct is prohibited.) *Bowers v. State*, 283 Md. 115, 389 A.2d 341 (1978).

C. Constitutional Rights

Because of the Constitution's respect for "family privacy" and the potentially punitive nature of state intervention to protect children from abusive parents, the U.S. Supreme Court has interpreted the Constitution to require special safeguards erroneous governmental intervention.

1. Vagueness of Statutory Standards

Neglect and dependency statutes have sometimes been attacked on the ground that they are unconstitutionally "vague," especially when termination of parental rights was at issue. Most often, courts have rejected these challenges. *E.g., State v. Watkins*, 659 N.W.2d 526 (Iowa 2003). Occasionally, however, these attacks have succeeded.

Examples: (1) Iowa's statute provided for the termination of parental rights where "the parents have substantially and continuously or repeatedly refused to give the child * * * care necessary for physical or mental health or morals of the child" and where "the parents are unfit by reason of * * * conduct found by the court likely to be detrimental to the physical or mental health or morals of the child." (Result: This statute was held to be unconstitutionally vague *both on its face and as applied.) Alsager v. District Court of Polk County, Iowa,* 406 F.Supp. 10 (S.D.Iowa 1975). On appeal, 545 F.2d 1137 (8th Cir.1976), the Circuit Court declined to resolve the important issue of facial unconstitutionality, but affirmed the holding *as applied to the facts of the case.*

(2) An Alabama statute that defined a neglected child as "any child, who, while under sixteen years of age * * * has no proper parental care or guardianship or whose home * * * is an unfit or improper place for such child" was struck down for vagueness. A provision authorized summary seizure of a child if it appears that "the child is in such condition that its welfare requires [seizure]." That provision was held to be an infringement on the fundamental right to family integrity and violating procedural due process, as well as unconstitutionally vague. A provision authorizing termination of parental rights as to a neglected child, defined as any child who has no proper parental care by reason of neglect, was also held unconstitutionally vague. *Roe v. Conn,* 417 F.Supp. 769 (M.D.Ala.1976).

2. Right to Counsel

The U.S. Supreme Court has held that due process does not necessarily require that counsel be provided to indigent parents in all termination of parental rights proceedings. In *Lassiter v. Department of Social Services of Durham County,* 452 U.S. 18, 101 S.Ct. 2153, 68 L.Ed.2d 640 (1981), William's (C) mother (M) had not provided proper medical care. C was adjudicated neglected and transferred to the custody of the County Department of Social Services. One year later, M was convicted of second degree murder and sentenced to imprisonment for forty years. The Department then petitioned to have M's parental rights terminated on the grounds that she had "willfully failed to maintain concern or responsibility for the welfare of the minor" and because termination was in the latter's best interests. Counsel was not appointed for M. The court concluded that M had had ample opportunity to obtain counsel, but had failed to do so "without just cause." M, however, had not averred that she was indigent. The court terminated her rights. On appeal, M argued that her due process rights were violated by not appointing counsel for her. The U.S. Supreme Court first explained its previous holdings to the effect that an indigent party is entitled to appointed counsel only when he may be deprived of his physical liberty. Applying the three-part *Mathews v. Eldridge* test, 424 U.S. 319, 96 S.Ct. 893, 47 L.Ed.2d 18 (1976), balancing the private interests at stake, the government's interest, and the risk that the procedures used will lead to erroneous decisions, the Court held that counsel did not have to be appointed in *this* case. The Court allowed that "[i]f, in a given case, the parent's interests were at their strongest, the State's interests were at their weakest, and the risks of error were at their peak, it could not be said that the *Eldridge* factors did not overcome the presumption against the right to appointed counsel and that due process did not therefore require the appointment of counsel." The question whether due process calls for the appointment of counsel for indigent parents in termination proceedings was left "to be answered in the first instance by the trial court, subject, of course, to appellate review." The Court added that "[a] wise public policy, however, may require that higher standards be adopted than those minimally tolerable under the Constitution," noting that thirty-four jurisdictions statutorily provide for the appointment of counsel in termination cases.

3.   Standard of Proof

The U.S. Supreme Court has held that, to terminate a parent's rights, the state must meet a "clear and convincing" standard of proof. *Santosky v. Kramer*, 455 U.S. 745, 102 S.Ct. 1388, 71 L.Ed.2d 599 (1982), reviewed a New York statute imposing the "fair preponderance of the evidence" standard. The U.S. Supreme Court looked to the burdens required in other states and noted that "a majority of the States have concluded that a 'clear and convincing evidence' standard of proof strikes a fair balance between the rights of the natural parents and the State's legitimate concerns." The Court went on to hold that New York's lower standard did not satisfy due process requirements. The Court did not consider whether the same "clear and convincing" standard of evidence is required in other adjudications involving lesser forms of state intervention, such as a temporary loss of custody.

Example: Court deprived M of custody of child, C, after finding abuse and neglect. Later, after reunification efforts failed, court terminated M's parental rights on grounds that M "fail[ed] to maintain a reasonable degree of interest" in C's welfare, deserted C, and "fail[ed] to make reasonable progress" toward addressing the conditions that led to the initial findings of abuse and neglect. M challenged the termination as unconstitutional on the ground that, although the court found the ultimate grounds for termination by "clear and convincing evidence," the initial findings of abuse and neglect were only by a "preponderance of the evidence." (Result: Termination affirmed. "Our courts, after considering and weighing each of these three factors, have concluded that a natural parent's due process rights are not violated where the grounds for termination of parental rights are established by clear and convincing evidence and the underlying abuse and neglect determinations are established by a preponderance of the evidence. . . . [A]n underlying finding of abuse or neglect does not affect the parental relationship to the same constitutionally significant degree as a termination proceeding because under [the statute], a parent cannot have his or her parental rights terminated based solely upon a finding of neglect or abuse. . . . Heightening the standard of proof for abuse and neglect proceedings could make it more difficult for the State to protect its children and could lessen the ability of courts and the State to fashion workable solutions to preserve family ties.") *In re Janira T.*, 368 Ill.App.3d 883, 307 Ill.Dec. 369, 859 N.E.2d 1046 (2006).

4. Freedom of Religion

Example: C fell ill and, motivated by her religious belief, M chose to treat the child's illness with prayer rather than medical care. Two weeks later, C died of meningitis. The state charged M with involuntary manslaughter and felony child endangerment, alleging that her negligence was criminal and proximately caused C's death. M's motion to dismiss was denied. M appealed. (Result: Criminal prosecution upheld. "The Legislature has determined that the provision of prayer is sufficient to avert misdemeanor liability for neglecting one's financial responsibility to furnish routine child support. This hardly compels the conclusion that in so doing the Legislature intended to create an unqualified defense to felony manslaughter and child endangerment charges for those parents who continue to furnish prayer alone in the rare instance when a gravely ill child lies dying for want of medical attention. * * * In sum, we reject the proposition that the provision of prayer alone to a seriously ill child cannot constitute criminal negligence as a matter of law.") *Walker v. Superior Court*, 47 Cal.3d 112, 253 Cal.Rptr. 1, 763 P.2d 852 (1988).

5. Home Visits and the Fourth Amendment

Recipients of welfare have attacked home visits required as a condition of eligibility for benefits. In *Wyman v. James,* 400 U.S. 309, 91 S.Ct. 381, 27 L.Ed.2d 408 (1971), the U.S. Supreme Court upheld a home visit against a Fourth Amendment challenge. The visit revealed that the child had a "skull fracture, a dent in the head and possible rat bite." The Court noted that the intrusion was reasonable in the circumstances, not an "early morning mass raid upon homes of welfare recipients."

6. State's Responsibility to Intervene—Liability for Failure to Protect?

Example: F beat five-year-old Joshua (C) into a life-threatening coma. C suffered brain damage so severe that he probably will spend his life in an institution for the profoundly retarded. During the proceeding two-year period, C had been hospitalized three times for suspicious injuries. Although the county caseworker visited the home and dutifully recorded numerous other suspicious injuries, she did nothing more and the Dept. of Social Services (D) took no action. Following C's first hospitalization, D had briefly taken C into its custody but C was returned to F three days later. Thereafter D failed utterly to protect C. C and his mother (M) brought a claim under 42 U.S.C.A. '1983, alleging that, by failing to intervene to protect him against a risk of violence of which they knew or should have known, D had deprived C of his liberty without due process of law, in violation of his rights under the Fourteenth Amendment. The district court entered summary judgment in favor of D, the court of appeals affirmed, and M appealed. (Held: D had no constitutional duty to protect C from F after receiving reports of possible abuse. "Petitioners concede that the harms Joshua suffered occurred not while he was in the State's custody, but while he was in the custody of his natural father, who was in no sense a state actor. While the State may have been aware of the dangers that Joshua faced in the free world, it played no part in their creation, nor did it do anything to render him any more vulnerable to them. That the State once took temporary custody of Joshua does not alter the analysis, for when it returned him to his father's custody, it placed him in no worse position than that in which he would have been had it not acted at all; the State does not become the permanent guarantor of an individual's safety by having once offered him shelter. Under these circumstances, the State had no constitutional duty to protect Joshua.") *DeShaney v. Winnebago County Dept. of Social Services*, 489 U.S. 189, 109 S.Ct. 998, 103 L.Ed.2d 249 (1989).

D. Parental Control Over a Child's Medical Care

1. Physical Health

Generally, parents must consent to any medical treatment given their minor child, except in an emergency. When a child requires medical treatment and the parents deny such treatment, the juvenile court may appoint a guardian for the child and direct the guardian to consent to necessary treatment.

Examples: (1) C was diagnosed as having a type of leukemia. C's parents refused to consent to chemotherapy. (Result: Natural parents do not have the authority of life and death over their children. The parental right to control the child's nurture is akin to a trust, subject to a correlative duty to care for and protect the child. It is terminable by the parents' failure to discharge their obligations. Even though the parents were loving and devoted in all other respects, their refusal to continue with chemotherapy for their child amounted to an unwillingness to provide necessary medical care and warranted an order removing legal custody from them.) *Custody of a Minor*, 375 Mass. 733, 379 N.E.2d 1053 (1978).

(2) F's nonmarital 3½–year-old twins lived with M, who had sole care and custody of them. The custody order obligated M to consult with F on all important matters concerning health, education, and welfare. F's 12–year-old son (S), who had a different mother, had leukemia and would die without a bone marrow transplant. The twins had met S only twice and did not know that he was their half-brother. F asked M to consent to testing the twins as potential bone marrow donors and to harvesting their bone marrow for transplant to S, if they were found to be compatible. M refused both procedures. F's emergency petition was denied, and he appealed. (Result: It was not in the best interest of the *twins* to submit to the bone marrow testing or to the harvesting procedure. "We hold that a parent or guardian may give consent on behalf of a minor * * * child to donate bone marrow to a sibling, only when to do so would be in the minor's best interest. * * * The evidence reveals three

critical factors which are necessary to a determination that it will be in the best interests of a child to donate bone marrow to a sibling. First, the parent who consents on behalf of the child must be informed of the risks and benefits inherent in the bone marrow harvesting procedure to the child. Second, there must be emotional support available to the child from the person or persons who take care of the child. * * * Third, there must be an existing, close relationship between the donor and recipient. The evidence clearly shows that there is no physical benefit to a donor child. If there is any benefit to a child who donates bone marrow to a sibling it will be a psychological benefit. * * * The psychological benefit is grounded firmly in the fact that the donor and recipient are known to each other as family. Only where there is an existing relationship between a healthy child and his or her ill sister or brother may a psychological benefit to the child from donating bone marrow to a sibling realistically be found to exist.") *Curran v. Bosze*, 141 Ill.2d 473, 153 Ill.Dec. 213, 566 N.E.2d 1319 (1990).

(3) Instead of seeking conventional therapy, parents took a seven year old child with Hodgkin's disease to Jamaica for nutritional therapy. The court refused to declare the child neglected and noted (1) that several qualified physicians were contributing to the child's care, (2) that great deference must be given a parent's choice as to the mode of medical treatment, (3) that conventional treatment (which would be administered if needed) had toxic effects, and (4) that the nutritional treatment was controlling his condition. *In re Hofbauer*, 47 N.Y.2d 648, 419 N.Y.S.2d 936, 393 N.E.2d 1009 (1979).

2. The First Amendment Issue

Numerous cases illustrate the potential tension between freedom of religion (typically the parent's) and the child's best interest. Ultimately such cases are resolved by balancing the care required (emergency blood transfusion vs. deferrable care or elective surgery not necessary for survival) against the parent's constitutional right to follow his or her religion in raising the child. The state steps in when the "exercise" of religion by the parent becomes life-threatening to the child. In extreme cases, a criminal prosecution may lie against the parent. (*Walker v. Superior Court*, p. 236). Some courts have accepted that "mature minors" may be constitutionally entitled to refuse life-saving treatment (thereby sparing their parents from liability), but others have rejected such an exception.

Examples: (1) 17–year-old girl, C, contracted leukemia and needed blood transfusions to survive. C, with the support of her mother, M, refused on the ground that receiving a transfusion would violate C's religious faith as a Jehovah's Witness. State filed a neglect petition and sought guardianship of C in order to consent to transfusions. (Result: No neglect. C, as a mature minor just months shy of her 18th birthday, was constitutionally entitled to refuse life-saving medical treatment, and her parents could not be criminally liable for neglect for acquiescing in her wishes.) *In re E.G.,* 133 Ill.2d 98, 139 Ill.Dec. 810, 549 N.E.2d 322 (1989).

(2) 16–year-old girl, C, fell seriously ill. M and F, consistent with their religious faith, prayed for C but refused medical treatment. C died from her condition, and parents were convicted of involuntary manslaughter and endangering the welfare of a child. (Result: Convictions affirmed. The court rejected a "mature minor" exception. "By mandating primary responsibility for the child's wellbeing upon the parents, the legislature has not only acted toward fulfilling its role as *parens patriae,* but also has recognized that parents have a duty to provide for their children which accompanies the right to raise children with minimal state encroachment." The constitutional rights of C and her parents must yield to the state's interest in preserving life. "A compelling interest in the welfare of minors may impinge upon the constitutional rights of both minors and adults simultaneously.") *Commonwealth v. Nixon,* 563 Pa. 425, 761 A.2d 1151 (2000).

3. Mental Health

A Georgia statute allowed a parent or guardian to apply for admission of his or her child to the state's mental hospital. The U.S. Supreme Court held that the risk of error inherent in a parental decision to have a child institutionalized for mental health care is sufficiently great that an inquiry should be made by a "neutral factfinder." It held, however, that Georgia's admission procedures were reasonable and consistent with constitutional guarantees, and that a formal or even quasi-formal hearing was not required. The Court suggested that the inquiry need not be conducted by a law-trained or judicial or administrative officer but must carefully probe the child's background, using all available sources. It is necessary that the decision maker have the authority to refuse to admit a child who does not satisfy medical standards for admission. The child's continuing need for commitment must be reviewed periodically by a similar procedure. *Parham v. J. R.*, 442 U.S. 584, 99 S.Ct. 2493, 61 L.Ed.2d 101 (1979).

4. Minor's Consent to Medical Treatment

Many states have enacted statutes granting minors the ability to give legal consent to a variety of medical procedures, especially relating to drugs, alcoholism and in the sexual sphere. The U.S. Supreme Court's concern with the minor's right to abortion has paved new inroads in this area.

a. Abortion

The U.S. Supreme Court has held that a "mature" minor may obtain an abortion without parental consent or notification if she establishes her "maturity" in an appropriate "bypass procedure." While numerous cases turn on this issue, the Court has not set a fixed age for "maturity" or provided a clear definition of "maturity." See also pp. 254–55.

Examples: (1) A Missouri abortion statute required the parent's written consent to an abortion requested by an unmarried woman under 18, unless a licensed physician certified that abortion was necessary to preserve the mother's life. (Result: The U.S. Supreme Court held the blanket parental consent requirement unconstitutional. No significant state interests, whether to safeguard family unity or parental authority or otherwise, were found to justify conditioning abortion on parental consent.) *Planned Parenthood of Central Missouri v. Danforth*, 428 U.S. 52, 96 S.Ct. 2831, 49 L.Ed.2d 788 (1976).

(2) A Utah statute required physicians to "notify, if possible," parents or guardians of minors upon whom abortion is to be performed. (Result: "A statute setting a 'mere requirement of parental notice' does not violate the constitutional rights of an immature, dependent minor." As applied here to an unemancipated minor girl living with and dependent upon her parents and making no claim or showing as to her maturity or as to her relations with her parents, the court held that the statute serves important state interests, is narrowly drawn to protect only those interests, and does not violate any guarantees of the Constitution. "We emphasized, however, 'that our holding

[in *Danforth*] does not suggest that every minor, regardless of age or maturity, may give effective consent for termination of her pregnancy.' [At 75, 96 S.Ct., at 2844, citing *Bellotti I.*] There is no logical relationship between the capacity to become pregnant and the capacity for mature judgment concerning the wisdom of an abortion. In *Bellotti II* [*Bellotti v. Baird*, 443 U.S. 622, 99 S.Ct. 3035, 61 L.Ed.2d 797 (1979)], dealing with a class of concededly mature pregnant minors, we struck down a Massachusetts statute requiring parental or judicial consent before an abortion could be performed on any unmarried minor. There the State's highest court had construed the statute to allow a court to overrule the minor's decision even if the court found that the minor was capable of making, and in fact had made, an informed and reasonable decision to have an abortion. We held, among other things, that the statute was unconstitutional for failure to allow mature minors to decide to undergo abortions without parental consent"). *H.L. v. Matheson*, 450 U.S. 398, 101 S.Ct. 1164, 67 L.Ed.2d 388 (1981).

(3) A Pennsylvania statute required a minor wishing to obtain an abortion to obtain the informed consent of one of her parents. A judicial "bypass" procedure was available. (Held: The one-parent consent requirement is constitutional. "Except in a medical emergency, an unemancipated young woman under 18 may not obtain an abortion unless she and one of her parents (or guardian) provides informed consent * * *. If neither a parent nor a guardian provides consent, a court may authorize the performance of an abortion upon a determination that the young woman is mature and capable of giving informed consent and has in fact given her informed consent, or that an abortion would be in her best interests. * * * Our cases establish, and we reaffirm today, that a State may require a minor seeking an abortion to obtain the consent of a parent or guardian, provided that there is an adequate judicial bypass procedure. Under these precedents, in our view, the one-parent consent requirement and judicial bypass procedure are constitutional.") *Planned Parenthood v. Casey*, 505 U.S. 833, 112 S.Ct. 2791, 120 L.Ed.2d 674 (1992).

(4) An Ohio statute, with certain exceptions, prohibited any person from performing an abortion on an unmarried, unemancipated, minor woman absent *notice* to one of the woman's parents or a court order of approval. (Held: The statute is constitutional. "[W]e determine that the statute accords with our precedents on parental notice and consent in the abortion context and does not violate the Fourteenth Amendment.") *Ohio v. Akron Center for Reproductive Health*, 497 U.S. 502, 110 S.Ct. 2972, 111 L.Ed.2d 405 (1990).

(5) A Minnesota statute provided, with certain exceptions, that no abortion could be performed on a woman under age 18 absent notification of *both* of her parents. (Held: The *two*-parent notice requirement is unconstitutional.) *Hodgson v. Minnesota*, 497 U.S. 417, 110 S.Ct. 2926, 111 L.Ed.2d 344 (1990).

b. Birth Control

Since a state may not impose a blanket prohibition on, or a blanket requirement of parental consent to, the choice of a minor to terminate her pregnancy, it follows that the blanket prohibition of distribution of contraceptives to minors is unconstitutional. *Carey v. Population Services*, 431 U.S. 678, 97 S.Ct. 2010, 52 L.Ed.2d 675 (1977). See pp. 260–61.

c. Life–Saving Medical Care

States have disagreed over whether "mature minors" are entitled to refuse medical care necessary to save life. *Compare In re E.G., supra* (recognizing such a right), *with Commonwealth v. Nixon, supra* (rejecting such a right).

E. Child Abuse

1. Abuse Reporting Statutes and Registries

Statutes encouraging and facilitating the reporting of child abuse and neglect are universal, but their content is not. Most states specify persons, such as physicians, school teachers and social workers, who are required to report suspected child abuse or neglect. Several states encourage everyone to report such situations. What must be reported is knowledge or suspicion of physical or mental injury, sexual abuse and neglect by a child's parent or immediate family member or any person responsible for the child's welfare or any person living in the same home. However, sanctions for failure to report generally are non-existent or weak.

Example: The Illinois statute provides: "Any [of a vast list of medical, school, social work, counseling professionals or state employees] having reasonable cause to believe a child known to them in their professional or official capacity may be an abused child or a neglected child shall immediately report or cause a report to be made to the Department. * * * The privileged quality of communication between any professional person required to report and his patient or client shall not constitute grounds for failure to report as required by this Act. In addition to the above persons required to report suspected cases of abused or neglected children, any other person may make a report if such person has reasonable cause to believe a child may be an abused child or a neglected child. * * * Any person who knowingly transmits a false report to the Department commits the offense of disorderly conduct * * *. Any person who violates this provision a second or subsequent time shall be guilty of a Class 4 felony. * * * A child whose parent, guardian or custodian in good faith selects and depends upon spiritual means through prayer alone for the treatment or cure of disease or remedial care may be considered neglected or abused, but not for the sole reason that his parent, guardian or custodian accepts and practices such beliefs." (325 ILCS § 5/4).

These registers can be very beneficial, but in practice they may store unsubstantiated rumors and suspicions. Possibly innocent parents have no opportunity to confront their accusers and cannot correct or expunge the record. They may not even know that such a record exists.

Example: "This court finds [the central child abuse registry statute] represents an unconstitutional infringement on the rights to privacy and the guarantees of due process. In implementing that section, the State Department of Public Welfare has devised the Child Abuse and Neglect Report and Inquiry System (CANRIS). CANRIS is a computerized system designed to collect and store the confidential information gathered by the state from the inception of an investigation through final disposition. It is clear from the expressed purpose of CANRIS that it goes far beyond the permissible maintenance of investigatory files. The mere filing of a report of child abuse is cause enough for the system to operate. The record in this case indicates that CANRIS places labels of 'perpetrator' on those parents who are ensnarled into this web—a conclusion reached by the state without any judicial determination. Similarly, CANRIS may label the report as 'validated,' which by the terms of its operation manual is appropriate where 'the investigating worker has proved that neglect or abuse exists.' This use of information gathering and dissemination absent a judicial determination of abuse or neglect is an impermissible violation of due process and right to privacy. Of course, the state may maintain investigative files. However, to the extent that CANRIS purports in any way to be a clearinghouse of child-abuse information without a judicial determination thereof, it is an unconstitutional infringement on the rights of the parents." *Sims v. State Dept. of Public Welfare*, 438 F.Supp. 1179, 1192 (S.D.Tex.1977), *rev'd on other grounds*, 442 U.S. 415, 99 S.Ct. 2371, 60 L.Ed.2d 994 (1979).

2. The Battered Child Syndrome

The "battered child syndrome," if accepted by the court, facilitates proof of child abuse in appropriate cases. Evidence of the syndrome is accepted more readily in civil than in criminal cases, but often plays a role in the latter.

Examples: (1) Two-year-old C was admitted to the hospital and placed in intensive care, where she had to be fed intravenously for 2 weeks. She was covered with bruises and abrasions, including an open lesion the size of a nickel under her left eye. She was severely dehydrated and had internal abdominal injuries that were later diagnosed as a fractured spleen, pancreatitis and liver dysfunction. The injuries had occurred approximately one week before C arrived at the hospital. C's medical history, as given by F to the physicians, was inconsistent with C's injuries. F and M were tried for injury to a child and convicted. They appealed, claiming that the trial court erred in admitting evidence of battered child syndrome. (Result: Convictions upheld. "Expert testimony is permitted, in the court's discretion, 'if the witness has a special skill or knowledge, beyond the ken of the average juror, that, as properly applied, would be helpful to the determination of an ultimate issue.' Battered child syndrome has become a well established medical diagnosis. Expert medical testimony that a child suffered from battered child syndrome has consistently been held admissible in other jurisdictions. '[T]he "battered child syndrome" simply indicates that a child found with [certain types of injuries] has not suffered those injuries by accidental means. This conclusion is based upon an extensive study of the subject by medical science.' A diagnosis of battered child syndrome is often indicated when a child's injuries do not jibe with the history given by the parent. A properly qualified expert medical witness, therefore, may appropriately explain the syndrome to the jury and express his opinion that the victim suffers from it.") *State v. Dumlao*, 3 Conn.App. 607, 491 A.2d 404 (1985).

(2) Parents took seven-week-old infant, C, to hospital, where he was found to have suffered severe brain damage leaving him in a permanent vegetative state. Parents were convicted of felony child abuse, based partly on expert testimony that infant suffered from "battered child syndrome." Parents appealed, challenging the sufficiency of the evidence. (Result: Convictions affirmed. "[U]pon a finding that the child suffered from 'battered child syndrome,' a logical presumption is raised 'that someone "caring" for the child was responsible for the injuries.' . . . This evidence is sufficient to establish that the event which caused [C's] brain injury occurred [during a period when] . . . [C] was under the sole care and supervision of Defendants.") *State v. Parker*, 185 N.C.App. 437, 651 S.E.2d 377 (2007).

F. Disposition by the Juvenile Court

After a finding of dependency, neglect or abuse, the court typically (1) appoints a guardian, and (2) may, if appropriate, return the child to the custody of its parents, or (3) put the child in foster care, or (4) institutionalize the child or (5) terminate parental rights.

1. Guardianship

An individual, a state agency or a private institution may be appointed guardian. The guardian may be given custody or the child's custody may be given to a third party or agency. In appropriate cases, the child may be returned to the custody of its parent under the supervision of the guardian. The guardian obtains all but complete parental authority in terms of making decisions regarding the child, and only "residual" parental rights and duties (such as the right to reasonable visitation, the duty to support and the right to consent or refuse to consent to adoption) are left with the parent.

2. Foster Care

The child may be placed in (state-licensed) foster care until the home situation has improved. In licensed foster homes, paid foster parents provide substitute family care for a planned period when the child's own family cannot provide appropriate care and when adoption is either not desirable or not possible. The state has the duty to monitor the foster care arrangement to ensure that the child is receiving whatever individual treatment it needs. Since foster parents do not have a constitutional right to procedural protections such as are afforded natural parents, contracts requiring foster parents to relinquish their wards are binding when the decision is made for any reason to transfer the child to another foster home or back to its natural parents.

Example: An organization of foster parents sought declaratory and injunctive relief, alleging that New York's statutory and regulatory procedures for removal of foster children from foster homes violated Due Process and Equal Protection. The foster parents' contention was that "when a child has lived in a foster home for a year or more, a psychological tie is created between the child and the foster parents which constitutes the foster family the true 'psychological family' of the child," and creates "a 'liberty interest' in its survival as a family that is protected by the Fourteenth Amendment." The lower court had concluded that "the pre-removal procedures presently employed by the State are constitutionally defective," and held that "before a foster child can be peremptorily transferred from the foster home in which he has been living, be it to another foster home or to the natural parents who initially placed him in foster care, he is entitled to a hearing at which all concerned parties may present any relevant information to the administrative decisionmaker charged with determining the future placement of the child." (Result: Reversed. Recognizing that "no one would seriously dispute that a deeply loving and interdependent relationship between an adult and child in his or her care may exist even in the absence of blood relationship," the U.S. Supreme Court nevertheless was "persuaded that, even on the assumption that appellees have a protected 'liberty interest,' the District Court erred in holding that the preremoval procedures presently employed by the State are constitutionally defective." The removal procedures were upheld.) *Smith v. Organization of Foster Families for Equality and Reform*, 431 U.S. 816, 97 S.Ct. 2094, 53 L.Ed.2d 14 (1977).

3. Institutionalization

Following a dependency, neglect or abuse adjudication, the child may be institutionalized in a state home or private institution. The parents' support obligation continues.

Example: S, nearly 15 years of age, left his parents' home and lived with various relatives. A juvenile court found S to be a dependent child. Temporary legal custody was awarded to the state but parental rights were not terminated. When the temporary order was lifted, S returned to his parents' custody. The state then filed a petition seeking reimbursement of monies it expended to support S. Relying on the common law doctrine of emancipation, the parents contested the petition and claimed that their duty to support S had ended when he voluntarily left home to pursue a homosexual lifestyle, of which they disapproved. Declining to apply the doctrine of emancipation, the trial court entered an order requiring repayment. The parents appealed. (Result: The doctrine of emancipation is part of the state's common law; further proceedings were necessary to determine whether S was emancipated and, if so, whether that would relieve parents of their responsibility to support S.) *State, In Interest of R.R. v. C.R. and R.R.*, 797 P.2d 459 (Utah App.1990).

4. Termination of Parental Rights

Where the possibility of rehabilitation of the parent appears to be remote and the parental neglect or abuse was severe, parental rights may be terminated. Statutes ordinarily require that the state prove that the parent is "unfit" because of repeated or severe abuse or neglect. With termination, the parent and child legally become "strangers" to each other. However, unless adoption is possible or likely, little may be gained by terminating a parent's rights even in serious cases. The child will lose his or her right to support from the parent and, adrift in the system of institutionalization or foster care, may never regain permanent family ties and legal rights. Termination of parental rights thus is a last resort and is resorted to only in severe cases. Special (constitutional) safeguards apply. (See pp. 238–41).

In 1997, concerned that excessive solicitude for parental rights and "family preservation" was causing many thousands of children to spend years in "foster care drift," Congress sought to push states to move faster to terminate the parental rights and free abused or neglected children for adoption into permanent homes. In the Adoption and Safe Families Act (ASFA), Congress mandated that, in the absence of special circumstances, states *must* seek to terminate parental rights if a child has been in foster care for 15 out of the past 22 months. Since the Act was enacted, the number of adoptions in the United States has nearly doubled.

G. Criminal Procedure

1. History and Development

The "delinquency track" of the juvenile court system developed as a means of protecting children who have committed a crime from being subjected to the same procedures, standards, and punishments applied to adults. The objective was to replace the adversarial nature of criminal proceedings with a "paternalistic" proceeding to determine what is in the best interest of the accused minor. Correction rather than punishment was sought at an age when the child was still impressionable and changeable and, perhaps, bore less than full responsibility for criminal acts. The bulk of delinquency and status offense cases are dealt with by informal supervision or unofficial handling, without an adjudication of delinquent behavior. Incarceration, if imposed, is in a "reform school" or similar institution rather than in a prison.

2. The Need for Reform

A major concern was that incarceration could be imposed on a juvenile potentially for a longer period than that for which an adult could have been sentenced for the same offense. Finding that the results in juvenile courts "have not been entirely satisfactory," the U.S. Supreme Court sought to provide more protection for juveniles by mandating that certain procedural rights accorded adult criminal defendants must be granted in the juvenile court system. *In re Gault*, 387 U.S. 1, 87 S.Ct. 1428, 18 L.Ed.2d 527 (1967). These rights include (1) adequate written notice, (2) advice as to right of counsel, (3) confrontation by sworn witnesses, (4) cross-examination of witnesses, and (5) the privilege against self-incrimination, in short, the "essentials of due process and fair treatment." The right to proof beyond a reasonable doubt was granted juveniles in cases involving "adult crimes." *In re Winship*, 397 U.S. 358, 90 S.Ct. 1068, 25 L.Ed.2d 368 (1970). Juveniles, however, do not have a constitutional right to jury trial in a juvenile court delinquency proceeding. *McKeiver v. Pennsylvania*, 403 U.S. 528, 91 S.Ct. 1976, 29 L.Ed.2d 647 (1971).

3. Status Offenses and Delinquency

"Status offenses," such as incorrigibility, truancy and running away from home, involve the child's status as a minor. They would not be crimes if committed by an adult. Offenders often are referred to as "persons," "minors" or "children" "in need of supervision" (PINS, MINS or CINS). A federal district court held in *Martarella v. Kelley,* 349 F.Supp. 575 (S.D.N.Y.1972), that PINS have a "right to treatment" while in detention, although no similar right has been established for juvenile delinquents.

Example: Following a finding that D had regularly disobeyed her parents, the juvenile court held D to be an undisciplined child in need of the discipline and supervision of the state. D was placed on probation, but she violated probation by keeping late hours, going to places and seeing people forbidden by her parents, and refusing to obey school rules. D was committed to a detention home for juveniles, and she appealed. (Result: "[D's] contention is that [the statute] violates the Equal Protection Clause of the Fourteenth Amendment in that it subjects an undisciplined child to probation and the concomitant risk of incarceration when the child has committed no criminal offense, while adults are subjected to probation and incarceration only for actual criminal offenses. * * * [T]he classification here challenged is based on differences between adults and children; and there are so many valid distinctions that the basis for challenge seems shallow. These differences are 'reasonably related to the purposes of the Act'—that is, to provide children the needed supervision and control. Consequently, the classification does not offend the Equal Protection Clause * * * and even if it be said that the classification here challenged affects 'fundamental interests' or is 'inherently suspect,' it is our view that the desire of the State to exercise its authority as parens patriae and provide for the care and protection of its children supplies a 'compellingly rational' justification for the classification.") *Matter of Walker,* 282 N.C. 28, 191 S.E.2d 702 (1972).

Review Questions

1. (T) or F   Status offenses are acts which, if committed by an adult, would not be a crime.

2. T or (F)   In a custody hearing, M, a Jehovah's witness, makes it clear that she would not consent to a blood transfusion for her child. For this reason alone, a court may find C to be neglected.

3. T or (F)   In proceedings to terminate their parental rights, parents have a constitutional right to counsel.

4. (T) or F   In proceedings to terminate parental rights, parental neglect or abuse must be proved by clear and convincing evidence.

5. T or (F)   Before a minor is committed to a mental institution by his/her parents, the minor is constitutionally entitled to a formal, adversary hearing before a neutral factfinder.

6. T or (F)   A judicial determination of child neglect and award of guardianship and custody to someone other than the parents, suspends the parents' support obligation.

7. T or (F)   Statutes requiring teachers, physicians and other professionals to report their reasonable suspicion of child abuse, usually carry severe criminal sanctions.

8. T or (F)   After foster parents have had custody of a foster child for a "substantial" period of time, they develop a constitutionally protected right to be "first in line" for the adoption of their foster child.

9. T or (F)   Under *In re Gault* and numerous U.S. Supreme Court cases that followed, minors being tried in juvenile courts have the same procedural protections that must be accorded adults in criminal prosecutions.

10. T or (F)   A parent who, for religious reasons, refuses to seek conventional medical care for his or her ill child may not be criminally prosecuted if the child dies or is harmed.

11. T or (F)   When a municipal or state child welfare agency fails to protect a child from serious or fatal child abuse or neglect, the agency is liable to the child or his estate.

12. **T** or **F**   A state's requirement that a minor seeking an abortion *notify* both parents has been held unconstitutional.

13. **T** or **F**   A state's requirement that a minor seeking an abortion obtain *consent* from *one* parent is constitutional.

*

X

Children's Rights

■ ANALYSIS

A. History of Parental Control
B. Constitutional Rights
C. Emancipation
D. Minor's Capacity to Contract
E. Children and Tort Law
    1. "Wrongful Life"
    2. Wrongful Death
    3. Suits Between Parent and Child—Erosion of the Tort Immunity
    4. "Heartbalm" Actions
    5. Childrens' Torts Against Third Parties—Parents' Liability?
    6. Parents' Criminal Liability?
F. Property Rights
G. Education: State and Parents
    1. Private Schooling
    2. Constitutional Objections to Obligatory Schooling
    3. Parental Control Over Classroom Content
    4. Discipline in Schools

A. History of Parental Control

"It is basic to our law that the court cannot regulate, by its processes, the internal affairs of the home. As we said more than 30 years ago, '[d]ispute [in the family] when it does not involve anything immoral or harmful to the welfare of the child is beyond the reach of the law. The vast majority of matters concerning the upbringing of children must be left to the conscience, patience and self-restraint of father and mother. No end of difficulties would arise should judges try to tell parents how to bring up their children.' " Jason, J., concurring in *Roe v. Doe*, 29 N.Y.2d 188, 324 N.Y.S.2d 71, 272 N.E.2d 567 (1971).

The old rule was that the father had all but absolute power over his offspring. Today, parents retain significant but not absolute control over their minor children. Limitations are defined by child "neglect," "dependency," "abuse" and compulsory school attendance laws. There is increasing judicial and statutory recognition of minor children as legal persons independent of their parents. Considerable strides have been made by the child in the area of criminal (juvenile delinquency) procedure and in a series of school-related situations. Vis-à-vis their parents, however, the definition of the child's own constitutional rights has not progressed very far, except in the area of sexual rights (*e.g.*, birth control, abortion).

B. Constitutional Rights

Children enjoy some protections under the United States Constitution, but their rights are not equal to or the same as those of adults. The U.S. Supreme Court has noted three reasons why children are treated differently than adults under the Constitution: "[T]he peculiar vulnerability of children; their inability to make critical decisions in an informed manner; and the importance of the parental role in child-rearing." *Bellotti v. Baird*, 443 U.S. 622, 99 S.Ct. 3035, 61 L.Ed.2d 797 (1979).

Examples: (1) A New York statute prohibited the sale or distribution of contraceptives to a minor under the age of sixteen years. (Result: Statute unconstitutional. "The question of the extent of state power to regulate conduct of minors not constitutionally regulable when committed by adults is a vexing one, perhaps not susceptible to precise answer. * * * Certain principles, however, have been recognized. 'Minors, as well as adults, are protected by the Constitution and possess constitutional rights.' '[W]hatever may be their precise impact, neither the Fourteenth Amendment nor the Bill of Rights is for adults alone.' On the other hand, we have held in a variety of contexts that 'the power of the state to control the conduct of children reaches beyond the scope of its authority over adults.' ") *Carey v. Population Services International*, 431 U.S. 678, 97 S.Ct. 2010, 52 L.Ed.2d 675 (1977). (See p. 248).

(2) The U.S. Supreme Court has struck down statutes requiring *parental consent* to a "mature" minor daughter's abortion. *Planned Parenthood of Central Missouri v. Danforth*, 428 U.S. 52, 96 S.Ct. 2831, 49 L.Ed.2d 788 (1976) and *Bellotti v. Baird*, 443 U.S. 622, 99 S.Ct. 3035, 61 L.Ed.2d 797 (1979). (See p. 246).

(3) In *H.L. v. Matheson*, 450 U.S. 398, 101 S.Ct. 1164, 67 L.Ed.2d 388 (1981), a statute requiring *notice* to parents of a minor seeking an abortion was upheld when applied to an unmarried, fifteen-year-old minor, who lived at home and was dependent on her parents. (See pp. 246–47).

(4) In *Planned Parenthood v. Casey*, 505 U.S. 833, 112 S.Ct. 2791, 120 L.Ed.2d 674 (1992), the U.S. Supreme Court held: ("Our cases establish, and we reaffirm today, that a State may require a minor seeking an abortion to obtain the consent of a parent or guardian, provided that there is an adequate judicial bypass procedure. Under these precedents, in our view, the one-parent consent requirement and judicial bypass procedure are constitutional.") (See p. 247).

(5) Approximately the same rule (notice to parents permitted but availability of bypass procedure for "mature minors" required) applies to parental *notice* statutes. *Ohio v. Akron Center for Reproductive Health*, 497 U.S. 502, 110 S.Ct. 2972, 111 L.Ed.2d 405 (1990); *Akron II*; *Hodgson v. Minnesota*, 497 U.S. 417, 110 S.Ct. 2926, 111 L.Ed.2d 344 (1990). (See p. 248).

(6) In *Troxel v. Granville*, 530 U.S. 57, 120 S.Ct. 2054, 147 L.Ed.2d 49 (2000), a divided U.S. Supreme Court upheld a parent's fundamental constitutional right to make basic decisions about his or her child's associations with others, including grandparents. Writing separately, Justice Stevens opined that it is likely that parents' rights should be balanced against the independent constitutional right of the child to maintain important family-like relationships. (See p. 225).

With respect to the parents' authority to commit their child to a psychiatric institution, the U.S. Supreme Court has held that a full, adversary hearing is *not* required under the Due Process clause, so long as certain basic safeguards are in place to prevent parents from "railroading their children into asylums." *Parham v. J.R.*, 442 U.S. 584, 99 S.Ct. 2493, 61 L.Ed.2d 101 (1979).

C. Emancipation → living on their own before (18)

As previously discussed (pp. 194–95), a minor's emancipation terminates the parental support obligation and eliminates minority as a legal defense to contractual obligations. Emancipation also involves the end of parental control over the minor.

D. Minor's Capacity to Contract

Contractual obligations incurred by unemancipated minors are voidable. Upon reaching majority, the obligation may be ratified. While it is the parent's duty to provide "necessaries" for a child and, if the parent fails to do so, the parent is liable under the infant's contract, the infant himself is liable on the contract if the parent is unable to provide for the necessaries.

Example: A child received necessary medical attention at a cost of $7,000. The mother (who was on welfare) could not pay the bill. (Result: The child—who had been awarded a judgment compensating for the injury that required the medical attention—was held liable on the contract.) *Gardner v. Flowers*, 529 S.W.2d 708 (Tenn.1975).

E. Children and Tort Law

1. "Wrongful Life"

Courts disagree whether parents can recover damages from a third party (physician, pharmacist) whose negligent performance or nonperformance of a duty (*e.g.*, sterilization, abortion, supply of medication) results in the conception and birth of an unwanted *healthy* child. (*Caveat*: Distinguish suits on behalf of the child or by the parents directly involving the birth of a disabled child.)

a. Recovery Allowed

Courts that allow recovery in a "wrongful life" action disagree as to the proper measure of damages. Many courts allow limited recovery for *direct* expenses associated with the pregnancy, sometimes including mental distress caused by the pregnancy. A few courts have allowed more, such as the cost of having and raising the child, reduced by the probable enjoyment the child will bring. The argument that the mother should mitigate damages by having an abortion or by putting the child up for adoption has not been favored.

Example: W and H decided not to have more children, and W underwent an unsuccessful tubal ligation. W became pregnant and delivered a healthy baby. The court held that W and H's damages properly included (1) all expenses associated with the birth, (2) a second sterilization operation, (3) W's lost earnings capacity, (4) day care costs for other children while W was incapacitated, (5) H's loss of consortium, (6) W's pain and suffering in connection with the birth and second surgery, and (7) the expense of raising the child. (Result: Affirmed. The Supreme Judicial Court of Massachusetts held: "The great weight of authority permits the parents of a normal child born as a result of a physician's negligence to recover damages directly associated with the birth (sometimes including damage for the parents' emotional distress), but courts are divided on whether the parents may recover the economic expense of rearing the child. * * * The judicial declaration that the joy and pride in raising a child always outweigh any economic loss the parents may suffer, thus precluding recovery for the cost of raising the child, simply lacks verisimilitude. The very fact that a person has sought medical intervention to prevent him or her from having a child demonstrates that, for that person, the benefits of parenthood did not outweigh the burdens, economic and otherwise, of having a child. The extensive use of contraception and sterilization and the performance of numerous abortions each year show that * * * large numbers of people do not accept parenthood as a net positive circumstance. We agree with those courts that have rejected the theory that the birth of a child is for all parents at all times a net benefit. * * * We conclude that * * * parents may recover the cost of rearing a normal, healthy but (at least initially) unwanted child if their reason for seeking sterilization was founded on economic or financial considerations. In such a situation, the trier of fact should offset against the cost of rearing the child the benefit, if any, the parents receive and will receive from having their child. We discern no reason founded on sound public policy to immunize a physician from having to pay for a reasonably foreseeable consequence of his negligence or from a natural and probable consequence of a breach of his guarantee, namely, the parents' expenses in rearing the child to adulthood.") *Burke v. Rivo*, 406 Mass. 764, 551 N.E.2d 1 (1990).

b. Recovery Denied

Examples: (1) H, W, and their five children brought a malpractice action against surgeon and hospital, alleging the improper performance of a sterilization operation on W. (Result: Recovery denied. To compel the allegedly negligent surgeon to assume financial responsibility for raising and educating the child would violate public policy and the law governing provable damages.) *Coleman v. Garrison*, 349 A.2d 8 (Del.1975).

(2) M and F filed a medical malpractice action against a physician, alleging that he had negligently performed a tubal ligation after which M had become pregnant and given birth to a healthy girl. They sought damages for the expenses of the pregnancy, delivery, postpartum care, and rearing the child. The trial court dismissed the part of their claim that asked damages for the expense of rearing the child. (Result: As a matter of public policy, M and F have suffered no legally cognizable harm by virtue of the birth of a healthy child, conceived after an unsuccessful surgical birth control procedure. Accordingly, there can be no recovery from the allegedly negligent physician, hospital, and clinic for pecuniary expenses of raising the healthy, normal, though unplanned, child.) *O'Toole v. Greenberg*, 64 N.Y.2d 427, 488 N.Y.S.2d 143, 477 N.E.2d 445 (1985).

c. Contract Actions

When a birth control device failed or a sterilization was unsuccessful, parents occasionally have sought to claim on a contract or warranty theory. Such claims generally have not met with success where the recovery sought was in excess of a refund of payments made.

d. Birth Defects

Where the baby suffered birth defects caused by a physician's negligence, courts have displayed more sympathy. Some courts term such cases "wrongful birth." (Note that these cases also may involve the child's *own* "damages" along with medical expenses the parents incur.)

Example: Baby suffered from congenital rubella syndrome. M brought a "wrongful birth" action against her physician, who allegedly had negligently failed to test for and discover that mother had rubella, had failed to advise mother regarding the risks of birth defects in a fetus exposed to rubella, and had thereby deprived mother of information which might have caused her to have an abortion. (Result: Damages for emotional distress and *ordinary* child-raising costs are not recoverable. Extraordinary medical and educational expenses attributable to the child's infirmities may be recovered.) *Smith v. Cote,* 128 N.H. 231, 513 A.2d 341 (1986).

2. Wrongful Death

A child may recover for pecuniary loss resulting from the wrongful death of a parent. Traditionally, in the absence of pecuniary damage resulting from the death of a minor child, parents could not recover. Today, parents generally may recover for the loss of "society and companionship" of their child, without specific proof of pecuniary damage or economic loss.

3. Suits Between Parent and Child—Erosion of the Tort Immunity

Traditional law prohibited tort suits between parents and children. Stated objectives were to preserve family harmony and to prevent collusive suits to collect insurance benefits. (Note: by comparison, the *interspousal* tort immunity rested on the additional notion of the spouses' "oneness.")

Many courts and legislatures have abolished the immunity doctrine, finding the underlying rationale unpersuasive. Other courts have created exceptions, allowing recovery when the child's injury results from the parents' "active" negligence or where the parents negligently entrusted the child with a "dangerous instrumentality." Still others have abrogated the immunity to the extent insurance will pay for the damage, on the assumption that domestic tranquility will not be affected adversely if an insurance company pays.

like Cav

Examples: (1) C sued F under intentional tort theories for sexually abusing him as a child. Trial court dismissed action, citing parent-child tort immunity. (Result: Action reinstated. "Although the majority of states in this country initially adopted the parental immunity doctrine in varying degrees, many have now either abrogated the doctrine completely or have established significant exceptions. . . . [T]he fear of disrupting the fabric and nucleus of families by allowing actions based upon intentional sexual abuse simply appears to be without merit. . . . [I]n those cases the inescapable conclusion is that the family fabric has already been tragically disrupted by the serious misconduct alleged.") *Herzfeld v. Herzfeld*, 781 So.2d 1070 (Fla. 2001).

(2) South Carolina's statutory partial abrogation of the immunity, creating an exception for automobile accidents, was held to violate Equal Protection. The court went on to abolish the immunity completely. *Elam v. Elam*, 275 S.C. 132, 268 S.E.2d 109 (1980).

4. "Heartbalm" Actions

Children may not recover for "alienation of parental affection" resulting in loss of parental society. Only a few cases have held to the contrary. Conversely, courts traditionally have not allowed a parent recovery for the loss of a child's society, although a growing number of states now recognize a tort for malicious interference with custodial or visitation rights.

Examples: (1) M sued her former employer for wrongful discharge and M's children added their own claim for loss of consortium with their mother arising from her discharge. (Result: Children's claim for parental consortium dismissed. "[T]he overwhelming weight of authority in the nation is against recognition of a cause of action for loss of parental consortium." In a related vein, "we have held that a minor child has no cause of action for alienation of his parent's affections by a third party.") *Mendillo v. Board of Educ. of East Haddam*, 246 Conn. 456, 717 A.2d 1177 (1998).

(2) F sued M and her parents for alienation of affections after they allegedly poisoned his relationship with his child. (Result: Dismissal affirmed. Florida law provides no tort remedy for alienation of affections, though it has recently recognized an action for intentional interference with a custodial relationship. "Tort litigation for alienation of affections carries the risk that litigation might increase intra-family disharmony and force children to testify in court, as pawns, testifying against a parent. . . . [O]nly where there is the additional element of interference

with parental physical custody by a third party is it in the child's best interest to allow a cause of action in tort.") *Davis v. Hilton*, 780 So.2d 974 (Fla.App. 2001).

→ three three another

5. Childrens' Torts Against Third Parties—Parents' Liability?

In general, parents are not *vicariously* liable for their child's tort against a third party. Exceptions include the "family purpose doctrine" and limited statutory liability. If it has requisite capacity (and money) a child, of course, is liable for its tort, and parents may be liable for their *own* negligence, if they negligently fail to supervise their child and damage results.

Under the "family purpose doctrine," vicarious liability may be imposed on a parent for the negligence of a family member, including a child, while driving the family car. In addition, a majority of states have enacted statutes that hold parents vicariously liable for damage caused by their children's torts, up to a statutory maximum amount, typically in the low thousands. Statutes of this type generally have been upheld against constitutional attack. A New Jersey court has held that a statute imposing *unlimited* strict liability on parents for damage done to school property by their children denied the parents due process. *Board of Education of Piscataway Twp. v. Caffiero*, 159 N.J.Super. 347, 387 A.2d 1263 (1978).

6. Parents' Criminal Liability?

Parents are not vicariously liable for *criminal* acts of their children. Concern over delinquency and violent crimes by juveniles, however, has led to the enactment of laws making it a crime for parents to fail to properly supervise an offending child.

Examples: (1) A municipal ordinance raised a presumption that a parent is responsible for the misbehavior of a child who twice within one year is adjudged guilty of acts defined as violations of the public peace. (Result: The presumption was held unconstitutional in view of evidence that parental actions are but one factor in the interaction of forces producing juvenile misconduct.) *Doe v. City of Trenton*, 143 N.J.Super. 128, 362 A.2d 1200 (1976).

(2) California Penal Code § 272 punishes causing, encouraging or contributing to delinquency of a minor and provides a fine "not exceeding * * * $2,500, or * * * imprisonment in the county jail for not more than one year, or * * * both such fine and imprisonment * * *, or [release] on probation for a period

not exceeding five years. *For purposes of this subdivision, a parent or legal guardian to any person under the age of 18 years shall have the duty to exercise reasonable care, supervision, protection, and control over their minor child"* (emphasis added).

(3) A 1995 Oregon statute criminalizes a parent's "failing to supervise a child" in cases where the child commits a juvenile offense, violates curfew, or fails to attend school. "[I]t is an affirmative defense that the [parent] took reasonable steps to control the conduct of the child." Ore. Rev. Stat. § 163.577.

F. Property Rights   Gifts or inheritance to Children are children.

Under the common law rule, the minor child's earnings belonged to the father while the child lived with and was maintained by him. Any property acquired by the child in any way other than by its own labor or services (*e.g.,* by gift or inheritance), belonged to the child. In order to provide effective, simple management of gifts to children, nearly all states have adopted the Uniform Transfers to Minors Act or a substantially similar statute.

G. Education: State and Parents

State laws require children to attend school for a designated period, typically expressed in terms of age, such as six to sixteen.

1. Private Schooling

If parents wish to send their children to a private school, a state may not require attendance at a public school. *Pierce v. Society of Sisters,* 268 U.S. 510, 45 S.Ct. 571, 69 L.Ed. 1070 (1925). States typically allow home instruction by parents, subject to minimal standards set by the state.

Example: Based on their religious beliefs, M and F decided to educate their children at home and sought a declaratory judgment that their home-school was a qualified nonpublic school under state law. M had attended college for one year and F had graduated from the U.S. Merchant Marine Academy with a degree in maritime science. M and F instructed their children in basic reading and writing, math, and Bible study. The children's standardized test scores were average or above average. (Result: Parents' home instruction met the statutory requirements for compulsory attendance at a nonpublic school. "[O]ur sister jurisdictions, when faced with the question of whether home instruction is prohibited by school attendance statutes which specify various standards for nonpublic schools, have almost always analyzed the question not in terms of any meaning intrinsic to the word 'school' but rather in terms of whether the particular home instruction in question met the statutory standards. In the absence of a clear legislative prohibition of home instruction, we think this is the better approach to the problem.") *Delconte v. State*, 313 N.C. 384, 329 S.E.2d 636 (1985).

2. Constitutional Objections to Obligatory Schooling

In *Wisconsin v. Yoder*, 406 U.S. 205, 92 S.Ct. 1526, 32 L.Ed.2d 15 (1972), the U.S. Supreme Court held that Wisconsin's compulsory school attendance law could not be applied to Amish parents who did not want their children to attend school beyond the eighth grade. The Court balanced the parents' interest in supervising their children's religious training with the state's interest in compulsory school attendance. The Court emphasized that the Amish religion provides a stable environment and noted the economic self-sufficiency of adherents of that religion.

3. Parental Control Over Classroom Content

Parents continue to voice concerns regarding classroom content, especially in the areas of religion, sex education, and the required use of certain books. Court decisions recognize broad latitude for school officials to determine curriculum. Although some school districts permit parents to "opt out" of objectionable programs, courts have been reluctant to find a constitutional entitlement to do so.

Examples: (1) The U.S. Supreme Court has decided a series of "school prayer" cases. In one case, the parent of three public school children challenged the constitutionality of an Alabama school prayer and meditation statute. The Court held that an Alabama statute authorizing a daily period of silence in public schools for meditation or voluntary prayer was an endorsement of religion that lacked any clearly secular purpose, and thus was in violation of the First Amendment. *Wallace v. Jaffree*, 472 U.S. 38, 105 S.Ct. 2479, 86 L.Ed.2d 29 (1985).

(2) Parents of children in kindergarten and first grade challenged public school's use of books designed to promote respect for families headed by gays and lesbians as a violation of their parental and free exercise rights. Parents claimed a

constitutional right to exempt their children from exposure to the books. The trial court dismissed their action. (Result: Dismissal affirmed. "While we accept as true plaintiffs' assertion that their sincerely held religious beliefs were deeply offended, we find that they have not described a constitutional burden on their rights, or on those of their children. . . . [T]he mere fact that a child is exposed on occasion in public school to a concept offensive to a parent's religious belief does not inhibit the parent from instructing the child differently. A parent whose 'child is exposed to sensitive topics or information [at school] remains free to discuss these matters and to place them in the family's moral or religious context, or to supplement the information with more appropriate materials.' ") *Parker v. Hurley,* 514 F.3d 87 (1st Cir. 2008).

(3) Parent of middle-school student challenged constitutionality of public school's dress code. Trial court granted summary judgment for school district. (Result: Dress code affirmed. "While parents may have a fundamental right to decide *whether* to send their child to a public school, they do not have a fundamental right generally to direct *how* a public school teaches their child. Whether it is the school curriculum, the hours of the school day, school discipline, the timing and content of examinations, the individuals hired to teach at the school, the extracurricular activities offered at the school or, as here, a dress code, these issues of public education are generally 'committed to the control of state and local authorities.' ") *Blau v. Fort Thomas Pub. Sch. Dist.,* 401 F.3d 381 (6th Cir. 2005).

(4) Facing a broader issue than *parental* control, the U.S. Supreme Court has restricted *legislative* control over the school curriculum. The Court struck down a Louisiana statute requiring the teaching of "creation science" alongside evolution, if the latter was to be taught at all. The Court held the law facially invalid because it lacked a clear secular purpose: "The legislative history documents that the Act's primary purpose was to change the science curriculum of public schools in order to provide persuasive advantage to a particular religious doctrine that rejects the factual basis of evolution in its entirety." *Edwards v. Aguillard,* 482 U.S. 578, 107 S.Ct. 2573, 96 L.Ed.2d 510 (1987).

4. Discipline in Schools

Discipline in schools has come under constitutional scrutiny. To illustrate, U.S. Supreme Court cases protect (1) the minor's freedom of political expression (*Tinker v. Des Moines Independent Community School Dist.*, 393 U.S. 503, 511, 89 S.Ct. 733, 739, 21 L.Ed.2d 731 (1969)); (2) the use of lewd and offensive language (*Bethel School District No. 403 v. Fraser*, 478 U.S. 675, 682, 106 S.Ct. 3159, 3164, 92 L.Ed.2d 549 (1986)); (3) censorship of a high school newspaper (*Hazelwood School Dist. v. Kuhlmeier*, 484 U.S. 260, 108 S.Ct. 562, 98 L.Ed.2d 592 (1988)). Further, hearing requirements govern suspensions (*Goss v. Lopez*, 419 U.S. 565, 95 S.Ct. 729, 42 L.Ed.2d 725 (1975)), and students may bring tort suits against school officials for being summarily expelled (*Wood v. Strickland*, 420 U.S. 308, 95 S.Ct. 992, 43 L.Ed.2d 214 (1975)); *cf. Carey v. Piphus*, 435 U.S. 247, 98 S.Ct. 1042, 55 L.Ed.2d 252 (1978). At the same time, the cases make clear that students' constitutional rights are qualified by the reasonable authority of school officials.

Example: High school student challenged his suspension for unfurling a banner at a school-sponsored event reading "Bong Hits 4 Jesus." (Result: Suspension upheld. "Our cases make clear that students do not 'shed their constitutional rights to freedom of speech or expression at the schoolhouse gate.' At the same time, we have held that 'the constitutional rights of students in public school are not automatically coextensive with the rights of adults in other settings,' and that the rights of students 'must be "applied in light of the special characteristics of the school environment." ' Consistent with these principles, we hold that schools may take steps to safeguard those entrusted to their care from speech that can reasonably be regarded as encouraging illegal drug use. We conclude that the school officials in this case did not violate the First Amendment by confiscating the pro-drug banner and suspending the student responsible for it.") *Morse v. Frederick*, ___ U.S. ___, 127 S.Ct. 2618, 168 L.Ed.2d 290 (2007).

Free Speech

The U.S. Supreme Court has held that the "cruel and unusual punishment" clause of the Eighth Amendment does not apply to corporal punishment in public schools. Specifically, "[w]e conclude that when public school teachers or administrators impose disciplinary corporal punishment, the Eighth Amendment is inapplicable. The pertinent constitutional question is whether the imposition is consonant with the requirements of due process. * * * We conclude that the Due Process Clause does not require notice and hearing prior to the imposition of corporal punishment in the public schools, as that practice is authorized and limited by the common law," *i.e.*, "to inflict only such corporal punishment as is reasonably necessary for the proper education and discipline of the child; any punishment going beyond the privilege may result in both civil and criminal liability. * * * As long as the schools are open to public scrutiny, there is no reason to believe that the common law constraints will not effectively remedy and deter excesses such as those alleged in this case." *Ingraham v. Wright,* 430 U.S. 651, 97 S.Ct. 1401, 51 L.Ed.2d 711 (1977).

Review Questions

1. **T or F** Unemancipated minors have no constitutional protections in their own right; what protection they have is derived from protections accorded their parents.

2. **T or F** For an emancipated minor, the fact that he or she is under the age of majority is not a legal defense to contractual obligations.

3. **T or F** Parents proving medical negligence that led to the birth of an unwanted healthy child, may collect for the expense of rearing the child in an action for "wrongful life."

4. **T or F** In the case of the wrongful death of their child, parents may recover for the loss of the child's society and companionship.

5. **T or F** To protect "family harmony," children may not sue their parents and parents may not sue their children for torts inflicted on each other.

6. **T or F** A minor may bring an action for alienation of affections against a third party who has caused the break-up of the minor's parents' marriage.

7. **T or F** Parents are not liable for the criminal acts of their dependent children.

8. **T or F** Under certain circumstances, parents may be held liable for torts committed by their minor children.

9. **T or F** The U.S. Supreme Court has upheld the lawfulness of corporal punishment in public schools.

10. **T or F** Parents are constitutionally entitled to prevent a public school from teaching sex education to their child.

*

XI

Legitimacy, Illegitimacy and Paternity

■ ANALYSIS

A.   **Legitimacy**
  1.   Definition
  2.   Presumption of Legitimacy
B.   **Illegitimacy**
  1.   Traditional Attitudes
  2.   The Constitutional Mandate
C.   **Establishing Paternity**
  1.   The Uniform Parentage Act
  2.   Constitutional Requirements
  3.   Statutes
  4.   The Unmarried Father's Custodial Interests
D.   **Conflicts of Laws**

A. Legitimacy

1. Definition

Legitimacy denotes the status of a child who enjoys a full legal relationship with both parents by virtue of the parents' marriage to each other at the time of the child's birth or conception.

2. Presumption of Legitimacy

The law presumes that a child born to a married woman is the child of her husband, absent convincing proof of his nonpaternity. This presumption was one of the strongest known to the common law and has become readily rebuttable only with the advent of modern blood tests. However, even if there is (or may be) proof of nonpaternity, estoppel may prevent its use (or production) as evidence. In recent years, traditional reluctance has given way in some states to a new willingness to allow presumed fathers to "disestablish" paternity based on blood or DNA tests, sometimes even after many years of acting as a child's father.

Examples: (1) H and W divorced. Custody of three of the four children was given to W. H was ordered to pay support. Attempting to defeat the support order, H alleged that two of the three children in W's custody were not his. H proposed to disprove his paternity with blood tests. (Result: Rules permitting presumption of legitimacy of children to be rebutted by blood tests did not apply so as to permit H to escape liability for support of children whom he had acknowledged as his own for more than fifteen years.) *Watts v. Watts,* 115 N.H. 186, 337 A.2d 350 (1975).

(2) Former H filed petition to disestablish paternity of child born during marriage that was dissolved 17 years ago and to terminate duty of support. The trial court dismissed on ground that there was no allegation of fraud or duress that would provide a basis for reopening divorce court's judgment establishing H's paternity. (Result: Reversed. A Florida statute enacted in 2006 "creates circumstances under which a male may disestablish paternity or terminate a child support obligation when he receives 'newly discovered evidence' demonstrating that he is not the biological father of the child. . . . [T]he plain language of this new statute demonstrates that the Legislature intentionally created a new cause of action in situations where

a father has 'newly discovered evidence,' rather than allegations of fraud, as previously required.") *Johnston v. Johnston*, 979 So.2d 337 (Fla.App. 2008).

B. Illegitimacy

Illegitimacy denotes the legal status of the child born outside of marriage, or of a child born to a married mother whose husband is not the father if the latter has legally disclaimed the child. In current usage, the term "nonmarital" child is replacing the terms "illegitimate" (unlawful) child or child "born out of wedlock" (archaic).

1. Traditional Attitudes

At early common law, the illegitimate child had no legal rights against either parent. As *filius nullius,* the child was kin to no one and was not entitled to support or inheritance from its parents or other blood relatives. However, the law has long recognized the relationship between a mother and her nonmarital child. Until the U.S. Supreme Court intervened in the late 1960s, most states continued to discriminate against the nonmarital child with regard to the child's legal relationship with its father. Of particular importance were the typical absence of a right of intestate succession, the presence of only a limited, if any, right of support, and limited, if any, eligibility under statutes (*e.g.,* social security, workmen's compensation, wrongful death) requiring proof of descent or specifically limited to legitimate offspring.

2. The Constitutional Mandate

Under the Equal Protection and Due Process Clauses, the U.S. Supreme Court has progressively invalidated nearly all forms of legal discrimination involving nonmarital children.

a. Standard of Review

The U.S. Supreme Court applies neither the "strict scrutiny" accorded racial classifications, nor the much less stringent "rational basis test," to classifications based upon the status of illegitimacy. Instead, the Court has employed an intermediate standard of review, under which the State must prove that the discriminatory classification is "substantially related" to the achievement of an "important" state interest.

b. Relationship to Mother

Levy v. Louisiana, 391 U.S. 68, 88 S.Ct. 1509, 20 L.Ed.2d 436 (1968), was the first U.S. Supreme Court case to apply the Equal Protection Clause to legal discrimination based on illegitimacy. Dealing with an unusual Louisiana law that denied a full legal relationship between the nonmarital child and its *mother,* the case established that a nonmarital child may recover for the wrongful death of its mother. Simultaneously, the Court held that a mother may recover for the wrongful death of her nonmarital child. *Glona v. American Guarantee and Liability Insurance Co.,* 391 U.S. 73, 88 S.Ct. 1515, 20 L.Ed.2d 441 (1968). Since discrimination in the legal relationship between mother and child was very unusual, the significance of these cases lies mainly in their applicability to the father and child relationship.

c.   U.S. Supreme Court Cases on the Father and Child Relationship

1)   Intestate Succession

Several U.S. Supreme Court cases have directly addressed the right of the nonmarital child to inherit from its deceased intestate father. In *Labine v. Vincent,* 401 U.S. 532, 91 S.Ct. 1017, 28 L.Ed.2d 288 (1971), the Court upheld a Louisiana law denying inheritance to a nonmarital child, even though the father had acknowledged the child during his lifetime. In *Trimble v. Gordon,* 430 U.S. 762, 97 S.Ct. 1459, 52 L.Ed.2d 31 (1977), the Court declared that an Illinois law that did not allow nonmarital offspring to inherit from their intestate fathers denied equal protection. (The Illinois Probate Act allowed nonmarital children to inherit only from their intestate mothers, whereas children born in wedlock could inherit by intestate succession from their mothers and their fathers.) The Court held that a classification based on illegitimacy must bear a rational relationship to a legitimate state purpose, and the provision could not be justified on the ground that it promoted legitimate family relationships. In a footnote, the Court stated that *Labine* had limited value as precedent. In *Lalli v. Lalli,* 439 U.S. 259, 99 S.Ct. 518, 58 L.Ed.2d 503 (1978), the Court held that, for purposes of intestate succession from an unmarried father, New York may require that paternity have been established during the father's lifetime.

2)   Right of Support

In *Gomez v. Perez,* 409 U.S. 535, 93 S.Ct. 872, 35 L.Ed.2d 56 (1973), the U.S. Supreme Court held that Texas law could not exclude nonmarital children from a generally enforceable right to paternal support.

3)   Wrongful Death

Parham v. Hughes, 441 U.S. 347, 99 S.Ct. 1742, 60 L.Ed.2d 269 (1979), involved a Georgia statute that precluded a father who had not legitimated a child from suing for the child's wrongful death. The statute was upheld on the ground that it provides a rational means of dealing with the problem of proving paternity, and that the father's situation is different from that of the child, in that the father's status is not immutable, and that he could have come forward to claim paternity. Moreover, the statute was found not to discriminate invidiously against a father simply because he is of the male sex.

4) Government Benefits Based on Father and Child Relationship

Examples: (1) A state may not discriminate against nonmarital children in distributing welfare benefits. *New Jersey Welfare Rights Organization v. Cahill,* 411 U.S. 619, 93 S.Ct. 1700, 36 L.Ed.2d 543 (1973).

(2) Nonmarital children, whether or not acknowledged, are eligible to collect workers' compensation benefits occasioned by their father's death. *Weber v. Aetna Cas. and Surety Co.,* 406 U.S. 164, 92 S.Ct. 1400, 31 L.Ed.2d 768 (1972).

(3) Federal law may require that unrecognized nonmarital children prove actual dependency to collect certain social security benefits even while legitimate children and those nonmarital children whose paternity is ascertained need not present such proof. *Mathews v. Lucas,* 427 U.S. 495, 96 S.Ct. 2755, 49 L.Ed.2d 651 (1976).

(4) Statute denying benefits to nonlegitimated nonmarital children who are born after the onset of the father's disability was not reasonably related to the valid governmental interest of preventing spurious claims. *Jimenez v. Weinberger,* 417 U.S. 628, 94 S.Ct. 2496, 41 L.Ed.2d 363 (1974).

(5) In *Fiallo v. Bell,* 430 U.S. 787, 97 S.Ct. 1473, 52 L.Ed.2d 50 (1977), unwed natural fathers and their nonmarital offspring sought to enjoin enforcement of sections of Immigration and Nationality Act that exclude the relationship between nonmarital child and its natural father from the special preference immigra-

tion status accorded a "child" or "parent" of a United States citizen or lawful permanent resident, whereas the *mother* and child relationship is covered. The Supreme Court rejected the claim on the grounds that (1) Congress' power to expel or exclude aliens is largely immune from judicial control (2) no factors in this case warranted more searching judicial scrutiny that generally applied in immigration cases, and (3) it is not for the Court to probe and test the justifications for legislative decisions in this area.

C. Establishing Paternity

1. The Uniform Parentage Act

About one half of the states have enacted the Uniform Parentage Act of 1973 or a variation. The Act provides procedures facilitating establishment of paternity. Considerable reliance is placed on improved, modern blood-typing procedures that contribute to certainty and ease of paternity determination. A successor Act, incorporating many provisions from the 1973 Act while also adding new provisions reflecting advances in the scientific determination of paternity, was promulgated in 2000. As of 2008, it had been enacted in eight states.

2. Constitutional Requirements

The Supreme Court has not done much to define acceptable procedures for paternity actions.

Examples: (1) In *Rivera v. Minnich*, 483 U.S. 574, 107 S.Ct. 3001, 97 L.Ed.2d 473 (1987), the Court held that Pennsylvania's legislative judgment allowing paternity to be established by a preponderance of the evidence, rather than requiring a higher standard, is entitled to a powerful presumption of validity, when challenged by an alleged father under the Due Process Clause.

(2) In *Lalli v. Lalli*, 439 U.S. 259, 99 S.Ct. 518, 58 L.Ed.2d 503 (1978), the Court did not question New York's imposition of a higher burden of proof (clear and convincing) than that normally required in a civil action (preponderance of the evidence).

(3) In several cases, the Court has struck down, as unduly short, several laws imposing various periods of limitations on

paternity actions. *Mills v. Habluetzel*, 456 U.S. 91, 102 S.Ct. 1549, 71 L.Ed.2d 770 (1982) (one year); *Pickett v. Brown*, 462 U.S. 1, 103 S.Ct. 2199, 76 L.Ed.2d 372 (1983) (two years); *Clark v. Jeter*, 486 U.S. 456, 108 S.Ct. 1910, 100 L.Ed.2d 465 (1988) (six years).

more evidence weight to your side

3. Statutes

a. Burden of Proof

Most states impose the civil standard of proof (preponderance of the evidence) in paternity actions. Several states still impose an enhanced burden of proof (such as clear and convincing evidence) that has its roots in the history of the paternity action as a criminal prosecution.

b. Statute of Limitations

The Uniform Parentage Act, in essence, suspends the statute of limitation during the child's minority. Under the federal child support laws, participating states are required to have an 18–year period of limitation. Accordingly, 18 years or longer is now the norm.

4. The Unmarried Father's Custodial Interests
(See also Adoption, pp. 298–301).

Before the U.S. Supreme Court got involved, the nonmarital child's custody, including any decision on adoption, had in most states been wholly under the mother's control. Only a few states heard the unwed father on the question of adoption when he had acknowledged the child in some way, when he had adequately contributed to the support of the child, or when paternity had been established by a court. By now, the U.S. Supreme Court has had a significant effect on adoptions of nonmarital children even while some uncertainty remains concerning the precise meaning in this context of Equal Protection as well as of substantive *and* procedural Due Process.

The U.S. Supreme Court has defined the unmarried father's rights in terms of his *actual relationship* with the child. *Stanley v. Illinois*, 405 U.S. 645, 92 S.Ct. 1208, 31 L.Ed.2d 551 (1972). In *Stanley*, a father who had long lived with the mother and his nonmarital children in a *de facto* family unit was held constitutionally entitled to notice and to a hearing in proceedings involving the custody of his children and, based on a footnote in *Stanley*, numerous states require a *published* notice of the birth of the nonmarital child, addressed "to unknown father" or "to whom it may concern," before an adoption may proceed. However, the "mere existence of a biological link does not merit equivalent constitutional protection." *Lehr v. Robertson*, 463 U.S. 248, 103 S.Ct. 2985, 77 L.Ed.2d 614 (1983).

Examples: (1) In 1978, the U.S. Supreme Court denied an unmarried father a "veto power" over the adoption of his nonmarital child, when for eleven years he had not availed himself of the opportunity under Georgia law to legitimate the child, had supported the child only irregularly and had never lived with the child in a *de facto* family setting. *Quilloin v. Walcott*, 434 U.S. 246, 98 S.Ct. 549, 54 L.Ed.2d 511 (1978).

(2) *Caban v. Mohammed*, 441 U.S. 380, 99 S.Ct. 1760, 60 L.Ed.2d 297 (1979), involved an unmarried father who had lived with the mother and two children for five years, had contributed to the children's support and had seen them frequently after he and the mother separated. The U.S. Supreme Court emphasized the father's *de facto* relationship with his children and allowed him to block the adoption of his children by the mother's new husband.

(3) An unmarried father had not supported and rarely seen his two-year old child. He sought to invalidate the child's adoption by the mother's husband on the ground that his right to due process was violated when he was not given advance notice of the adoption proceeding nor an opportunity to be heard. The Supreme Court found the distinction between *Caban* and *Stanley* on one side, and this case and *Quilloin* on the other "both clear and significant." "When an unwed father demonstrates a full commitment to the responsibilities of parenthood by 'com[ing] forward to participate in the rearing of his child,' his interest in personal contact with his child acquires substantial protection under the due process clause. * * * But the mere existence of a biological link does not merit equivalent constitutional protection." *Lehr v. Robertson*, cited *supra*.

(4) An unmarried father had briefly enjoyed "the blessings of the parent-child relationship" while he cohabited with the *married* mother. When he sought custodial rights to his daughter, the mother's husband objected. The Supreme Court upheld the traditional presumption of legitimacy that applies to a child born to a married mother and denied the unmarried father any and all rights. *Michael H. v. Gerald D.*, 491 U.S. 110, 109 S.Ct. 2333, 105 L.Ed.2d 91 (1989).

D. Conflicts of Laws

Legitimacy status generally is respected across state lines as a matter of policy. A *judicial* determination of legitimate status must be accorded "Full Faith and Credit" in other states.

Review Questions

1. **T or F** A child born to a married woman is presumed to be her husband's child.

2. **T or F** Under traditional American law, a nonmarital child was entitled to inherit from his mother, but not from his father.

3. **T or F** Today, illegitimacy is deemed a suspect classification under the Equal Protection Clause and classifications based on illegitimacy are subject to strict scrutiny.

4. **T or F** A judicial determination of legitimacy is entitled to Full Faith and Credit nationwide.

5. **T or F** States need not afford unwed fathers the same custodial rights vis-à-vis their nonmarital children as married fathers have vis-à-vis their legitimate children.

6. **T or F** Many sources indicate that, at early common law, a nonmarital child was not legally deemed its mother's child.

7. **T or F** For purposes of intestate succession, a state may require that a child's paternity must have been established during the father's life.

8. **T or F** Nonmarital children have a more limited right to paternal support than legitimate children have.

9. **T or F** In terms of providing government derived financial benefits, a statute may not distinguish between nonmarital children who have and those who have not been recognized by the father.

10. **T or F** Once a child meets the definition of legitimacy in the state of its domicile, the Full Faith and Credit Clause requires courts everywhere (in the U.S.) to recognize the child's legitimate status.

XII

Adoption

■ ANALYSIS

A. **History and Development**
B. **Social Functions**
C. **The Adoption Process**
    1. Agency Placement
    2. Independent Adoption
    3. "Sale" of Children and "Black Market" Adoption
    4. Subsidized Adoption
    5. Adult Adoption
    6. Equitable Adoption
D. **Qualifications of Adoptive Parents**
    1. Marital Status
    2. Sexual Orientation
    3. Age
    4. Physical and Emotional Disabilities
    5. Religion
    6. Race
E. **Consent to Adoption**
    1. Consent of Parents
    2. Consent of Unmarried Father
    3. Unreasonable Refusal of Consent
    4. Adoption by Stepparent: Consent of the Noncustodial Parent

5.   Consent of Agency or Guardian
6.   Consent of the Child
7.   Formalities of Consent
8.   Finality and Revocation of Consent
F.   **Anonymity**
G.   **Revocation of Adoption**
H.   **Legal Effect of Adoption**
1.   Custody
2.   Name and Birth Certificate
3.   Incest Laws
4.   Obligation of Support
5.   Inheritance

A. History and Development

Adoption did not exist under the common law and was established by statute, beginning in the U.S. in the mid-nineteenth century.

B. Social Functions

Adoption (1) serves the adopted child's interest in being raised in a presumably better environment than would be the case without adoption, (2) provides childless couples with children, (3) relieves the natural parent of an unwanted child, and (4) relieves the taxpayer of a potential welfare burden.

C. The Adoption Process

Statutory regulation of the adoption process is detailed and strict. The two main *Test* interests are the protection of the child's best interests and the biological parents' rights. The first requires careful scrutiny of where the child goes, and the second ensures that existing parental rights are properly terminated before new parental rights are created in the adoptive parents.

1. Agency Placement

In many adoptions by unrelated persons, state agencies or state-regulated private agencies act as intermediaries between natural and adoptive parents. Advantages of agency placement (as opposed to independent, private placement) typically include: (1) professional investigation and approval of the adoptive parents and their home; (2) continuing supervision of the adoption by the agency for a period of time following the adoption; and (3) maintenance of confidentiality concerning the natural and adoptive parents' identity.

2. Independent Adoption

Many states prohibit independent adoption by non-relatives and closely regulate independent placement even with relatives. In other states, natural parents may contract to place their children directly with adoptive parents. Proponents of independent adoptions argue that they provide immediate placement for the child with less intrusion into the privacy of the adoptive parents. Critics of independent adoption argue that (1) such adoptions may be challenged more easily than professionally arranged adoptions, (2) there may be inadequate or no professional investigation into the suitability of the adoptive parents, and (3) there may not be the confidentiality typically maintained in agency adoptions. Since court approval to complete the adoption legally is needed in any case, a court may exercise considerable control over the suitability of any given adoption, depending on the statutes in force and the practices followed.

3. "Sale" of Children and "Black Market" Adoption

Most state laws specifically prohibit and criminalize the payment of consideration in connection with adoption. Prohibited payments include payments to the natural mother or father (with exceptions for out-of-pocket expenses involving the pregnancy) or to middlemen (with exceptions permitting appropriate legal and medical fees). So-called "black market" adoptions involve the "sale" of children.

Examples: (1) Utah Stat. § 76–7–203 provides that any person with custody or control of a child who "sells, or disposes of the child . . . in consideration of the payment of money or another thing of value" is guilty of a felony. The statute expressly permits, however, the payment of reasonable expenses incurred by birth parents relating to pregnancy, childbirth, and facilitating the adoption, including "temporary living expenses during the pregnancy."

(2) D presented herself to a prospective adoptive couple as an intermediary working with an adoption attorney and offered to help arrange an adoption of a three-year-old girl whose parents were both incarcerated. D informed the couple that the attorney's fees and other costs would likely total $5,000. Thereafter, the prospective adoptive couple learned that D was not associated with the attorney, was not authorized to arrange the adoption, and had misrepresented several material facts about the child's availability for adoption. D was convicted under a Mississippi statute of arranging the "placing out" of a child for compensation and was fined and sentenced to one year in jail and two years supervised release. The intermediate appellate court reversed, finding insufficient evidence of guilt. (Result: Conviction reinstated. "The Court of Appeals stated that [D] had to *receive* something of value to be guilty," but "the State need only prove she directly or indirectly requested a thing of value." Here, the suggestion that the adoption would cost $5,000 was sufficient.) *Balouch v. State*, 938 So.2d 253 (Miss. 2006).

(3) Defendant bought a used car and offered it to the mother of a small child in exchange for the child. The mother gave defendant the child. Defendant pleaded guilty to inducing a mother to part with her child, but reserved the right to challenge the constitutionality of the applicable statute on vagueness grounds. (Result: Statute constitutional. The statute "defines the term 'inducement' to include any direct or indirect financial assistance except 'payment or reimbursement of the medical expenses directly related to the mother's pregnancy and hospitalization for the birth of the child and medical care for the child.' Thus, [the statute] provides clear warning that if a person provides any financial assistance to a parent other than that specifically excluded from the definition set forth in the statute, that person provides an 'inducement' to the parent. * * * Based on the clear language of the statute and assigning the ordinary meaning to the words used in the statute, we hold that the challenged terms have meanings sufficiently precise for a person or ordinary intelligence to understand that offering an automobile to a parent in exchange for physical custody or control of a child is proscribed.") *Douglas v. State*, 263 Ga. 748, 438 S.E.2d 361 (1994).

4. Subsidized Adoption

In recent years, both federal and state governments have stepped up their efforts to promote adoption, including through the use of subsidies and financial incentives. A federal tax credit, instituted in 1997, reimburses adoptive parents for many of the expenses involved in the adoption process. And states, supported by federal funding, typically offer additional subsidies to families that adopt harder-to-place children with "special needs," including health insurance, college tuition waivers, and counseling or other services. Beginning in 1999, the federal government began paying large bonuses directly to states that moved more children from foster care into adoption. Partly as a result of this combination of incentives, the number of adoptions in the United States has more than doubled since 1995 and now exceeds 50,000.

Example: D.C. Code § 3–115(b) provides: "(1) The Mayor may make adoption subsidy payments to an adoptive family (irrespective of the state of residence of the family), as needed, on behalf of a child with special needs, where such child would in all likelihood go without adoption except for the acceptance of the child as a member of the adoptive family, and where the adoptive family has the capability of providing the permanent family relationships needed by such child in all areas except financial, as determined by the Mayor. * * * (2) For the purpose of this subsection—(A) The term 'child with special needs' includes any child who is difficult to place in adoption because of age, race, or ethnic background, physical or mental condition, or membership in a sibling group which should be placed together. A child for whom an adoptive placement has not been made within six months after he is legally available for adoptive placement shall be considered a child with special needs within the meaning of this section. (B) The term 'adoptive family' includes single persons."

5. Adult Adoption

Many states allow adults to be adopted. Adults are typically adopted in order to create inheritance rights or sometimes to create a family relationship where marriage is disallowed, as in the case of same-sex couples. Adult adoptions may be accomplished by consent of the parties and entry of a court decree following a simple proceeding. Since the concerns designed to promote the best interests of children are absent in adult adoption, states impose much less supervision on adult adoptions. Very occasionally, however, courts have refused adoptions on policy grounds.

Example: H and W, a married couple aged 50 and 53 years respectively, sought to adopt A, a 52–year-old single woman who had been living with them for more than 10 years. H, W, and A described themselves as "a team of three equals" and stated that they simply wished to formalize their common family status. (Result: Adoption denied. New Jersey statute governing adult adoption requires an age difference of at least 10 years between adopter and adoptee unless court finds that adoption is nevertheless in best interests of adoptee. "Because this court believes that the age difference requirement was enacted by the New Jersey Legislature as a means of ensuring a semblance of a parent-child relationship, it logically follows that, if this age difference cannot be met, the court must examine whether the parties' purpose is to legally solidify their already-existing parent-child relationship. If the parties do not have a [de facto] parent-child relationship and are not separated in age by ten years, the adoption petition must necessarily be denied, as it is contrary to the Legislature's intent. Otherwise, courts would be providing a legal stamp of approval to illogical and on some occasions bizarre relationships without any consideration or weight given to the statutory age difference requirement."). *In re P.B. for Adoption of L.C.*, 392 N.J.Super. 190, 920 A.2d 155 (2006).

6. Equitable Adoption

Occasionally, persons take a child into their home and, over time, treat the child as their own without formal adoption. In other cases, would-be adoptive parents have agreed to adopt a child and failed to complete the legal formalities needed to finalize the adoption, but they have treated the child as though it had been adopted. In the case of intestate death, the question is whether, for purposes of inheritance, the child should be treated as an adopted child. In the case of divorce or other family dissolution, the question is whether a child support obligation or custodial rights may be recognized in the absence of a formal adoption. Traditionally, most courts refused to do so, being persuaded that because adoption did not exist at common law, a valid adoption may be accomplished only by compliance with the relevant statute. Today, however, most states recognize "equitable adoptions" for certain limited purposes, such as inheritance, standing to recover in tort, and, less often, child support or visitation rights.

Examples: (1) After M was negligently killed in a traffic accident, F filed a petition to recognize C as M's child by equitable adoption. The court found that M had lived with F and C for four years with the intention of marrying F and adopting C, but had not done so by the time of her death. It recognized an equitable adoption, and C was then added as a plaintiff in a wrongful death action against the driver who caused the fatal accident. The driver's insurance company contested C's standing as a child of M. (Result: Equitable adoption upheld. "To prove an equitable adoption, the plaintiff must show that a promise to adopt was made, but the adoption had not occurred prior to the promisor's death. * * * An equitable adoption differs from a legal adoption in that it is only valid and binding upon the parties involved in the equitable proceeding." Here, there was sufficient testimony by M's survivors of her intention to adopt C.) *Coon v. American Compressed Steel*, 207 S.W.3d 629 (Mo.App. 2006).

(2) C was conceived as a result of a brief nonmarital relationship between M and F. While pregnant, M married H, who

agreed to adopt C and to assume full parental responsibility with F's consent. The marriage between M and H dissolved after three years, however, and no formal adoption ever occurred. When M then sought child support from F, he defended on the ground that H had "equitably adopted" C and therefore should be substituted for F as C's father. (Result: Equitable adoption doctrine does not apply in child support matters. "New Mexico courts have recognized the doctrine of equitable adoption. Where the doctrine is applied, no formal adoption occurs; rather, the purpose of the doctrine is to permit the court to apply equity and to create a status that confers certain benefits to a child." In applying the doctrine, "the best interests of the child are paramount." "The biological father cannot freely contract away his parental obligation. In the absence of a formal adoption under the Adoption Act, the biological father cannot voluntarily effect a relinquishment of his parental duties imposed upon him by law.") *Poncho v. Bowdoin*, 138 N.M. 857, 126 P.3d 1221 (N.M.App. 2005).

D. Qualifications of Adoptive Parents

Statutes govern the qualifications of adoptive parents. Courts and practice have added detail. The best interests of the child control. Traditional factors include marital status, age, fitness to be a parent, religion, race, and economic status of the prospective adopter(s). The trend however, is against a narrow or rigid conception of who should qualify as a "suitable" adoptive parent.

1. Marital Status

Some states allow adoption only by married couples. Many states, however, allow single persons to adopt, and a growing number have allowed unmarried couples to adopt *jointly*. In all events, courts recognize that the marital status of prospective adopting parents is a legitimate factor for consideration and prefer adoption by married couples. When a married couple adopts, statutes usually require that *both* parents join in the adoption.

Example: An unmarried couple who had lived together for 20 years sought to adopt the woman's 15–year-old nephew, who had been living with the couple since the death of his custodial grandmother several years earlier. The trial court denied the petition on the grounds that New York's adoption statute permitted adoption only by a single person or by a married couple jointly. (Result: Reversed. The adoption statute "opens with a declaration that 'An adult unmarried person or an adult husband and his adult wife together may adopt another person.' " By requiring that both spouses join in an adoption petition, the legislature did not intend to preclude joint adoption by unmarried persons.) *In re Adoption of Emilio R.*, 293 A.D.2d 27, 742 N.Y.S.2d 22 (2002).

2. Sexual Orientation

An intending adopter's gay or lesbian sexual orientation has figured as a qualifying factor either on its own or in terms of the intending adopter's single marital status. A Florida statute flatly prohibiting adoptions by homosexuals was upheld against constitutional attack. Most other states, however, take a more flexible view, and indeed a growing number now allow "second-parent adoptions," whereby the same-sex partner of a gay or lesbian parent may adopt in much the same way as a stepparent.

Examples: (1) "Under the New York adoption statute, a single person can adopt a child. Equally clear is the right of a single homosexual to adopt. These appeals call upon us to decide if the unmarried partner of a child's biological mother, whether heterosexual or homosexual, who is raising the child together with the biological parent, can become the child's second parent by means of adoption. Because the two adoptions sought—one by an unmarried heterosexual couple, the other by the lesbian partner of the child's mother—are fully consistent with the adoption statute, we answer this question in the affirmative. To rule otherwise would mean that the thousands of New York children actually being raised in homes headed by two unmarried persons could have only one legal parent, not the two who want them." *Matter of Jacob*, 86 N.Y.2d 651, 636 N.Y.S.2d 716, 660 N.E.2d 397 (1995).

(2) M and her female partner (A) decided to have and raise children together. M was artificially inseminated with sperm from an anonymous donor and gave birth to two children. A became a second parent to the first child through adoption, with M's consent, and petitioned to adopt the second child as well. Before the second adoption became final, however, M and A's relationship dissolved. M then moved to block A's adoption, contending there was no legal basis for A to adopt. (Result:

Second-parent adoption is permitted without terminating the rights of the existing parent. "Second parent adoption can secure the salutary incidents of legally recognized parentage for a child of a nonbiological parent who otherwise must remain a legal stranger. Second parent adoptions also benefit children by providing a clear legal framework for resolving any disputes that may arise over custody and visitation. Our explicitly recognizing their validity will prevent uncertainty, conflict, and protracted litigation in this area, all of which plainly are harmful to children caught in the middle."). *Sharon S. v. Superior Court*, 31 Cal.4th 417, 2 Cal.Rptr.3d 699, 73 P.3d 554 (2003).

(3) F had served as an "exemplary" foster parent to three children since their infancy. His petition to adopt, however, was denied on the ground that he is gay and that a Florida statute prohibits adoption by homosexuals. F challenged the constitutionality of the Florida statute. (Result: Statute upheld. Florida's law burdens no fundamental rights. "There is no precedent for appellants' novel proposition that long-term foster care arrangements and guardianships are entitled to constitutional protection akin to that accorded to natural and adoptive families." Nor do homosexuals constitute a suspect class. Accordingly, the rational-basis test applies, and Florida's law is rationally related to the state's "legitimate interest in encouraging a stable and nurturing environment for the education and socialization of its adopted children.") *Lofton v. Secretary of Dep't of Children & Family Services*, 358 F.3d 804 (11th Cir. 2004).

3. Age

Courts consider the age of the adopting parent, both in terms of legal capacity and in relation to the age of the child proposed to be adopted. The adopting parent must be of legal age, although some statutes allow exceptions upon showing of good cause. Many agencies prefer that the age span between adoptive parents and the adopted child approximate a "normal" age span between natural parents and their children. The facts of the particular case control.

Examples: (1) Solely because of their ages, H (aged 68) and W (aged 55) were denied adoption of a 3–year-old who had been a foster child in their home for virtually her whole life. (Result: Reversed. The court looked past the age factor and recognized that to "separate the child from her established home" would invite risk of grave harm to her.) *In re Haun,* 31 Ohio Misc. 9, 277 N.E.2d 258 (1971).

(2) H and W took newborn C into their home with the stated intent of adopting her. When C was 3 years old, the State Department of Health recommended that H and W's petition for adoption be denied on the sole ground that H was 70 years old and W was 54 years old. (Result: Adoption granted. The court took notice of the fact that C had been living with H and W for three years and that, aside from their ages, H and W had no negative characteristics in relation to the adoption.) *In re Adoption of Michelle Lee T.,* 44 Cal.App.3d 699, 117 Cal.Rptr. 856 (1975).

4. Physical and Emotional Disabilities

Courts consider physical and emotional disabilities of prospective adoptive parents. If the would-be parents are otherwise qualified, courts do not deny an adoption solely on the basis of a disability that does not directly involve ability to care for the child.

5. Religion

It is disputed what role (if any) the religion of the adopting parents and the religion of the child may or should play in the adoption decision. Some statutes specifically provide that, when practicable or possible, a child should be placed with adoptive parents of the same religious beliefs as the child or birth mother. Such statutes have been defended on the ground that they increase a religious mother's willingness to place her child for adoption. If the child to be adopted is of an age where it has its own religious understanding, religious matching obviously is in the child's best interest.

Examples: (1) H and W were refused permission to file an application as adoptive parents solely because they did not have a religious affiliation. Article VI § 32 of New York's Constitution specified that children be placed *when practicable* in the custody of a person of the same religion as the child. (Result: H and W's right to profess no religion was not violated. H and W would still be eligible, under Article VI, to adopt a child when the natural parents were indifferent to the religious placement of their child or when the child's religious background was unknown.) *Dickens v. Ernesto,* 30 N.Y.2d 61, 330 N.Y.S.2d 346,

281 N.E.2d 153 (1972). (*Caveat:* Twenty years after *Dickens*, a New York court ruled that the use of religion as "the sole or determinative factor" in making adoptive placements *would* state a claim for violation of the Establishment Clause of the First Amendment. *Orzechowski v. Perales,* 153 Misc.2d 464, 582 N.Y.S.2d 341 (Sup. Ct. 1992).)

(2) H and W, both Episcopalian, petitioned for the adoption of a Cambodian refugee orphan. The adoption agency denied H and W's request because the agency placed children only with members of evangelical Protestant churches. (Result: Although an agency may attempt to match the religion of the child to the religion of the adoptive parents, the agency may not impose any additional religious requirements on adoptive parents.) *Scott v. Family Ministries,* 65 Cal.App.3d 492, 135 Cal.Rptr. 430 (1976).

(3) H and W petitioned to adopt baby C. Although they were otherwise well qualified as adoptive parents, the trial judge denied H and W's petition solely because they had no religious affiliation. (Result: Reversed. The New Jersey Supreme Court held that, while religion may be considered as a *factor* in determining the suitability of adoptive parents, denial of an adoption solely because the prospective parents have no religious affiliation violates the First Amendment.) *In re Adoption of "E",* 59 N.J. 36, 279 A.2d 785 (1971).

6. Race

Since 1996, the federal Multiethnic Placement Act (MEPA) (42 U.S.C. § 1996b) has made it unlawful for states or private adoption agencies receiving federal funds to "delay or deny" an adoptive placement on the basis of race. This mandate attacks what had been a common practice among agencies and social workers of matching children with adoptive parents by race, even if finding a match required that the child wait for months or years. Congress included an exception in the law, however, for children of Native American ancestry. Those children remain subject to another federal statute, the Indian Child Welfare Act, which mandates a preference for tribal placement of Indian children available for adoption.

Examples: (1) Twenty children who had been in foster care for years sued New Jersey's child welfare agency for systemic failures to live up to its legal obligations, including violating the federal Multiethnic Placement Act (MEPA) by placing children according to their race. Agency moved to dismiss. (Result: Dismissal denied. MEPA provides a private right of action for individuals injured by agency decisions to "delay or deny" an adoptive or foster care placement because of race. Plaintiffs, who claimed that Hispanic children who spoke only English were placed in Spanish-speaking homes out of a desire to achieve an ethnic match, stated a claim for a violation of MEPA.) *Charlie H. v. Whitman*, 83 F. Supp. 2d 476 (D.N.J. 2000).

(2) M and F were members of the Mississippi Band of Choctaw Indians and residents of the Choctaw reservation. Twin babies were born to M and F in a county 200 miles from the reservation. Because M and F did not want the children to grow up on the reservation, they both consented to the twins' adoption by a non-native-American couple. The county court at the twin's place of birth finalized the adoption. Two months later, the Choctaw Tribe moved to vacate the adoption decree on the ground that under the Indian Child Welfare Act of 1978 (ICWA) the tribal court had exclusive jurisdiction over child custody proceedings involving Indian children domiciled on the reservation. The county court denied the motion. The state supreme court affirmed. (Result: Reversed and remanded to the tribal court. "It remains to give content to the term 'domicile' in the circumstances of the present case. The holding of the Supreme Court of Mississippi that the twin babies were not domiciled on the Choctaw Reservation appears to have rested on two findings of fact by the trial court: (1) that they had never been physically present there, and (2) that they were 'voluntarily surrendered' by their parents. The question before us, therefore, is whether under the ICWA definition of 'domicile' such facts suffice to render the twins nondomiciliaries of the reservation. * * * It is undisputed in this case that the domicile of the mother (as well as the father) has been, at all relevant times, on the Choctaw Reservation. Thus, it is clear that at their birth the twin babies were also domiciled on the reservation, even though they themselves had never been there. * * * The appellees in this case argue strenuously that the twins' mother went to great lengths to give birth off the reservation so that her children could be adopted by the Holyfields. But that was

precisely part of the Congress' concern. Permitting individual members of the tribe to avoid tribal exclusive jurisdiction by the simple expedient of giving birth off the reservation would, to a large extend, nullify the purpose the ICWA was intended to accomplish. * * * We are not unaware that over three years have passed since the twin babies were born and placed in the Holyfield home, and that a court deciding their fate today is not writing on a blank slate in the same way it would have in January 1986. Three years' development of family ties cannot be undone, and a separation at this point would doubtless cause considerable pain. Whatever feelings we might have as to where the twins should live, however, it is not for us to decide that question. We have been asked to decide the legal question of *who* should make the custody determination concerning these children—not what the outcome of that determination should be. The law places that decision in the hands of the Choctaw tribal court.") *Mississippi Band of Choctaw Indians v. Holyfield*, 490 U.S. 30, 109 S.Ct. 1597, 104 L.Ed.2d 29 (1989).

E. Consent to Adoption

Proper consent to adoption is essential to accomplish a valid adoption. Consent must be obtained from the biological parents of the child or, if parental rights have been legally terminated, from the agency or guardian entrusted with the care of the child. If the parents are minors, their consent to the adoption typically is valid. If the child is above a certain age, its own consent may be required.

1. Consent of Parents

Except where their rights have been legally terminated (or are legally terminated as part of the adoption proceeding), the consent of both parents is a universal prerequisite to the adoption of a marital child. With respect to a nonmarital child, the mother's consent traditionally sufficed. Importantly, in recent decades, the *unmarried* father has gained substantial rights that must be carefully respected if an adoption is to be secure from challenge.

2. Consent of Unmarried Father

At common law, the mother had custody of a nonmarital child. Under statutes, the unmarried father could be held liable for support, but had no rights to the child. Consequently, he had no right to notice of (or to consent to) the adoption of the child.

a. Judicial (U.S. Supreme Court) Intervention

Since the 1970's, the U.S. Supreme Court has held in a series of landmark cases that the unmarried father has a significant and constitutionally protected interest in the custody and adoption of his nonmarital child. While the unmarried father's interest has not yet been precisely defined, it is clear that for constitutional purposes, there is a difference between (1) an unmarried father who has lived with and/or contributed to the support of his child, and (2) one who did not have or was not given that opportunity, and (3) one who did not seize an opportunity that was available to him to show his serious interest in his child. An adjudication that an adoption should not have proceeded without an unmarried fathers's consent does *not* automatically mean that he must be awarded custodial rights.

Examples: (1) M and F lived together intermittently for 18 years and had three children. They were not married. Under Illinois law, children of unwed mothers became wards of the state upon the death of their mother. M died. F sought custody of his children. (Result: F prevails. The U.S. Supreme Court ruled that "all Illinois parents are constitutionally entitled to a hearing on their fitness before their children are removed from their custody." The opinion contained the following footnote: "Extending opportunity for hearing to unwed fathers who desire and claim competence to care for their children creates no constitutional or procedural obstacle to foreclosing those unwed fathers who are not so inclined. Unwed fathers who do not promptly respond cannot complain if their children are declared wards of the State. Those who do respond retain the burden of proving their fatherhood.") *Stanley v. Illinois*, 405 U.S. 645, 92 S.Ct. 1208, 31 L.Ed.2d 551 (1972).

(2) Georgia law provided an unwed father the right to legitimate his child and gain full parental rights with respect to the child's adoption. Here the putative father had not attempted to recognize the child until the adoption process began (eleven years after the child's birth), and the U.S. Supreme Court denied an unwed father the right to veto the adoption of his child. *Quilloin v. Walcott*, 434 U.S. 246, 98 S.Ct. 549, 54 L.Ed.2d 511 (1978).

(3) Where the putative father had lived with the mother for five years, had admitted paternity, and had participated in the raising of the two children, the U.S. Supreme Court

allowed him to veto a proposed adoption. *Caban v. Mohammed*, 441 U.S. 380, 99 S.Ct. 1760, 60 L.Ed.2d 297 (1979).

(4) Where, for two years after the birth of his child, the putative father had never contributed to the support of or visited the child, the U.S. Supreme Court denied him the right to veto the child's adoption by the mother's husband. Significantly, the putative father could have gained a voice in the adoption process by adding his name to New York's "putative father registry," but had failed to do so. The Court held that "[w]hen an unwed father demonstrates a full commitment to the responsibilities of parenthood by 'com[ing] forward to participate in the rearing of his child' [quoting from *Caban*], his interest in personal contact with his child acquires substantial protection under the due process clause * * *. *But the mere existence of a biological link does not merit equivalent constitutional protection.*" (Emphasis added). *Lehr v. Robertson*, 463 U.S. 248, 103 S.Ct. 2985, 77 L.Ed.2d 614 (1983).

(5) An unmarried father sought custodial rights to his daughter by a *married* mother. While the father *had* actually cohabited with the mother and child, the U.S. Supreme Court upheld the traditional presumption of legitimacy and denied the unmarred father's claim. *Michael H. v. Gerald D.*, 491 U.S. 110, 109 S.Ct. 2333, 105 L.Ed.2d 91 (1989).

(6) In the "Baby Jessica" and "Baby Richard" cases, the unmarried mother deliberately frustrated the putative father's interest in coming forward. In both cases, the unmarried mothers had surrendered their children for adoption. Baby Jessica's mother had lied about the father's identity. Baby Richard's father had been told that the baby had died. In each case, the father asserted his paternal rights as soon as he found out the truth, and the mother subsequently married the father. While Jessica's adoption had been denied by the trial court, the intending adopters had held Jessica in Michigan for some two years, in defiance of the Iowa court's contempt ruling. In Richard's case, the trial court had ordered the adoption despite the

mother's refusal to name the father, and the adopters had retained custody of Richard for more than 3 years. The legal issue in both cases was whether the father's justifiable ignorance of his child's birth was a circumstance that should weigh in his favor when measured against the U.S. Supreme Court's *(Lehr)* standard of giving him at least a chance to "grasp" "the opportunity to develop a relationship with his offspring." Since neither Baby Jessica's nor Baby Richard's father had had any such chance, both cases were ultimately decided in favor of the fathers. (These disputes spawned numerous cases; important citations include: *In Interest of B.G.C.,* 496 N.W.2d 239 (Iowa 1992)*(Jessica)*; *Petition of Kirchner,* 164 Ill.2d 468, 208 Ill.Dec. 268, 649 N.E.2d 324 (1995) *(Richard)).*

b. Uniform Parentage Act, Uniform Putative and Unknown Fathers Act, Uniform Adoption Act

The Uniform Parentage Act, the Uniform Putative and Unknown Fathers Act, and the Uniform Adoption Act (§§ 2–401, 2–402) similarly (1) provide for termination of the rights of an *uninterested* putative father, (2) protect the *interested* putative father, and (3) seek to keep interference with the adoption process at a minimum. The UPA provides a procedure by which the court may ascertain the identity of the father and permit speedy termination of his potential rights *if he shows no interest in the child.* If, on the other hand, the natural father or a man representing himself to be the natural father claims custodial rights, the court is given authority to determine custodial rights. It is contemplated that there may be cases in which the man alleging himself to be the father is so clearly unfit to take custody of the child that the court would proceed to terminate his potential parental rights without deciding whether the man actually is the father of the child. If, on the other hand, the man alleging himself to be the father and claiming custody is *prima facie* fit to have custody of the child, an action to ascertain paternity is indicated.

3. Unreasonable Refusal of Consent

In very exceptional cases, a few courts have held (or appear to have held) that an adoption may proceed without parental consent, if consent is withheld unreasonably in violation of the child's best interest.

Example: At C's birth, M tried to place him for adoption but, for unknown reasons, failed to do so. M never took C home from the hospital, and C spent the next four years in foster homes. When C's foster parents petitioned to adopt him, M refused to consent. M argued that the adoption petition could not be granted without her consent unless she was found to be unfit. (Result: Petition granted. M's consent was withheld unreasonably where C had never known M. In such a case, the test is the best interest of the child.) *In re J.S.R.*, 374 A.2d 860 (D.C.App.1977). (*Caveat:* Almost certainly, M's parental rights could have been terminated on the ground of abandonment.)

4. Adoption by Stepparent: Consent of the Noncustodial Parent

If adoption is sought by the new spouse of the custodial parent, some courts seem to attach less importance to obtaining the noncustodial parent's consent. If he or she has not substantially contributed to the support of the child or has otherwise "abandoned" the child, his or her consent may not be needed. *In any case, the noncustodial parent is entitled to notice and an opportunity to be heard.*

Examples: (1) When H_1 and W divorced, W received custody of C. W's second husband (H_2) petitioned to adopt C without notifying H_1, on the ground that H_1 had not substantially contributed to C's support for over two years. At the time of the petition, both W and H_2 knew of H_1's whereabouts. H_1 appealed from the granting of the adoption petition. (Result: Adoption set aside on the ground that H_1 had been denied Due Process, *i.e.*, notice and an opportunity to be heard.) *Armstrong v. Manzo*, 380 U.S. 545, 85 S.Ct. 1187, 14 L.Ed.2d 62 (1965).

(2) When H_1 and W divorced, W received custody of the children. For several years, H_1 continued to support and to help care for the children. Following a bitter argument with H_1, W gave information to the police that led to H_1's arrest and incarceration. W then thwarted H_1's attempts to communicate with his children from jail. W's second husband (H_2) petitioned to adopt the children over H_1's objections. W and H_2 claimed that H_1 had failed to substantially contribute to the support of the children or to communicate meaningfully with them. (Result: Adoption denied. Indigency—due here to incarceration—is a valid excuse for non-support, and H_1 had not communicated with his children because he was unable, not unwilling, to do so.) *R.N.T. v. J.R.G.*, 666 P.2d 1036 (Alaska 1983).

5. Consent of Agency or Guardian

The refusal of consent to adoption by an agency or guardian may be overridden more easily than a parent's refusal of consent. If the adoption is determined to be in the best interests of the child, courts tend to permit an adoption over the objection of an agency or guardian.

6. Consent of the Child

Many state statutes provide that if a child is above a certain age (*e.g.*, 10–14 years), the child's consent also is required for adoption.

7. Formalities of Consent

Consent to adoption usually must be written, witnessed, and acknowledged or notarized. Consent to adoption is not binding unless given *after* the child's birth, with statutory requirements ranging from 24 to 72 hours after birth. Many statutes are quite detailed and most courts insist on exact compliance. Properly executed consent papers must be submitted with the adoption petition. If an agency is involved in the adoption, the parent's consent is given to the agency; *i.e.*, the child is "surrendered" to the agency and the agency consents to the specific adoption. Anonymity is thus preserved, and the risk of harm to the child's best interest minimized. In connection with private adoptions, "blank consents" are considered to promote "black market" dealing in babies, and many though not all states prohibit consent to be given in a form that omits indication of the identity of the adoptive parents.

8. Finality and Revocation of Consent

a. Birth Parents

If a birth parent has properly consented to the adoption of his or her child, but has a later change of mind, revocation is sometimes allowed, especially if fraud, duress, or undue influence can be shown. After the final decree has been issued, reversal of the adoption is very narrowly restricted.

Example: Unmarried M voluntarily gave custody of her two-year-old son, C, to her mother, G. G then raised C for the next nine years, while M lived in other states. G and M discussed the possibility of G adopting C, and M executed a formal consent form. Some months later, G filed a petition to adopt C, based on M's consent, while M filed an action to regain custody and revoke her consent to the adoption. Trial court granted adoption. (Result: Adoption affirmed. M claimed to have told G that she changed her mind about the adoption shortly after executing the consent, but this was legally ineffective. The governing statute "provides, in its entirety: 'Parental consent to an adoption shall be revocable prior to the final order of adoption (i) upon proof of fraud or duress or (ii) after placement of the child in an adoptive home, upon written, mutual consent of the birth parents and prospective adoptive parents.' Mother does not contend grandmother engaged in either fraud or duress in relation to mother's execution of the consent to adoption. * * * There is also no evidence of a revocation of her consent by written, mutual consent between her and grandmother. Thus, mother does not meet the terms of [the statute] for effecting a revocation of her consent.") *T.S.G. v. B.A.S.*, 52 Va.App. 583, 665 S.E.2d 854 (2008).

b. Reversal of Placement by Agency

Examples: (1) An adoption agency placed 18–month-old C with H and W on the condition that they not file for adoption until C had been with them for a year. During that year, the agency discovered that H was being treated for a drinking problem. In earlier interviews with the agency, H had denied his drinking problem. The agency canceled C's placement on the grounds that H and W had lied. (Result: Revocation of placement must be measured in terms of the best interests of the child, and H and W are entitled to a hearing on this issue.) *C.V.C. v. Superior Court for County of Sacramento*, 29 Cal.App.3d 909, 106 Cal.Rptr. 123 (1973).

(2) Shortly after being screened, qualified and accepted as prospective adoptive parents, H and W began experiencing marital difficulties. H and W did not reveal this to the adoption agency, nor did they seek marriage counseling. A child was placed with H and W on a "quasi-adoptive" basis. Within one year of the placement, H and W separated. After being anonymously notified of this separation, the agency determined that the deteriorated family situation was not in C's best interests. "Because of the likelihood that the wife would flee with the minor child," C was removed from the home without advance notice. (Result:

Prior notice may be waived only when the child is in "imminent danger." Such imminent danger encompasses the possibility that a prospective parent would flee with the child if notice were given.) *Marten v. Thies*, 99 Cal.App.3d 161, 160 Cal.Rptr. 57 (1979), *cert. denied*, 449 U.S. 831, 101 S.Ct. 99, 66 L.Ed.2d 36 (1980).

F. Anonymity

Most states follow the tradition that adoption records are to be sealed in order to secure the relationship between adopter and child, and to protect the privacy of the biological parents. Adopted children generally have no access to names, addresses, or other information concerning their natural parents. Exceptions may be made for good cause, such as medical need, psychological trauma or crisis of religious identity. Increasingly, however, states have been "opening" up the adoption process. A number of states now allow "open adoptions," in which biological parents maintain regular contact with a child following the adoption. A handful of states, moreover, now permit adult adoptees to find out the identities of their birth parents on demand. In several states, adoption is *not* anonymous, *i.e.*, "open." The following interests are in the balance: (1) the adoptee's interest (and curiosity) in knowing his/her origin; (2) the natural parents' interest in privacy; and (3) the adoptive parents' interest in being undisturbed. Most states have balanced these interests by permitting adopted children and biological parents who wish information to register. If both sides register, information is exchanged. The Uniform Adoption Act would maintain anonymous adoption and recommends release only of *non*-identifying, typically genetic, information. It also provides a matching registry that is to be available to adopted children over 18 years of age and their former parents. Constitutional attacks on legislative choices in this area have generally failed.

Examples: (1) To discover his natural identity, C sought access to his sealed adoption records. C claimed that the Illinois statute that required adoption files to be sealed, and allowed them to be examined only upon court order, violated his constitutional rights. (Result: The Illinois Supreme Court found the statute to be rationally related to the legitimate legislative purpose of protecting the adoption process. C's interest in knowing his origins "should not prevail over the potential infringement of the rights of other parties," such as C's natural and adoptive parents.) *In re Roger B.*, 84 Ill.2d 323, 49 Ill.Dec. 731, 418 N.E.2d 751 (1981).

(2) In 1998, Oregon voters approved an initiative measure that allowed all adoptees access to their original birth certificates upon

reaching the age of 21. A group of birth mothers who had previously surrendered their children for adoption challenged the law as an unconstitutional invasion of their privacy. (Result: The Oregon Supreme Court upheld the open-records law. Although the decision to relinquish a child for adoption is "intensely personal," it "may not be made unilaterally by a birth mother or by any other party. It requires, at a minimum, a willing birth mother, a willing adoptive parent, and the active oversight and approval of the state. Given that reality, it cannot be said that a birth mother has a fundamental right to give birth to a child and then have someone else assume legal responsibility for that child," much less to demand anonymity in making that choice). *Does v. State*, 164 Or.App. 543, 993 P.2d 822 (1999).

G. Revocation of Adoption

Revocation of adoption challenges the adoption *after* a final decree has been entered. (Distinguish revocation of consent *before* entry of an adoption decree.) Unless there was a defect in the process of adoption (*e.g.*, invalid or absent consent, inadequate notice), courts rarely set aside a final adoption decree. The purpose is to provide stability for the adopted child. Depending on the substance of the challenge, due process questions may arise. Occasionally, adoptive parents have been allowed to revoke an adoption on the ground that they adopted the child without knowledge that the child was seriously "defective," or they may have recourse to tort law to "remedy" a "wrongful adoption." An adoption agency may be allowed to attack an adoption decree on the ground that the adoptive parents had fraudulently misrepresented their qualifications. The overriding policy is to avoid "punishing" the child for someone else's violation of the adoption laws, and many states set specific time frames after which an adoption may no longer be challenged (*e.g.*, Uniform Parentage Act: 6 months).

Examples: (1) C was placed in institutional care at age eight because of neglect and was later adopted by M. After the adoption, C's behavior worsened, ultimately including "promiscuity, drinking alcohol, destruction of property, petty theft, deterioration of academic performance and violence toward [M]." After C ran away from home, authorities placed her in a residential care facility, where C revealed that she had been sexually abused in her original home. M petitioned to revoke the adoption on the ground that the adoption agency had not disclosed that C had been abused as well as neglected. (Result: Revocation denied. "[P]ublic policy disfavors a revocation of an adoption because an adoption is intended to bring a parent and child together in a permanent relationship, to bring stability to the child's life, and to allow laws of intestate succession to apply with certainty to adopted children. Although public policy abhors the idea of being able to 'send the child back,' we recognize that an order of adoption is a judgment and may be set aside pursuant to Indiana Trial Rule 60(B) [in the event of fraud]." Here, C did not reveal the abuse to anyone until after the adoption. "Although the record may support a finding that [the agency] acted negligently in failing to discover the alleged sexual abuse, it does not support a finding that [the agency] committed fraud. Consequently, the attempt to set aside the adoption based upon fraud must fail.") *In Matter of Adoption of T.B.*, 622 N.E.2d 921 (Ind. 1993).

(2) M and F adopted an infant, C, in 1961 through an adoption agency. The agency assured M and F that C was a "healthy baby" and, despite inquiries, did not disclose that C's birth parents both had a family history of schizophrenia. C later developed serious behavioral and emotional difficulties and was diagnosed as a young man as schizophrenic. M and F sued the agency in tort for fraud and wrongful adoption. (Result: Adoptive parents were entitled to recover compensatory but not punitive damages in tort. The agency "acknowledges that plaintiffs have raised a cognizable claim under common-law fraud principles in the adoption setting." Tort recovery for wrongful adoption requires "not simply an agency's silence but 'the deliberate act of misinforming' a couple who were deprived of their right to make informed parenting decisions." Here, agency's deliberate misrepresentations about C's family history warranted compensatory damages, but did not show malice necessary to support punitive damages.) *Ross v. Louise Wise Services*, 8 N.Y.3d 478, 836 N.Y.S.2d 509, 868 N.E.2d 189 (2007).

H. Legal Effect of Adoption

The legal relationship between adoptive parent and child is equivalent to the legal relationship between parent and biological child. With rare exceptions, adoption terminates all rights and obligations existing between the adopted child and the biological parents.

1. Custody

Adoption gives adoptive parents the same right to custody as if the child were their biological child. Some statutes and courts allow exceptions for visitation by biological grandparents, especially in the case of a stepparent adoption.

Example: Following F's death, a trial court awarded F's parents (G) visitation with F and M's daughter (D). The order was conditional, and was to have no effect if M remarried and M's new husband adopted D. Following M's remarriage and D's adoption by her new stepfather, G appealed the termination of their visitation rights. (Result: Visitation reinstated. "A trial court's authority to grant grandparent visitation * * * continues even after subsequent adoption. The statute allows the trial court, in the best interest of the child, to order grandparental visitation in direct opposition to the wishes of the custodian regardless of who the custodian is. To hold that an adoptive parent has rights to override the [grandparents' visitation statute], would be to apply an exception to the statute that does not exist. To judicially impose such an exception would create rights for an adoptive parent superior to those that exist for a natural parent. Once the grandparents in this case were ordered visitation rights with their minor grandchild, they should not have been deprived of those rights without due process.") *Matter of Visitation of C. G. F.,* 168 Wis.2d 62, 483 N.W.2d 803 (1992). (*Caveat*: Any such order of visitation must comply with the constitutional requirements respecting parents' rights as delineated in *Troxel v. Granville*, 530 U.S. 57, 120 S.Ct. 2054, 147 L.Ed.2d 49 (2000). See pp. 225–26.)

2. Name and Birth Certificate

The adopted child's name ordinarily is changed to that of the adopting parents. Statutes typically provide for the sealing of the original and the issuance of a new birth certificate that designates the adoptive parents as the parents and omits any reference to the biological parents, usually retaining only the actual place and date of the child's birth.

3. Incest Laws *No marriage between biological and adopted child*

Under state incest statutes, for purposes of criminal prosecution and eligibility to marry, both the biological and adoptive families are typically treated as related to the adopted child.

4. Obligation of Support

Adoptive parents incur the same obligation to support the adopted child as if the child were their biological child. A few states may continue to recognize (at least in theory) a subsidiary support obligation on the part of the biological parents that becomes enforceable if the adoptive parents default in their support obligation. As a practical matter, the practice of anonymous adoption makes any such obligation unenforceable. No case has been found where adoption records were unsealed to enforce a biological parent's support obligation.

5. Inheritance

a. From Adoptive Parents

The adopted child's right to inherit from an adoptive parent and the latter's family depends upon state adoption and inheritance laws. Today it is virtually universal that the adopted child is treated as "issue" of the adoptive parents for purposes of intestate succession from the latter as well as from the latter's relatives. Similarly, the trend favors interpreting potentially ambiguous terms in wills, such as "child," "issue," and "descendant," to include adopted children.

b. From Kin of Adoptive Parents

While few statutes deal specifically with the right of the adopted child to inherit from the adoptive parent's lineal or collateral kin, the modern rule is to allow such inheritance.

c. From Natural Parents

The right of the adopted child to inherit from its biological parents and their kin typically is terminated by the adoption. In a few states, the child, even though adopted, retains an inheritance relationship with its natural parent, in addition to inheriting from adoptive parents. (Note that the practice of anonymous adoption makes it difficult or often impossible to learn the identity of the natural parents.)

Example: When C was one year old, she was adopted by her paternal aunt. Decades later, when her birth mother died intestate, C sought to inherit. (Result: C was entitled to inherit from her birth mother's estate. In New York, "adopted persons retained the right to inherit from their birth parents until 1963, 'when the Legislature severed the adopted child's right to inherit from biological kindred, except from a custodial and natural parent who had remarried and consented to the child's adoption by a stepparent.' The statutory provision at issue here was enacted in 1987 and restored the right of an adopted person to inherit from biological parents under limited circumstances [when they are adopted by a close relative]. * * * [T]he laws of intestacy attempt to distribute the decedent's property to persons whom the decedent would likely have chosen had he or she executed a will. Accordingly, in cases where a child is adopted by a close family member, '[t]he Legislature has chosen not to cut off inheritance ties between the adopted-out child and the natural family that has been replaced because of the likelihood of continued contact with that family.' ") *In re Estate of Johnson*, 18 Misc.3d 898, 850 N.Y.S.2d 855 (Sur. Ct. 2008).

d. From Adoptee

Adoption statutes and statutes of descent and distribution generally have been construed to allow adoptive parents and often their kin to inherit from their adopted child to the exclusion of the biological parents.

Review Questions

1. The following factor(s) may not be used in evaluating prospective adoptive parents:

    A. Race

    B. Marital status

    C. Religion

    D. Age

2. **T or F**   Adoptive parents usually cannot rescind a completed adoption even if they later discover that, at the time of adoption, the child suffered from an unknown condition, such as mental illness.

3. **T or F**   Adoption terminates all of the natural parents' rights and responsibilities toward the child.

4. **T or F**   Adoption was well established under the common law.

5. **T or F**   Court approval is needed to complete the adoption process.

6. **T or F**   Adults may be adopted.

7. **T or F**   Minor parents are not legally required to consent to the adoption of their child.

8. **T or F**   Courts may not consider race in an adoption proceeding.

9. **T or F**   If their child has been adjudicated "neglected" or "abused" and a guardian has been appointed for the child, the adoption of their child may proceed without the natural parents' consent.

10. **T or F**   A noncustodial parent who has not substantially contributed to the child's support or who has otherwise abandoned the child is subject to having his/her child adopted without consent.

11. **T or F**   The minor but "mature" child's consent to its own adoption is required in an adoption proceeding.

12. **T or F**   A parent's revocation of consent to a child's adoption will be allowed only if the consent was obtained by fraud, duress, or undue influence.

13. **T or F** The practice of sealing adoption records and allowing neither child nor natural parent access, has been attacked on constitutional grounds.

14. **T or F** The right of an adopted child to inherit from its natural parents terminates with the adoption.

15. **T or F** Subsidized adoption produces a legally incomplete parent and child relationship, only somewhat more secure than foster care.

16. **T or F** The unmarried father has no standing to challenge the mother's decision to place her child for adoption.

17. **T or F** The goal of state adoption statutes is the protection of the rights of adoptive parents.

18. **T or F** Some courts seem to attach less importance to a noncustodial parent's consent to the adoption of his or her child when the prospective adoptive parent is the child's stepparent.

19. **T or F** In a private adoption, parents consent to the adoption of their child by a specific person or persons.

XIII

Procreation

■ ANALYSIS

A. **Constitutional Underpinnings**
   1. Contraception
   2. Abortion
   3. Sterilization
B. **Assisted Reproduction**
   1. Artificial Insemination
   2. *In Vitro* Fertilization and Ovum Transplantation
   3. Surrogate Motherhood for Pay

A. Constitutional Underpinnings

1. Contraception

Since 1965, the U.S. Supreme Court has recognized a protected privacy interest in the use of contraceptives by *married* couples. *Griswold v. Connecticut,* 381 U.S. 479, 85 S.Ct. 1678, 14 L.Ed.2d 510 (1965). *Griswold,* invoking the "penumbras" and "emanations" of and from the 1st, 3rd, 4th, 5th and 9th Amendments, brought marriage under the U.S. Constitution: "We deal with a right of privacy older than the Bill of Rights * * *. Marriage is a coming together for better or for worse, hopefully enduring, and intimate to the degree of being sacred. It is an association that promotes a way of life, not causes; a harmony in living, not political faiths; a bilateral loyalty, not commercial or social projects. Yet it is an association for as noble a purpose as any involved in out prior decisions."

In 1972, the U.S. Supreme Court constitutionally extended access to birth control devices to *unmarried* persons. The Court reasoned that the protected interest in whether or not to conceive a child is an *individual* right: "[W]hatever the rights of the individual to access to contraceptives may be, the rights must be the same for the unmarried and the married alike. If under *Griswold* the distribution of contraceptives to married persons cannot be prohibited, a ban on distribution to unmarried persons would be equally impermissible. It is true that in *Griswold* the right of privacy in question inhered in the marital relationship. Yet the marital couple is not an independent entity with a mind and heart of its own, but an association of two individuals each with a separate intellectual and emotional make-up. If the right of privacy means anything, it is the right of the *individual,* married or single, to be free from unwarranted governmental intrusion into matters so fundamentally affecting a person as the decision whether to bear or beget a child." *Eisenstadt v. Baird,* 405 U.S. 438, 92 S.Ct. 1029, 31 L.Ed.2d 349 (1972).

In 1977, the Court struck down New York legislation criminalizing the distribution of contraceptives to minors under the age of 16 years: "The question of the extent of state power to regulate conduct of minors not constitutionally regulable when committed by adults is a vexing one, perhaps not susceptible to precise answer. * * * Certain principles, however, have been recognized. 'Minors, as well as adults, are protected by the Constitution and possess constitutional rights.' *Planned Parenthood of Central Missouri v. Danforth,* 428 U.S. 52, 96 S.Ct. 2831, 49 L.Ed.2d 788 (1976). '[W]hatever may be their precise impact, neither the Fourteenth Amendment nor the Bill of Rights is for adults alone.' *In re Gault,* 387 U.S. 1, 87 S.Ct. 1428, 18 L.Ed.2d 527 (1967). On the other hand, we have held in a variety of contexts that 'the power of the state to control the conduct of children reaches beyond the scope of its authority over adults.' Of particular significance to the decision of this case, the right to privacy in connection with decisions affecting procreation extends to minors as well as to adults." *Carey v. Population Services International,* 431 U.S. 678, 97 S.Ct. 2010, 52 L.Ed.2d 675 (1977).

2. Abortion

In the original decision recognizing the woman's right to abortion (*Roe v. Wade,* 410 U.S. 113, 93 S.Ct. 705, 35 L.Ed.2d 147 (1973)), Justice Blackmun summarized the U.S. Supreme Court's majority view:

> "A state criminal abortion statute of the current Texas type, that excepts from criminality only a *life saving* procedure on behalf of the mother, without regard to pregnancy stage and without recognition of the other interests involved, is violative of the Due Process Clause of the Fourteenth Amendment.

> "(a) For the stage prior to approximately the end of the first trimester, the abortion decision and its effectuation must be left to the medical judgment of the pregnant woman's attending physician.

> "(b) For the stage subsequent to approximately the end of the first trimester, the State, in promoting its interest in the health of the mother, may, if it chooses, regulate the abortion procedure in ways that are reasonably related to maternal health.

> "(c) For the stage subsequent to viability the State, in promoting its interest in the potentiality of human life, may, if it chooses, regulate, and even proscribe, abortion except where it is necessary, in appropriate medical judgment, for the preservation of the life or health of the mother."

In 1992, the Supreme Court reaffirmed *Roe*'s recognition of abortion as a constitutional right, but substantially refigured the scope of judicial protection. *Planned Parenthood v. Casey,* 505 U.S. 833, 112 S.Ct. 2791, 120 L.Ed.2d 674 (1992). *Casey* "reject[ed] the rigid trimester framework of *Roe,*" and replaced it with a test that permits states wider leeway to regulate abortion. Under *Casey*'s "undue burden" test, states are permitted to impose regulations at any time during the pregnancy meant to protect fetal or maternal health so long as the regulation does not constitute an "undue burden" on a woman's free choice. "An undue burden exists, and therefore a provision of law is invalid, if its purpose or effect is to place a substantial obstacle in the path of a woman seeking an abortion." After the point of viability, however, the state is permitted to prohibit abortion altogether, so long as it makes an exception for abortions necessary to protect the life or health of the pregnant woman. In 2000, the Supreme Court invalidated a Nebraska ban on so-called "partial birth," late-term abortions because it failed to make an exception for maternal health. *Stenberg v. Carhart*, 530 U.S. 914, 120 S.Ct. 2597, 147 L.Ed.2d 743 (2000). Three years later, President George W. Bush signed into law the first federal ban on "partial-birth" abortions, also omitting an exception for maternal health. In 2007, the Supreme Court upheld this law, distinguishing *Stenberg v. Carhart* on the ground that the federal law was more narrowly targeted than the Nebraska statute in defining the proscribed method of abortion and that Congress made specific findings that the prohibited method is not medically necessary. *Gonzales v. Carhart*, 550 U.S. 124, 127 S.Ct. 1610, 167 L.Ed.2d 480 (2007).

A succession of decisions has emphasized that abortion is very much the *woman's* right. Neither the husband (nor an unmarried would-be father), nor parents of a pregnant minor may be required to consent or even be notified, and thus be put in a position to prevent the exercise of the pregnant female's right to abort. *Planned Parenthood of Missouri v. Danforth*, 428 U.S. 52, 96 S.Ct. 2831, 49 L.Ed.2d 788 (1976); *Planned Parenthood v. Casey*, 505 U.S. 833, 112 S.Ct. 2791, 120 L.Ed.2d 674 (1992). With respect to minors, the U.S. Supreme Court has complicated the picture by limiting autonomy to "mature" minors, without doing much to define a "mature" minor, leaving that to individualized case-by-case determination. See pp. 246–248, 261.

3. Sterilization

a. Compulsory Sterilization

In 1927, the U.S. Supreme Court upheld a state statute providing for compulsory sterilization of an insane or retarded person, provided there is notice and a hearing, and the action is not arbitrary or in punishment of a crime. *Buck v. Bell*, 274 U.S. 200, 47 S.Ct. 584, 71 L.Ed. 1000 (1927). If *Buck v. Bell* were challenged today at the U.S. Supreme Court level, change should be expected, at least in the breadth of the holding. However, attempts to litigate such a challenge into the U.S. Supreme Court have not succeeded, and the case still stands. (See *In re Sterilization of Moore*, 289 N.C. 95, 221 S.E.2d 307 (1976)). In *Skinner v. Oklahoma*, 316 U.S. 535, 62 S.Ct. 1110, 86 L.Ed. 1655 (1942), the U.S. Supreme Court held:

"We are dealing here with legislation which involves one of the basic civil rights of man. Marriage and procreation are fundamental to the very existence and survival of the race. The power to sterilize, if exercised, may have subtle, far-reaching and devastating effects. In evil or reckless hands it can cause races or types which are inimical to the dominant group to wither and disappear. There is no redemption for the individual whom the law touches. Any experiment which the State conducts is to his irreparable injury. He is forever deprived of a basic liberty. We mention these matters not to reexamine the scope of the police power of the States. We advert to them merely in emphasis of our view that strict scrutiny of the classification which a State makes in a sterilization law is essential, lest unwittingly, or otherwise, invidious discriminations are made against groups or types of individuals in violation of the constitutional guaranty of just and equal laws."

b. Voluntary Sterilization

Courts have held that a state may not deny elective sterilization.

Example: A city hospital's policy barring use of facilities in connection with consensual sterilization was challenged. (Result: City hospital's prohibition violated the Equal Protection Clause. (1) A fundamental interest was involved, (2) no other surgical procedures were prohibited outright, and (3) other procedures of equal risk and nontherapeutic procedures were permitted.) *Hathaway v. Worcester City Hospital,* 475 F.2d 701 (1st Cir.1973).

B. Assisted Reproduction

New techniques for noncoital reproduction encompass artificial insemination, ovum donation, *in vitro* fertilization, embryo transfer, and "surrogate motherhood." The availability of these techniques presents legal issues regarding the relationship of a child so conceived to the various "actors" who may be involved. Depending on the facts of the case and the technique used, these actors may include (1) the biological (sperm-supplying) father, (2) the biological father's wife, (3) the biological mother's husband, (4) the biological (ovum-supplying) mother; and (5) the "surrogate mother" who carries (a) another woman's ovum (the sperm donor's wife's or an ovum donor's) or (b) her own ovum/fetus/child to term under an agreement (possibly for hire) calling for the relinquishment of the child upon birth to one or both of the biological parent(s) and/or to an adoptive parent or parents.

As one court observed in 2008, "[m]arvelous advances in assisted reproductive technologies ('ART') have joined with rapidly evolving social structures so as to implode many traditional legal assumptions about parentage, custody, and responsibility for children. Such assumptions, formed when the only means of reproduction was that designed by nature, have proven too brittle to fit around the myriad new combinations of sperm and egg, on the one hand, and of married, unmarried, opposite-sex and same-sex partnerships on the other. The pace of all this change has resulted in a crazy quilt of legal theories, statutes, and decisional law." *Oleski v. Hynes*, 2008 WL 2930518 (Conn.Super. 2008).

1. Artificial Insemination

a. Married Couple

Not terribly long ago, courts disagreed as to whether a child conceived by way of artificial insemination was legitimate. (*Gursky v. Gursky*, 39 Misc.2d 1083, 242 N.Y.S.2d 406 (1963)(no), and *People v. Sorensen*, 68 Cal.2d 280, 66 Cal.Rptr. 7, 437 P.2d 495 (1968)(yes)). At the extreme, artificial insemination was held to be akin to adultery. The Uniform Parentage Act of 1973, § 5, provides:

> "(a) If, under the supervision of a licensed physician and with the consent of her husband, a wife is inseminated artificially with semen donated by a man not her husband, the husband is treated in law as if he were the natural father of a child thereby conceived. The husband's consent must be in writing and signed by him and his wife. The physician shall certify their signatures and the date of the insemination, and file the husband's consent with the [State Department of Health], where it shall be kept confidential and in a sealed file. However, the physician's failure to do so does not affect the father and child relationship. (b) The donor of semen provided to a licensed physician for use in artificial insemination of a married woman other than the donor's wife is treated in law as if he were not the natural father of a child thereby conceived."

This legislation, or legislation patterned after the UPA, now is in effect in most states.

In 2000, the Uniform Law Commissioners substantially revised the UPA, initially expanding its scope to cover all artificial insemination involving a married couple, even if not done under the supervision of a physician. In response to criticism, the Commissioners again revised the Act in 2002 to drop its limited focus on married couples (see below).

b. Unmarried Persons

The legal situation vis-à-vis the sperm donor of the offspring of an unmarried woman who was artificially inseminated at her request and for her own purposes, remains largely unclear. If the sperm donor can be identified, a paternity action may lie. Conversely, the sperm donor may assert custody or visitation rights.

The 2002 revision of the Uniform Parentage Act (§ 703) provides that "[a] man who provides sperm for, or consents to, assisted reproduction by a woman . . . with the intent to be the parent of her child, is a parent of the resulting child," without regard for whether the couple is married.

2. *In Vitro* Fertilization and Ovum Transplantation

Medical advances have made it possible to extract ova from a woman and fertilize them with male sperm in a so-called Petri dish—*not* the proverbial test tube. The ova thus fertilized may be (1) reimplanted into the woman from whom they came, (2) implanted into another woman (surrogate mother), or (3) frozen, for later use in accordance with (1) or (2) above. The technique (1) enables a fertile woman to bear a child if, for any reason, she cannot conceive naturally; (2) makes it possible for a pregnancy to be "farmed out" to another woman, perhaps to avoid a medical problem that prevents the ovum-producing woman from successfully completing pregnancy. In most states there appears to be no serious problem with *in vitro* fertilization in terms of the legality of using the technique, although potential complications have arisen relating to laws restricting fetal research or the sale or donation of ova.

Example: A (now repealed) Illinois law directed that "any person who intentionally causes the fertilization of a human ovum by a human sperm outside the body of a living human female shall, with regard to the human being thereby produced, be deemed to have care and custody of a child for the purposes * * * of the Act to Prevent and Punish Wrongs to children * * * except that nothing in that Section shall be construed to attach any penalty to participation in the performance of a lawful pregnancy termination." Ill.Rev.Stat. ch. 38 § 81–26(7)(1983). The Attorney General of Illinois indicated his unwillingness to apply this statute to *in vitro* fertilization, and a federal court held that the statute did not prohibit *in vitro* fertilization, but applied only to willful endangerment or injury during the period prior to implantation, through willfully destructive laboratory experimentation. *Smith v. Hartigan,* 556 F.Supp. 157 (N.D.Ill.1983). 720 ILCS § 510/6 (7) now provides: "No person shall sell or experiment upon a fetus produced by the fertilization of a human ovum by a human sperm unless such experimentation is therapeutic to the fetus thereby procured. * * * Nothing in this subsection (7) is intended to prohibit the performance of in vitro fertilization."

If actors other than husband and wife are involved, legal issues arise regarding the status of offspring conceived by *in vitro* fertilization. Assume now that a husband and wife wish to have a child but cannot have one the usual way:

a. Husband's Sperm—Wife's Ovum

If the husband's sperm is used in *in vitro* fertilization of the wife's ovum and the fertilized ovum is re-implanted into her, and they are thereby enabled to have their own child, no question arises regarding their child's legal status: The child is their legitimate child.

b. Donor's Sperm—Wife's Ovum

If donor sperm, not the husband's sperm, is used in *in vitro* fertilization of the wife's ovum, and the ovum is reimplanted into the wife, the response should be the same as that given by Uniform Parentage Act § 5 for artificial insemination: The child should be their legitimate child, provided proper procedures were followed.

c. Donor's Ovum—Husband's or Donor's Sperm

If a fertilized donated ovum, not the wife's, is used for implantation into the wife, the response should be analogous to that given under b., above, *i.e.,* the child should be the husband's and wife's legitimate child and any donors should be out of the picture, if proper procedures were followed.

d. Surrogate Mother—Husband's Sperm and Wife's Ovum

If a surrogate mother is used to carry a fertilized ovum to term that is genetically the husband's and the wife's, the legal answer should follow the genetic relationship, *i.e.,* the child should legally become the husband and wife's child, after appropriate procedures terminate the potential interests of the surrogate mother and her husband, if she is married.

Example: W and H were unable to conceive a child because W had had a partial hysterectomy. They and a surrogate mother signed a contract providing that an embryo created from the ovum of W and the sperm of H would be implanted in the surrogate, and when the child was born it would live with W and H "as their child." The surrogate mother agreed to relinquish all parental rights. During the pregnancy, the relationship between W and H and the surrogate mother deteriorated, and each woman filed suit seeking a declaratory judgment that she was the legal mother of the unborn child. (Result: The court relied upon California's Uniform Parentage Act and held that, legally, W is, and the surrogate mother is not, the mother of the child. Consequently, the surrogate mother had no claim to visitation or any continued relationship with the child. "We conclude that although the Act recognizes both genetic consanguinity and giving birth as means of establishing a mother and child relationship, when the two means do not coincide in one woman, she who intended to procreate the child—that is, she who intended to bring about the birth of a child that she intended to raise as her own—is the natural mother under California law. * * * The surrogate mother's argument depends on a prior determination that she is indeed the child's mother. Since [W] is the child's mother under California law because she * * * provided the ovum for the *in vitro* fertilization procedure, intending to raise the child as her own, it follows that any constitutional interests [the surrogate mother] possesses in this situation are something less than those of a mother. * * * Moreover, if we were to conclude that [the surrogate mother] enjoys some sort of liberty interest in the companionship of the child, then the liberty interests of [H and W], the child's natural parents, in their procreative choices and their relationship with the child would perforce be infringed.") *Johnson v. Calvert*, 5 Cal.4th 84, 19 Cal.Rptr.2d 494, 851 P.2d 776 (1993).

3. Surrogate Motherhood for Pay

a. Surrogate Mother and Child

There are two distinct scenarios: (1) The "surrogate mother" is artificially inseminated with the sperm of a man who has contracted with her to have her surrender her rights to the child upon birth, and (2) the "surrogate mother" carries to birth a child that is not genetically hers, *i.e.,* a fertilized ovum (whether or not stemming from the couple contracting with her) was transplanted into her for "carriage and delivery." Note that in (1) nothing is "surrogate" about the mother's biological relationship to her child, whereas in (2) the term seems more appropriate. The second scenario was litigated in *Johnson v. Calvert*, above, but "carriage only" surrogacy remains relatively infrequent. Highly publicized litigation has centered, under scenario (1), on the question of the enforceability of a so-called surrogacy contract. The ultimate issue is whether a mother can contract so as to be *compelled* to surrender her genetic child to the father (or to a contractor who instigated the pregnancy by having donated sperm used in the mother's artificial insemination). Statutes against "baby selling" have been drawn upon to strike down such bargains. One difficulty is that where the father himself "purchases" his own biological child, such statutes may not apply.

Examples: (1) Infertile couples and prospective surrogate mothers sought a declaratory judgment that Michigan's Surrogate Parenting Act was not an outright ban on surrogacy contracts for pay. Plaintiffs argued that an outright ban would violate their constitutionally protected privacy rights and the due process and equal protection clauses of the state and federal constitutions. (Result: Only contracts that call for the surrogate's relinquishment of her parental rights to the child are illegal. "Plaintiffs * * * maintain that the state has no compelling interest in intervening in this conduct. We disagree. * * * The first interest is that of preventing children from becoming mere commodities. * * * The best interest of the child is also an interest that is sufficiently compelling to justify government intrusion. * * * A third compelling state interest is that of preventing the exploitation of women. * * * We affirm the lower court's ruling to the extent it holds that the Legislature intended to make void and unenforceable those arrangements that provide both for conception or surrogate gestation services and for the relinquishment of parental rights. The statutory language clearly defines 'a surrogate parentage contract' as consisting of two elements: (1) conception, through either natural or artificial insemination, of, or surrogate gestation by, a female and (2) her voluntary relinquishment of her parental rights to the child. Only a contract, agreement, or arrangement combining these two elements constitutes a 'surrogate parentage contract' that is void and unenforceable under the act. Section 9 of the act provides that a 'surrogate parentage contract' for compensation is unlawful and prohibited. Hence, a contract agreement, or arrangement providing compensation solely for conception or surrogate gestation services is not unlawful and prohibited, because the element of 'relinquishment of parental rights' is lacking.") *Doe v. Attorney General*, 194 Mich.App. 432, 487 N.W.2d 484 (1992).

(2) In 1986, the Kentucky Supreme Court refused to hold that the statute prohibiting the sale of children for adoption applies to surrogate parenting: "The question for us to decide is one of statutory interpretation: Has the legislature spoken? The fundamental question is whether SPA's involvement in the surrogate parenting procedure should be construed as participation in the buying and selling of babies as prohibited by KRS 199.590(2). We conclude that it does not, that there are fundamental differences between the surrogate parenting procedure in which SPA participates and the buying and selling of children as prohibited by KRS 199.590(2) which place this surrogate parenting procedure beyond the purview of present legislation." *Surrogate Parenting Associates, Inc. v. Commonwealth, ex rel. David Armstrong*, 704 S.W.2d 209 (Ky.1986).

(3) F, a single, gay man who wished to become a father, contracted with his niece, N, to serve as a gestational surrogate. The contract called for an egg from an anonymous donor to be fertilized with F's sperm and implanted in N; N agreed to disclaim any parental rights to the child and F agreed to pay N a $20,000 fee plus expenses. During N's pregnancy, the parties had a falling out and N refused to surrender the baby upon its birth. (Result: Surrogacy contract is enforceable and requires that F be recognized as child's only parent. "[N] argues that the district court erred by giving any effect to the GSA [gestational surrogacy agreement] because there is 'no statutory or case law authority under Minnesota law which sanctions the determination of a child's parentage and custody pursuant to a

private contract.' But as noted above, there is no Minnesota statute or case law that prohibits GSAs. And the legislature has expressly protected the rights of individuals who use assisted-reproduction technologies [by way of artificial insemination]. * * * Because there is no Minnesota legislative or judicial pronouncement that prohibits such agreements, we conclude that GSAs do not violate any articulated public policy of this state.") *In re Paternity and Custody of Baby Boy A.*, 2007 WL 4304448 (Minn.App. 2007).

(4) The famous "*Baby M*" case involved a surrogacy contract under which a married woman had been inseminated with the "purchasing" father's sperm in exchange for a fee of $10,000. Her husband had consented. When the "surrogate" mother refused to give up the child, the trial court ordered it to be turned over to the father and his wife, for adoption by the latter. The trial court held that (1) the "baby selling" law did not apply and (2) the father's right to procreate noncoitally and to contract for surrogacy is constitutionally protected. The contract was held specifically enforceable, the surrogate mother's rights were terminated, custody of the child was awarded to the father, and the latter's wife was allowed to adopt the child. (Result: The New Jersey Supreme Court reversed on all issues except custody. The surrogacy contract was held to violate public policy and the "baby selling" prohibition as well as statutes regulating revocation of consent to adoption and those regulating termination of parental rights. In the child's best interest, however, the court allowed custody of the child to remain with the father and his wife, and remanded the case for appropriate definition of the (surrogate) mother's visitation rights. The court added: "Nowhere, however, do we find any legal prohibition against surrogacy when the surrogate mother volunteers, without any payment, to act as a surrogate and is given the right to change her mind and to assert her parental rights.") *In the Matter of Baby M*, 109 N.J. 396, 537 A.2d 1227 (1988).

b. Legal Relationship Between "Purchaser's" Spouse/Partner and Child

Several cases have struggled with the question how the "purchased" child is to be brought into a legal relationship with its biological father and, more importantly, his wife or nonmarital partner. Paternity and adoption statutes have sometimes been brought into the picture. Generally, the laws on the books are not well suited to this purpose, and the cases point to the need for appropriate legislation.

Examples: (1) A and B, an unmarried, gay couple involved in a longterm relationship, entered into a contract with SM and her husband, H, under which SM would serve as a gestational surrogate of twins conceived with A's sperm. During the pregnancy, A and B sued SM and H, seeking to obtain a court judgment validating their agreement and directing the state to issue a birth certificate recognizing A and B as the twins' legal parents. The litigating parties were not actually adverse, but all desired the resulting court judgment validating their arrangement. (Result: A alone recognized as twins' legal father. "The foremost problem with the manner in which this court has been asked to approve the parties' contract stems from the reality that in a few days when the twins themselves become lives in being and in need of the care of a custodial parent for at least the next eighteen years, the determination of who is the appropriate custodian will already have been made as a function of directing whose names go on the children's birth certificates. By the process employed here, the court is effectively being asked to approve [SM's] transfer of the custody of the children to whom she will have given birth to not only their biological father, but also to an individual not related to them except by his untested declaration that he intends to parent them. * * * If the children here were one day old, and [SM] then turning them over to a stranger, no court in the world would approve that transfer *solely* on the basis of her contract with that third party, and without any evidence as to whether such a transfer accommodated the children's interests.") *Oleski v. Hynes*, 2008 WL 2930518 (Conn.Super. 2008).

(2) In Michigan in 1985, SM gave birth to her third child, C. All parties assumed that C was conceived when SM was artificially inseminated with the plaintiff's (F's) semen. SM had agreed to bear F's child in return for his promise to pay her $10,000 over and above all medical and confinement expenses. F and his wife had physical custody of C. SM and her H had consistently cooperated with F's efforts to obtain a court order acknowledging F's paternity. (Result: The Michigan Supreme Court allowed use of the paternity act to establish F's paternity with a view to bringing the child into his home. "The plaintiff seeks only a paternity act determination that he is the biological father of Teresa Syrkowski. The act was created as a procedural vehicle for determining the paternity of children 'born out of wedlock,' and enforcing the resulting support obligation. The plaintiff is requesting the court to determine the status of the child and his biological paternity. The act allows fathers to seek and receive such determinations.") *Syrkowski v. Appleyard*, 420 Mich. 367, 362 N.W.2d 211 (1985).

c. Intermediary's Liability

Intermediaries ("baby brokers"), especially attorneys, run serious risk of civil or criminal liability.

Example: Attorney Keane set up a surrogacy contract between SM (a married surrogate mother), F (the prospective father), and W (F's wife). SM was artificially inseminated with F's sperm and became pregnant. Later in the pregnancy it was discovered that (1) SM's husband, not F, was the father of the child, and (2) SM carried a virus that can be sexually transmitted. Keane's surrogacy program did not call for any testing. At birth, the child had an active virus infection and, due to that exposure, suffered from multiple birth defects, including mental retardation, hearing loss, and neuro-muscular disorders. SM and F brought a negligence action against Keane and associates, claiming that the source of SM's and the child's exposure was the artificial insemination. SM and F appealed from the district court's dismissal on summary judgment. (Result: Reversed and remanded for a jury trial. "We have noted that this negligence case poses questions of first impression concerning the rights and duties of those involved in surrogacy arrangements. The courts have not yet developed a set of precedents defining these rights and duties. * * * Courts traditionally have imposed an affirmative duty in special relationship cases because the person upon whom the duty to act is imposed has assumed some special task or role and expects a benefit or profit. * * * In addition courts impose a duty to protect in special relationships because one party is in control and the other has entrusted himself to the party in control. * * * Keane and his program fall within the principles found in these negligence cases imposing a duty to act. As the facts make clear, Keane assumed a task and role as a surrogacy broker, and the other professionals participated in the program Keane designed. The group were in this sense joint venturers engaged in an entirely new kind of project. * * * Keane, as well as the doctors and the lawyer, expected to profit from their roles in the program. Keane held out the services of his program. He should not be allowed to wash his hands of responsibility by turning the project over to others, as the dissent argues.") *Stiver v. Parker*, 975 F.2d 261 (6th Cir.1992).

Review Questions

1. **T or F**   An individual's decision to use contraceptives is constitutionally protected.

2. **T or F**   A state may forbid the sale of contraceptives to minors.

3. **T or F**   A state may constitutionally require that parents of an "immature" minor daughter be notified of her decision to have an abortion.

4. **T or F**   A state statute mandating compulsory sterilization of the mentally retarded is constitutional.

5. **T or F**   In order to give legal protection to the best interests of the child, modern statutes provide that both the sperm donor and the husband of a woman artificially inseminated legally are fathers of the child.

6. **T or F**   There is no question as to the legality of *in vitro* fertilization.

7.   Which of the following combinations involving "assisted reproduction" pose no serious legal question as to the parent and child relationship?

    A.   Husband's sperm, wife's ovum, wife carries child to term.

    B.   Donor's sperm, wife's ovum, wife carries child to term.

    C.   Donor's ovum, husband's sperm, wife carries child to term.

    D.   Husband's sperm, wife's ovum, surrogate mother carries child to term.

    E.   Husband's sperm, surrogate mother's ovum, surrogate mother carries child to term.

    F.   Donor's ovum, donor's sperm, surrogate mother carries child to term.

8. **T or F**   Statutes forbidding "baby selling" may apply to contracts with a surrogate mother to deliver a child.

9. **T or F**   Non-coital reproduction is a right protected by the U.S. Supreme Court.

10. **T or F**   Policy encourages intermediaries to facilitate "surrogacy" for pay.

APPENDIX A

Answers to Review Questions

■ I. THE NATURE OF MARRIAGE

1. *False.* The states have established the rights and obligations of marriage primarily by statutes.

2. *False.* Although entered by contract, marriage is also a status. Courts have held that new laws may redefine rights to (or grounds for) divorce, or realign property and support rights upon divorce, even if reasonable expectations of a party are defeated.

3. *False.* The *validity* of a marriage generally is determined under the law of the place of celebration. However, *legal incidents* (rights to property, support, grounds for divorce) generally are determined by the parties' marital domicile.

4. *True.* Today's majority view enforces antenuptial agreements if not "unconscionable" when made (UPAA, UMPA). Traditionally, however, courts did not uphold antenuptial agreements that violated traditional "public policies." Today, some jurisdictions still do not enforce an antenuptial agreement if it "encourages" divorce, or alters the "essence" of marriage, such as the marital support obligation. Courts generally insist that there be full disclosure and/or independent legal advice and/or fair provisions for the economically weaker party.

5. *True.* Although UPAA permits all manner of contracts regarding "personal rights and obligations not in violation of public policy or a statute imposing a criminal penalty" (§ 3(a)(8)), courts remain loath to involve themselves with day-to-day aspects of marriage, such as requiring certain support levels, or church attendance, or vacation plans. Parties may generally contract freely with regard to property.

6. *False.* Under the UPAA and UMPA, financial provisions are reviewed as of the date of execution of the agreement. Ohio's Supreme Court, in *Gross,* evaluated the fairness of property provisions as of the time of execution of the agreement, but scrutinized support provisions as of the time they are sought to be enforced.

7. *True.* True, although UPAA and UMPA dispense with the consideration requirement. Moreover, the promise of marriage is not effective consideration for federal gift tax purposes.

8. *True.* That may often be the case. However, reconciliation (*e.g.,* withdrawing a divorce petition) or a business relationship may provide sufficient new consideration. Under UPAA and UMPA, consideration is not required for antenuptial or postnuptial agreements nor for the postnuptial modification of antenuptial agreements.

9. *False.* The surrounding circumstances and the donor's intent determine whether a particular gift is so clearly in contemplation of (and thus conditional on) marriage that it must be returned if the marriage is not entered. To illustrate, an engagement ring is often held to be returnable, whereas a birthday or holiday gift may typically be retained.

10. *True.* These statutes also granted married women numerous other rights, such as contracting and bringing law suits in their own names, and more recently, these statutes abolished or limited interspousal tort immunities.

11. *True.* UMDA § 207(b) expressly validates a previously invalid marriage once the impediment to the marriage is removed. The previously invalid marriage becomes valid as of the time the impediment is removed.

12. *False.* UPAA § 6(a) allows the spouse against whom enforcement is sought to invalidate the agreement only if the agreement was unconscionable *when made.* In addition, the complaining spouse (1) must not have been provided adequate disclosure, (2) did not waive disclosure, and (3) had no independent knowledge

of the other spouse's financial circumstances.

13. *False.* Courts are not bound by provisions that affect children.

14. *True.* Under UMDA § 306(b), provisions that concern support and the disposition of property are binding on the court, unless the court finds that the agreement is unconscionable.

■ II. MARRIAGE REQUISITES

1. *False.* There are many levels of mental incompetence. (1) Even though a person may not be able to carry on his/her ordinary affairs, if he/she has the capacity to understand the nature of marriage, he/she may give valid consent to marriage. (2) If the incompetent's difficulties go deeper, a guardian must consent to his/her marriage. (3) At some level, substantive marriage prohibitions against marriage of "feebleminded," *etc.,* persons apply, and even a guardian cannot supply valid consent.

2. *False.* Most states require more. The fraud also must go to the "essence of marriage." Misrepresentations as to fertility, pregnancy or important religious beliefs have sufficed to allow annulment, whereas misrepresentations concerning wealth, income or professional position typically have not.

3. *True.* Solemnization is not needed in a jurisdiction that recognizes common law marriage. In addition, since many policies coalesce in favor of upholding the parties' expectations or protecting an existing relationship, courts have been lenient in their interpretation of applicable laws. To illustrate: (1) Even a short-term sojourn to another jurisdiction that recognizes common law marriage sometimes has been held to create one; (2) When the parties had *either* a marriage license *or* had undergone a ceremony, a marriage has occasionally been found; (3) Various presumptions regarding the validity of an alleged marriage may uphold what otherwise would be difficult or impossible to prove to be a valid marriage; (4) Where applicable, the putative spouse doctrine protects the innocent party to an invalid marriage, so long as he/she remains in good faith unaware of the defect. Many states, however, specifically (or by interpretation) limit the applicability of the putative spouse doctrine to ceremonial "marriage."

4. *False.* If specific requirements are met, some states recognize proxy marriages. In any event, proxy marriages are not considered to be sham marriages.

5. Answer: *B.* So long as the parties intended to be married, cohabited, and held themselves out as married, they will be deemed to have created a valid common law marriage. There is no minimum period of cohabitation or requirement that the parties have children.

6. *False.* The putative spouse doctrine protects a partner to an invalid marriage who has participated in a marriage ceremony only for so long as he/she believes in good faith that the marriage is valid.

7. *False.* All states prohibit marriage between a parent and his/her child; most states also prohibit marriage between an aunt and her nephew.

8. *True.* Parental consent usually is required up to the age of majority.

9. *True.* While adoption simulates the legal relationships created by blood, the genetic argument is inapplicable in the adoption situation. Accordingly, a Colorado Supreme Court decision has allowed siblings by adoption to marry. Generally, however, such marriages remain prohibited.

10. *False.* No state allows polygamy. The state has an interest in protecting monogamous relationships, and statutes prohibiting polygamy do not violate the First Amendment.

11. *False.* A common law marriage that is valid where entered is generally recognized in all other states, even in those that have abolished common law marriage.

12. *False.* Only the underage spouse (and in many states his or her parents) may attack the validity of an underage marriage.

■ III. COHABITATION WITHOUT MARRIAGE

1. *False.* Divorce statutes do not govern a non-marital relationship.

2. *True.* Under *Marvin*, support and property obligations may arise in connection with nonmarital cohabitation on the basis of express or implied agreements, or on the theories of unjust enrichment, quasi-contract, or resulting or constructive trusts.

3. *False.* Although courts are divided on the question, most recent decisions have held such marriages to be void on the ground that gender for purposes of marriage laws is determined at birth. Of course, in the minority of jurisdictions permitting same-sex marriage, Francine's gender would be immaterial to the validity of the marriage.

4. *False.* Joanne should recover the *quantum meruit* value of her services less the reasonable value of her support.

■ IV. SPOUSES

1. *False.* A 1979 U.S. Supreme Court decision (*Orr v. Orr*) invalidated an Alabama statute that restricted alimony to women. Gender-based classifications may reinforce stereotypes and must be carefully tailored. A gender-neutral statute based on need would serve legitimate state purposes better than a gender-based statute.

2. *True.* However, depending on the parties' standard of living, many courts may not consider this item "necessary." In the alternative, the creditor should proceed on an agency theory (actual or by estoppel).

3. *False.* So long as the marriage continues, property acquired by each spouse before *or after* marriage is that spouse's separate property. Only at divorce is some property classified as "marital" and subject to division.

4. *False.* The concept of "marital property" is used in many separate property states to define the (divisible) gains of the marriage. Courts typically take into account the separate (non-marital) property held by each spouse in deciding how to "equitably" divide the marital property. In a minority of states, *all* property owned by either spouse is potentially subject to distribution at divorce.

5. *False.* Today, spouses can take title in any of these forms.

6. *True.* If *bona fide* transfers are involved, W generally can deplete her estate, so that H takes nothing, if nothing is left. (The "augmented estate" concept of the Uniform Probate Code seeks to guard against this.) If property is left in W's estate and her will makes no or inadequate provision for H, H can renounce the will and take a statutory share, usually one-third.

7. *False.* Separate property typically also includes property acquired after marriage by inheritance, gift, or personal injury recovery. "Commingling" of property after marriage may transform separate property into community property. There is a split in authority whether post-marriage income from and/or appreciation of separate property is separate or community property.

8. *True.* Texas, for instance, provides for sole management of community property by the spouse who earned that property. Other states require joint

management of community property, with some states excepting business property from joint management. Special exceptions also may govern disposition of community property.

9. *False.* W also can distribute her half of the community property. Since H owns his half of the community property, no provision is made for him to renounce W's will and take a statutory share.

10. *False.* A number of states still allow such actions, even while many states have abolished the actions. Some statutes limit recovery severely.

11. *False.* The husband-wife testimonial privilege has been restricted in many states, abolished altogether in at least one (New Jersey), and is disfavored by influential commentators. In a federal prosecution, the U.S. Supreme Court has held that the witness spouse alone has the right to decide whether or not to testify (*Trammel*).

12. *True.* With few statutory exceptions that (should) no longer apply (*e.g.,* driver's license, voter's registration), a wife has never been *compelled* by law to take the husband's surname. While the father's name traditionally became the child's (and some cases spoke of this as the father's common law right), cases now hold that parents may give their children any surname they choose. If one parent later seeks to change the child's name over the other parent's objection, courts typically resolve the conflict based on the child's best interests.

13. *False.* Unless the parties are separated, courts are unwilling to enforce the spousal support obligation by ordering one spouse to provide support directly to the other. However, in most states a financially dependent spouse may purchase *necessary* items on the other spouse's account.

14. *False.* The 8 original community property states are Arizona, California, Idaho, Louisiana, New Mexico, Nevada, Texas, Washington and their property regimes were derived from or influenced by civil law sources. Wisconsin, however, enacted the Uniform Marital Property Act prepared by the Commissioners on Uniform State Laws who were influenced by the laws of the original 8 community property states.

15. *False.* So far, only a small minority of jurisdictions have recognized a cohabitant's right of consortium.

16. *True.* Several states have amended rape statutes, while in others the courts have reinterpreted existing statutes or used constitutional arguments to bring down the exemption.

17. *False.* A gift of nonmarital property by one spouse to the other is typically classified as marital property upon divorce. (Under earlier law, a wife's gift to her husband was subject to the "presumption of advancement" which, unless overcome, returned property W had given to H during the marriage to W on divorce).

18. *True.* Recent amendments to the UPC promulgated by the Uniform Laws Commissioners provide a graduated scale under which the spouse's forced share reaches one-half of the decedent spouse's estate after 15 years of marriage.

■ V. DIVORCE—STATUS

1. *False.* The *ex parte* divorce decree based on H's domicile is valid and entitled to full faith and credit in all other states. However, the effect of an *ex parte* divorce extends to status only, not to consequences. In short, H's divorce is entitled to full faith and credit, the denial of alimony to W is not.

2. *False.* If an Iowa statute gives the Iowa court jurisdiction ("long-arm" statutes based on maintenance of matrimonial domicile are common and have been upheld against due process challenge), the divorce is valid as to status *and* consequences. In short, the alimony award would be enforceable against H in Wisconsin.

3. *A.*

4. *B.*

5. *True.* Under no-fault divorce statutes in effect in all states a finding of fault is not required. A divorce will be granted on the basis of "incompatibility," or "breakdown of the marriage," or proof of a specified period of time during which the spouses have lived apart. Only a small minority of jurisdictions require mutual consent for a no-fault divorce.

6. *True.* Despite nominal prohibitions on "collusion," the typical fault-based divorce proceeded by prior arrangement of the parties. Grounds were invented or defenses to existing grounds were not interposed. The courts largely acquiesced. A significant difference between consensual divorce under a fault-based system and a no-fault system was that the "guilty" party or the party desiring a divorce but not having grounds had to make financial or child support and custody concessions to the other spouse in negotiating for consent.

7. *False.* In addition or instead, most states require proof of separation for a specific period of time.

8. *False.* The majority of states continue to provide for fault divorce as an alternative to no-fault divorce. While in some states there has been some change in fault grounds, others continue pretty much on the historical model. Defenses, on the other hand, have been more readily abolished or reduced in relevance. Financial consequences may depend on fault.

9. *False.* Provocation requires a causal connection, recrimination does not. Provocation is a defense and, while recrimination has been converted into a defense in many states, traditionally it constituted a bar to divorce. Provocation need not and recrimination must constitute a ground for divorce.

10. *False.* Desertion requires "fault," *i.e.*, it must be against the will of the other spouse, whereas "living apart" may be consensual.

11. *False.* Traditionally, federal courts have declined jurisdiction in family law matters. This abstention rule was recently reaffirmed by the U.S. Supreme Court. However, under specific statutes, family law matters may be heard (*e.g.*, interstate child support enforcement).

12. *False.* Personal service does not require minimum contacts. (As reaffirmed in 1990 by the U.S. Supreme Court in *Burnham v. Superior Court.*)

13. *False.* By provoking W's departure, H has constructively deserted W. If H's provocation was adequate, W has not deserted H.

14. *False.* W's appropriate defense is "connivance."

■ VI. DIVORCE—FINANCIAL CONSEQUENCES

1. *False.* If the dependent spouse has no realistic employment opportunities or adequate assets and the marriage was of considerable duration, courts still extend alimony payments for indefinite duration, including life.

2–3. *False.* Although all states provide for no-fault divorce in some form, fault grounds are still available as an alternative in a majority of states. If a fault ground is used to litigate the status issue, the consequences may also be affected, although alimony generally is more vulnerable than property division. In addition, in some pure no-fault states, the amount of an alimony award may be reduced by proof of the claimant's severe fault, such as adultery. With regard to property division, the concept of economic fault ("dissipation") is increasingly applied, regardless of the reason for the marital break-up.

4. *False.* H's obligation was contractual, *i.e.,* subject only to contract defenses, until it was incorporated (merged) into the judgment. As an alimony judgment, it would be held generally modifiable in the light of new circumstances. Here, however, H's change in circumstances was voluntary. Worse, H may even have intended to avoid payment of the alimony obligation. In such circumstances, H's obligation will not be modified.

5. *True.* Unless the separation agreement and decree expressly provide otherwise, the alimony obligation terminates at the death of either the payor or payee. Some courts may view the designation as "rehabilitative alimony," along with the six-year limitation, as sufficient to express an intent that death is *not* to terminate the obligation.

6. *Close call.* Remarriage typically terminates an alimony obligation either by operation of law, under the terms of the decree, or based on changed circumstances. Here, because it is paid for a specific purpose, *rehabilitative* alimony may not necessarily be terminated by the recipient's remarriage.

7. *True.* Note, however, that although obligations arising from a property settlement generally remain dischargeable in bankruptcy, federal legislation limits the discharge in bankruptcy of marital property obligations in some circumstances.

8. *True.* The change in circumstances must occur after the alimony decree, and the decree must not expressly or impliedly rule out modifiability.

9. *True.* In a sense, this approach reflects, up to the amount of the alimony paid, the income splitting rationale of the joint return.

10. *True.* The recipient of property in a divorce settlement takes the transferor's adjusted basis for that property. (In 1984, Congress abolished the rule under which the transfer by one spouse to the other of property on divorce was a taxable event, *i.e.,* if the property had appreciated in value, a capital gains tax was due.)

11. *False.* The vast majority of courts do not classify a professional license or degree as property. Instead, many courts consider one spouse's contribution to the other spouse's education or professional training as an important factor influencing the division of marital and even of separate property or, if there is inadequate property, in the allocation of alimony. Very few courts (prominently in New York) have classified a professional degree or license as a marital asset and "divided" it upon divorce, by awarding to the other spouse *as property* a specific percentage of the "present value" of the degree or license, or even the value of an "enhanced career."

12. *False.* Reconciliation generally terminates a separation agreement. The traditional rationale is that, upon reconciliation, the separation agreement turns into a post-nuptial agreement contemplating divorce and therefore is invalid. A more reasonable rationale is that reconciliation constitutes a change of circumstances amounting to an implied revocation of the separation agreement.

■ VII. THE PARENTAL CHILD SUPPORT OBLIGATION

1. *False.* A child's independent wealth or income normally does not relieve parents of their support obligation.

2. *True.* Most states impose no support duty on a stepparent who has married the custodial parent, but who has not adopted the child. Several states impose a support duty while the relationship continues.

3. *False.* The Uniform Reciprocal Enforcement of Support Act (URESA) permits a support action to be filed where the dependent resides. The action will be heard and enforced where the obligor resides. Any award collected is sent to the initiating court for disbursement. The newer Uniform Interstate Family Support Act (UIFSA) provides a similar procedure and, in addition, relies heavily on comprehensive long-arm provisions that give a court where the dependent resides exclusive jurisdiction if there is a "significant connection" to the obligor.

4. *True.* Traditionally, the mother had only a secondary child support obligation.

5. *False.* If the "child" cannot care for itself after the age of majority, the obligation of support may be open-ended.

6. *False.* Such statutes have been upheld on the rationale that there is an increased likelihood that a divorced parent will refuse to pay for a college education and that such legislation therefore bears a rational relationship to the permissible legislative objective of protecting children whose parents are divorced. (*Caveat:* In at least one state, such a statute was held to deny equal protection).

7. *False.* If the state of facts that caused the emancipation ceases to exist, a minor may revert to unemancipated status, reviving a parent's support obligation.

8. *False.* Child support obligations are modifiable if a change of circumstances is proved.

9. *False.* Such statutes have been upheld because they further the legitimate legislative purpose of alleviating some of the state's burden of caring for the indigent.

10. *True.* However, the UMDA and similar statutes allow a support order entered in the context of divorce to continue support payments to the child from the parent's estate or, for higher education, past the child's majority.

11. *False.* Some state guidelines have a built-in cap. In some no-cap states, rather remarkably high amounts of child support have been ordered when the obligated parent's income was very high. In other states, courts have deviated from guidelines in cases of exceptionally high-earning parents and determined a reasonable amount that should be paid for child support.

■ VIII. CHILD CUSTODY

1. *False.* When the custodial parent dies, the noncustodial parent is next in line for custody, unless there are very special circumstances.

2. *True.* While not binding on the court, absent special circumstances, courts will honor the deceased parents' designation of a guardian. (If one parent predeceased the other, the latter's sole designation will usually be honored.) Note also that the parents' agreement regarding child custody (or support) is not binding on the court even if expressed in a separation agreement or in a premarital agreement.

3. Answer: All except E. Note that in recent cases and under the UMDA the parent's (im)moral conduct matters only if the conduct directly affects his/her relationship to the child. The child's preference is given weight only if the child is sufficiently mature to express a reasonable opinion.

4. *True.* A noncustodial parent has a right to visitation which, under the UMDA, may be denied only if it would "endanger seriously the child's physical, mental, moral or emotional health."

5. *False.* Joint custody typically means shared legal custody (*i.e.*, shared decisionmaking authority), even if one parent is awarded primary physical custody.

6. *True.* If the other parent has custody, typically only a significant, very negative change in the *custodial* parent's circumstances will result in a change of custody. Stability in the child's environment is viewed as a very important factor in itself. If, however, a third party (*e.g.*, a grandparent) has custody, the natural parent's primary right to custody is given great weight.

7. *False.* UMDA § 407 does not impose a time frame and allows modification of the visitation order if it would be in the best interest of the child.

8. *True.* Generally, this is correct, although under the UMDA, while it invokes the child's best interests, visitation may be *restricted* only if it would seriously endanger the child's "physical, mental, moral, or emotional health."

9. *True.* Vis-á-vis third parties, one important (bootstrapping) presumption is that it is in the child's best interests to be in a parent's custody. For disputes between two parents, UMDA § 402, quoted in the text, provides detailed standards.

10. *True.* The parents' right to the custody, care, and control of their child has been held to be a fundamental liberty protected by the Fourteenth Amendment.

11. *True.* The child may live with one parent permanently or with both parents for alternating periods of time; however, both parents have legal custody and decisions regarding the child's welfare must be made jointly by both parents.

12. *False.* Even before the U.S. Supreme Court's decision in *Troxel v. Granville* in 2000, very few courts enforced grandparental visitation in an *ongoing* marriage. *Troxel* holds that courts are constitutionally required to give "special weight" to a parent's objections to grandparent visitation, and some state courts have held that the Constitution bars use of a "best interest" standard in this context.

13. *True.* It remains true, however, that mothers are more likely than fathers to obtain custody, partly because of the "primary caretaker" preference and partly because of residual gender stereotyping.

14. *True.* Parents are *prima facie* entitled to have custody. Most states favor custody with parents over third parties unless parent custody would cause harm or serious detriment to a child.

15. *True.* The court is guided by the child's best interests and is not bound by the parents' wishes.

16. *False.* The remedy available to F is judicial enforcement of the visitation order. In extreme cases, some states would also permit F to seek recovery in tort against M.

17. *False.* F's improved circumstances may be taken into account, but will not eliminate the non-custodial parent's obligation.

18. *True.* In response to widespread parental "child snatching," Congress legislated Full Faith and Credit protection for custody judgments.

■ IX. PARENTAL OBLIGATION OF CARE AND CONTROL AND THE JUVENILE COURT SYSTEM

1. *True.* Such "offenses" involve the child's status as a child and include "incorrigibility", "truancy", running away from home, being beyond the discipline of the parents, *etc.*

2. *False.* A custody order should make the least possible intrusion upon constitutionally protected interests of the parent, in this case First Amendment rights. In similar situations, some courts have required the custodial parent to agree to provide standard medical care, as a condition to custody.

3. *False.* In *Lassiter v. Department of Social Services*, the U.S. Supreme Court did not define an unconditional right to counsel. Instead, it did not rule out the possibility of a constitutional right to counsel if special circumstances combine to make counsel necessary to assure Due Process. The Court also noted that the majority of states statutorily provides the parents counsel in termination of parental rights cases.

4. *True.* In *Santosky v. Kramer*, the U.S. Supreme Court invalidated on Due Process grounds a New York statute that allowed parental rights to be terminated by a "fair preponderance of the evidence." The court noted that a majority of states imposes a "clear and convincing" standard of evidence and concluded that this standard is called for by the Due Process Clause.

5. *False.* In *Parham v. J.R.*, the U.S. Supreme Court held that a formal or even quasi-formal commitment hearing is not required. However, a determination should be made by a neutral factfinder, who must have the authority to deny admission and who should carefully probe the minor's background.

6. *False.* The child support obligation continues. By contrast, a judicial termination of parental rights would end the support obligation.

7. *False.* The typical child abuse reporting statute carries relatively weak or no criminal sanctions.

8. *False.* The U.S. Supreme Court found in *Smith v. OFFER* that New York procedures for the removal of a foster child from the foster parents' custody were not constitutionally defective, "even on the assumption that the [foster parents] have a protected 'liberty interest.'"

9. *False.* Many but not all constitutional protections have been extended to minors being tried in juvenile courts; prominently missing is the right to jury trial.

10. *False.* Generally, when the physical welfare (especially the life) of a child is jeopardized by a parent's religious belief, the state may intervene to provide conventional medical care and, depending on state statutes, may prosecute the parent if serious harm has come to the child. A tort action may be another option: In 1995, the U.S. Supreme Court let stand a Minnesota decision that upheld a $1.5 million judgment in favor of the father of a child whose custodial mother relied on Christian Science prayer with the result that the child died from untreated diabetes. (*McKown v. Lundman*).

11. *False.* Unless a special duty to protect the specific child can be found, the agency is not responsible for harm done to the child. As demonstrated by the U.S. Supreme Court in *DeShaney v. Winnebago City Department of Social Services*, the burden of finding such a duty is very difficult to meet.

12. *True.* The requirement that she notify *one* parent, however, is constitutional, provided an adequate judicial bypass procedure is available to a mature minor.

13. *True.* However, an adequate judicial bypass option must be available to a mature minor.

■ X. CHILDREN'S RIGHTS

1. *False.* Increasingly, the U.S. Supreme Court as well as state courts have recognized a broad spectrum of constitutional rights of minors, sometimes (particularly in the context of abortion) in direct opposition to rights asserted by their parents.

2. *True.* This is what emancipation is about. Note also that the contract of an unemancipated minor is ratified when the age of majority is reached without disavowal.

3. *False.* Typically, though with some exceptions, the birth of a healthy child has been held not to give rise to an action by the parents. However, where a baby suffers birth defects caused by a third party's negligence, an action typically is available.

4. *True.* Under older law, only pecuniary harm was compensated. Since in our economy parents do not usually suffer pecuniary harm from the loss of their child, the old rule has been generally abandoned and monetary recovery is allowed for intangible harm.

5. *False.* The traditional immunity doctrine has been generally restricted or abandoned. However, various limitations on tort recovery remain in effect, especially in the area of parental discretion and control.

6. *False.* The general rule remains that minors may not bring such actions, even though an occasional court has held to the contrary. (Remember: There is a strong tide running against similar "heart balm" actions in the wife/husband context.)

7. *True.* Parents may not be held criminally responsible for the criminal acts of their children. (Caveat: Under exceptional statutes that focus on parental failure to supervise their children, parents may incur some limited criminal liability.)

8. *True.* When the "family purpose doctrine" applies, parents may be held responsible for torts committed by their child while driving the family car. Beyond that, statutes commonly impose liability up to a certain amount on parents for certain torts committed by their children. Finally, parents may be liable for their own negligence in failing to supervise their child.

9. *True.* If appropriate safeguards are followed. (*Ingraham v. Wright*).

10. *False.* Nevertheless, many school systems permit parents to opt their children out of sex education or condom distribution programs.

■ XI. LEGITIMACY, ILLEGITIMACY, AND PATERNITY

1. *True.* This rule is intended to protect marriage and children. It is rooted in the old common law.

2. *True.* Note, however, that a few states until relatively recently still denied the "illegitimate" child a right to take by intestate succession from the mother's kin.

3. *False.* The U.S. Supreme Court has called for heightened, but not the strict scrutiny that applies to a "suspect classification," such as race. The applicable standard is "intermediate scrutiny."

4. *True.* Any final judgment is entitled to Full Faith and Credit.

5. *True.* The U.S. Supreme Court has not defined precisely the extent of the unwed father's interest. While it is clear that an unmarried father has significant (Due Process) rights with regard to his child, it also is clear that a distinction is permissible between unmarried fathers who have lived with or supported their child and those who have not.

6. *True.* At common law, an illegitimate child was considered *filius nullius*—the child of no one, and was not entitled to support or inheritance from either parent or other blood relatives.

7. *True.* The U.S. Supreme Court has held that such a requirement does not violate the Equal Protection Clause in that it is substantially related to important state interests, such as preventing fraudulent claims on estates. (*Lalli v. Lalli*).

8. *False.* While the U.S. Supreme Court has not made this completely clear, it is probable that, once paternity is established, an illegitimate child has the same support rights as a legitimate child. (*Gomez v. Perez*). This result also follows from state child support formulas and tables.

9. *False.* The U.S. Supreme Court has upheld such a distinction, because it allows governmental agencies to avoid the burden and expense of case-by-case determination. (*Mathews v. Lucas*, but *cf. Jimenez v. Weinberger*).

10. *False.* Only a *judicial* determination of legitimacy is entitled to Full Faith and Credit. As a matter of conflicts law and good policy, however, once achieved, legitimate status achieved in one state is generally recognized in others.

■ XII. ADOPTION

1. *False.* All of these factors have been held relevant in determining the best interests of a child in relation to a prospective adopter. Federal law, however, makes it unlawful to "delay or deny" an adoptive placement on the basis of race.

2. *True.* Courts typically do not allow adoptive parents to relieve themselves of responsibility for an adopted child more easily than a natural parent could relieve himself of responsibility for a natural child. A tort action against the adoption agency, however, may be available.

3. *True.* In a few states, however, the natural parent may retain a subsidiary support obligation, enforceable if the adoptive parents fail to support the child.

An inheritance relationship may also subsist.

4.   *False.* Adoption was established by statute.

5.   *True.* Court approval for adoption is mandated in all states. Depending upon the statute and court practices, a court may exercise considerable discretion in approving an adoption.

6.   *True.* Many states allow adult adoption. Such adoptions are typically subject to little supervision; however, permission has sometimes been denied in cases where the closeness of age between the parties seems to preclude any semblance of a parent-child relationship.

7.   *False.* A minor parent's consent to the adoption of his/her child is required.

8.   *False.* Race has generally been considered as a *factor* in adoption, but federal law mandates that it cannot be used to "delay or deny" an adoptive placement, except in cases falling under the Indian Child Welfare Act. (The relevance of *Palmore* v. *Sidoti*—the U.S. Supreme Court's interracial custody decision—in regard to interracial adoptions has not been fully determined.)

9.   *False.* A neglect or abuse adjudication does not terminate parental rights and the parents retain a "residual" legal relationship to their child. Adoption may not proceed without either their consent or involuntary termination of the parents' rights.

10.   *True.* "Abandonment" generally is a ground for terminating parental rights and unexcused failure to render support may constitute abandonment.

11.   *True.* Typical state statutes require the child's consent if he/she is above a certain age, often set at 14 years.

12.   *False.* A parent's consent to adoption typically is scrutinized *very* closely. Even seemingly minor formal flaws in the consent may suffice to set aside parental consent.

13.   *True.* Constitutional challenges on anonymous adoption have been mounted, but they generally have not succeeded. However, numerous states permit some access to adoption information, some by a "registry matching" process, whereby adopted child and biological parent are brought together if *both* file requests for information.

14.   *True.* Typically, the adoption or descent and distribution statute explicitly denies or is held implicitly to deny the right of inheritance from natural parents.

However, in a few states an inheritance relationship survives the adoption.

15. *False.* Subsidized adoptions are available in many states to provide financial assistance to families who adopt a "hard-to-place" child. The legal relationship between the adopter and the adopted child is complete and permanent.

16. *False.* Very false. The *interested* unmarried father may not be ignored, as the prospective adoptive parents of *Baby Jessica* and *Baby Richard* learned to their and, more importantly, to the children's disadvantage.

17. *False.* Statutory regulation of the adoption process is focused primarily on the child's best interests, as well as on the rights of the child's biological parents, specifically that their rights be terminated properly and finally before the adoption takes place.

18. *True.* The noncustodial parent, in any event, is entitled to notice and an opportunity to be heard. Moreover, when he or she has complied with a support obligation and maintained contact with the child, termination of the absent parent's rights is very difficult or impossible.

19. *True.* Unless the child is surrendered to an agency, most states prohibit consent to be given in "blank" or a form that does not identify the identity of the adoptive parent(s).

■ XIII. PROCREATION

1. *True.* The U.S. Supreme Court has protected the decision not to have a child as a privacy interest inherent in marriage (*Griswold*) and as an individual right of unmarried persons (*Eisenstadt*).

2. *False.* State restrictions inhibiting privacy rights of minors are valid only if they serve a significant state interest (*Carey*). Indeed, some schools now distribute free condoms to students.

3. *True.* The parental right to control an *immature* minor daughter has not been affected by various U.S. Supreme Court decisions striking down statutes interfering with the autonomy of a *mature* minor daughter.

4. *False.* While *Buck* v. *Bell*, the U.S. Supreme Court's 1927 decision upholding a compulsory sterilization statute, has not been overruled, today's Supreme Court would subject any such law to strict constitutional scrutiny, under which it would

be exceedingly difficult to justify an across-the-board mandate.

5. *False.* Under § 5 of the Uniform Parentage Act (that provision or similar legislation has been enacted by a majority of the states), only the woman's husband is treated as the child's legal father provided he has consented to his wife's insemination.

6. *False.* Laws forbidding or restricting fetal research and experimentation on embryos or utilization of discarded fetal material possibly may apply to *in vitro* fertilization.

7. A, and in a majority of states, B, and by analogy to sperm donation, probably C and, under *Johnson v. Calvert*, D. E and F, however, remain fraught with legal uncertainty.

8. *True.* However, where the child is the result of inseminating the surrogate mother with the "purchasing" father's sperm, the situation is less clear. Some courts have held that such a transaction is not covered by a "baby selling" statute.

9. *False.* The U.S. Supreme Court has not ruled on the constitutional status of "assisted reproduction." Commentators are divided on the applicability of a right to procreate in the context of assisted reproduction, or the extent of any such right. It seems noteworthy that the U.S. Supreme Court decisions most often cited to support such a right primarily involve protection of decisions *not* to procreate.

10. *False.* While intermediaries (*e.g.*, sperm banks) are permitted to act and may be regulated in a number of states, courts and statutes have increasingly disfavored "profiteers" in this sensitive area (*Doe v. Atty. Gen.*).

*

APPENDIX B

Practice Essay Questions

QUESTION I

George comes to you and requests your legal advice. His story is that, for several years, he had been living with Linda more or less openly in her apartment. During that time, "to keep up appearances", he had not given up his rented room nearby. Eleven months ago, Linda told him that she had become pregnant, that he was not the father and "would [he] please move out immediately." George then moved back to his room. Within weeks, Linda proceeded to marry Bill, an older, rather wealthy local lawyer. When her child was born three months ago, Bill was delighted and raised no questions.

George wants you to file a paternity suit and obtain visitation rights to the child or, preferably, full custody. He is willing to pay child support out of his income of about $20,000/year. He has moved in with his mother who he says is willing to provide day-to-day care for the baby, while George is at his job. He offers you $5,000 (borrowed from his mother) as a cash retainer—and he is the first potential client you have seen in days. Advise George.

QUESTION II

To save taxes on divorce, Ann and Jack agreed in their separation agreement (subsequently incorporated into their divorce decree) that Jack would pay substantial ($5,000/month) combined alimony and child support to Ann, but that essentially all property, consisting primarily of a major real estate investment, would be retained by Jack, except for Ann's jewelry and personal items. The real property had been purchased for about $150,000 with savings from Jack's earnings as a physician and had appreciated in value substantially, to about $600,000 at the time of the divorce. Ann and Jack had been married seven years and had two children, the custody of whom was awarded to Ann. Ann had been trained as a hamburger helper at McDonald's, but has not worked there or anywhere else for five years.

Now, three years after the divorce, Ann (39 years of age) is cohabiting with Joe (30 years of age), in the apartment Ann rents with the funds received monthly from Jack. Ann and Joe have no jobs and no income, other than the alimony paid by Jack. They do not seem interested in marriage.

Jack consults you regarding his wish to stop paying Ann alimony and child support. He also seeks custody of his two children, a boy of 9 years of age and a girl of 7. His current expenses are high, involving a new wife, their two-year old child and her three children from a previous marriage that had ended with her husband's death. Jack's income situation also has deteriorated since his divorce. While he had earned $300,000/year at the time of divorce, he now is down to $220,000/year, because his group practice was absorbed by an H.M.O. Worst of all, Jack lost all his real estate in a fire two years ago, after forgetting to pay his insurance premiums. (The value of the lots barely paid for the removal of the debris). Advise Jack.

QUESTION III

Conrad Grebel's wife, Anna, wishes to divorce him. Anna declares she has fallen in love with Dr. Jaime Mendoza, a university professor of comparative religion, with no particular religion of his own, whom she met when he came to Amishtown, PA, to buy cheese. She also complains that she has never seen much of Conrad as he works on the farm all day, and every evening he works as a blacksmith, by candlelight. The Grebels have never had electricity, radio, telephone, nor TV.

The Grebels and their extended families have been Old Order Amish since time immemorial, and Conrad and Anna have raised their two children (a girl 10 years old, a boy 12 years old) in that religion. Conrad has always taken a strong interest in his children, somewhat sternly, and both parents have raised the children rather strictly in accordance with the Amish religion.

Before their separation, the Grebels resided in a 5–room farm house on 1000–acres, the latter now worth about $200,000. The house was built by Conrad just before the marriage from materials supplied by his father. It has a current replacement cost of about $40,000. The acreage is composed of 300 acres each spouse inherited from his/her family, 200 acres Conrad purchased during the marriage (from profits earned in the farming operation and savings from his evening job as a blacksmith), plus 200 acres Anna received as a wedding gift from her father when she was married. Their inherited acreage had a tax basis of $1,000 per acre, the wedding gift was then worth $2,000 an acre, and the acreage purchased during the marriage cost $3,000 per acre. All the acreage is now and always was of equal value on a per-acre basis. All the acreage was farmed as one unit by Conrad. No separate operating records were kept, and joint tax returns were filed. Anna has never had a job outside of the home, and did not participate in the operation of the farm in any way. Conrad's net profit is $10,000 per year from his farming (supplementing the ample in kind production from the farm that has always supplied most of the family's food and other daily needs), plus $10,000 cash income per year from his evening work as a blacksmith.

When she moved to Universitytown Anna requested and was awarded temporary alimony, child custody and child support. She now is staying at a motel, along with the children. Recently, the children have become a little more difficult to handle, due perhaps to the excitement of the impending divorce and their change to a wholly secular school in Universitytown. They have now been at that school for one month. Already the boy is talking of becoming an astronaut and the girl an ocean geographer. Her attraction to Dr. Mendoza has solidified into a "steady dating" relationship, but she asserts that she has no intention of marrying him. Specifically, they carry on their "affair"—Conrad admits to uncertainty as to whether adultery has occurred or is occurring—in Dr. Mendoza's home during the day, while the children are in school and Mendoza is between classes. Anna now wants to proceed with a divorce.

Advise Conrad regarding (1) child custody (which both parents desire intensely); (2) his liability for alimony to Anna; (3) Anna's property rights in their home and farm; and (4) his child support obligation should he fail to win custody. (NOTE: Discuss (3) in terms of property law prevailing in (a) typical separate property states and (b) typical community property states. Discuss the other issues (1), (2), (4), in terms of "prevailing" law in the U.S., giving important divisions in authority due play).

QUESTION IV

Your first job after graduation is as law clerk to Chief Justice Lavender of the Oklahoma Supreme Court. The trial court holding excerpted below is up on appeal. The Justice has asked you to write a memorandum discussing the relevant issues and suggesting the proper analysis and disposition of the case. (Do not be concerned how the case got to the Supreme Court from the trial court or whether, in real life, Justice Lavender actually would follow your advice).

In making the award in question, the trial court stated the following: "The Court finds that the plaintiff helped support the defendant and the family by being employed throughout the time the defendant attended pre-medical school and medical school, and has contributed to such support during the defendant's training to be a doctor, and has contributed materially to his medical education. The Court further finds that during the more than twelve years that plaintiff worked and helped defendant obtain this medical degree and train to be a doctor, she could look forward to the time when she would enjoy the prestige and position, as well as the financial comfort, of a doctor's wife. That the granting of a divorce, through no fault of plaintiff, prevents her from reaping those awards. She is relegated to her pre-marital status, except for the acquiring of an insubstantial amount of property, not recompensed for the years she has helped the defendant to attain his professional standing. The Court further finds that the defendant is now on the threshold of a successful professional life, an able-bodied man, and has a present income of some $20,000 annually. That as a medical doctor his reasonable anticipated income will be $80,000 to $120,000 per year. The Court finds that the plaintiff has a vested interest in the defendant's medical profession, which is deemed to be a valuable property right. The only means of awarding her that property right is by alimony in lieu of division of property. * * * The Court further finds that the defendant is reasonably expected to earn $1,000,000 over the first twelve years of his beginning practice of medicine, with a net income of not less than $500,000. That the plaintiff is entitled to forty percent (40%) thereof as alimony in lieu of division of property. That plaintiff is therefore entitled to judgment as permanent alimony in lieu of a division of property in the amount of $200,000." (Facts adapted from *Hubbard v. Hubbard*, 603 P.2d 747 (1979)).

QUESTION V

Anna Marie Sappington, who was being paid $750 per month in alimony by her ex-husband, was sharing the former marital home with Lyle Montgomery. They shared the responsibilities of home upkeep, attended social activities together, and occupied the same room when traveling. He had access to the entire house and kept his clothes there. Lyle contended that he originally moved in to protect Anna Marie, as she was afraid of being alone. He argued that he has no interest in women and has been impotent for three or four years. Both parties denied having any sexual interest in the other and denied any sexual conduct toward the other, claiming instead that their relationship was solely that of friends.

This case involves the interpretation and application of the Marriage and Dissolution of Marriage Act which, in pertinent parts, provides: "Unless otherwise agreed by the parties in a written separation agreement set forth in the judgment or otherwise approved by the court, the obligation to pay future maintenance is terminated upon the death of either party, or the remarriage of the party receiving maintenance, or if the party receiving maintenance cohabits with another person on a resident, continuing conjugal basis."

Plaintiff Mr. Sappington has petitioned the court to relieve him of further alimony payments and has brought in Dr. Carol Moy, a professor of psychiatry and family practice at Southern University School of Medicine as his expert witness. She testified at the trial in this case. She counsels couples who are dissatisfied with their relationships and assists people in developing a conjugal relationship, including males who are impotent. She indicated that penile penetration is not the only form of sexual intercourse, that there are verbal and non-verbal ways of expressing sexuality. While indicating that a conjugal relationship does not necessarily involve sexual intercourse or sexual gratification, she defined a conjugal relationship as "a total family relationship * * * between a male and a female [is] usually understood to be a relationship of two people living, functioning together in a mutually supportive atmosphere."

1. You are the judge! Decide this case, giving reasons. (Facts from *In re Marriage of Sappington*, 478 N.E.2d 376 (1985)).

2. As a legislative assistant to Representative X, make recommendation as to whether, how and why the statute should be retained, amended or repealed.

QUESTION VI

George and LaVon Feisthamel were married on October 18, 1974. They entered into an antenuptial agreement dated October 5, 1974, prior to the marriage. They separated in July, 1994.

The respondent, LaVon Feisthamel, is a 62 year old woman in fair health. LaVon has had a history of problems relating to high blood pressure, depression, post-menopausal problems, and osteoarthritis. She underwent eye surgery for glaucoma shortly before the trial in this matter and further surgery may be needed. LaVon has not been in the employment market significantly. While she was a registered nurse, she is not currently licensed since her training occurred many years ago and she has never worked in that capacity. LaVon worked as a housewife and homemaker in a previous marriage and, following her first husband's death, was employed for a short time as a secretary/receptionist in a Chiropractic Office. During her marriage to the appellant, she worked as a homemaker and housewife. She has made numerous attempts to obtain full employment and obtained a temporary Vista volunteer job for which she received $357 per month. That job ended in May, 1987.

The appellant, George Feisthamel, is a 59 year old male in generally good health. George has been employed by Long Construction Company and Western Energy for many years as a heavy equipment mechanic. He is a member of the International Union of Operating Engineers. He continues to reside in the family home. LaVon moved from the family home in July, 1994.

Both of the parties owned certain properties, both real and personal, prior to their marriage. The trial court found that the antenuptial agreement dated October 5, 1974, excluded from consideration all real and personal property owned by either party prior to the marriage in determining the issues of maintenance and division of marital assets.

The provision involving the maintenance issue in the October 5, 1974 antenuptial agreement states:

"That in the event, after entering into the marriage, said parties find they cannot live together congenially as husband and wife and decide to separate and/or to secure a divorce, and it is necessary to make an equitable division of their property rights and a determination of the rights, if any, of Second Party to separate maintenance or temporary or permanent alimony, all real and personal property now owned by the parties shall not be taken into consideration. Provided, however, in event of such separation and/or divorce, Second Party shall be entitled to an equitable division of the property accumulated and acquired as a result of and in connection with their marriage. Provided, further when said accumulated property has been equitably divided said parties shall execute and deliver to each other, a release of any and all right, title and interest which they may have or claim in and to the property now owned or hereafter accumulated by either party. Provided, further that in the event a divorce is granted by a Court of competent jurisdiction to either party the terms of this contract shall be binding upon said Court, and at the time of granting said divorce this contract shall be incorporated in said decree."

This provision was honored in the final decree. The trial court divided the net marital assets equally between the parties and awarded LaVon maintenance in the amount of $1,000 per month commencing November 1, 1995, and ending November 30, 1999.

George and LaVon contest the award of maintenance and the property disposition. George claims that the District Court should have considered a certain annuity of $500 as well as other income or benefits LaVon might receive from a trust provided by her deceased first husband. LaVon's position is that the annuity income of $500 per month and any trust benefits are covered by the antenuptial agreement and should not be considered for determining the appropriateness of maintenance. LaVon further argues that the maintenance awarded is too low and for too short a time even if the annuity were to be considered because she lacks sufficient property to provide for her reasonable needs and is unable to support herself through appropriate employment.

Decide on appeal and give reasons. (Facts adapted from *In re Marriage of Feisthamel*, 739 P.2d 474 (1987)).

QUESTION VII

In 1977, Lois Smith and Max Michoff became romantically involved, even though Max was already married. Their relationship continued, and Max divorced his wife. Lois and Max then decided to, and did, live together. At the time, Lois was employed by Max as a prototype technician, working forty hours per week and earning eleven dollars per hour.

In 1979, Lois and Max moved from California to your state. That same year, Lois Smith legally changed her name to Lois Michoff. Max's attorney handled the name change. Lois claimed that she changed her name at Max's request; he believed that if they had a woman-owned construction-type business, they would "fare better in getting jobs." For example, according to Lois, they could bid five percent over the low bid and nevertheless be classified as the low bidder. Moreover, Max wanted Lois to be the sole owner so that his ex-wife could not make a claim against the business. It is uncontroverted that Max had concealed $50,000 from his former wife and the court in which he obtained his divorce. The record, however, does not indicate whether Max had defrauded his former wife out of other assets.

The parties started a construction equipment rental business called L & M Rentals (named for Lois and Max). Lois obtained the business license and paid the licensing fees. The business license listed Lois as the sole owner. When the parties started L & M Rentals, Max transferred all of his assets from a former business to L & M Rentals. Most of the cash was then used to purchase a certificate of deposit in the name of L & M Rentals. Although Max thus had contributed a large portion of the funds to start L & M Rentals and Lois was listed as sole owner, Lois and Max had orally agreed that they really were to be co-equal owners of the business. Consequently, Lois devoted her efforts and time toward running the business, including such integral functions as bookkeeping and maintaining the equipment.

Approximately six months after starting L & M Rentals, Lois and Max discovered that they needed a contractor's license to operate the business. Lois therefore applied for such a license. Lois was listed as the owner of the business and Max was listed as the "qualified employee." Lois testified that they had agreed that it was their company; thus, again, Lois provided much of the skill and labor necessary for the business' success. Her services included doing all of the office work (bookkeeping, payroll, and paperwork) and assisting in the maintenance, service, and running of the equipment. The profits from the business were either invested into the business or retained as savings.

Lois continued to do the bookkeeping, and she also updated the records, reviewed bids, negotiated contracts and labored in the field—performing such jobs as flagging and running heavy equipment. Whenever L & M Rentals sought a license increase, it was Lois who applied for the increase. In order to obtain the necessary contractor's bonds from the Contractor's Board, Lois personally guaranteed the bonds.

During their relationship, Max held Lois out as his wife. In fact, in 1984, Max entered a partnership agreement with Robert Frybarger and requested that Lois sign a consent of spouse. This provision provided: "We, the undersigned, being the respective wives to the parties to the foregoing partnership agreement, have read and understand said agreement executed by our husbands. Each of us hereby approves and consents to the said partnership agreement and agrees to be bound by all of its provisions."

Max and Lois filed joint tax returns as husband and wife commencing in 1980 and continuing through 1995. For the years 1983 through 1995, they also filed tax returns under L & M Rentals, showing Lois as an officer and owner. Moreover, L & M Rentals incorporated and elected to file a sub-chapter S election on March 24, 1983. The election was signed by Lois and Max and designated the holdings of the corporation as jointly owned property.

After Lois and Max terminated their sexual relationship earlier this year (Lois apparently left Max because he had been physically abusing her), she brought this action, seeking a declaration and judgment that she owns one-half of all of the parties' assets, including of course L & M, their home and furnishings and various investments. She also seeks long-term support from Max.

As best you can, decide this case under your state's law, giving reasons. To the extent you do not know your state's law, apply "national" law. To the extent you do know your state's law, compare "national" law. (Facts are adapted from *Western States Construction, Inc. v. Michoff*, 108 Nev. 931, 840 P.2d 1220 (1992)).

*

APPENDIX C

Text Correlation Chart

	Abrams, Cahn, Ross & Meyer	Areen & Regan (5th ed.)	Clark & Estin (7th ed.)	Davis, Scott, Waddlington & Whitebread (4th ed.)	Ellman, Kurtz, Scott, Weithorn & Bix (4th ed.)	Gardner & Dupre (2d ed.)	Harris & Teitelbaum (2d ed.)	Harris, Teitelbaum & Carbone (3d ed.)	Krause, Elrod, Garrison & Oldham (6th ed.)	Mnookin & Weisberg (5th ed.)	Schneider & Brinig (3d ed.)	Wadlington & O'Brien (6th ed.)	Wardle & Nolan	Weisberg & Appleton (3d ed.)	Weyrauch, Katz & Olsen
1. THE NATURE OF MARRIAGE AND MARITAL CONTRACTS															
A. Religious Influence		408-14			003-004				75-76		003-014	58-60	003-004		
B. Contract or Status	819-21							725-28	182-85		447-58	62-63		114-16	74-91
C. Controlling Factors Affecting the Marriage Contract	444														
D. Marriage and the Constitution	80-135	58-83	64-89		95-118			176-84	77-85		1260-66	68-74; 153-64	67-72; 95-112	140-60	464-96; 537-68
E. The Marital Relationship at Common Law	168-70, 460	151-69	594-604						140-44		299-320	278-81	409-10; 447-48	237-42	309-10
F. Married Women's Property Acts	370-72		604						141-42				448-49		
G. The Antenuptial Agreement	822-52	201-16	011-039		734-83			728-53	185-217		402-46	595-621	165-76	128-40	41-73
H. Agreements During Marriage	852-66		30					98-112	217-26		404-14	621-22			006-41
I. Conflicts Aspects of Marital Agreements	823								212-13						
J. Breach of Promise to Marry	398-408				148-51				259-60			180-89	176-77; 182-83	116-23	002-006
K. Gifts in Contemplation of Marriage	465								260-62			189-92	177-83	123-28	
2. MARRIAGE REQUISITES AND COMMON LAW MARRIAGE															
A. Formal Requirements	145-51	132-41	89-98		73-78			155-71	118-27		14-19	60-61; 207-10	72-75; 141-59	212-19	157-87
B. Substantive Requirements for Valid Marriage	76-145	83-132	114-61		95-147			184-218	86-118		19-77	164-78; 225-65	75-139	160-212	513-86
C. Conflicts of Laws	113-15, 133-34, 947-53				129-34			218-27				265-77	206-18		
D. Annulment	453-56		114					171-75	599-600			210-25			502-12
3. COHABITATION WITHOUT MARRIAGE															
A. Unmarried Cohabitation	252-78	11-15; 769-81	40-63		870-943			246-83	227-59		512-94	20-58	200-05; 803-24	377-405	213-308
B. Same-Sex Relationships	275-78		57-63		928-44			267-83	251-59		89-94; 557-63	53-58; 175-78	185-205	438-47	304-08
4. SPOUSES															
A. Support Obligations During Marriage	228-38	146-51			152-61			63-85	36-43		299-308	300-11	425-42	242-50	

	Abrams, Cahn, Ross & Meyer	Areen & Regan (5th ed.)	Clark & Estin (7th ed.)	Davis, Scott, Waddlington & Whitebread (4th ed.)	Ellman, Kurtz, Scott, Weithorn & Bix (4th ed.)	Gardner & Dupre (2d ed.)	Harris & Teitelbaum (2d ed.)	Harris, Teitelbaum & Carbone (3d ed.)	Krause, Elrod, Garrison & Oldham (6th ed.)	Mnookin & Weisberg (5th ed.)	Schneider & Brinig (3d ed.)	Wadlington & O'Brien (6th ed.)	Wardle & Nolan	Weisberg & Appleton (3d ed.)	Weyrauch, Katz & Olsen
B. Property Rights	238-40, 460-62		594-605		162-67			98-107	159-76			297-301	410-25	238-43	310-18
D. Marriage and Criminal Law	347-63	281-345	633-44		201-02			113-37	45-53		233-76	317-43	475-88; 799, 802	320-61	341-48; 466-77
E. Family Names	189-93	1053-58	981		634-35			175-76	144-46			281-97	448	250-58	325-40
5. DIVORCE -- STATUS ISSUES															
A. Access to and Jurisdiction of Courts	936-48	415-19; 817-30	661-701		681-732			769-800	600-25			383-430	639-70	540-47; 573-92	587-88; 975-1039
B. Traditional Grounds and Defenses	412-31	357-74	645-46; 656, 661		204-11			293-308	573-80		115-20	359-79	671-75	494-516	587-88; 613-22
C. Divorce Reform	431-53	372-92; 420-28	646-56		232-68			323-44	588-98		121-42		675-96	516-39	589-602
D. Separation	456-58								598-99						
6. DIVORCE -- FINANCIAL CONSEQUENCES															
A. Alimony on Divorce	514-58	730-57	785-805		363-409			430-58	815-63		330-70	457-88	727-50	606-34	461-65, 623-44
B. Property Division on Divorce	459-513	697-730	701-65		269-362			398-429; 459-500	751-814		321-30; 346-94	431-57, 488-548	697-726	595-605, 640-59	92-156
C. Separation Agreements	866-75	846-60	823-57		783-835			754-68	920-47		404-14	621-38	775-84	715-21	
7. THE PARENTAL CHILD SUPPORT OBLIGATION															
A. Definition of the Parental Obligation	559-66	782-91	865-95		447-48			501-03	864-80	172-85	1192-1247		517-19	666-68	
B. Stepparent's Duty to Support	566-70	809-15	437, 874		455-56			911-21		183-84		574-84	519-24		
C. Duration of the Obligation	570-74	791-98	896-902		448-54			533-41	880-85	185-90; 192-94	1126-30	559-74		676-81	917-24
D. Traditional Criteria for Awarding Support	574-75	784			459				888-89	190-91	1193-94	548-49	924		
E. Child Support Guidelines	575-84	782-84	865-95		459-96			504-33	888-919	190-94	1193-1247	549-59	924-42	668-76	898-907
F. Modification	594-611	798-809	892-95		497-507			549-77	991-1021	195-97			943-49	681-91	908-17
G. Child Support Enforcement Sanctions	611-30	830-46	902-37		508-29			578-601	1022-32	197-203	1247-66	584-95	950-63	691-703	924-37

	Abrams, Cahn, Ross & Meyer	Areen & Regan (5th ed.)	Clark & Estin (7th ed.)	Davis, Scott, Wadlington & Whitebread (4th ed.)	Ellman, Kurtz, Scott, Weithorn & Bix (4th ed.)	Gardner & Dupre (2d ed.)	Harris & Teitelbaum (2d ed.)	Harris, Teitelbaum & Carbone (3d ed.)	Krause, Elrod, Garrison & Oldham (6th ed.)	Mnookin & Weisberg (5th ed.)	Schneider & Brinig (3d ed.)	Wadlington & O'Brien (6th ed.)	Wardle & Nolan	Weisberg & Appleton (3d ed.)	Weyrauch, Katz & Olsen
H. Conflicts of Laws Aspects of Child Support: The Uniform Interstate Family Support Act	989-1009	825-30	858-65		530-57			787-800	625-33		1266-75	660	917-24	703-15	
I. Federal Child Support Enforcement Legislation	611-18	831-34, 842-46	436-37, 909-11		496-97, 510-15				1023-30	199-203	1275-87	584-95	960-62	699-703	
J. Full Faith and Credit	1002-09				555-56								920-22		
K. Reciprocity: The Child's Duty to Support Parents	565-66		437					542-48	885-87						
8. CHILD CUSTODY															
A. Child Custody During Marriage					559-600; 609-19		575-628; 717-49	621-42; 660-94		460-74; 534-71					
B. Child Custody Upon Divorce	634-749	429-94	959-1015	375-432	600-09	62-78		643-60	661-98	571-83	800-952	1038-60	849-91	723-67; 808-22	831-90
C. Joint Custody	749-63	574-79	972-81	432-37	619-34	78-80		695-715	699-711	583-95	895-907	1060-69, 1153-57	865	767-77	891-97
D. Rights of the Noncustodial Parent	764-87	602-30	972-83; 988-95	437-40; 447-68	636-55	107-08			711-18	615-16	713-24	1114-25	891-92	777-89	
E. Standards for Modification	798-812	594-612	995-1009	447-68	655-78			715-24	740-50	595-603	907-25		899-909	822-33	
F. Visitation Rights of Third Parties	787-98	621-30	1016-33	52-62	698-728	108-24		841-50	718-40	616-22	690-713	1125-46	580-600; 892-97	789-808	
G. Interstate Recognition of Custody Decrees	961-88	663-81	939-58	474-83				801-30	633-46		847-50	1158-1201	829-48	833-45	1040-87
9. THE PARENTAL OBLIGATION OF CARE AND CONTROL, AND THE JUVENILE COURT SYSTEM															
A. Child Dependency				504-27								889-94	604		
B. Child Neglect and Abuse	363-68	1189-1237	488-560	527-693	1127-1221	124-62, 204-384			488-524	223-360	1024-1187	889-952	603-20	873-999	938-52
C. Constitutional Rights	14-16; 636-48; 787-98	1022-30; 1276-96	562-72		1077-97	147-162	50-64		504-07		1121-43	1202-21			
D. Parental Control over Medical Care Rendered Their Child	224-25	1074-1107	447-76	639-93	1104-26; 1141-55	204-384	203-69		455-87	361-438	728-99	952-1023	555-71		672-92
E. Child Abuse	363-68	1189-1214	488-526	527-638	1156-1221	827-970; 1107-75	575-99; 614-28; 717-49			243-98	1051-1118	902-52	628-30	873-95	
F. Disposition by the Juvenile Court		1043-53		857-1018			273-356; 479-540			698-782			620-35		938-52
G. Criminal Procedure				1018-1228			403-78			782-851					
10. CHILDREN'S RIGHTS															
A. History of Parental Control	14-16	1017-30	425-26	001-052	1077-97		008-015		431-44	47-68	601-10; 746-60		529-31	15-20; 857-67	661-71

	Abrams, Cahn, Ross & Meyer	Areen & Regan (5th ed.)	Clark & Estin (7th ed.)	Davis, Scott, Waddington & Whitebread (4th ed.)	Ellman, Kurtz, Scott, Weithorn & Bix (4th ed.)	Gardner & Dupre (2d ed.)	Harris & Teitelbaum (2d ed.)	Harris, Teitelbaum & Carbone (3d ed.)	Krause, Elrod, Garrison & Oldham (6th ed.)	Mnookin & Weisberg (5th ed.)	Schneider & Brinig (3d ed.)	Wadlington & O'Brien (6th ed.)	Wardle & Nolan	Weisberg & Appleton (3d ed.)	Weyrauch, Katz & Olsen
B. Constitutional Rights	14-16; 224-25		438-42; 487-88	001-052; 117-64	1077-97	10-28; 439-69	004-008; 113-201			76-142	760-78		550-52		693-719
C. Emancipation	565	1179-88	426-31; 893-94	228-52	1101-03	196-204	337-38		882-83	731-32		1033-37	503-11	1000-05	
D. Minor's Capacity to Contract		1142-46		110-15						659-61					
E. Children and Tort Law	376-81	1130-41	445-46	115-17		180-95				234-36; 652-58	1144-50	1023-33	511-17	1005-14	
F. Property Rights	583	1147-54								209-12			524-28		
G. Education: State and Parents	14-16	1058-73		002-052	1097-98		39-111		444-55	47-68	601-10; 1289; 1318	848-76		15-20	646-61
11. LEGITIMACY, ILLEGITIMACY AND PATERNITY															
A. Legitimacy	278-79	1107-14	228-62	790-92				850-51	295-307	143-48		666-75	257-60; 262-64		
B. Illegitimacy	278-79; 299	1107-14	228-62	103-07	1035-38				307-11	154-72		666-87	264-73	447-78	743-83
C. Establishing Paternity	279-99		262-85		949-72			877-88	311-22	167-70		687-736	247-61	452-85	
D. Conflicts of Laws															
12. ADOPTION															
A. History and Development	1013-15	1304-06		790-92		169-71		943-46	323-27		926	1264-66	305-10	1021-23	
B. Social Functions									323-27			1264-66	332-33		
C. The Adoption Process	1027-33	1306-23	321-52	802-34	1254-58			957-61	367-75	506-07		1326-42	323-32	1060-67	
D. Qualifications of Adoptive Parents	1021-26; 1049-53	1356-85	352-66	792-801; 818-32	1043-66; 1254-73	174-80		961-80	353-67	515-34	1318-60	1267-78	337-49; 378-80	1038-60	
E. Consent to Adoption	1040-42	1316-17	321-31	62-103; 801-02	1223-53	171-73		946-56	327-53	476-505		1279-1326	310-23; 331-32	1024-38	
F. Anonymity	1042-48; 1056; 1061	1340-46; 1396-99	389-90	834-42	1300-04			953-56	364-66	513-15		1345-52; 1362-64	352-60	1091-97	953-59
G. Revocation of Adoption	1054-56	1385-96	390-98	808-18	1297-99					508-09			352	1097-1102	
H. Legal Effect of Adoption	1012-13	1305	398-400	842-44	1294-97	169						1342-45	349-52	1084-85	953-59
13. PROCREATION															
A. Constitutional Underpinnings	16-34	238-43	162-227					140-49	60-66; 272-95	674-87	610-71	74-153	381-98; 449-59	001-015; 20-56	350-401
B. Assisted Reproduction	1061-1100	954-1016	400-24	737-846	1305-30	81-106		981-1009	376-430	439-49; 622-35	952-98	737-846	275-304	1102-48	

*

APPENDIX D

Glossary*

* Based on Black's Law Dictionary.

A

Adoption Legal process pursuant to which a child's legal rights and duties toward his natural parents are terminated and similar rights and duties toward his adoptive parents are substituted. The procedure is entirely statutory and has no historical basis in common law.

Affinity Relation which one spouse because of marriage has to blood relatives of the other. The connection existing, in consequence of marriage, between each of the married persons and the kindred of the other. Degrees of relationship by affinity are computed as are degrees of relationship by consanguinity. The doctrine of affinity grew out of the canonical maxim that marriage makes husband and wife one. The husband has the same relation, by affinity, to his wife's blood relatives as she has to them by consanguinity and vice versa. Affinity is distinguished into three kinds: (1) Direct, or that subsisting between the husband and his wife's relations by blood, or between the wife and the husband's relations by blood; (2) secondary, or that which subsists between the husband and his wife's relations by marriage; (3) collateral, or that which subsists between the husband and the relations of his wife's relations.

Alienation of Affections "Alienation of affections" is a tort based upon willful and malicious interference with marriage relation by third party, without justification or excuse. The elements constituting the cause of action are wrongful conduct of defendant, plaintiff's loss of affection or consortium of spouse and causal connection between such conduct and such loss. See also Consortium; Heartbalm Statutes.

Alimony Comes from Latin "alimonia" meaning sustenance, and means, therefore, the sustenance or support of the wife by her divorced husband and stems from the common-law right of the wife to support by her husband. Allowances which husband or wife by court order pays other spouse for maintenance while they are separated, or after they are divorced (permanent alimony), or temporarily, pending a suit for divorce (pendente lite). Generally, it is restricted to money unless otherwise authorized by statute. But it may be an allowance out of the spouse's estate.

Alimony in Gross Alimony in a lump sum, is in the nature of a final property settlement, and hence in some jurisdictions is not included in the term "alimony," which in its strict or technical sense contemplates money payments at regular intervals. Refers to those alimony arrangements where entire award is a vested and determined amount and not subject to change.

Alimony Pendente Lite An allowance for temporary alimony made pending a suit for divorce or separate maintenance including a reasonable allowance for preparation of the suit as well as for support.

Annulment To nullify, to abolish, to make void an attempted or purported marriage by competent authority. An "annulment" differs conceptually from a divorce in that a divorce terminates a legal status, whereas an annulment establishes that a marital status never existed.

Antenuptial Before marriage.

Antenuptial Agreement A contract between spouses made before and in contemplation of marriage. Antenuptial agreements are generally entered into by people about to enter marriage in an attempt to resolve issues of support, distribution of wealth and division of property in the event of the death of either or the failure of the proposed marriage resulting in either separation or divorce. Commonly, the statute of frauds requires a writing and signing to be enforceable.

Arbitration The reference of a dispute to an impartial (third) person chosen by the parties to the dispute who agree in advance to abide by the arbitrator's award issued after a hearing at which both parties have an opportunity to be heard. See also Conciliation; Mediation.

Augmented Estate Estate reduced by funeral and administration expenses, homestead allowance, family allowances, exemptions, and enforceable claims to which is added value of property transferred to anyone other than bona fide purchaser and value of property owned by surviving spouse at decedent's death. This concept is used in the Uniform Probate Code.

B

Banns of Matrimony Public notice or proclamation of a matrimonial contract, and the intended celebration of the marriage of the parties in pursuance of such contract. Such announcement is required by certain religions to be made in a church or chapel, during service, on three consecutive Sundays before the marriage is celebrated. The object is to afford an opportunity for any person to interpose an objection if he knows of any impediment or other just cause why the marriage should not take place.

Bigamy The criminal offense of willfully and knowingly contracting a second marriage (or going through the form of a second marriage) while the first marriage, to the knowledge of the offender, is still subsisting and undissolved. The state of a man who has two wives, or of a woman who has two husbands, living at the same time. A married person is guilty of bigamy, a misdemeanor, if he contracts or purports to contract another marriage, unless at the time of the subsequent marriage: (a) the actor believes that the prior spouse is dead; or (b) the actor and the prior spouse have been living apart for five consecutive years throughout which the prior spouse was not known by the actor to be alive; or (c) a court has entered a judgment purporting to terminate or annul any prior disqualifying marriage, and the actor does not know that judgment to be invalid; or (d) the actor reasonably believes that he is legally eligible to remarry. Model Penal Code, § 230.1. See also Polygamy.

C

Capacity Legal qualification (e.g., legal age), competency, power or fitness. Ability to understand the nature and effects of one's acts. The ability of a particular individual or entity to use, or to be brought into, the courts of a forum.

Civil Union A formal legal status available in some states for same-sex or other couples through which the parties may obtain state recognition and many or all of the tangible legal incidents of marriage. State laws vary concerning whether civil unions are available only to same-sex partners and the extent of the marriage-like benefits provided. See also Domestic Partnership.

Cohabitation To live together as spouses. The mutual assumption of those marital rights, duties and obligations which are usually manifested by married people, including but not necessarily dependent on sexual relations. See also "Palimony."

Collusion In divorce proceedings, collusion is an agreement between spouses that one of them shall commit, or appear to have committed, or be represented in court as having committed, acts constituting a cause of divorce, for the purpose of enabling the other to obtain a divorce. But it also means connivance or conspiracy in initiating or prosecuting the suit, as where there is a compact for mutual aid in carrying it through to a decree.

Comity Recognition that one sovereignty allows within its territory to the legislative, executive, or judicial act of another sovereignty, having due regard to rights of its own citizens. In general, principle of "comity" is that courts of one state or jurisdiction will give effect to laws and judicial decisions of another state or jurisdiction, not as a matter of obligation but out of deference and mutual respect.

Common–Law Marriage One not solemnized in the ordinary way (i.e. nonceremonial) but created by an agreement to marry, followed by cohabitation. A consummated agreement to marry, between persons legally capable of making marriage contract, *per verba de praesenti*, followed by cohabitation. Such marriage requires a positive mutual agreement, permanent and exclusive of all others, to enter into a marriage relationship, cohabitation sufficient to warrant a fulfillment of necessary relationship of spouses, holding out to the public as such, and an assumption of marital duties and obligations.

Community Property Property owned in common by spouses each having an undivided one-half interest by reason of their marital status. Nine states have community property systems. The rest of the states are classified as common law jurisdictions. The difference between common law and community property systems centers around the property rights possessed by married persons. In a common law system, each spouse owns whatever he or she earns. Under a community property system, one-half of the earnings of each spouse is considered "earned" by the other spouse.

Conciliation The adjustment and settlement of a dispute in a friendly, unantagonistic manner. See also Arbitration; Mediation.

Condonation The conditional remission or forgiveness, by means of continuance or resumption of marital cohabitation, by one of the married parties, of a known matrimonial offense committed by the other, that would constitute a cause of divorce; the condition being that the offense shall not be repeated. Condonation to constitute valid defense in divorce action, must be free, voluntary, and not induced by duress or fraud.

Conjugal Of or belonging to marriage or the married state; suitable or appropriate to the married state or to married persons; matrimonial; connubial.

Connivance The secret or indirect consent or permission of one person to the commission of an unlawful or criminal act by another. As constituting defense in divorce action, is plaintiff's corrupt consent, express or implied, to offense charged against defendant.

Consanguinity Kinship; blood relationship; the connection or relation of persons descended from the same stock or common ancestor. Consanguinity is distinguished from "affinity," which is the connection existing in consequence of a marriage, between each of the married persons and the kindred of the other. Lineal consanguinity is that which subsists between persons of whom one is descended in a direct line from the other, as between son, father, grandfather, great-grandfather, and so upwards in the direct ascending line; or between son, grandson, great-grandson, and so downwards in the direct descending line. Collateral consanguinity is that which subsists between persons who have the same ancestors, but who do not descend (or ascend) one from the other. Thus, father and son are related by lineal consanguinity, uncle and nephew by collateral consanguinity.

Consortium Conjugal fellowship of spouses, and the right of each to the company, society, cooperation, affection, and aid of the other in every conjugal relation. Damages for loss of consortium are commonly sought in wrongful death actions, or when a spouse has been seriously injured through negligence of another, or by a spouse against a third person alleging that he or she has caused the break-up of the marriage. "Loss of consortium" means loss of society, affection, assistance and conjugal fellowship, and includes loss or impairment of sexual relations. Cause of action for "consortium" occasioned by injury to marriage partner, is a separate cause of action belonging to the spouse of the injured married partner and though derivative in the sense of being occasioned by injury to spouse, is a direct injury to the spouse who has lost the consortium.

Covenant Marriage An alternative form of marriage offered in some states through which the parties elect to bind themselves through more restrictive laws governing entry into and exit from marriage.

Criminal Conversation Sexual intercourse of an outsider with husband or wife. Tort action based on adultery, considered in its aspect of a civil injury to the husband or wife entitling him or her to damages; the tort of debauching or seducing of a wife or husband. See also Alienation of Affections; Heartbalm statutes.

Curtesy The estate to which by common law a man was entitled, on the death of his wife, in the lands or tenements of which she was seised in possession in fee-simple or in tail during her coverture, provided they have had lawful issue born alive which might have been capable of inheriting the estate. It was a freehold estate for the term of his natural life. In some jurisdictions, there was no requirement that issue have been born of the union. The estate has gradually lost much of its former value.

D

Desertion As used in statute providing that parental consent to adoption is not required when parent has wilfully deserted child evinces settled purpose to forego, abandon, or desert all parental duties and parental rights in child. Constructive desertion: That arising where an existing cohabitation is put an end to by misconduct of one of the parties, provided such misconduct is itself a ground for divorce. For example, where one spouse, by his or her words, conduct, demeanor, and attitude produces an intolerable condition which forces the other spouse to withdraw from the joint habitation to a more peaceful one. Divorce law: As a ground for divorce, an actual abandonment or breaking off of matrimonial cohabitation, by either of the parties, and a renouncing or refusal of the duties and obligations of the relation, with an intent to abandon or forsake entirely and not to return to or resume marital relations, occurring without legal justification either in the consent or the wrongful conduct of the other party. The elements of offense of "desertion" as grounds for divorce are a voluntary intentional abandonment of one party by the other, without cause or justification and without consent of party abandoned.

Dissolution of Marriage (See Divorce, Annulment).

Divisible Divorce Decree of divorce may be divided as between provisions for support and alimony and provisions dissolving the marriage. Doctrine applied in cases under Full Faith and Credit Clause in connection with effect of foreign divorce on support provisions.

Divorce The legal separation of spouses, effected by the judgment or decree of a court, and either totally dissolving the marriage relation, or suspending its effects so far as concerns the cohabitation of the parties.

Divorce *a Mensa et Thoro* A divorce from table and bed, or from bed and board. A partial or qualified divorce, by which the parties are separated and forbidden to live or cohabit together, without affecting the marriage itself.

Divorce *a Vinculo Matrimonii* A divorce from the bond of marriage (annulment). A total divorce of spouses, dissolving the marriage tie, and releasing the parties wholly from their matrimonial obligations.

Domestic Partnership A formal legal status available under the laws of some states and municipalities through which the parties can obtain public recognition and some or all of the legal incidents of marriage. See also Civil Union.

Domicile That place where a person has his true, fixed, and permanent home and principal establishment, and to which whenever he is absent he has the intention of returning. The permanent residence of a person or the place to which he intends to return even though he may actually reside elsewhere. A person may have more than one residence but only one domicile. Matrimonial domicile: The place where spouses have established a home, in which they reside in the relation of spouses, and where the matrimonial contract is being performed.

Dower The provision which the law makes for a widow out of the lands or tenements of her husband, for her support and the nurture of her children. A species of life-estate which a woman is, by law, entitled to claim on the death of her husband, in the lands and tenements of which he was seised in fee during the marriage, and which her issue, if any, might by possibility have inherited. The life estate to which every married woman is entitled on death of her husband, intestate, or, in case she dissents from his will one-third in value of all lands of which husband was beneficially seized in law or in fact, at any time during coverture. Dower has been widely abolished.

E

Equitable Adoption "Equitable adoption" refers to situation involving oral contract to adopt child, fully performed except that there was no statutory adoption, and in which rule is applied for benefit of child in determination of heirship upon death of person contracting to adopt.

Emancipation The term is principally used with reference to the emancipation of a minor child by its parents, which involves an entire surrender of the right to the care, custody, and earnings of such child as well as a renunciation of parental duties. The emancipation may be express, as by voluntary agreement of parent and child, or implied from such acts and conduct as import consent, and it may be conditional or absolute, complete or partial. Complete emancipation is entire surrender of care, custody, and earnings of child, as well as renunciation of parental duties. A "partial emancipation" frees a child for only a part of the period of minority, or from only a part of the parent's rights, or for some purposes, and not for others.

Estoppel "Estoppel" means that party is prevented by his own acts from claiming a right to detriment of other party who was entitled to rely on such conduct and has acted accordingly. An inconsistent position, attitude or course of conduct may not be adopted to loss or injury of another. Estoppel is a bar or impediment which precludes allegation or denial of a certain fact or state of facts, in consequence of previous allegation or denial or conduct or admission, or in consequence of a final adjudication of the matter in a court of law. It operates to put party entitled to its benefits in same position as if thing represented were true.

Estover An allowance (more commonly called "alimony") traditionally granted to a woman divorced a mensa et thoro, for her support out of her husband's estate.

***Ex Parte* Divorce** Divorce proceeding in which only one spouse participates or one in which the other spouse does not appear.

F

Fornication Unlawful sexual intercourse between two unmarried persons. Further, if one of the persons be married and the other not, it is fornication on the part of the latter, though adultery for the former.

Forum Non Conveniens Term refers to discretionary power of court to decline jurisdiction when convenience of parties and ends of justice would be better served if action were brought and tried in another forum. The doctrine is patterned upon the right of the court in the exercise of its powers to refuse the imposition upon its jurisdiction of the trial of cases even though the venue is properly laid if it appears that for the convenience of litigants and witnesses and in the interest of justice the action should be instituted in another forum where the action might have been brought. The doctrine presupposes at least two forums in which the defendant is amenable to process and furnishes criteria for choice between such forums.

Full Faith and Credit Clause The clause of the U.S. Constitution (Art. IV, Sec. 1) which provides that the various states must recognize legislative acts, public records, and judicial decisions of the other states within the United States. There are exceptions to this, a major one being that a state need not recognize a divorce decree of a state where neither spouse was a legal resident. Doctrine means that a state must accord the judgment of a court of another state the same credit that it is entitled to in the courts of that state. See also Comity.

H

Heartbalm Statutes State statutes abolishing or restricting common law right of action for alienation of affections, breach of promise to marry, criminal conversation, and seduction of person over legal age of consent.

I

Illegitimate Child Child who is born to parents who are not married to each other.

Incest The crime of sexual intercourse or cohabitation between a man and woman who are related to each other within the degrees wherein marriage is prohibited by law. A person is guilty of incest, a felony of the third degree, if he knowingly marries or cohabits or has sexual intercourse with an ancestor or descendant, a brother or sister of the whole or half blood (or an uncle, aunt, nephew or niece of the whole blood). "Cohabit" means to live together under the representation or appearance of being married. The relationships referred to herein includes blood relationships without regard to legitimacy, and relationship of parent and child by adoption. Model Penal Code, § 230.2.

Intestacy The state or condition of dying without having made a valid will, or without having disposed by will of a part of his property.

J

Joint Tenancy An estate in fee-simple, feetail, for life, for years, or at will, arising by purchase or grant to two or more persons. Joint tenants have one and the same interest, accruing by one and the same conveyance, commencing at one and the same time, and held by one and the same undivided possession. The primary incident of joint tenancy is survivorship, by which the entire tenancy on the decease of any joint tenant remains to the survivors, and at length to the last survivor. Type of ownership of real or personal property by two or more persons in which each owns an undivided interest in the whole and attached to which is the right of survivorship. Single estate in property owned by two or more persons under one instrument or act.

L

Legal Separation (See Separate Maintenance; Divorce *a mensa et thoro*).

Legitimacy Lawful birth; the condition of being born in wedlock; the opposite of illegitimacy or bastardy.

"Long Arm" Statute Various state legislative acts which provide for personal jurisdiction over persons who are nonresidents of the state and who have contacts within the state deemed sufficiently significant (measured under the due process clause) to have them brought before the courts of the state for litigation.

M

Maintenance The furnishing by one person to another, for his support, of the means of living, or food, clothing, shelter, etc., particularly where the legal relation of the parties is such that one is bound to support the other, as between father and child, or husband and wife. The supplying of the necessaries of life. Term "maintenance" means primarily food, clothing and shelter.

Marriage Traditionally defined as legal union of one man and one woman as husband and wife; in states recognizing same-sex marriage defined as legal union of two persons as spouses. A contract, according to the form prescribed by law, by which two parties capable of entering into such contract, mutually engage with each other to live their whole lives (or until divorced) together in the state of union which ought to exist between spouses. The word also signifies the act, ceremony, or formal proceeding by which persons take each other for husband and wife (or spouses). Marriage which follows all the statutory requirements of blood tests, license, waiting period, and which has been solemnized before an official (religious or civil) capable of presiding at the marriage. See also Voidable Marriage; Void Marriage.

Mediation Intervention; interposition; the act of a third person in intermediating between two contending parties with a view to persuading them to adjust or settle their dispute. Settlement of dispute by action of intermediary (neutral party). See also Arbitration; Conciliation.

Meretricious Of the nature of unlawful sexual connection.

Migratory Divorce Term used to describe a divorce secured by a spouse or spouses who leave(s) his/their domicile and move(s) to, or reside(s) temporarily in, another state or country for purpose of securing the divorce. See also *Ex parte* divorce.

Miscegenation Term formerly applied to marriage between persons of different races.

Monogamy The marriage of one spouse only, or the state of such as are restrained to a single spouse. The term is used in opposition to "bigamy" and "polygamy."

N

Necessaries An article which a party actually needs. Things indispensable, or things proper and useful, for the sustenance of human life. The word has no hard and fast meaning, but varies with the accustomed manner of living of the parties. Necessaries consist of food, drink, clothing, medical attention, and a suitable place of residence, and they are regarded as necessaries in the absolute sense of the word. However, liability for necessaries is not limited to articles required to sustain life; it extends to articles which would ordinarily be necessary and suitable, in view of the rank, position, fortune, earning capacity, and mode of living of the household.

Neglected Child A child is "neglected" when his parent or custodian, by reason of cruelty, mental incapacity, immorality or depravity, is unfit properly to care for him, or neglects or refuses to provide necessary physical, affectional, medical, surgical, or institutional or hospital care for him, or he is in such condition of want or suffering, or is under such improper care or control as to endanger his morals or health.

Nonmarital Child See "Illegitimate Child."

P

"Palimony" Slang term with meaning similar to "alimony" except that award, settlement or agreement arises out of nonmarital relationship of parties (*i.e.*, nonmarital partners). *Marvin v. Marvin* held that courts should enforce express contracts between nonmarital partners except to the extent the contract is explicitly founded on the consideration of meretricious sexual services, despite contention that such contracts violate public policy; that in the absence of express contract, the court should inquire into the conduct of the parties to determine whether that conduct demonstrates implied contract, agreement of partnership or joint venture, or some other tacit understanding between the parties, and may also employ the doctrine of quantum meruit or equitable remedies such as constructive or resulting trust, when warranted by the facts of the case.

Paternity The state or condition of a father; the relationship of a father.

Peonage A condition of servitude (prohibited by 13th Amendment) compelling persons to perform labor in order to pay off a debt.

Per Verba de Futuro By words of the future (tense). A phrase applied to contracts of marriage.

Per Verba de Praesenti By words of the present (tense). A phrase applied to contracts of marriage.

Plural Marriage In general, any bigamous or polygamous union, but particularly, a second or subsequent marriage of a man who already has one wife living under system of polygamy.

Polygamy The offense of having several wives or husbands at the same time, or more than one wife or husband at the same time. Bigamy literally means a second marriage distinguished from a third or other, while polygamy means many marriages. See also monogamy.

Postnuptial After marriage.

Prenuptial Before marriage. See also Antenuptial.

Pretermitted Heir A child or other descendant omitted by a testator. Where a testator unintentionally fails to mention in his will, or make provision for, a child, either living at the date of the execution of the will or born thereafter, a statute may provide that such child, or the issue of a deceased child, shall share in the estate as though the testator had died intestate.

Putative Marriage A marriage contracted in good faith and in ignorance (on one or both sides) that impediments exist which render it unlawful.

Putative Spouse One, in an invalid marriage, believing, in good faith, to be the spouse of another.

Proxy Marriage A marriage contracted or celebrated through agents acting on behalf of one or both parties. A proxy marriage differs from the more conventional ceremony only in that one or both of the contracting parties are represented by an agent, all the other requirements having been met.

R

Reconciliation The renewal of amicable relations between two persons who had been at variance; usually implying forgiveness on one or both sides. In law of domestic relations, a voluntary resumption of marital relations in the fullest sense.

Recrimination A charge made by an accused person against the accuser; in particular a counter-charge of adultery or cruelty made by one charged with the same offense in a suit for divorce, against the person who has charged him or her. Under doctrine of "recrimination", if conduct of both husband and wife has been such as to furnish grounds for divorce neither is entitled to relief.

Res Judicata A matter adjudged; a thing judicially acted upon or decided; a thing or matter settled by judgment. Rule that a final judgment rendered by a court of competent jurisdiction on the merits is conclusive as to the rights of the parties and their privies, and, as to them, constitutes an absolute bar to a subsequent action involving the same claim, demand or cause of action. And to be applicable, requires identity in thing sued for as well as identity of cause of action, of persons and parties to action, and of quality in persons for or against whom claim is made. The sum and substance of the whole rule is that a matter once judicially decided is finally decided.

S

Separate Maintenance Money paid by one married person to the other for support if they are no longer living as husband and wife, but are not divorced. See also Alimony.

Separate Property Property owned by married person in his or her own right during marriage.

Solemnization To enter marriage publicly before witnesses in contrast to a clandestine or common law marriage.

Sua Sponte Of his or its own will or motion; voluntarily; without prompting or suggestion.

T

Tenancy by the Entirety A tenancy which is created between a husband and wife and by which together they hold title to the whole with right of survivorship so that, upon death of either, other takes whole to exclusion of deceased heirs. It is essentially a "joint tenancy," modified by the common-law theory that

husband and wife are one person, and survivorship is the predominant and distinguishing feature of each.

V

Voidable Marriage One which is not void when entered into and which remains valid until either party secures lawful court order dissolving the marital relationship. A voidable marriage is one where there is an imperfection which can be inquired into only during the lives of both of the parties in a proceeding to obtain a judgment declaring it void.

Void Marriage One not good for any legal purpose, the invalidity of which may be maintained in any proceeding between any parties. Such marriage is invalid from its inception, and parties thereto may simply separate without benefit of court order of divorce or annulment.

*

APPENDIX E

Table of Cases

Acheampong v. Keisler, 2007 WL 2913927 (6th Cir.2007), 74

Adoption of (see name of party)

Alsager v. District Court of Polk County, Iowa, 545 F.2d 1137 (8th Cir.1976), 239

Alsager v. District Court of Polk County, Iowa (Juvenile Division), 406 F.Supp. 10 (S.D.Iowa 1975), 239

Andrew A., In re, 149 Md.App. 412, 815 A.2d 931 (Md.App.2003), 238

Ankenbrandt v. Richards, 504 U.S. 689, 112 S.Ct. 2206, 119 L.Ed.2d 468 (1992), 131

Anonymous v. Anonymous, 37 Misc.2d 773, 236 N.Y.S.2d 288 (N.Y.Sup.1962), 142

Appeal of (see name of party)

Application for Change of Name by Bacharach, In re, 344 N.J.Super. 126, 780 A.2d 579 (N.J.Super.A.D.2001), 125

Armstrong v. Manzo, 380 U.S. 545, 85 S.Ct. 1187, 14 L.Ed.2d 62 (1965), 302

Arnold, Marriage of v. Arnold, 270 Wis.2d 705, 679 N.W.2d 296 (Wis.App.2004), 219

Baby M, Matter of, 109 N.J. 396, 537 A.2d 1227 (N.J.1988), 324

Baehr v. Lewin, 74 Haw. 530, 74 Haw. 645, 852 P.2d 44 (Hawai'i 1993), 23

Baehr v. Miike, 1996 WL 694235 (Hawai'i Cir.Ct.1996), 23

Baker v. Combs, 248 S.W.3d 581 (Ky.App.2008), 215

Baker v. State, 170 Vt. 194, 744 A.2d 864 (Vt.1999), 24

Balouch v. State, 938 So.2d 253 (Miss.2006), 288

Barbara Haven, In re, 86 Pa. D. & C. 141 (Pa.Orph.1954), 65

Barndt v. Barndt, 397 Pa.Super. 321, 580 A.2d 320 (Pa.Super.1990), 228

Barnes v. Barnes, 16 Va.App. 98, 428 S.E.2d 294 (Va.App.1993), 157

Beaudette v. Frana, 285 Minn. 366, 173 N.W.2d 416 (Minn.1969), 111

Bell v. Bell, 393 Mass. 20, 468 N.E.2d 859 (Mass.1984), 162

Bell v. Bell, 38 Md.App. 10, 379 A.2d 419 (Md.App.1977), 180

Bellotti v. Baird, 443 U.S. 622, 99 S.Ct. 3035, 61 L.Ed.2d 797 (1979), 247, 260, 261

Bennett v. Jeffreys, 40 N.Y.2d 543, 387 N.Y.S.2d 821, 356 N.E.2d 277 (N.Y.1976), 214

Berger v. Berger, 277 Mich.App. 700, 747 N.W.2d 336 (Mich.App.2008), 174, 213

Berle v. Berle, 97 Idaho 452, 546 P.2d 407 (Idaho 1976), 170

Bethel School District No. 403 v. Fraser, 478 U.S. 675, 106 S.Ct. 3159, 92 L.Ed.2d 549 (1986), 271

Bicknell, In re, 96 Ohio St.3d 76, 771 N.E.2d 846 (Ohio 2002), 125

Bilowit v. Dolitsky, 124 N.J.Super. 101, 304 A.2d 774 (N.J.Super.Ch.1973), 73

Blau v. Fort Thomas Public School Dist., 401 F.3d 381 (6th Cir.2005), 270

Blixt v. Blixt, 437 Mass. 649, 774 N.E.2d 1052 (Mass.2002), 226

Board of Education of Piscataway Tp. v. Caffiero, 159 N.J.Super. 347, 387 A.2d 1263 (N.J.Super.L.1978), 267

Boddie v. Connecticut, 401 U.S. 371, 91 S.Ct. 780, 28 L.Ed.2d 113 (1971), 130

Bodne v. Bodne, 277 Ga. 445, 588 S.E.2d 728 (Ga.2003), 221

Boettcher, United States v., 780 F.2d 435 (4th Cir.1985), 229

Boris v. Blaisdell, 142 Ill.App.3d 1034, 97 Ill.Dec. 186, 492 N.E.2d 622 (Ill.App. 1 Dist.1986), 198

Boswell v. Boswell, 497 So.2d 479 (Ala.1986), 60

Bowers v. State, 283 Md. 115, 389 A.2d 341 (Md.1978), 238

Brabec v. Brabec, 181 Wis.2d 270, 510 N.W.2d 762 (Wis.App.1993), 158

Brady v. Brady, 64 N.Y.2d 339, 486 N.Y.S.2d 891, 476 N.E.2d 290 (N.Y.1985), 136

Bronson v. Swensen, 394 F.Supp.2d 1329 (D.Utah 2005), 19

Buck v. Bell, 274 U.S. 200, 47 S.Ct. 584, 71 L.Ed. 1000 (1927), 316

Buckley v. Buckley, 50 Wash. 213, 96 P. 1079 (Wash.1908), 75

Burke v. Rivo, 406 Mass. 764, 551 N.E.2d 1 (Mass.1990), 264

Burnham v. Superior Court of California, County of Marin, 495 U.S. 604, 110 S.Ct. 2105, 109 L.Ed.2d 631 (1990), 132

Burns v. Burns, 518 So.2d 1205 (Miss.1988), 114

Butler v. Butler, 464 Pa. 522, 347 A.2d 477 (Pa.1975), 104

Byers v. Mount Vernon Mills, Inc., 268 S.C. 68, 231 S.E.2d 699 (S.C.1977), 59

Caban v. Mohammed, 441 U.S. 380, 99 S.Ct. 1760, 60 L.Ed.2d 297 (1979), 282, 300

Capps v. Capps, 216 Va. 382, 219 S.E.2d 898 (Va.1975), 135

Carabetta v. Carabetta, 182 Conn. 344, 438 A.2d 109 (Conn.1980), 51

Carey v. Piphus, 435 U.S. 247, 98 S.Ct. 1042, 55 L.Ed.2d 252 (1978), 271

Carey v. Population Services, International, 431 U.S. 678, 97 S.Ct. 2010, 52 L.Ed.2d 675 (1977), 248, 261, 315

Carter v. Carter, 584 P.2d 904 (Utah 1978), 158

Castle Rock, Colo., Town of v. Gonzales, 545 U.S. 748, 125 S.Ct. 2796, 162 L.Ed.2d 658 (2005), 122

Catalano v. Catalano, 148 Conn. 288, 170 A.2d 726 (Conn.1961), 61

C.G.F., Matter of, 168 Wis.2d 62, 483 N.W.2d 803 (Wis.1992), 308

Chafino v. Chafino, 228 S.W.3d 467 (Tex.App.-El Paso 2007), 152, 169

Change of Name of Slingsby, In re, 276 Neb. 114, 752 N.W.2d 564 (Neb.2008), 126

Charlie H. v. Whitman, 83 F.Supp.2d 476 (D.N.J.2000), 297

Choin v. Mukasey, 537 F.3d 1116 (9th Cir.2008), 74

Cladis v. Cladis, 512 So.2d 271 (Fla.App. 4 Dist.1987), 31

Clark v. Jeter, 486 U.S. 456, 108 S.Ct. 1910, 100 L.Ed.2d 465 (1988), 281

Clark, State v., 88 Wash.2d 533, 563 P.2d 1253 (Wash.1977), 96

Clayton v. Clayton, 231 Md. 74, 188 A.2d 550 (Md.1963), 76

Cochran v. Cochran, 106 Cal.Rptr.2d 899 (Cal.App. 2 Dist.2001), 86

Cole v. Cushman, 946 A.2d 430 (Me.2008), 230

Coleman v. Garrison, 349 A.2d 8 (Del.Supr.1975), 264

Commonwealth v. _____ (see opposing party)

Connor v. Southwest Florida Regional Medical Center, Inc., 668 So.2d 175 (Fla.1995), 97

Cook v. Cook, 342 U.S. 126, 72 S.Ct. 157, 96 L.Ed. 146 (1951), 131

Cook v. Cook, 209 Ariz. 487, 104 P.3d 857 (Ariz.App. Div. 1 2005), 62

Coon v. American Compressed Steel, Inc., 207 S.W.3d 629 (Mo.App. W.D.2006), 291

C.P., In re, 836 A.2d 984 (Pa.Super.2003), 237

Curran v. Bosze, 141 Ill.2d 473, 153 Ill.Dec. 213, 566 N.E.2d 1319 (Ill.1990), 244

Curtis v. Kline, 542 Pa. 249, 666 A.2d 265 (Pa.1995), 193

Custody of a Minor, 375 Mass. 733, 379 N.E.2d 1053 (Mass.1978), 243

Custody of Dallenger, In re, 173 Mont. 530, 568 P.2d 169 (Mont.1977), 224

C.V.C. v. Superior Court, 29 Cal.App.3d 909, 106 Cal.Rptr. 123 (Cal.App. 3 Dist.1973), 304

Dallman's Estate, In re, 228 N.W.2d 187 (Iowa 1975), 54

Das v. Das, 133 Md.App. 1, 754 A.2d 441 (Md.App.2000), 136

Davis v. Hilton, 780 So.2d 974 (Fla.App. 4 Dist.2001), 267

Davis, United States v., 370 U.S. 65, 82 S.Ct. 1190, 8 L.Ed.2d 335 (1962), 171

Dean v. District of Columbia, 653 A.2d 307 (D.C.1995), 23

Decker v. Decker, 2008 WL 2854820 (Ala.Civ.App.2008), 161

Delconte v. State, 313 N.C. 384, 329 S.E.2d 636 (N.C.1985), 269

DeLorean v. DeLorean, 211 N.J.Super. 432, 511 A.2d 1257 (N.J.Super.Ch.1986), 41

Demetz, State ex rel. Dept. of Economic Sec. v., 212 Ariz. 287, 130 P.3d 986 (Ariz.App. Div. 1 2006), 196

Department of Human Resources v. Williams, 130 Ga.App. 149, 202 S.E.2d 504 (Ga.App.1973), 39

Dept. of Economic Sec., State ex rel. v. Demetz, 212 Ariz. 287, 130 P.3d 986 (Ariz.App. Div. 1 2006), 196

DeShaney v. Winnebago County Dept. of Social Services, 489 U.S. 189, 109 S.Ct. 998, 103 L.Ed.2d 249 (1989), 243

Devaney v. L'Esperance, 195 N.J. 247, 949 A.2d 743 (N.J.2008), 86

DeVito v. DeVito, 967 So.2d 74 (Miss.App.2007), 213

DewBerry v. George, 115 Wash.App. 351, 62 P.3d 525 (Wash.App. Div. 1 2003), 27

Dexter v. Dexter, 2007 WL 1532084 (Ohio App. 11 Dist.2007), 211

Dickens v. Ernesto, 30 N.Y.2d 61, 330 N.Y.S.2d 346, 281 N.E.2d 153 (N.Y.1972), 295

Diemer v. Diemer, 8 N.Y.2d 206, 203 N.Y.S.2d 829, 168 N.E.2d 654 (N.Y.1960), 137

Doe v. Attorney General, 194 Mich.App. 432, 487 N.W.2d 484 (Mich.App.1992), 323

Doe v. City of Trenton, 143 N.J.Super. 128, 362 A.2d 1200 (N.J.Super.A.D.1976), 267

Does v. State, 164 Or.App. 543, 993 P.2d 822 (Or.App.1999), 306

Dominy, State v., 6 S.W.3d 472 (Tenn.1999), 121

Douglas v. State, 263 Ga. 748, 438 S.E.2d 361 (Ga.1994), 289

Downs v. Downs, 154 Vt. 161, 574 A.2d 156 (Vt.1990), 172

Drews, In re Marriage of, 115 Ill.2d 201, 104 Ill.Dec. 782, 503 N.E.2d 339 (Ill.1986), 50

Dumlao, State v., 3 Conn.App. 607, 491 A.2d 404 (Conn.App.1985), 251

"E", In re Adoption of, 59 N.J. 36, 279 A.2d 785 (N.J.1971), 296

Edmunds v. Edwards, 205 Neb. 255, 287 N.W.2d 420 (Neb.1980), 48

Edwards v. Aguillard, 482 U.S. 578, 107 S.Ct. 2573, 96 L.Ed.2d 510 (1987), 270

Edwardson v. Edwardson, 798 S.W.2d 941 (Ky.1990), 35

E.G., In re, 133 Ill.2d 98, 139 Ill.Dec. 810, 549 N.E.2d 322 (Ill.1989), 245

Eickhoff v. Eickhoff, 263 Ga. 498, 435 S.E.2d 914 (Ga.1993), 183

Eisenstadt v. Baird, 405 U.S. 438, 92 S.Ct. 1029, 31 L.Ed.2d 349 (1972), 25, 314

Elam v. Elam, 275 S.C. 132, 268 S.E.2d 109 (S.C.1980), 266

Elkins v. Elkins, 262 Ark. 63, 553 S.W.2d 34 (Ark.1977), 192

Elkus v. Elkus, 169 A.D.2d 134, 572 N.Y.S.2d 901 (N.Y.A.D. 1 Dept.1991), 175

Ellam v. Ellam, 132 N.J.Super. 358, 333 A.2d 577 (N.J.Super.Ch.1975), 144

Ellis v. Estate of Ellis, 169 P.3d 441 (Utah 2007), 115

Emilio R., In re Adoption of, 293 A.D.2d 27, 742 N.Y.S.2d 22 (N.Y.A.D. 1 Dept.2002), 293

Estate of (see name of party)

Estevez v. Superior Court, 27 Cal.Rptr.2d 470 (Cal.App. 2 Dist.1994), 199

Estin v. Estin, 334 U.S. 541, 68 S.Ct. 1213, 92 L.Ed. 1561 (1948), 130

Faasse, United States v., 265 F.3d 475 (6th Cir.2001), 201

Fadgen v. Lenkner, 469 Pa. 272, 365 A.2d 147 (Pa.1976), 118

Fiallo v. Bell, 430 U.S. 787, 97 S.Ct. 1473, 52 L.Ed.2d 50 (1977), 279

Figueiredo–Torres v. Nickel, 321 Md. 642, 584 A.2d 69 (Md.1991), 120

Fish v. Fish, 285 Conn. 24, 939 A.2d 1040 (Conn.2008), 216

Flaherty v. Smith, 87 Mich.App. 561, 274 N.W.2d 72 (Mich.App.1978), 209

Fletcher v. Fletcher, 68 Ohio St.3d 464, 628 N.E.2d 1343 (Ohio 1994), 34

Fort v. Fort, 270 S.C. 255, 241 S.E.2d 891 (S.C.1978), 137

Foster/Dixon, United States v., 509 U.S. 688, 113 S.Ct. 2849, 125 L.Ed.2d 556 (1993), 122

Fournier v. Fournier, 376 A.2d 100 (Me.1977), 165

Fredo v. Fredo, 49 Conn.Supp. 489, 894 A.2d 399 (Conn.Super.2005), 77

Friedrich v. Friedrich, 983 F.2d 1396 (6th Cir.1993), 231

Friedrich v. Katz, 73 Misc.2d 663, 341 N.Y.S.2d 932 (N.Y.Sup.1973), 66

Funkhouser v. Funkhouser, 158 W.Va. 964, 216 S.E.2d 570 (W.Va.1975), 210

Gambla and Woodson, In re Marriage of, 367 Ill.App.3d 441, 304 Ill.Dec. 770, 853 N.E.2d 847 (Ill.App. 2 Dist.2006), 212

Gardner v. Flowers, 529 S.W.2d 708 (Tenn.1975), 262

Gardner v. Gardner, 110 Nev. 1053, 881 P.2d 645 (Nev.1994), 153

Gastineau v. Gastineau, 151 Misc.2d 813, 573 N.Y.S.2d 819 (N.Y.Sup.1991), 168

Gault, In re, 387 U.S. 1, 87 S.Ct. 1428, 18 L.Ed.2d 527 (1967), 254, 315

Gearhart v. Gearhart, 2008 WL 62286 (Ohio App. 5 Dist.2008), 53

Geitner v. Townsend, 67 N.C.App. 159, 312 S.E.2d 236 (N.C.App.1984), 49

Gerrits v. Gerrits, 167 Wis.2d 429, 482 N.W.2d 134 (Wis.App.1992), 159

Gilley v. McCarthy, 469 N.W.2d 666 (Iowa 1991), 198

Gillmore, In re Marriage of, 174 Cal.Rptr. 493, 629 P.2d 1 (Cal.1981), 177

Gleason v. Gleason, 26 N.Y.2d 28, 308 N.Y.S.2d 347, 256 N.E.2d 513 (N.Y.1970), 16, 146

Glidden v. Conley, 175 Vt. 111, 820 A.2d 197 (Vt.2003), 226

Glona v. American Guarantee & Liability Insurance Co., 391 U.S. 73, 88 S.Ct. 1515, 20 L.Ed.2d 441 (1968), 278

Gomez v. Perez, 409 U.S. 535, 93 S.Ct. 872, 35 L.Ed.2d 56 (1973), 278

Gonzales v. Carhart, 550 U.S. 124, 127 S.Ct. 1610, 167 L.Ed.2d 480 (2007), 316

Goode v. Goode, 183 W.Va. 468, 396 S.E.2d 430 (W.Va.1990), 84

Goodridge v. Department of Public Health, 440 Mass. 309, 798 N.E.2d 941 (Mass.2003), 17, 19, 24

Goss v. Lopez, 419 U.S. 565, 95 S.Ct. 729, 42 L.Ed.2d 725 (1975), 271

Greene v. Greene, 15 N.C.App. 314, 190 S.E.2d 258 (N.C.App.1972), 141

Greenlaw, In re Marriage of, 123 Wash.2d 593, 869 P.2d 1024 (Wash.1994), 228

Greenwood v. Greenwood, 2008 WL 3983852 (Ala.Civ.App.2008), 223

Greger v. Greger, 22 Conn.App. 596, 578 A.2d 162 (Conn.App.1990), 181

Griswold v. Connecticut, 381 U.S. 479, 85 S.Ct. 1678, 14 L.Ed.2d 510 (1965), 25, 314

Gross v. Gross, 11 Ohio St.3d 99, 464 N.E.2d 500 (Ohio 1984), 36

Gursky v. Gursky, 39 Misc.2d 1083, 242 N.Y.S.2d 406 (N.Y.Sup.1963), 318

Hagerty v. Hagerty, 281 N.W.2d 386 (Minn.1979), 145

Hakkila v. Hakkila, 112 N.M. 172, 812 P.2d 1320 (N.M.App.1991), 113

Hall v. Hall, 655 S.E.2d 901 (N.C.App.2008), 218

Hamlet v. Hamlet, 583 So.2d 654 (Fla.1991), 155

Hansen, In re Marriage of, 733 N.W.2d 683 (Iowa 2007), 214, 219

Hardy v. Hardy, 235 F.Supp. 208 (D.D.C 1964), 101

Harrison v. Harrison, 2008 WL 943915 (Ark.App.2008), 214

Hatch v. Hatch, 113 Ariz. 130, 547 P.2d 1044 (Ariz.1976), 169

Hathaway v. Worcester City Hospital, 475 F.2d 701 (1st Cir.1973), 317

Haun, In re, 277 N.E.2d 258 (Ohio Prob.1971), 295

Hazelwood School Dist. v. Kuhlmeier, 484 U.S. 260, 108 S.Ct. 562, 98 L.Ed.2d 592 (1988), 271

Hernandez v. Robles, 7 N.Y.3d 338, 821 N.Y.S.2d 770, 855 N.E.2d 1 (N.Y.2006), 25

Herzfeld v. Herzfeld, 781 So.2d 1070 (Fla.2001), 266

Hewitt v. Hewitt, 77 Ill.2d 49, 31 Ill.Dec. 827, 394 N.E.2d 1204 (Ill.1979), 88

Hicks on Behalf of Feiock v. Feiock, 485 U.S. 624, 108 S.Ct. 1423, 99 L.Ed.2d 721 (1988), 201

Hightower, In re Marriage of, 358 Ill.App.3d 165, 294 Ill.Dec. 450, 830 N.E.2d 862 (Ill.App. 2 Dist.2005), 141

H. L. v. Matheson, 450 U.S. 398, 101 S.Ct. 1164, 67 L.Ed.2d 388 (1981), 247, 261

Hodgson v. Minnesota, 497 U.S. 417, 110 S.Ct. 2926, 111 L.Ed.2d 344 (1990), 248, 261

Hofbauer, Matter of, 47 N.Y.2d 648, 419 N.Y.S.2d 936, 393 N.E.2d 1009 (N.Y.1979), 244

Hollandsworth v. Knyzewski, 353 Ark. 470, 109 S.W.3d 653 (Ark.2003), 221

Holm, State v., 137 P.3d 726 (Utah 2006), 20

Hopkins v. Hopkins, 597 S.W.2d 702 (Mo.App. W.D.1980), 168

Howard, In re Marriage of, 661 N.W.2d 183 (Iowa 2003), 225

Hoye v. Hoye, 824 S.W.2d 422 (Ky.1992), 119

Humphrey v. Humphrey, 293 Ala. 118, 300 So.2d 376 (Ala.1974), 53

Hunsaker, In re, 291 Mont. 412, 968 P.2d 281 (Mont.1998), 54

Huss, In re Marriage of, 888 N.E.2d 1238 (Ind.2008), 216

Ingraham v. Wright, 430 U.S. 651, 97 S.Ct. 1401, 51 L.Ed.2d 711 (1977), 272

In Interest of B.G.C., 496 N.W.2d 239 (Iowa 1992), 301

In re (see name of party)

Israel v. Allen, 195 Colo. 263, 577 P.2d 762 (Colo.1978), 64

Jacob, Matter of, 86 N.Y.2d 651, 636 N.Y.S.2d 716, 660 N.E.2d 397 (N.Y.1995), 293

Janda v. Janda, 984 So.2d 434 (Ala.Civ.App.2007), 72

Janira T., In re, 368 Ill.App.3d 883, 307 Ill.Dec. 369, 859

N.E.2d 1046 (Ill.App. 1 Dist.2006), 241

Jech v. Burch, 466 F.Supp. 714 (D.Hawai'i 1979), 125

Jennifer S. v. Marvin S., 150 Misc.2d 300, 568 N.Y.S.2d 515 (N.Y.Fam.Ct.1991), 195

Jimenez v. Weinberger, 417 U.S. 628, 94 S.Ct. 2496, 41 L.Ed.2d 363 (1974), 279

Johnson, In re Estate of, 18 Misc.3d 898, 850 N.Y.S.2d 855 (N.Y.Sur.2008), 310

Johnson v. Calvert, 19 Cal.Rptr.2d 494, 851 P.2d 776 (Cal.1993), 321

Johnson v. La Grange State Bank, 73 Ill.2d 342, 22 Ill.Dec. 709, 383 N.E.2d 185 (Ill.1978), 105

Johnson v. Muelberger, 340 U.S. 581, 71 S.Ct. 474, 95 L.Ed. 552 (1951), 131

Johnston v. Johnston, 297 Md. 48, 465 A.2d 436 (Md.1983), 183

Johnston v. Johnston, 979 So.2d 337 (Fla.App. 1 Dist.2008), 277

Joseph S., In re, 25 A.D.3d 804, 808 N.Y.S.2d 426 (N.Y.A.D. 2 Dept.2006), 48

Joye v. Yon, 355 S.C. 452, 586 S.E.2d 131 (S.C.2003), 77

J. S. R., Matter of Adoption of, 374 A.2d 860 (D.C.1977), 302

Kantaras v. Kantaras, 884 So.2d 155 (Fla.App. 2 Dist.2004), 90

Kelley v. Iowa Department of Social Services, 197 N.W.2d 192 (Iowa 1972), 191

Kelly, State v., 97 N.J. 178, 478 A.2d 364 (N.J.1984), 123

Khalifa v. Shannon, 404 Md. 107, 945 A.2d 1244 (Md.2008), 223

Kirchberg v. Feenstra, 450 U.S. 455, 101 S.Ct. 1195, 67 L.Ed.2d 428 (1981), 108

Kirchner, Petition of, 164 Ill.2d 468, 208 Ill.Dec. 268, 649 N.E.2d 324 (Ill.1995), 301

Knight v. Radomski, 414 A.2d 1211 (Me.1980), 49

Knight, State v., 3 S.D. 509, 54 N.W. 412 (S.D.1893), 200

Kolmosky v. Kolmosky, 631 A.2d 419 (Me.1993), 182

Kruzel v. Podell, 67 Wis.2d 138, 226 N.W.2d 458 (Wis.1975), 124

Kuhns' Estate v. Kuhns, 550 P.2d 816 (Alaska 1976), 160

Kujawinski v. Kujawinski, 71 Ill.2d 563, 17 Ill.Dec. 801, 376 N.E.2d 1382 (Ill.1978), 165, 193, 197

Kukafka, United States v., 478 F.3d 531 (3rd Cir.2007), 201

Kulko v. Superior Court of California In and For City and County of San Francisco, 436 U.S. 84, 98 S.Ct. 1690, 56 L.Ed.2d 132 (1978), 132

Labine v. Vincent, 401 U.S. 532, 91 S.Ct. 1017, 28 L.Ed.2d 288 (1971), 278

Laing v. Laing, 741 P.2d 649 (Alaska 1987), 178

Lalli v. Lalli, 439 U.S. 259, 99 S.Ct. 518, 58 L.Ed.2d 503 (1978), 278, 280

Lash v. Lash, 307 So.2d 241 (Fla.App. 2 Dist.1975), 153

Lassiter v. Department of Social Services of Durham County, N. C., 452 U.S. 18, 101 S.Ct. 2153, 68 L.Ed.2d 640 (1981), 239

Lawrence v. Texas, 539 U.S. 558, 123 S.Ct. 2472, 156 L.Ed.2d 508 (2003), 23, 26

Lehr v. Robertson, 463 U.S. 248, 103 S.Ct. 2985, 77 L.Ed.2d 614 (1983), 281, 300

Leonard v. Leonard, 259 So.2d 529 (Fla.App. 3 Dist.1972), 135

Levy v. Louisiana, 391 U.S. 68, 88 S.Ct. 1509, 20 L.Ed.2d 436 (1968), 277

Lewis v. Lewis, 69 Haw. 497, 748 P.2d 1362 (Hawai'i 1988), 33

Liberta, People v., 64 N.Y.2d 152, 485 N.Y.S.2d 207, 474 N.E.2d 567 (N.Y.1984), 122

Lieb v. Lieb, 53 A.D.2d 67, 385 N.Y.S.2d 569 (N.Y.A.D. 2 Dept.1976), 132

Lofton v. Secretary of Dept. of Children and Family Services, 358 F.3d 804 (11th Cir.2004), 294

Loving v. Virginia, 388 U.S. 1, 87 S.Ct. 1817, 18 L.Ed.2d 1010 (1967), 21, 61

Lozoya v. Sanchez, 133 N.M. 579, 66 P.3d 948 (N.M.2003), 115

L.S.K. v. H.A.N., 813 A.2d 872 (Pa.Super.2002), 191

Lucas v. Lucas, 166 Cal.Rptr.

853, 614 P.2d 285 (Cal.1980), 110

Mahoney v. Mahoney, 91 N.J. 488, 453 A.2d 527 (N.J.1982), 176

Marmelstein v. Kehillat New Hempstead, 11 N.Y.3d 15, 862 N.Y.S.2d 311, 892 N.E.2d 375 (N.Y.2008), 120

Marriage Cases, In re, 76 Cal.Rptr.3d 683, 183 P.3d 384 (Cal.2008), 17, 19, 24

Marriage of (see name of party)

Martarella v. Kelley, 349 F.Supp. 575 (S.D.N.Y.1972), 255

Marten v. Thies, 99 Cal.App.3d 161, 160 Cal.Rptr. 57 (Cal.App. 4 Dist.1979), 305

Marvin v. Marvin, 122 Cal.App.3d 871, 176 Cal.Rptr. 555 (Cal.App. 2 Dist.1981), 83

Marvin v. Marvin, 134 Cal.Rptr. 815, 557 P.2d 106 (Cal.1976), 82

Mason v. Rostad, 476 A.2d 662 (D.C.1984), 88

Mass, In re Marriage of, 102 Ill.App.3d 984, 58 Ill.Dec. 941, 431 N.E.2d 1 (Ill.App. 1 Dist.1981), 161

Massey v. Massey, 867 S.W.2d 766 (Tex.1993), 112

Mathews v. Eldridge, 424 U.S. 319, 96 S.Ct. 893, 47 L.Ed.2d 18 (1976), 240

Mathews v. Lucas, 427 U.S. 495, 96 S.Ct. 2755, 49 L.Ed.2d 651 (1976), 279

Matter of (see name of party)

May v. Anderson, 345 U.S. 528, 73 S.Ct. 840, 97 L.Ed. 1221 (1953), 226

Maynard v. Hill, 125 U.S. 190, 8 S.Ct. 723, 31 L.Ed. 654 (1888), 15

McGuire v. McGuire, 157 Neb. 226, 59 N.W.2d 336 (Neb.1953), 98

McKee–Johnson v. Johnson, 444 N.W.2d 259 (Minn.1989), 32

McKeiver v. Pennsylvania, 403 U.S. 528, 91 S.Ct. 1976, 29 L.Ed.2d 647 (1971), 254

McLane v. Paul, 189 P.3d 1039 (Alaska 2008), 225

Meadows v. Meadows, 2008 WL 3582691 (Ala.Civ.App.2008), 220, 222

Meagher and Maleki, In re Marriage of, 31 Cal.Rptr.3d 663 (Cal.App. 1 Dist.2005), 72

Mendillo v. Board of Educ. of Town of East Haddam, 246 Conn. 456, 717 A.2d 1177 (Conn.1998), 266

MEW and MLB, In re Marriage of, 4 Pa. D. & C.3d 51, 27 Fiduc.Rep. 416 (Pa.Com.Pl.1977), 64

Michael H. v. Gerald D., 491 U.S. 110, 109 S.Ct. 2333, 105 L.Ed.2d 91 (1989), 282, 300

Michelle T., Adoption of, 44 Cal.App.3d 699, 117 Cal.Rptr. 856 (Cal.App. 1 Dist.1975), 295

Miller, In re, 824 A.2d 1207 (Pa.Super.2003), 125

Mills v. Habluetzel, 456 U.S. 91, 102 S.Ct. 1549, 71 L.Ed.2d 770 (1982), 281

Milne v. Milne, 383 Pa.Super. 177, 556 A.2d 854 (Pa.Super.1989), 194

Mississippi Band of Choctaw Indians v. Holyfield, 490 U.S. 30, 109 S.Ct. 1597, 104 L.Ed.2d 29 (1989), 298

Moe v. Dinkins, 533 F.Supp. 623 (S.D.N.Y.1981), 66

Mogged v. Mogged, 55 Ill.2d 221, 302 N.E.2d 293 (Ill.1973), 139

Moore's Sterilization, In re, 289 N.C. 95, 221 S.E.2d 307 (N.C.1976), 316

Moran v. Beyer, 734 F.2d 1245 (7th Cir.1984), 114

Morgan v. Morgan, 52 A.D.2d 804, 383 N.Y.S.2d 343 (N.Y.A.D. 1 Dept.1976), 155

Morris v. Morris, 201 Neb. 479, 268 N.W.2d 431 (Neb.1978), 156

Morse v. Frederick, ___ U.S. ___, 127 S.Ct. 2618, 168 L.Ed.2d 290 (2007), 271

Mpiliris v. Hellenic Lines, Ltd., 323 F.Supp. 865 (S.D.Tex.1969), 73

M.S.R., In re, 2007 WL 3228072 (Tex.App.-Corpus Christi 2007), 220

M. T. v. J. T., 140 N.J.Super. 77, 355 A.2d 204 (N.J.Super.A.D.1976), 91

Murga, In re Marriage of, 103 Cal.App.3d 498, 163 Cal.Rptr. 79 (Cal.App. 4 Dist.1980), 219

Nash v. Mulle, 846 S.W.2d 803 (Tenn.1993), 199

National Account Systems, Inc. v. Mercado, 196 N.J.Super. 133, 481 A.2d 835 (N.J.Super.A.D.1984), 99

New Jersey Welfare Rights Organization v. Cahill, 411 U.S. 619, 93 S.Ct. 1700, 36 L.Ed.2d 543 (1973), 279

Nichols v. Funderburk, 881 So.2d 266 (Miss.App.2003), 88

Nixon, Commonwealth v., 563 Pa. 425, 761 A.2d 1151 (Pa.2000), 245

Nordberg, In re Marriage of, 265 Mont. 352, 877 P.2d 987 (Mont.1994), 191

Nott v. Flemming, 272 F.2d 380 (2nd Cir.1959), 78

O'Brien v. O'Brien, 66 N.Y.2d 576, 498 N.Y.S.2d 743, 489 N.E.2d 712 (N.Y.1985), 174

Ohio v. Akron Center for Reproductive Health, 497 U.S. 502, 110 S.Ct. 2972, 111 L.Ed.2d 405 (1990), 248, 261

Oldham v. Morgan, 372 Ark. 159 (Ark.2008), 226

Oleski v. Hynes, 2008 WL 2930518 (Conn.Super.2008), 318, 325

Olver v. Fowler, 161 Wash.2d 655, 168 P.3d 348 (Wash.2007), 83

O'Rourke, Appeal of, 310 Minn. 373, 246 N.W.2d 461 (Minn.1976), 59

Orr v. Bowen, 648 F.Supp. 1510 (D.Nev.1986), 58

Orr v. Orr, 440 U.S. 268, 99 S.Ct. 1102, 59 L.Ed.2d 306 (1979), 95, 99, 151

Orzechowski v. Perales, 153 Misc.2d 464, 582 N.Y.S.2d 341 (N.Y.Sup.1992), 296

Osier v. Osier, 410 A.2d 1027 (Me.1980), 211

Otis v. Otis, 299 N.W.2d 114 (Minn.1980), 152

O'Toole v. Greenberg, 64 N.Y.2d 427, 488 N.Y.S.2d 143, 477 N.E.2d 445 (N.Y.1985), 264

Painter v. Bannister, 258 Iowa 1390, 140 N.W.2d 152 (Iowa 1966), 216

Palmore v. Sidoti, 466 U.S. 429, 104 S.Ct. 1879, 80 L.Ed.2d 421 (1984), 212

Parham v. Hughes, 441 U.S. 347, 99 S.Ct. 1742, 60 L.Ed.2d 269 (1979), 278

Parham v. J. R., 442 U.S. 584, 99 S.Ct. 2493, 61 L.Ed.2d 101 (1979), 246, 262

Parker v. Hurley, 514 F.3d 87 (1st Cir.2008), 270

Parker v. Stage, 43 N.Y.2d 128, 400 N.Y.S.2d 794, 371 N.E.2d 513 (N.Y.1977), 195

Parker, State v., 185 N.C.App. 437, 651 S.E.2d 377 (N.C.App.2007), 251

Parkinson v. J. & S. Tool Company, 64 N.J. 159, 313 A.2d 609 (N.J.1974), 56

Pater v. Pater, 63 Ohio St.3d 393, 588 N.E.2d 794 (Ohio 1992), 211

Paternity and Custody of Baby Boy A., In re, 2007 WL 4304448 (Minn.App.2007), 324

Patey v. Peaslee, 99 N.H. 335, 111 A.2d 194 (N.H.1955), 71

P.B. for Adoption of L.C., In re, 392 N.J.Super. 190, 920 A.2d 155 (N.J.Super.L.2006), 291

Peddy v. Montgomery, 345 So.2d 631 (Ala.1977), 101

People v. _____ (see opposing party)

Petition of (see name of party)

Pfohl v. Pfohl, 345 So.2d 371 (Fla.App. 3 Dist.1977), 151

Phelps v. Bing, 58 Ill.2d 32, 316 N.E.2d 775 (Ill.1974), 22, 66

Pickett v. Brown, 462 U.S. 1, 103 S.Ct. 2199, 76 L.Ed.2d 372 (1983), 281

Pierce, People v., 61 Cal.2d 879, 40 Cal.Rptr. 845, 395 P.2d 893 (Cal.1964), 120

Pierce v. Society of the Sisters of the Holy Names of Jesus and Mary, 268 U.S. 510, 45 S.Ct. 571, 69 L.Ed. 1070 (1925), 268

Planned Parenthood of Central Missouri v. Danforth, 428 U.S. 52, 96 S.Ct. 2831, 49 L.Ed.2d 788 (1976), 246, 261, 314, 316

Planned Parenthood of Southeastern Pennsylvania v. Casey, 505 U.S. 833, 112 S.Ct. 2791, 120 L.Ed.2d 674 (1992), 247, 261, 315, 316

Poncho v. Bowdoin, 138 N.M. 857, 126 P.3d 1221 (N.M.App.2005), 292

Postema v. Postema, 189 Mich.App. 89, 471 N.W.2d 912 (Mich.App.1991), 174

Potter v. Murray City, 760 F.2d 1065 (10th Cir.1985), 19

Quilloin v. Walcott, 434 U.S. 246, 98 S.Ct. 549, 54 L.Ed.2d 511 (1978), 282, 299

R.E.G. v. L.M.G., 571 N.E.2d 298 (Ind.App. 1 Dist.1991), 167

Renshaw v. Heckler, 787 F.2d 50 (2nd Cir.1986), 57

Reynolds v. United States, 98 U.S. 145, 25 L.Ed. 244 (1878), 18, 19

Rivera v. Minnich, 483 U.S. 574, 107 S.Ct. 3001, 97 L.Ed.2d 473 (1987), 280

R.N.T. v. J.R.G., 666 P.2d 1036 (Alaska 1983), 302

Roberts v. Roberts, 200 Neb. 256, 263 N.W.2d 449 (Neb.1978), 145

Robison, In re Marriage of, 311 Mont. 246, 53 P.3d 1279 (Mont.2002), 220

Rodriguez v. Bethlehem Steel Corp., 115 Cal.Rptr. 765, 525 P.2d 669 (Cal.1974), 115

Roe v. Conn, 417 F.Supp. 769 (M.D.Ala.1976), 239

Roe v. Doe, 29 N.Y.2d 188, 324 N.Y.S.2d 71, 272 N.E.2d 567 (N.Y.1971), 260

Roe v. Wade, 410 U.S. 113, 93 S.Ct. 705, 35 L.Ed.2d 147 (1973), 315

Roger B., In re, 84 Ill.2d 323, 49 Ill.Dec. 731, 418 N.E.2d 751 (Ill.1981), 305

Ross v. Louise Wise Services, Inc., 8 N.Y.3d 478, 836 N.Y.S.2d 509, 868 N.E.2d 189 (N.Y.2007), 307

Sanditen v. Sanditen, 496 P.2d 365 (Okla.1972), 105

Santolino, In re Estate of, 384 N.J.Super. 567, 895 A.2d 506 (N.J.Super.Ch.2005), 68, 71

Santosky v. Kramer, 455 U.S. 745, 102 S.Ct. 1388, 71 L.Ed.2d 599 (1982), 240

Sappington, In re Marriage of, 106 Ill.2d 456, 88 Ill.Dec. 61, 478 N.E.2d 376 (Ill.1985), 162

S.B. v. S.J.B., 258 N.J.Super. 151, 609 A.2d 124 (N.J.Super.Ch.1992), 135

Schauer, In re, 391 B.R. 430 (Bkrtcy.E.D.Wis.2008), 171

Schiffman, In re Marriage of, 169 Cal.Rptr. 918, 620 P.2d 579 (Cal.1980), 125

Schultz v. Schultz, 145 Idaho 859, 187 P.3d 1234 (Idaho 2008), 217

Schutz v. Schutz, 581 So.2d 1290 (Fla.1991), 223

Scott v. Family Ministries, 65 Cal.App.3d 492, 135 Cal.Rptr. 430 (Cal.App. 2 Dist.1976), 296

Shapiro v. Thompson, 394 U.S. 618, 89 S.Ct. 1322, 22 L.Ed.2d 600 (1969), 130

Sharma v. Sharma, 8 Kan.App.2d 726, 667 P.2d 395 (Kan.App.1983), 18

Sharon H., State v., 429 A.2d 1321 (Del.Super.1981), 63

Sharon S. v. Superior Court, 2 Cal.Rptr.3d 699, 73 P.3d 554 (Cal.2003), 294

Sharpe Furniture, Inc. v. Buckstaff, 99 Wis.2d 114, 299 N.W.2d 219 (Wis.1980), 96

Sherrer v. Sherrer, 334 U.S. 343, 68 S.Ct. 1087, 92 L.Ed. 1429 (1948), 131

Shramek v. Shramek, 901 A.2d 593 (R.I.2006), 103

Simeone v. Simeone, 525 Pa. 392, 581 A.2d 162 (Pa.1990), 30

Simmons, In re Marriage of, 355 Ill.App.3d 942, 292 Ill.Dec. 47, 825 N.E.2d 303 (Ill.App. 1 Dist.2005), 91

Simmons v. Simmons, 98 Ark.App. 12, 249 S.W.3d 843 (Ark.App.2007), 38

Sims v. State Dept. of Public Welfare of State of Tex., 438 F.Supp. 1179 (S.D.Tex.1977), 250

Sininger v. Sininger, 300 Md. 604, 479 A.2d 1354 (Md.1984), 192

Skinner v. State of Oklahoma ex rel. Williamson, 316 U.S. 535, 62 S.Ct. 1110, 86 L.Ed. 1655 (1942), 316

Skipworth v. Skipworth, 360 So.2d 975 (Ala.1978), 53

Smith v. Cote, 128 N.H. 231, 513 A.2d 341 (N.H.1986), 265

Smith v. Hartigan, 556 F.Supp. 157 (N.D.Ill.1983), 320

Smith v. Lee, 2008 WL 906323 (W.D.N.C.2008), 117

Smith v. Organization of Foster Families For Equality and Reform, 431 U.S. 816, 97 S.Ct. 2094, 53 L.Ed.2d 14 (1977), 252

Smith v. State, 247 Ga. 612, 277 S.E.2d 678 (Ga.1981), 123

Sommers, Matter of Marriage of, 246 Kan. 652, 792 P.2d 1005 (Kan.1990), 156

Sorensen, People v., 68 Cal.2d 280, 66 Cal.Rptr. 7, 437 P.2d 495 (Cal.1968), 318

Sosna v. Iowa, 419 U.S. 393, 95 S.Ct. 553, 42 L.Ed.2d 532 (1975), 130

Spence v. Spence, 930 So.2d 415 (Miss.App.2005), 135

Stanard v. Bolin, 88 Wash.2d 614, 565 P.2d 94 (Wash.1977), 117

Stanley v. Illinois, 405 U.S. 645, 92 S.Ct. 1208, 31 L.Ed.2d 551 (1972), 281, 299

Stanton v. Stanton, 429 U.S. 501, 97 S.Ct. 717, 50 L.Ed.2d 723 (1977), 66

Stanton v. Stanton, 421 U.S. 7, 95 S.Ct. 1373, 43 L.Ed.2d 688 (1975), 66

State v. _____ (see opposing party)

State ex rel. v. _____ (see opposing party and relator)

State in Interest of R.R. v. C.R. and R.R., 797 P.2d 459 (Utah App.1990), 253

Steinke v. Steinke, 238 Pa.Super. 74, 357 A.2d 674 (Pa.Super.1975), 139

Stenberg v. Carhart, 530 U.S. 914, 120 S.Ct. 2597, 147 L.Ed.2d 743 (2000), 316

Stewart, State v., 243 Kan. 639, 763 P.2d 572 (Kan.1988), 124

Stiver v. Parker, 975 F.2d 261 (6th Cir.1992), 327

Sullivan v. Rooney, 404 Mass. 160, 533 N.E.2d 1372 (Mass.1989), 87

Sumners, In re Marriage of, 645 S.W.2d 205 (Mo.App. S.D.1983), 69

Surrogate Parenting Associates, Inc. v. Commonwealth ex rel. Armstrong, 704 S.W.2d 209 (Ky.1986), 323

Swain v. Swain, 179 N.C.App. 795, 635 S.E.2d 504 (N.C.App.2006), 159

Swoap v. Superior Court of Sacramento County, 111 Cal.Rptr. 136, 516 P.2d 840 (Cal.1973), 203

Syrkowski v. Appleyard, 420 Mich. 367, 362 N.W.2d 211 (Mich.1985), 326

T___ T—-, 216 Va. 867, 224 S.E.2d 148 (Va.1976), 28

T.B., Matter of Adoption of, 622 N.E.2d 921 (Ind.1993), 307

Thompson v. Thompson, 576 So.2d 267 (Fla.1991), 173

Thornhill, In re Marriage of, 2008 WL 3877223 (Colo.App.2008), 184

Tinker v. Des Moines Independent Community School Dist., 393 U.S. 503, 89 S.Ct. 733, 21 L.Ed.2d 731 (1969), 271

Town of (see name of town)

Trammel v. United States, 445 U.S. 40, 100 S.Ct. 906, 63 L.Ed.2d 186 (1980), 121

Trimble v. Gordon, 430 U.S. 762, 97 S.Ct. 1459, 52 L.Ed.2d 31 (1977), 278

Troxel v. Granville, 530 U.S. 57, 120 S.Ct. 2054, 147 L.Ed.2d 49 (2000), 225, 261, 308

T.S.G. v. B.A.S., 52 Va.App. 583, 665 S.E.2d 854 (Va.App.2008), 304

Turner v. Safley, 482 U.S. 78, 107 S.Ct. 2254, 96 L.Ed.2d 64 (1987), 22, 61

United States v. _____ (see opposing party)

United States Fidelity & Guaranty Co. v. Industrial Commission, 25 Ariz.App. 244, 542 P.2d 825 (Ariz.App. Div. 1 1975), 78

Vanderbilt v. Vanderbilt, 354 U.S. 416, 77 S.Ct. 1360, 1 L.Ed.2d 1456 (1957), 131

Veazey v. Veazey, 560 P.2d 382 (Alaska 1977), 210

Walker, In re, 114 B.R. 847 (Bkrtcy.N.D.N.Y.1990), 22

Walker, Matter of, 282 N.C. 28, 191 S.E.2d 702 (N.C.1972), 255

Walker v. Superior Court, 253 Cal.Rptr. 1, 763 P.2d 852 (Cal.1988), 241

Walker v. Walker, 330 Mich. 332, 47 N.W.2d 633 (Mich.1951), 75

Wallace v. Jaffree, 472 U.S. 38, 105 S.Ct. 2479, 86 L.Ed.2d 29 (1985), 269

Walton, In re Marriage of, 28 Cal.App.3d 108, 104 Cal.Rptr. 472 (Cal.App. 4 Dist.1972), 16

Ware v. Ware, 10 Va.App. 352, 391 S.E.2d 887 (Va.App.1990), 195

Watkins, State v., 659 N.W.2d 526 (Iowa 2003), 238

Watts v. Watts, 250 Neb. 38, 547 N.W.2d 466 (Neb.1996), 77

Watts v. Watts, 137 Wis.2d 506, 405 N.W.2d 303 (Wis.1987), 85

Watts v. Watts, 115 N.H. 186, 337 A.2d 350 (N.H.1975), 276

Webb v. Hillsborough County Hospital Authority, 521 So.2d 199 (Fla.App. 2 Dist.1988), 100

Weber v. Aetna Cas. & Surety Co., 406 U.S. 164, 92 S.Ct. 1400, 31 L.Ed.2d 768 (1972), 279

White v. Marciano, 190 Cal.App.3d 1026, 235 Cal.Rptr. 779 (Cal.App. 2 Dist.1987), 198

Whitman v. Kiger, 139 N.C.App. 44, 533 S.E.2d 807 (N.C.App.2000), 191

Whorton v. Dillingham, 202 Cal.App.3d 447, 248 Cal.Rptr. 405 (Cal.App. 4 Dist.1988), 90

Wickham v. Byrne, 199 Ill.2d 309, 263 Ill.Dec. 799, 769 N.E.2d 1 (Ill.2002), 225

Wife, B. T. L. v. Husband, H. A. L., 287 A.2d 413 (Del.Ch.1972), 179

Wildey v. Springs, 47 F.3d 1475 (7th Cir.1995), 117

Williams v. State of North Carolina, 325 U.S. 226, 65 S.Ct. 1092, 89 L.Ed. 1577 (1945), 130

Williams v. State of North Carolina, 317 U.S. 287, 63 S.Ct. 207, 87 L.Ed. 279 (1942), 130

Williams v. Williams, 120 Nev. 559, 97 P.3d 1124 (Nev.2004), 60

Winship, In re, 397 U.S. 358, 90
S.Ct. 1068, 25 L.Ed.2d 368
(1970), 254

Wisconsin v. Yoder, 406 U.S. 205,
92 S.Ct. 1526, 32 L.Ed.2d 15
(1972), 269

Wolfe v. Wolfe, 62 Ill.App.3d 498,
19 Ill.Dec. 306, 378 N.E.2d
1181 (Ill.App. 1 Dist.1978),
73

Wood v. Strickland, 420 U.S.
308, 95 S.Ct. 992, 43 L.Ed.2d
214 (1975), 271

Wyman v. James, 400 U.S. 309,
91 S.Ct. 381, 27 L.Ed.2d 408
(1971), 242

Zablocki v. Redhail, 434 U.S.
374, 98 S.Ct. 673, 54 L.Ed.2d
618 (1978), 21, 61

Zagarow v. Zagarow, 105 Misc.2d
1054, 430 N.Y.S.2d 247
(N.Y.Sup.1980), 137

Zellmer v. Zellmer, 164 Wash.2d
147, 188 P.3d 497
(Wash.2008), 191

Zeolla v. Zeolla, 908 A.2d 629
(Me.2006), 17

APPENDIX F

Index

ABORTION
Constitutional law, 246–
48, 260–61, 315–16
Husband's consent or
notification, 316
Minor's right (parent's
consent), 246–48,
260–61

ABUSE
"Battered Child
Syndrome", 250–51
"Battered Spouse
Syndrome", 122–24
Children, 248–54
Reporting statutes,
registries, 248–50
Spousal, 122–24

ADOPTION
Adoptive relationship as
marriage impediment,
63–64
Adult, 290–91
Age of adopter, 294–95
Agency's role, 287, 303,
304–05
Anonymity, 297–98
"Black market" babies,
288–89
Compensation for
placement, 288–89
Consent, 298–304
Child's, 303

Form, 303
Revocation, 303–04
Unmarried father's,
298–301
Equitable adoption,
291–92
Gays or lesbians, 293–94
Grandparents, 309
History, 287
Indian Child Welfare Act,
296–98
Inheritance, 309–10
Legal effects, 307–08
Marital status of adoptive
parents, 292–93
Open Adoption, 305–06
Race as factor, 296–97
Religion as factor, 295–96
Revocation, 306–07
Same-sex couples, 293–94
Single parent, 292–93
Stepparent, 301
Subsidization, 289–90
Uniform Adoption Act,
301
Unmarried father, 281–
82, 296–99, 298–301

ADULTERY
Factor in alimony or
property distribution,
156–58

Ground for divorce,
134–35
Tort, 117–20

AFFINITY, 63–64

**ALIENATION OF
AFFECTIONS,** 118–19

ALIMONY
Adultery as factor, 156–58
Bankruptcy, 159, 163
Cohabitation terminating,
161–62
Death terminating,
159–60
Enforcement, 162
Factors, 153–58
Fault as factor, 156–58
Gender, 99, 151
History, 99, 151
Modifiability, 158–59
Professional license as
factor, 171–72
Remarriage terminating,
160–61
Revival following
termination, 76–77
Sex discrimination, 99,
151
Taxation, 163
Uniform Marriage and
Divorce Act, 151–56

Waiver in antenuptial agreement, 35–36

AMERICAN LAW INSTITUTE (ALI) PRINCIPLES
Approximation standard for custody, 214
Domestic partners, 88–89

ANNULMENT, 70–78
Consequences, 71, 75–78
Defenses, 70–71
Duress, 73
Fraud, 72–73
Grounds, 66–68, 70
History, 70
Legal effects of void or voidable marriage, 75–78
Retroactivity, 76
Sham marriage, 73–74
Uniform Marriage and Divorce Act, 70, 72
Void marriage, 66–68, 70–72
Voidable marriage, 66–68, 70–72

ANTENUPTIAL AGREEMENTS, 17, 26–37
Conflicts of laws, 40–41
Consideration, 28
Disclosure obligation, 30–31
Statute of Frauds, 27–28
Subject matter, 26, 34–37
Unconscionability, 31–33
Uniform Acts, 28, 30, 31–33, 35–37
Validity, 27–37
Voluntariness, 33–34
Waiver of support and property rights, 28–30

ARTIFICIAL INSEMINATION, 318–19

ASSISTED REPRODUCTION, 317–27

ATTORNEY
Antenuptial agreements, 33–34
Child custody, 209–10
Termination of parental rights, 239–40

BANKRUPTCY, 22, 170–71

BATTERED CHILDREN, 250–51
See also Abuse, Neglect and Dependency

BATTERED SPOUSES, 120–24
Criminal offense, 121–22
Divorce, grounds for, 135–36
Order of protection, 122
Rape by husband, 121–22
"Syndrome", 122–24

BIGAMY
See also Annulment
Civil effects, 20–21, 138
Crime, 20
Marriage prohibition, 18–21, 59–60
Putative marriage, 60–61

BIRTH CONTROL
Constitutional privacy, 248, 260–61, 314–15
Minor's rights, 248, 260–61, 314–15

BLOOD TESTS
Marriage license, 67
Paternity, 276

BREACH OF PROMISE TO MARRY, 41, 115–17

CAPACITY TO MARRY, 47–50, 67–68
See also Annulment

CHILD CUSTODY
See Custody

CHILD SUPPORT
Conflict of laws, 201–02

Contempt of court, 200–01
Criminal penalty, 201
Criteria, 197–99
Death of parent, 196–97
Duration, 191–97
Emancipation, 194–95
Enforcement, 200–01
Federal enforcement legislation, 201, 202
Formula, 197–99
Full Faith and Credit, 202–03
Grandparents, 191
Guidelines, 197–99
Majority, 192–94
Modification, 199
Revival following termination, 195
Stepparent, 191
Uniform Acts, 197, 201–02

CIVIL UNIONS, 23–24, 90

COHABITATION (Unmarried)
See also Common Law Marriage
Contracts, 82
Invalid ceremonial marriage, 60–61
Marvin doctrine, 82–89
Names, 124–25
Presumption of valid marriage, 58–59
Putative spouse, 60–61
Same-sex couples, 89–91

COLLUSION (Divorce), 139

COMMON LAW MARRIAGE, 52–58, 83–85

CONNIVANCE, 140

CONSANGUINITY, 61–63

CONSENT
Abortion (minor's), 246–48, 260–61, 315–16

Adoptions, 298–304
Marriage, 47–50

CONSORTIUM, LOSS OF, 115

CONTRACT CLAUSE, 15

CONTRACT COHABITATION, 82–89

COUNSEL
See Attorney

COVENANT MARRIAGE, 145

CRIMINAL CONVERSATION, 117–18

CRUELTY
Ground for divorce, 135–36, 137–38
Spouse abuse, 122–24

CUSTODY
Adoptive parents, 308
ALI "Approximation Standard", 214
"Best interests" standard, 208–10
Child's preference, 208–09
Conflicts of laws, 226–30
Enforcement, 229–30
Expert testimony, 209
Factors, 208–16
Gays and lesbians, 212–13
Gender, 209–10
Grandparents, 214–16, 225–26
Hague Convention, 230–31
Joint custody, 217–19
"Kidnapping" by parent, 227–28
Modification, 223–25
"Morality" of parent, 212–14
Non-parents, 214–16, 225–26
Parental Kidnapping Prevention Act, 227–28

Parental rights, 207, 214–16, 260, 308
"Primary caretaker rule", 210
Race of parent, 211–12
Religion of parent, 210–11
Relocation of custodial parent, 220–22
Residence (jurisdiction), 226–30
Role of the judge, 208–09
Sex of parent, 210
Sexual "morality" as factor, 212–14
"Tender years doctrine", 210
Third party vs. natural parent, 214–16
Uniform Child Custody Jurisdiction Act, 227
Uniform Child Custody Jurisdiction & Enforcement Act, 229–30
Unmarried father, 281–82, 296–99, 298–301
Visitation rights, 219–23, 225–26

DESERTION, 136–37

DIVORCE
A mensa et thoro, 145
Adultery, 134–35
Bars, 139–42
Breakdown of marriage, 144–45
Conflicts of laws, 16–17
Sherrer rule, 131
Cruelty,
    Mental, 137–38
    Physical, 135–36
Defenses, generally, 139–42
    Collusion, 139
    Condonation, 141–42
    Connivance, 140
    Provocation, 140
    Recrimination, 139–40
Desertion, 136–37
Fault grounds, 132–39

Full faith and credit for sister state divorce, 130–31
History, 132–33
Insanity, 138–39, 142
Jurisdiction, 130–32
"Living apart", 143–44
No-fault divorce, 134, 143–45
Reform, 142–45
Residence requirements, 130
State Power to Revise Law, 15–16
Tort law, 111–12

DIVORCE FROM BED AND BOARD, 145
Convertibility into full divorce, 146

DOMESTIC PARTNERSHIPS, 88–89, 90
See also Cohabitation

DOMESTIC VIOLENCE, 122–24
See also Battered Spouses

DOMICILE
Child custody, 226–30
Divorce, 16–17, 40–41, 130

EMANCIPATION, 194–95, 262

EMBRYO TRANSPLANT, 319–24

ENGAGEMENT GIFTS, 41–43

EQUITABLE DISTRIBUTION, 163–78

FOSTER CARE, 251–52

FULL FAITH AND CREDIT
Child Custody, 226
Child Support, 202–03
Divorce, 130–31

Legitimacy, 283
Marriage, 69–70

GAYS AND LESBIANS
Adoption, 293–94
Child custody, 212–14
Civil Unions, 23–24, 90
Cohabitation, 23–26,
    89–90
Constitutional law, 23–26
Crime, 25–26
Marriage, 23–26

GIFTS
Premarital, 41–42
Spousal, 39, 101, 103–04
Tax treatment, 39

**GRANDPARENTS'
    VISITATION
    RIGHTS,** 225–26

GUARDIANSHIP, 49–50,
    237, 251

HEALTH
Medical treatment of
    child, 243–46
Qualification for
    marriage, 67–68

**HEART BALM
    ACTIONS,** 115–20,
    266–67

HUSBAND AND WIFE
See SPOUSES

ILLEGITIMACY
Defined, 277
Conflicts of laws, 283
Equal protection, 277–80
Father's custodial rights,
    273–74
Inheritance, 278
Paternity, 280–82
Support, 278

INCEST
Adoptive relationships,
    308
Definition, 61, 308
Marriage prohibition,
    61–64
Crime, 62

**IN VITRO
    FERTILIZATION,**
    319–20

INHERITANCE
Adopted child, 309–10
Child, 278
Intestacy, 105–06, 109,
    278
Spouse, 105–06, 109–10

INTENT TO MARRY, 50

JOINT CUSTODY,
    217–19

JURISDICTION
Child custody, 226–30
Child support, 132,
    201–02
Divorce, 130–32

JUVENILE COURT
Civil, 237–38, 251–54
Criminal (delinquency),
    237, 254–55

LAWYER
See Attorney

**LEGITIMACY AND
    LEGITIMATION,**
    276–83
Conflicts of laws, 283
Presumption of
    legitimacy, 276
Uniform Parentage Act,
    280

LESBIANS
See Gays and Lesbians

**LICENSES,
    PROFESSIONAL
    (Treatment on
    divorce),** 171–74

LIMITED DIVORCE,
    146

MARITAL CONTRACTS
See also Antenuptial
    Agreements;
    Postnuptial
    Agreements;
    Separation
    Agreements

Conflicts of laws, 40–41
Consideration, 38
Fair dealing, 39
Legislation, 38–39
Reconciliation
    agreements, 40, 184–85
Separation agreements,
    40, 176–84

MARRIAGE
See also Annulment;
    Antenuptial
    Agreements; Marital
    Contracts
Affinity, 63
Age, 24, 64–67
Bigamy, 20–21
Capacity, 47–50
Common law, 52–60
Conflicts of laws, 16–17,
    56–58, 68–70
Consent, 47–50
Constitutional right to
    marry, 21–26
Contract or status?, 15
Covenant Marriage, 145
Formalities, 47–52
Fraud, 72–73
Gays and lesbians, 23–25
Incestuous, 61–64
Legal effect of invalid
    marriage, 60–61
License, 50–51
Polygamy, 18–21
Prerequisites, 47–68
Presumptions regarding
    validity, 58–59
Proxy, 51
Putative spouse, 60–61
Religious influence, 15,
    17–18
Right to marry, 21–26
Same-sex, 23–25
Sham, jest, 73–74
Solemnization, 50–52
Testimonial privilege,
    120–21
Void vs. voidable, 71–72

**MARRIED WOMEN'S
    PROPERTY ACTS,**
    26, 38–39, 100–01

MONOGAMY, 18–21

NAME
Child's, 125–26, 308
Spouse's, 124
Unmarried partners, 124–25

NEGLECT AND DEPENDENCY
See also Termination of Parental Rights
Defined, 237–39
Constitutional law, 238–43
Criminal prosecution, 238
Dependency, 237
Juvenile court, 237–38, 251–54
Medical neglect, 241–42, 243–46
Neglect, 241–42
Reporting statutes, 248–50
Right to counsel, 239–40
Standard of proof, 240–41
Termination of parental rights, 253–54

PARENT AND CHILD
See also Adoption; Child Support; Custody; Guardianship; Neglect and Dependency
Assisted reproduction, 317–27
Child's emancipation, 194–95, 262
Child's name, 125–26, 308
Compulsory schooling, 269
Consent to medical treatment, 207, 241–42, 243–46, 260–61
Education, 268–72
Parental consent to minor child's abortion, 246–48, 260–62
Parental liability for child's crime, 267–68
Parental liability for child's torts, 267

Termination of parental rights, 253–54
Tort immunity, 265–66

PATERNITY
See also Illegitimacy; Legitimacy and Legitimation
Artificial insemination, 318–20
Blood tests, 276
Burden of proof, 281
Constitutional law, 280–82
Father's right to ascertain, 280–82
Standard of proof, 281
Statute of limitations, 281
Unmarried father's custodial rights, 280–82
Uniform Parentage Act, 280, 281

PENSIONS
Divisibility on divorce, 176–78
ERISA, 178
QDRO, 178
Timing of pay-out, 178

POSTNUPTIAL AGREEMENTS, 38–39

PREMARITAL AGREEMENTS
See Antenuptial Agreements

PRIVACY
Right to marital, 21–22, 25–26
Sexual privacy of unmarried persons, 25–26

PROFESSIONAL LICENSES
Alimony, 171–72
"Divisibility" on divorce, 173–74

PROPERTY
See also Antenuptial Agreements; Pensions
Bankruptcy, 179–71
Common law (separate property) systems, 100–06, 163–64
Community property, 106–10, 168–69
Conflicts of laws, 110, 169–70
Dissipation of marital property, 166–68
Divorce, 163–78
Equitable distribution, 163–78
Fault affecting distribution on divorce, 166–68
Inheritance by spouse, 104–06, 109
Joint ownership, 102–04, 168
Management, 108–09
Marital property, 110, 164–65
Married Women's Property Acts, 26, 38–39, 100–01
Professional license, 173–74
Taxation, 171
Uniform Acts, 105–07, 165–66

PUTATIVE SPOUSE, 60–61

RACE
Adoption, 296–98
Custody, 211–12
Marriage, 21

RAPE (Marital), 121–22

RECONCILIATION AGREEMENTS, 40, 184–85

RECRIMINATION (Divorce), 139–40

RESIDENCE
Custody, 220–22, 226–30
Divorce, 16–17, 130

SAME-SEX MARRIAGE, 23–25

SCHOOLING (Child's), 268–72

SEPARATE MAINTENANCE, 146

SEPARATION AGREEMENTS
See also Antenuptial Agreements; Marriage Contracts
Consideration, 179
Reconciliation, 184–85
Relationship to divorce decree, 182–83
Uniform acts, 40, 180, 182
Validity, 179

SEXUAL PRIVACY
Gays and lesbians, 23–26
Marital, 25–26
Unmarried persons, 25–26

SOLEMNIZATION OF MARRIAGE, 50–52

SPOUSES
Abortion (husband's consent), 316
Agency, 97
"Battered women's syndrome", 122–24
Confidential communication (privilege), 120–21
Consortium, loss of, 115
Criminal law, 120–24
Inheritance, 105–06, 109–10
Name, 124
Necessaries doctrine, 95–97, 98–99
Property, 26, 100–10
Rape, 121–22
Support, 95–100
Testimonial privilege, 120–21

Tort law, 111–20

STEP-RELATIONSHIP
Adoption by stepparent, 302
As marriage impediment, 63–64
Stepparent's support obligation, 191

STERILIZATION, 316–17

SUPPORT OBLIGATIONS
See Child Support, Alimony

SURROGATE MOTHERHOOD, 317, 320–26

TAXATION
Alimony, 163
Gift tax, 39
Postnuptial agreements, 39
Property distribution, 171

TERMINATION OF PARENTAL RIGHTS
See also Adoption; Neglect and Dependency
Constitutional safeguards, 238–41, 253
Grounds, 253–54
Right to counsel, 239–41
Standard of proof, 240–41

TORTS AND THE FAMILY, 111–20, 262–67

TRANSSEXUALS
Capacity to marry, 90–91

UNIFORM ACTS
See specific subjects and titles

UNIFORM CHILD CUSTODY JURISDICTION ACT, 227

UNIFORM CHILD CUSTODY JURISDICTION & ENFORCEMENT ACT, 229–30

UNIFORM DISPOSITION OF COMMUNITY PROPERTY RIGHTS AT DEATH ACT, 110

UNIFORM INTERSTATE FAMILY SUPPORT ACT, 200–01

UNIFORM MARITAL PROPERTY ACT, 37, 106–07

UNIFORM MARRIAGE AND DIVORCE ACT
See specific topics

UNIFORM MARRIAGE EVASION ACT, 69

UNIFORM PARENTAGE ACT, 280–81, 301, 318–19

UNIFORM PREMARITAL AGREEMENTS ACT, 28–37

UNIFORM PROBATE CODE
Spouse's elective share, 105–09

UNIFORM PUTATIVE AND UNKNOWN FATHERS ACT, 301

UNIFORM RECIPROCAL ENFORCEMENT OF SUPPORT ACT, 132, 201–02

UNMARRIED COHABITATION
See Cohabitation, unmarried

VISITATION RIGHTS
See Custody

**VOID AND VOIDABLE
   MARRIAGES**
See Annulment

"WRONGFUL LIFE",
   262–64

WRONGFUL DEATH,
   265

†